D1600315

JUSTIN

I

LCL 557

JUSTIN

EPITOME OF POMPEIUS TROGUS

BOOKS 1–20

EDITED AND TRANSLATED BY

J. C. YARDLEY

INTRODUCTION AND NOTES BY

DEXTER HOYOS

HARVARD UNIVERSITY PRESS

CAMBRIDGE, MASSACHUSETTS
LONDON, ENGLAND
2024

First published 2024

Library of Congress Control Number 2023051825
CIP data available from the Library of Congress

ISBN 978-0-674-99760-8

*Composed in ZephGreek and ZephText by
Technologies 'N Typography, Merrimac, Massachusetts.
Printed on acid-free paper and bound by
Maple Press, York, Pennsylvania*

CONTENTS

CONTENTS

GENERAL INTRODUCTION

JUSTIN

The Author of the Epitome

Justin—Marcus Iunianius (or, less likely, Iunianus) Iusti-nus—is a shadowy figure whose fame rests entirely on the work of an earlier writer. His name is not stated anywhere in his *Epitome* (as moderns call his work): it is supplied in the headings of two late-medieval manuscripts, and in the genitive case (*m. iuniani iustini epithoma historiarum*)—hence uncertainty over whether his *nomen* was Iunianius or Iunianus. In Sir Ronald Syme's lapidary phrase, he was "Justin, a text rather than a personality."[1]

In one of his few personal statements, the epitomator tells the story of how his *Epitome* came about. An admirer of the Augustan historian Pompeius Trogus, "a man with

---

[1] "*m*" is in only a single MS. The form "Iunianus" is the major-ity preference among scholars; but if Justin was writing around AD 200, his *nomen* would be Iunianius (and might have been so even two hundred years later). The MSS' "M. Iuniani Iustini" point to a standard Roman name with the *tria nomina*, which fit a second- or third-century dating and in which the *nomen* ends in *-ius* and not *-us*, except for certain old Etruscan or Italic names such as Perperna, Salvidienus, and Vipstanus; see also n. 9 below. "A text [etc.]": Syme (1988, 370). Valuable remarks on epitoma-tors' methodologies, and flaws, in Brunt (1980).

the eloquence of the ancients" (*vir priscae eloquentiae*), and of Trogus' forty-four-book world history called *Historiae Philippicae*,

> I, during some free time that we were spending in the City, took excerpts from all his finest work, and, omitting what did not make pleasurable reading or serve to provide a moral, I have produced a brief anthology (*breve veluti florum corpusculum*) to refresh the memory of those who had studied history in Greek, and provide instruction for those who had not. (*Praef.* §4)

These comments indicate that Justin was not a resident of Rome but had visited there with some others for a sojourn, probably a lengthy one—his anthologizing would have taken time—and that he had, at least by his own description, compiled the *corpusculum* to be a manual of information on Greek and earlier history. The person he addresses is left unnamed but seems not to have been one of the group with him at Rome but instead a respected mentor. A minority view is that he was merely a rhetorical trope.[2]

The Historiae Philippicae

Pompeius Trogus' *Historiae Philippicae*, a name not fully understood (see "Why *Philippicae*?" below), told the story

---

[2] That the addressee had been a companion of Justin's at Rome is, however, held by (e.g.) Yardley and Heckel (1997, 9 and n. 26). For Elliott (2018, 114–20), the addressee is a fictitious rhetorical device.

of the world—meaning in practice the Mediterranean and the Middle Eastern world—from mythical beginnings to the early decades of the first century BC, with one striking omission: Roman history save for intermittent mentions of Rome's interactions with the kingdoms of Hellenistic times. This was a remarkable feat in Latin literature, surviving now only in the pared-down version put together by the mysterious Justin and in *Prologi*, brief lists of the books' contents by some other compiler.

The *Historiae Philippicae* open in legendary times with Assyria, the Medes, and the rise of the Persian Empire, move on via Scythians and Amazons to early Greece, Athens, and Sparta, and then progress through fifth-century and fourth-century eastern Mediterranean events (mainly those of Greece and Persia) to the rise of Macedon under Alexander's father, Philip II. From Book 11 on we are in Alexander's and then Hellenistic times, along with excursions: to Persia again; to Carthage, starting with its foundation by Dido; and then to Sicily, under the notorious Syracusan tyrants Dionysius and Agathocles. The eastern Mediterranean monarchies of the third and second centuries BC, with their sensational wars and internal coups, form the bulk of the second half (Books 24–40), but Trogus rounded off his work—perhaps in a second edition—with four additional books: two on the Parthians, successor-rulers to the Persians, and the Parthian kings, and two on legendary Italy and Spain; with a brief coda on how Spain came under Carthaginian and then Roman rule.

Forty-four books were a sizable achievement, matching the large-scale world histories of past Greek historians such as Ephorus, Theopompus, Timaeus, of Trogus' older contemporary Diodorus, and the sizable works on shorter periods by notable authors such as Hieronymus, Duris, Polybius, Poseidonius, and Trogus' contemporary Dionysius of Halicarnassus. (Roman historians in the third, second, and first centuries were mostly voluminous too, but they kept to Rome's own history.) A work on a world scale as large as the *Historiae Philippicae* was a novelty, as Justin notes ("the originality of such a work," *Praef.* §1).

Epitome *and* Prologi

Justin's *corpusculum* represents (at best) only perhaps one-fifth—and more likely it amounts to barely one-tenth—of the original *Historiae*. His selectivity is quite varied. Book 2, on the Scythians and early Greeks, for instance, is fifteen chapters long and covers twenty-two pages in Otto Seel's Teubner edition; Book 38, with the sole full-length Trogan speech in the work, is thirteen pages long. However, Book 10 (on mid-fourth century BC Persia) Justin must have found so dull he allowed it barely a page and a half. Yet in the *Prologi*, brief surviving summaries of Trogus' original content, *Prol.* 10 is almost as stocked with content as *Prol.* 9 and is longer than *Prol.* 11. (By contrast, Justin allots seven pages to Book 9, and to Book 11 a respectable thirteen.) Justin's selections thus do not necessarily respect the proportions of Pompeius Trogus' original material.

It is noteworthy too that the first half of the *Epitome*, Books 1–21, takes up 176 Teubner pages, the second half (Books 22–42) a much shorter 124. The reverse holds for the corresponding groups of *Prologi*, eight and ten Latin pages, respectively; so it is not likely that Trogus' original second half was as economical with space as Justin's *corpusculum* would imply.

In two of its three classes of manuscripts[3] this "anthology" is followed, as in our edition, by the *Prologi* mentioned above. They consist of one-paragraph summaries of the books, not of the *Epitome* but of Trogus' original work and deriving from a separate ancient tradition, since they often mention topics that Justin does not (as can be seen in the differences between his Book 10 and *Prol.* 10), omit items that he includes, and situate the episode of Hanno the Great (Book 21.4) in *Prol.* 20; there are also many differences in proper names. In places too the *Prologi* correctly state a detail that Justin gets wrong, as shown by fuller ancient sources, e.g., his habitual transfers to Polyperchon, one of Alexander the Great's successor-generals, of actions (usually crimes) committed by another, Craterus (and see "The *Epitome*: Structure and Flaws," below).[4]

In their formulaic and condensed structure, the *Prologi* differ from such similar summaries as the fuller Livian *Periochae* or the even briefer chapter-headings (*capitula*) often found in manuscripts in late antiquity; perhaps they were originally labels for the *volumina* in a Roman library, or made for its catalog. Who compiled them and when is unknown.

Paradoxically, the hard-to-identify Justin's "anthology" became one of the most widely read and influential books

---

[3] See further "A Note on the Text," below.

[4] Polyperchon for Craterus: (e.g.) Justin 12.10.1, 15.1.1; *Prol.* 14–15; cf. Yardley and Heckel (1997, 24, 39), for fuller lists.

in the Middle Ages and Renaissance. Justin was treated as a major authority on ancient history apart from Rome's. Rather more than two hundred manuscripts of his work, complete or incomplete, survive.

The Date of Justin's "Anthology"

The minimal information in the *Preface* has opened a wide range of modern views on Justin's date and aims, how he carried out these aims, and how far they reflect (or distort) Pompeius Trogus' own intentions. That the two lived at least a century apart is certain, but widely varied dates—AD 144/5, circa 200 or 320, and 390/400—have been canvased for the epitomator. Efforts to find a plausible era have been made, for instance, by assessing terms that would not have been in Trogus' Augustan-age Latin: to mention only a few, *ad instar*, "similar to" (classical Latin uses just *instar*); *adunare*, "to unite" (2.12.18 and eight later occurrences); *adtaminare*, "to defile" (21.3.4); *fungi* in the sense "to complete" one's lifespan (19.1.1); *medela*, "remedy, antidote" (11.1.7); *stagnare*, "to fortify" (37.2.6). But this approach is inconclusive, since these terms appear in other authors from as early as the later second century AD onward to the fifth, which leaves the field for dating Justin inconveniently broad.[5]

[5] Examples in Syme (1988, 367–69), who uses them as part of his case for the late fourth century (he adds to the list *deleticius* [*HP* 2.10.13], but that is a nineteenth-century conjecture); cf. Syme (1992). Also favoring the late fourth century: P. L. Schmidt, *BNP* s.v. Iustinus 5 (accessed February 23, 2023); Zecchini (2016); Hofmann (2020, 750). Alonso-Núñez (1995, 355–57), hovers between choosing circa 200 or circa 400.

Other dating criteria have been tried. In Book 41 Justin introduces "the Parthians, between whom and the Romans the world is more or less divided, and who now rule the East" (41.1.1). Taken literally, this places him earlier than the mid-220s AD, for then the Parthian Arsacid monarchy was displaced by a revived Persian (Sassanid) dynasty. However, supporters of a fourth-century Justin stress that Latin writers of all eras could use the names Parthians and Persians interchangeably.

A chronologically nebulous remark soon after must be Justin's too—that while the Parthians name all their kings Arsaces, "the Romans have used the name Caesar and Augustus [*Caesares Augustosque*, plural] for theirs" (41.5.8). In Trogus' day only a single person bore both those names, the emperor Augustus, and it would have been a serious *faux pas* to refer to him as a king. But for dating Justin the remark is unhelpful, for "Caesar" and "Augustus" continued in use for half a millennium as epithets for ruling emperors and their designated heirs.

One intriguing item is sometimes invoked to support a date for the *Epitome* before, and maybe close to, AD 321. In that year Nazarius, a Gallic orator at Rome, delivered an elaborately flattering and still surviving speech in honor of the emperor Constantine (then absent) and his two older sons. At one point Nazarius recounts a not very relevant story of how the early Macedonians once saved the day against invading Illyrians by bringing into battle their infant king Aeropus, in his cradle, to inspire them—an item strikingly close in language to the same story in Justin. Does it mean that this early-fourth-century orator had been reading Justin's *Epitome*, and therefore it had recently appeared? Nazarius' passage is the basis for urging both. But, contrarily, Nazarius could be channeling Trogus' original; and in any case, even if Justin's version of Trogus was available by the year 321, that still leaves open how long it had been available.[6] As J. C. Yardley and W. Heckel put it after discussing the inadequate but suggestive evidence, "we have enough to suggest a date towards the latter part of the second century (or, possibly, the early part of the third)."[7]

A Provincial Epitomator

Justin's homeland is likewise unknown. The *Epitome*'s plentiful coverage of North African affairs, from early Carthaginian history to the murderously squabbling Ptolemies of Egypt, shows that the Gallic-descended Pompeius Trogus was much interested in that region's history, but it is no clue to Justin's provenance. Nor does Book 43's

---

[6] *HP* 7.2.7–12; Nazarius, *XII Panegyrici Latini* 10.20 (Teubner edition) = 4.20 (Oxford Classical Text); cf. Nixon and Rodgers (1994, 334–42, 366n89). Ammianus Marcellinus seventy years later told the story too, more briefly (Amm. 26.9.3). Syme (1988, 362–63), holds that Nazarius took the tale directly from Trogus, not through Justin.

[7] Yardley and Heckel (1997, 10–14 [quoted from 12], 16); so too (e.g.) Yardley (2000; 2003, 5); Alonso-Núñez (2002, 105); Baynham (2009, 292); Alidoust (2016, 912). By contrast Seel (1985, iv, and elsewhere) urges "fine tertii vel fortasse initio quarti saeculi"; similarly Barnes (1998); also Borgna (2018, 37–44, 107–27; 2020a, §§32–35), favoring publication sometime before Nazarius' oration (AD 321 "andrebbe considerato come il *terminus ante quem* per l'esistenza della *Epitoma*": [2018, 127]); Horn (2019, 175).

lengthy attention to the Iberian peninsula help, as again this must come from Trogus. Improbably, even a homeland in northern Asia Minor has been proposed for the epitomator.[8]

It is more likely that like Trogus' father, uncle, and grandfather, Justin was from Gaul. True, the work has little to say about that region, but this was Trogus' choice even though we know (thanks to Justin: 43.5.11–12) that Gaul was his ancestral home. As mentioned earlier, Iunianius rather than Iunianus was probably his family name (*nomen*). The *nomen* is recorded by several persons in Gaul and in the Roman Rhineland in the second and third centuries AD: for instance, a Iunianius Bassinus is commemorated on a family epitaph just outside Augustodunum (Autun); and the pleasantly named Iunianius Amabilis, a *sevir Augustalis*, is known at Forum Hadriani (Voorburg, next to The Hague). At Augusta Treverorum

---

[8] Africa: Zecchini (2016); contrast Syme (1988, 369–70); Yardley and Heckel (1997, 10, 32n30—both doubtful). Horn (2021, 42n33), cites M.-P. Arnaud-Lindet (*Histoire et politique à Rome: Les historiens romains IIIe ap. J.-C.–Ve siècle ap. J.-C.* [Paris, 2001]—not accessible to D. H.) for two North African senators named Iulius Iunianus on inscriptions. But with that *cognomen* one can equally note the Baetican L. Iunius L.f. Iunianus (*ILS* 5498) and the Bithynian(?) C. Iulius C.f. Iunianus (*ILS* 7192). Gaul: W. Kroll, *Paulys Realencyclopädie der Klassischen Altertumswissenchaft*, s.v. "Iunianus (4)"; Mócsy (1982–1984, 379–81, with maps). Olbia Pontica is urged by Ballesteros Pastor (2017, 83–84), viewing Justin, not Trogus, as interested in the Scythians and also as the true author of *HP*'s various speeches criticizing Rome. Borgna (e.g., 2020b, 38–39) stays noncommittal on the question.

(Trier) there lived Iunianius Modestus, another *Augustalis*. The *nomen* is rare, but *nomina* formed from Latin *cognomina* were certainly plentiful in Roman Gaul.[9]

The Epitome: *Structure and Flaws*

More debated is why our epitomator calls his work "a brief anthology" or "little body of flowers." As is often pointed out, he does not present it as an epitome even if his manuscripts, and moderns, do; and Augustine paid him the compliment of calling it a history.[10] As an abridgment, anthology, or *florilegium*, it has many flaws—drawing harsh condemnation from several frustrated readers.[11] The *Pro-*

---

[9] Bassinus: Gaillard (1985, 267) = *Année Épigraphique* 1993, no. 1196 (St-Symphorien-lès-Autun). Amabilis: *ILS* 7065 (not "Iunianus" as Móczy [1982–1984, 379]). Modestus: Raepset-Charlier (2002, 114) (= *CIL* 13.3695). *Nomen* from *cognomen*: e.g., Drinkwater (1978, 847); cf. Syme (1988, 370), but dismissing it in Justin's case as he dates the latter to the late empire. In the Rhineland and western Gaul, note several such *nomina*: Ianuarinius Ambacthus (*ILS* 4750, among the Batavi), two Honoratii (ib. 4687 Belgica; 9119 Rhineland), C. Crispinius Cladaeus (3931 Confluentes [Coblenz]), T. Genialinius Crescens (7084 Moguntiacum), Genialius Saturninus (4705 near Metz), Verecund(ius) Cornutus (7066 near The Hague), Victorinius Longinus (2526 near Augsburg), Vitalinius Felix and his son Felicissimus (7531 Lugdunum), and C. Vitalinius Victorinus (2412 near Geneva).

[10] *De civ. D.* 4.6. Cf. Yardley and Heckel (1997, 12, 15–19); Elliott (2018, 111n4).

[11] Harsh criticism: notably F. R. D. Goodyear's—"Justin excerpted hurriedly and carelessly"; he "contributed little, except his blunders and a scattering of synonyms, from the language of

logues show that Justin left a good deal out—for instance, most of Trogus' plentiful excursuses on eastern geography and peoples; and blurred or cut out all too many topographical and chronological details of events, preferring to focus on exciting, uplifting, or tragic moments within events (as discussed in *"Unsatisfactory Omissions,"* below). Various Roman wars in the Mediterranean east are ignored, even though the *Prologues* show most were in Trogus—including the war of Actium and the defeat of Antony and Cleopatra.[12]

Chronology too suffers repeatedly in the *Epitome.* Avoiding the tedium of actual dating by regnal years or magistrates, Justin very often marks sequences of events with generalized (and sometimes misleading) phrases, such as, "while this was taking place" (16.2.4), "while this was going on" (32.1.4), "at about the same time" (34.4.1). His favorite phrase, according to Yardley—used ten times—is *interiecto deinde tempore,* meaning "then, some time later" or the like. These phrases must, at least largely, be Justin's way of linking selected episodes while

his own day, which he substituted consciously or unconsciously for Trogus' words" (quoted by Yardley and Heckel [1997, 14]); cf. Bartlett (2014, 251). Also, "epitomatore mediocre e pedissequo" (Forni and Angeli Bertinelli [1982, 1311]); Justin "abbreviated, conflated, and often garbled Trogus" (Baynham [2009, 292]); and still other censures cited by Borgna (2020b, §18 and n. 9).

[12] Lengthy list of Trogus' excursuses in Bartlett (2014, 252–53n27). Cf. Yardley and Heckel (1997, n. 63) for omissions in *HP* 15–27 of topics that the *Prologues* mention; and Yardley, Wheatley, and Heckel (2011, 331–34) for omissions in *HP* 13–15 of items known from Diodorus and others. Borgna (2020a, §14 and n. 25), notes the silence on several later Roman wars.

passing over intervening items that, to him, "did not make pleasurable reading or serve to provide a moral" (*Praef.* §4). Yet in various places there are actual (if occasionally fanciful) time indicators. The Assyrian Empire lasted thirteen hundred years (1.2.13), the Second Messenian War came eighty years after the First (3.5.2), the great Athenian invasion of Sicily lasted for two (5.1.1), Philip II of Macedon "died at the age of forty-seven after reigning for twenty-five years" (9.8.1), Macedon's thirty kings ruled for nine hundred and twenty-four years but the Macedonian Empire for only a hundred and fifty-two (33.2.6; or maybe "one hundred and ninety-two"); so it seems that Trogus' chronology was much clearer and in its own terms fairly careful.[13]

Justin's fuzzy phrases can hide leaps in time. The Carthaginian defeat at Himera in Sicily in 480 BC (4.2.7) is followed in the next sentence, via "meanwhile" (*medio tempore*, 4.3.1), by events at Rhegium in 461/0 (4.3.1–3) and then, without any time marker at all, by actions in Sicily during the mid-420s (4.3.4–7); next, "some time later" (*interiecto deinde tempore*)—in fact, in 416—the Athenians decide on their ill-fated expedition to the island (4.4.1). Dramatizing intra-familial discord among the later Ptolemies, Justin tells how, after Ptolemy X Alexander

[13] *interiecto deinde tempore*: Yardley (2003, 94), cites its occurrences, e.g., 1.5.8, 3.6.7, 13.7.4, et al. For "a hundred and fifty-two years" of Macedonian Empire, the starting point would thus have been 320/19, a date difficult to explain; so some editors emend the figure to one hundred and ninety-two (see textual note to *HP* 33.2.6).

killed his lethal mother, Cleopatra III (before she could murder him instead), "as soon as [the crime] became known" his subjects drove him from the kingdom (39.4.5–5.1; *ubi primum conpertum est*, 5.1); but in reality Ptolemy slew his mother in 101 BC and was expelled thirteen years later for other reasons.[14]

There are plain mistakes too, which must be Justin's and not Trogus', and due to the former's efforts at compressing the latter: for instance, chronologically distorting the origins of Athens' famous expedition against Syracuse (4.4.1–2); having the Macedonian leader Cassander murder both of Alexander the Great's sons (15.2.1–5—the second son was the victim of another leader, Polyperchon; correctly, *Prol.* 15); and making two kings of Pergamum kings of neighboring Bithynia instead (27.3.2 and 3.5; 33.1.2) even though elsewhere he gets the realm right (38.6.2). It is careless to call the Persian satrap Pharnabazus, allied with Sparta against Athens, a Spartan general along with the actual Spartan general Mindarus (5.4.1). At 42.5.11–12 he makes the Parthian king Phraates not only restore to Augustus' Rome the captives and legionary standards taken in earlier wars—as happened in 20 BC—but simultaneously hand over his sons and grandsons as hostages, something Phraates did ten years later.[15]

---

[14] Blurry chronology: Yardley and Heckel (1997, 25–26); Borgna (2020b, 25–27). Cleopatra III and her son: G. Hölbl, *A History of the Ptolemaic Empire* (London and New York, 2001), 204–11.

[15] Useful, if disconcerting, lists of errors in, e.g., Forni and Angeli Bertinelli (1982, 1307–8); Bartlett (2014, 266–69).

Unsatisfactory Omissions

Justin regularly favors exciting, tragic, or emotive anecdotes at the expense of context. Much of his battle of Marathon is the tale of the valiant Cynegirus, who fought on with his teeth when both hands were cut off (2.9.9–21); and Justin—probably not Trogus—also kills in the battle the ousted Athenian tyrant Hippias, which is almost certainly wrong.[16] Reporting the conflict between the Carthaginian authorities and their exiled, but vengefully returned, general "Malchus" (18.7.3–18), he lavishes most of his narrative, complete with a (rare) speech in *oratio recta*, on how the general denounced his undutiful son, the city's high priest, and then crucified him in his vestments (18.7.6–15). Most details of the battle of Cynoscephalae are sacrificed—even the battle's name—in favor of two speeches by the Roman proconsul Flamininus and his opponent Philip V of Macedon, followed by comments on the clashing armies' emotions (30.4.5–16). So too the decisive battle of Pydna that ended the ancient kingdom of Macedon: it is left unnamed while Justin focuses almost entirely on how Cato the Censor's son lost his sword in the fight but forced his way through enemy ranks to recover it (33.2.1–4). Trogus can hardly have been so cavalier.[17]

Then again, an often-cited example of narrowed focus raises a different question. At 38.4.1–7.10 Justin famously reproduces verbatim the long speech (in *o. obliqua*), bit-

[16] Cicero makes the same error about Hippias, but not in a historical work (*Att.* 9.10.3).

[17] Cf. Forni and Angeli Bertinelli (1982, 1304).

terly critical of Rome, which Trogus gave to Mithridates of Pontus before the start of the First Mithridatic War—but all three Mithridatic Wars, from 88 to 63 BC, are then summed up in a single sentence: "after thus stimulating the men Mithridates, twenty-three years after taking power, embarked on his Roman wars" (38.8.1).[18] Justin never mentions Mithridates or his wars again. Is it another case of clipping out from Trogus "what did not make pleasurable reading or serve to provide a moral"? But the *Prologues* make no mention of the long and complex Mithridatic Wars either—only a remark in *Prol.* 40 of Tigranes of Armenia, Mithridates' son-in-law, losing Syria after being defeated by Rome, which happened after he joined in the final one. Is it possible that Trogus himself left these wars out?

Rhetoric and Language in Justin

Ancient historians' partiality for rhetoric extended to speeches, in which Trogus' and Justin's work abounds. Trogus had criticized Livy and Sallust, his older contemporaries, for indulging in direct-speech inventions written in their own distinctive style (so Justin reports: 38.3.11). By contrast, all but three of the many orations in the *Historiae Philippicae* are suitably in indirect speech, *oratio obliqua*, including the one given to Mithridates denouncing Rome's misdeeds (38.4.1–7.10). Ironically—or self-

---

[18] Justin's "twenty-three years" (*annos tres et XX*) is also a mistake for thirty-three years; there seems no reason to suspect a copyist's slip.

subvertingly?—all, Mithridates' included, are in standard Latin rhetorical style, as indeed they had to be if they were to be included at all.

The other three, in *oratio recta*, are Themistocles' "speech" (rather bizarrely inscribed on coastal rocks) urging the Ionians to desert Xerxes (2.12.3–6), Eumenes' to his mutinous troops before they hand him over to his enemies (14.4.2–14), and the rebuke of the Carthaginian "Malchus" to his recalcitrant priestly son (18.7.10–14). Were these Justin's own inventions? Eumenes' speech, it has been noted, includes details of his career that Justin's own abridgment does not have. Even if his own composition, he must have based it on material in Trogus. The same probably holds for the other two.[19]

The choice of terminology in all three offers very few "Justinisms"—words or phrases that are found only in later Latin, therefore cannot be Trogus'—and this suggests Justin kept these speeches largely as he found them. Mithridates' oration in its turn has a number of phrases recalling Livian ones, with again nothing identifiably "Justinist."[20] J. C. Yardley has shown that plentiful words and

[19] Eumenes' speech: Bartlett (2014, 271–74); Yardley, Wheatley, and Heckel (2011, 186–88, 318).

[20] "Justinisms" rare in the three speeches: cf. Yardley (2003, 125, 147, 154)—although he sees Themistocles' message as Justin's invention *because* in *oratio recta* (Yardley [1998, 106–7; (2003, 190]). Mithridates' speech has echoes of Livy: (Yardley (2003, 21–22). Ballesteros Pastor (2017) argues the entire opposite: Justin's statement about Trogus' speeches (38.3.11) is false; in reality, he rewrote them from Trogus' *oratio recta* into *oratio obliqua*, and the three in *oratio recta* are Justin's own composition to hide the fact.

phrases throughout the *Historiae Philippicae* echo words and phrases in Livy's surviving books, many more in fact than terms shared with Cicero, Caesar, Sallust, and Virgil. They cannot all be imports by Justin, and perhaps none is.

Caution must apply. Post-Augustan vocabulary peppers the text as well, with notable contributions from the pseudo-Quintilianic *Major* and *Minor Declamations* (model speeches on varied topics, wrongly claimed by their authors to be by Quintilian), and from the second-century-author Apuleius, third-century legal texts, and even verse, such as the first-century didactic piece *Aetna* and the poets Statius and Silius Italicus. Yardley finds, too, a number of items that can be credited to the epitomator himself. The literary style of the *Historiae Philippicae*— competent, rarely flashy, fond of lengthy periods (and ablatives absolute), occasionally obscure—is thus a blend: mainly Augustan and with heavy input from Livy, speckled with Silver-Age and later tints.[21]

The picture is a little disconcerting. It reveals Trogus, while collecting his historical materials from a variety of Greek sources recent and older, also regularly looking up current and older Latin literary works for verbal inspiration, including scrutinizing newly released books of the history by his almost exact coeval (and friend?) Livy. There may in fact well be much more of Livy in the *Historiae* than scholars can identify, for everything that that historian wrote after his Book 45 has been lost. Later on, Trogus' anthologist-epitomator, in turn, when paring down the monumental work, intermittently blends its lan-

---

[21] For a friendlier verdict on Trogus' style: Syme (1992, 17)—"fluent and elegant, albeit conventional."

guage with coloring borrowed from literature of the generations after its author's own time.

Justin Occasionally Speaks

Justin very occasionally puts himself into his *florum corpusculum*. The *Preface* is the most obvious and lengthy example, with its lavish praise of Pompeius Trogus, "a man with the eloquence of the ancients," "great intellectual and great physical stamina," and "Herculean enterprise" (§§1–2), followed by Justin's description (§§4–6) of when and why he undertook his project, and by proper diffidence over what both his unnamed addressee and future ages will make of it. Even so, some commentators suggest that he uses part of Trogus' own presumed preface to fill his out. Later, the comment about Roman rulers being named "Caesar" and "Augustus" (41.5.8) must be his own, as noted above; so may a few cross-references to other parts of the work (e.g., 20.5.1, 23.3.2). Definitely Justin's again is the introduction (38.3.11) to Mithridates' anti-Roman speech with its remark about Trogus' antipathy to speeches in direct discourse. And of course he reports Trogus' succinct account of his Vocontian family background at the close of Book 43—though, incongruously, Justin says that Trogus had it in Book 44.

A Manual for Rhetoricians or Historians?

The impression of slapdash or clumsy filleting by Justin of the original *Historiae Philippicae* has been contested. Arguably, the epitomator-anthologist consciously pursued an aim not historical but rhetorical: to omit even important details, or subordinate them, in favor of episodes of drama and pathos, with the aim of compiling materials usable by orators—with Nazarius' little anecdote about the Macedonians and their cradled king a convenient example of this. All the same, in his *Preface* Justin stresses that he compiled his *breve florum corpusculum* because Trogus had succeeded in encompassing "the [Greek] annals (*res gestae*) of all ages, kings, nations and peoples" (§2) and he, Justin, wished "to refresh the memory of those who had studied history in Greek, and provide instruction for those who had not" (§4). This rationale takes for granted that the readers Justin wants to reach will be interested in the *res gestae*, literally the affairs and achievements, of past states—in effect, their history.[22]

Nonetheless, it is true that for Greek and Roman historians history was closely bound up with oratory ("since this is an undertaking uniquely fitted for oratory," as Atticus says in Cicero's *de Legibus*, written when Trogus was probably a youth). Speeches were essential elements in these productions; likewise, dramatic scenes of action, pathos, terror, or excitement. Justin may thus have expected that his anthology would both convey world history to readers unable to possess or access Pompeius Trogus directly and become a storehouse of appealing historical examples for Latin orators.[23]

[22] Justin as intentional rhetorical excerptor: e.g., Yardley and Heckel (1997, 15–19); Bartlett (2014, 269–74); Horn (2019, 175: "Justin se soucie de rhétorique et non d'histoire"; 2021, 43–44); Borgna (2018; 2020a; 2020b, 34: "a collection of materials for use by future rhetors").

[23] Cic. *Leg.* 1.5 (*quippe cum sit opus, ut tibi quidem videri solet, unum hoc oratorium maxime*); cf. Laird (2009). On essential elements in Roman historiography: Feldherr (2009); J. Marincola, ed., *A Companion to Greek and Roman Historiography*, 2

If he did hope for this latter, he would have been disappointed. In the copious speeches (not to mention Christian sermons) that survive from the later Roman centuries, Nazarius' brief retelling of the infant Macedonian king seems the only borrowing from him—if it is from him and not from Trogus. This even though, by the later fourth century anyway, the *Historiae* were well known: praised by the author of the *Historia Augusta*, mentioned by Jerome, Augustine, and Orosius, and later still by Cassiodorus and Isidore of Seville—not as a rhetorical source but as history.[24]

POMPEIUS TROGUS

A Gallic Roman Historian

The author of the original *Historiae Philippicae* was not, in his own mind, a Gaul, as moderns usually term him. At the start of Book 43, Justin, in one of his rare personal interventions, writes:

> Trogus now returns home to the beginnings of the city of Rome as if from a long trip abroad, thinking himself an ungrateful citizen (*ingrati civis officium existimans*) if, after he had illuminated every other nation's history, he remained silent only about his

---

vols. (Maldon and Oxford, 2010); elsewhere Marincola stresses "the omnipresent influence of rhetoric" on historians (*Authority and Tradition in Ancient Historiography* [Cambridge, UK, 1997], 5, cf. 21–22, 128–30).

[24] Syme (1988, 365–66; 1992, 13); Yardley and Heckel (1997, 8, 15, 20).

own country (*de sola tantum patria*). He therefore touches briefly on the beginnings of the Roman Empire [etc.]. (43.1.1–2)

At the end of the same book, as remarked earlier, he lets Trogus speak again:

> In his last book Trogus says that his ancestors were of Vocontian origin, his grandfather, Pompeius Trogus, received Roman citizenship from Gnaeus Pompeius in the war with Sertorius, his uncle had been a cavalry squadron leader under the same Pompeius in the Mithridatic War, and his father had also served under Gaius Caesar (*sub C. Caesare militasse*) and been responsible for his correspondence, diplomatic missions, and official seal. (43.5.11–12)

Gaining citizenship from Pompey the Great, grandfather Trogus' *praenomen* will have been Gnaeus. Probably the historian's father and the historian himself bore it too. The Celtic *cognomen* Trogus, it has been suggested, meant "clan" or—another suggestion—"miserable."[25]

---

[25] "Clan": Klotz (1952, 2300–2301). "Miserable": K. H. Schmidt, *Die Komposition in gallischen Personnamen* (Tübingen, 1957), 262. Several persons with the noteworthy *nomina* Trogius/Troccius are found in Narbonese Gaul: e.g., *CIL* 12.2758, 3142a, 3145, 3961, 3962. Whether the Cn. Pompeius, an interpreter for Caesar's legate Titurius in Gaul in 54 (*de Bello Gallico* 5.36.1), was the historian's father or uncle is not known (Mineo [2016b, 197], suggests his father); if so he must have survived Titurius' disaster that winter, though few did (*BG* 5.37.7). Against identifying the C. Caesar of 43.5.12 with Augustus' grandson who died in AD 2: Mineo (2016b, 196–97).

The Vocontii lived between the middle Rhône River and the Vercors massif, with not one but two cantonal capitals, Vasio (Vaison-la-Romaine) and Lucus Augusti (Luc-en-Diois), and an inscription related to the historian's family exists near Vaison.[26] The Roman province of Transalpine Gaul—renamed Narbonese Gaul in Augustus' time—had been conquered in the late second century BC, then was rapidly flooded with Italian settlers and investors. Julius Caesar and Augustus founded Roman colonies there, and so by the 70s AD it could be termed "more truly an Italy than a province" (Plin. *HN* 3.31, a play on its popular nickname, Provincia).

Significantly nonetheless, Trogus the historian, if Justin cites him rightly, regarded himself as a Roman. In other words, while his ancestors were Gauls, no doubt eminent Vocontian Gauls, he was as Roman as (for example) his older contemporary, Catullus' and Cicero's learned friend Cornelius Nepos from Transpadana, the Gallic region of Italy beyond the River Po; or the renowned Q. Ennius, one of the founding fathers of Latin poetry and drama, who had come to Rome almost two centuries earlier from Rudiae in the Sallentine heel of Italy and claimed to have "three hearts" (*tria corda*): native Oscan, Roman, and Greek. Pompeius Trogus probably could claim the same, with Gallic in lieu of Ennius' Oscan.

As his father had been a personal secretary to Julius Caesar—at least so Trogus said, though his father never appears in our copious sources on Caesar—the historian

---

[26] *CIL* 12.1371, dedicated to a "Q. Pom[peio]" by his daughter Pompeia after AD 14 or 28 (photograph in Yardley, Wheatley, and Heckel [2011, v]).

will have lived through the Augustan age. As mentioned earlier, the last clearly datable event in the *Historiae* is the Parthian king sending his sons to Rome as hostages in 10 BC. The medieval English historian Matthew Paris averred that Trogus "ended his chronicles" in AD 9, and some think this means his death; but, whether career or death, the source for Matthew's report is totally unknown.[27]

Nature and Purpose of the Historiae

Gnaeus(?) Pompeius Trogus was author not only of the *Historiae Philippicae* but of a sizable work on zoology, *De animalibus*, drawing on Aristotle; Pliny the Elder often mentions it, as well. Nevertheless, the *Historiae* were Trogus' magnum opus, forty-four books of world history—

---

[27] *Prol.* 42 includes an entry for "the end of the Saraucae" (*interitusque Saraucarum*; Justin does not have it), taken as a reference to the collapse of a short-lived kingdom of the nomadic Sacaraucae in Afghanistan and neighboring lands. Though widely dated to circa AD 6 (cf. Horn [2021], 37]), J. Wiesehöfer (*BNP* s.v. Sacaraucae) puts it in the mid-first century BC, and U. Ellerbrock, *The Parthians: The Forgotten Empire* (London, 2021), 118, dates it still earlier, to around 100 BC. Cf. A. D. H. Bavar, *Encyclopaedia Iranica* (online), s.v. Gondophares (accessed February 10, 2023). By contrast, P. Callieri (*Encyclopaedia Iranica*, s.v. Sakas: in Afghanistan) dates the *interitus* to around AD 20. The item clearly cannot be used to help date Trogus' *HP*.—Matthew Paris: *Flores Historiarum, sub anno* AD 9; Mineo (2016b, 198). (But "of Westminster" is a mistaken sobriquet: S. Lloyd and R. Reader, *Oxford Dictionary of National Biography*, online [2010], s.v. Matthew Paris.)

"world" in ancient eyes: the Mediterranean and the Middle East—from mythical times to his own day. As Justin explains,

> [he] composed his history of Greece and the whole world in the Latin language; . . . enticed either by a wish to rival these [Greek] authors' fame or by the originality (*varietate et novitate*) of such a work, and in order to make Greek history as accessible in our language as ours is in Greek. (*Praef.* §1)

Trogus' history told the Mediterranean past as seen through Greek eyes, using Greek sources (which ones are much debated). Rome is absent apart from sporadic mention of its dealings with, mostly, Hellenistic states together with an account, at the start of Book 43, of its mythical antecedents (43.1.2–3.2)—an account shorter, at least in Justin's reduction, than the story of the Greek city of Massilia in Narbonese Gaul (43.3.3–5.10). The reduced *Historiae Philippicae* fairly certainly does not do justice to its original author's achievement, which earned Trogus the rank—at any rate in the eyes of the eccentric composer of the *Historia Augusta*—of one of Rome's four leading historians.[28]

Why Philippicae?

The title of the work, given in manuscripts though never mentioned by Justin, remains opaque. Theopompus of

---

[28] *Hist. Aug. Aurelian* 2.2, and *Probus* 2.7 (Livy, Sallust, Tacitus, Trogus); Syme (1988, 364–65; 1992).

Chios, a historian contemporary with and critical of Philip II of Macedon, had termed his fifty-eight books *Philippica*, "History of Philip," even though its surviving fragments show that he ranged far more widely, giving space like several other large-scale historians (Herodotus being a famous example) to digressions on peoples, mores, marvels, and other topics of interest—features frequent in Trogus' own *Historiae Philippicae*. But as Alexander's father is only one figure in Trogus' work, though a major one, another suggestion is that the title is a reminiscence of, or a tribute to, Cicero's renowned speeches opposing Antony in 44 and 43 BC, which he nicknamed the *Philippics* to recall Demosthenes' classic denunciations of Philip II three centuries before.

Other proposals see *Philippicae* as acknowledging the many Philips, starting with Alexander's father and ending with two negligible Seleucid Philips in first-century BC Syria, who earn mention in the work's Hellenistic-era books (though if so, it could equally have been named *Alexandricae* or even *Ptolomeicae*). Or, a similar idea, that *Philippicae* refers to the Macedonian Empire and its post-Alexander successors, all originating from Philip II—or even that it is an allusion to the battle of Philippi in 42 BC, which ended all hope of restoring the free Republic and opened the road ultimately to the monarchy of Augustus.[29] These efforts at solving the puzzle all pose difficulties, and

[29] Theories about *HP*'s name: e.g., Klotz (1952, 2303); Urban (1982b); Alonso-Núñez (1987, 58–59; 2002, 105); Yardley and Heckel (1997, 24–25); Landucci (2014); Mineo (2016b, 200–204); Borgna (2018, 31–36); Horn (2019, 176–77).

it may be best to leave it unsolved, while trusting that Trogus gave an explanation at the start of his work that Justin failed to transmit.

Trogus' Sources

Another fraught question is what predecessors Pompeius Trogus consulted. All were Greek historians, Justin states (*Praef.* §3); but nowhere in the *Historiae* are any named. Trogus would certainly have had an embarrassment of riches to choose from. Not only Herodotus, Thucydides, Xenophon, and Polybius—historians in earlier times whose works we still have, complete or in part, and whose occasional echoes in Trogus are varyingly identified by scholars—but also other large-scale works especially of classical and Hellenistic Greek historians, which have disappeared save for scattered extracts quoted by extant authors. Ephorus, Philistus, and Theopompus from the fourth century, Timaeus, Duris, and Hieronymus from the third, and Poseidonius from the first are all candidates. But without more than fragments of their works, and with Trogus' own history surviving only as a *breve corpusculum*, it is problematic to identify what he took from them.[30]

For the bulk of the *Historiae*, the Alexandrian Timagenes, an older and opinionated contemporary of Trogus, and at one time a protégé of none other than Augustus, has been confidently identified as Trogus' source by many

[30] Cf. Brunt (1980, 477–78, 494). Trogus and his sources: Forni and Angeli Bertinelli (1982); Yardley and Heckel (1997, 30–34); Borgna (2018, 131–55); Horn (2021, 36–41).

scholars, including Yardley and Heckel. In one older and for a time influential view, the *Historiae* were even judged to be simply Timagenes' world history *On Kings* turned into Latin.[31] Close resemblances between a few items in Trogus and their matches in Polyaenus, the later-second-century AD Greek military anecdotalist, suggest that both were taking these from the same earlier source, economically identified by many as Timagenes. Still, if the items came from him—or another ultimate source—we might have expected a more plentiful range of matching stratagems in the *Historiae* and Polyaenus' *Stratagems*. Disappointingly, even in his Book 4, an inventory of Macedonian stratagems, Polyaenus lacks the tale of the infant king Aeropus that appealed to both Trogus and Nazarius.[32]

For particular periods or regions, Trogus seems to have turned to other authorities besides his main source or sources. Thus for the era, achievements, and crimes of

[31] McInerney and Roller, *FGrH*, "Timagenes (88)," in *Jacoby Online* (accessed February 20, 2023); L. Capponi, *OCD* s.v. (accessed February 20, 2023); cf. Balsdon (1979, 183–85). Trogus virtually translated Timagenes: von Gutschmid (1882). Timagenes as Trogus' main source: (e.g.) for Yardley and Heckel (1997, 33), it would be surprising "if a history of similar scope and emphasis, completed shortly before Trogus set about creating his own in Latin, did not influence or, indeed, form the basis of the latter."

[32] *HP* 1.7.11–19, 1.5.10, 2.5.1–7; Polyaenus, *Strat.* 7.6.4, 7.7, 7.44.2 (some Persian and Scythian stratagems). If these items ultimately go back to Timagenes—or another primary source for both—we might have expected *HP* and Polyaenus to furnish more plentifully matching stratagems, yet there are none.

Philip II he looks likely to have drawn on the king's contemporary (and critic) Theopompus.[33] As his chief source on Alexander the Great, scholarly consensus agrees again on Cleitarchus, a contemporary of the conqueror: Cleitarchus' history of Alexander's reign, though lost, fairly certainly comes through in many surviving sources (not only Justin but Diodorus, Curtius, and Plutarch)—but, noteworthily, they are much less critical than Trogus is of the king. In fact, Trogus almost certainly drew on another account or accounts too. Writings on Alexander by contemporaries and then by later authors were exceptionally plentiful; and the increasingly dark depiction of the king and the detailed claim—stated as plain fact—that he was murdered by Antipater point to a different and subversive account that Trogus, for reasons of his own, chose either to follow or at any rate to combine with Cleitarchus'.[34]

[33] Cf. M. Ostwald (1994), in *CAH* 6, 601–2; K. Meister, "Theopompus (3) of Chios, Greek historian," in *OCD* (accessed March 17, 2023). Another late-fourth century BC author, Anaximenes of Lampsacus, wrote a history called *Philippica* too, most of it lost, as usual—an eight-book account of Philip II (*FGrH* 72; cf. M. F. Williams, s.v., *Jacoby Online* (2013) (accessed March 22, 2023). He was in Alexander the Great's entourage, so this work and other writings must have been Philip-friendly, in contrast to Theopompus'.

[34] Horn (2021, 146–212, 275–94) argues that much of this dark portrayal is Trogus' own work, not from a source, and is colored to reflect the political upheavals of Trogus' own time. Cleitarchus: L. Prandi (2016), *FGrH*, "Kleitarchos of Alexandria (137)," *Jacoby Online* (accessed March 24, 2023); Horn (2021, 295–98).

Other sections of the *Historiae* may likewise be based on sources specific to their topics or periods. As mentioned earlier, Trogus shows a particular interest in Carthage, even though the city was neither a kingdom nor one of the world empires. Its foundation, domestic history over several centuries, and the memorable obituary-encomium of Hannibal all figure notably (see also below). Trogus' accounts of Massilia and Spain, tacked on almost as appendices to the bulk of the *Historiae*—as suggested earlier, maybe in a second edition—may again have come from works other than Theopompus, Timagenes, and their ilk. For although the idea of Trogus using more than one sole source, or else very few sources, is not universally accepted, a wider range of them—if Justin has not completely invented the account of his methodology—well fits Trogus' research and compositional processes as described in the *Preface* (§§1–3).[35]

Trogus' Themes

One theme in the *Historiae Philippicae* is the (supposed) regular succession of empires, starting with the semi-fabled Assyrians and narrating those of the Medes and Persians, Egyptians, Scythians (rulers of the steppes), Athenians, and Spartans—all these in Books 1 to 6—be-

---

[35] The Massiliots put in a unique earlier appearance in 129 BC (37.1.1), persuading Rome to pardon their founder-city Phocaea for supporting the Pergamene-pretender Aristonicus: a case of Trogus adding an item from his preparatory readings for the final books?

fore devoting the next thirty-four books to the Macedonian and then the Macedonian-descended Hellenistic empires, from Alexander the Great's father, Philip II, onward. Justin claims that Trogus structured his narrative chronologically:

> what Greek historians treated piecemeal . . . Pompeius arranged chronologically with items laid out in order. (*Praef.* §3)

But in fact this would not have been possible where events in different states overlapped, or where it was more rational to follow the fortunes of a particular state or region. Thus in Book 2 Persia's early history is paused after the battle of Marathon, and Trogus then recounts Athens' mythical origins and early history; next, after a return to the Persians' Greek wars in the second half of Book 2 (the longest book in the work) and the first of Book 3, he switches to the origins of Sparta and other Peloponnesian states. After that come Greek events down to the rise and dominance of Macedon under Philip II (Books 3–9). This is the start of the Macedonian Empire, but Persia during the same period returns in Book 10—before being overwhelmed by the careers of Alexander the Great and his bloodthirsty successors (Books 11–18.6).

The rest of Book 18 and then Book 19 move to the origins and early history of Carthage and to its ensuing fifth-century wars in Sicily. From Books 20 to 23 we read the checkered and violent stories of the fourth-century Sicilian tyrants Dionysius and Agathocles, before returning to the lengthy and no-less violent fortunes of the Macedonian Empires (with a pause, Books 37–38, for the early career of the famous Mithridates VI of Pontus), until the last of them, Ptolemaic Egypt, falls to Rome in Book 40.[36]

Trogus on Gaul, Gauls, and Africa

Surprisingly for a Gallic Roman, Trogus largely ignored the history of Gaul (written sources for it must have been thin, in any case), limiting himself to an account in Book 43 of Greek Massilia and Massilia's intermittently stressful dealings with its Ligurian and Gallic neighbors. He was much more informative, though not wholly enthusiastic, about the largely predatory Gallic tribes who migrated eastward in Hellenistic times. "A violent, reckless, bellicose race" (24.4.4) who practiced a "ferocity . . . that was terrifying Asia and Italy" (32.1.3), most of their activities in the *Historiae* are unscrupulous and disruptive. Gallic mercenaries, for example, win a victory for Antiochus Hierax in 240/39 BC, but then turn against him and have to be bought off like "bandits" (27.2.11–12). Gallic depredations extend (in 279) even to attacking the sacred site of Delphi, a sacrilege for which they are duly and comprehensively punished (24.6.1–8.16), with the episode ending solemnly: "So it turned out that from such a huge army, which . . . had felt contempt even for the gods, none survived even to record such a massive defeat." In the west, even after the Gauls around Massilia learn the benefits of Greek civilization, they continue to make war on the city (43.4.1–2, 5.1). The territory of Gaul itself scarcely en-

---

[36] Summaries of *HP* contents: Yardley and Heckel (1997, 22–23); Alonso-Núñez, *The Idea of Universal History in Greece* (Leiden, 2002), 133–34.

thused its descendant: Trogus—unless it was Justin—judged even Spain's climate as superior to that of Gaul, a land "buffeted by incessant winds" (44.1.4).[37]

Had Justin not included the information that Trogus was Gallic by ancestry, readers might have thought him a North African (just as the epitomator himself has occasionally been thought to be), for as just noted there is much attention to that region. Trogus writes an excursus on Cyrene (13.7.1–11), narrates the story of Carthage, as just mentioned, also Agathocles' invasion of Africa (22.3.1–8.15), and later the career after the Second Punic War of Carthage's famed leader Hannibal, and his death (31.1.7–2.8, 3.5–6.9; 32.4.2–10). One (or more than one) of Trogus' sources must have devoted significant space to Carthaginian affairs, and he was interested enough to exploit it. The Sicilian Timaeus may be the authority for most of it, but he ended his history with 265 BC; one of the "Hannibal historians," such as Sosylus of Sparta, was conceivably another. We might wonder whether Trogus drew on some of the same source materials as Livy did for his own excursus on Carthage in his lost sixteenth book.

Trogus' Criticisms of Rome

Composed to inform readers of Latin about Greek and related histories, the *Historiae Philippicae* deliberately

[37] Trogus seen as much more favorable to the Gauls: e.g., Alonso-Núñez (1987, 69: [he] "does not miss any opportunity to stress the importance of the Gauls"); Bartlett (2014, 270), holding that the praise from the Aetolians, Hannibal, and Mithridates for Gallic victories over Rome (e.g., 28.2.3–7, 31.5.9, 38.4.7–10) "must represent Trogus' patriotism"; Borgna (2018, 203–10) on "l'orgoglio gallico."

excluded Rome's. Even so, Rome itself comes in for moments of specific criticism—enough of them to convince some readers that Trogus was really an anti-Roman Gaul.[38] The Aetolians deride the Romans (28.2.1–13), the Illyrian ruler Demetrius criticizes them (29.2.2–6), Hannibal insists to Antiochus III that they are easy to beat (31.5.2–9), and—most strikingly of all—Trogus gives to Mithridates and Justin reproduces in full the already-mentioned and long oration excoriating Roman greed, aggression, and faithlessness (38.4.1–7.10).

In a few other places Trogus himself is censorious: for instance, marking the annexation of the kingdom of Pergamum (which Justin, no doubt rather than Trogus, persistently calls "Asia" when not calling it Bithynia) with the comment, "Thus Asia, now made the property of the Romans, passed its vices as well as its riches on to Rome"—this because the consuls sent to carry out the task quarreled, through greed for its wealth (36.4.12). A little earlier comes the rather snide remark about Rome's friendship enabling Judaea to gain freedom from the weakened Seleucid Empire, "the Romans at that time readily distributing the property of others" (36.3.9). When Trogus turns in Book 41 to the Parthians, who had replaced the old Persian monarchy with their own, they are the people "between whom and the Romans the world is more or less divided" (41.1.1). That he ascribes the victory over Macedon at Cynoscephalae as due to *Romana Fortuna* (30.4.16), rather than Roman valor, has been claimed as criticism too.

[38] Alonso-Núñez (1987, 68–69); Balsdon (1979, 183–85); similar interpretations cited critically by Urban (1982a, 1435n63); Yardley and Heckel (1997, n. 72).

Nonetheless, the notion of an anti-Roman Trogus has largely fallen away as its supposed examples are more closely examined.[39] For example, Fortune, Greek *Tyche*, as an omnipresent and often decisive force was both a literary commonplace and, for some, a serious historical concept (Polybius being perhaps its best-known exponent).[40] In Book 39, *Fortuna Romana* decides to extend Rome's reach beyond Italy to the kingdoms of the East (39.5.3): given the vicious internecine behavior of the eastern monarchs, major and minor, whose fortunes and crimes Trogus has been reporting over more than half the *Historiae*, he quite likely saw this as an improvement.

In Rome's own embryonic history in Book 43, Fortune plays a crucially benign role: the infant twins Romulus and Remus are saved by it, and so by implication is the future Rome (43.2.5). As for *Romana Fortuna* at Cynoscephalae, if Trogus unlike his epitomator reported it in even modest detail, readers would have learned how the Romans were near to losing the struggle until a military tribune seized

[39] Cf. Urban (1982a) citing and rejecting views that for *Romana Fortuna* to defeat the Macedonians is anti-Roman criticism. Hostility of Trogus to Rome: rejected by Klotz (1952, 2308); Urban (1982a, 1433–41); Yardley and Heckel (1997, 29–30); Borgna (2018, 157–202); Horn (2019, 178–81). Adler (2006) judges Sallust's composition of Mithridates' letter to the Parthian king denouncing Rome (*Hist.* 4.69 M) as more effectively anti-Roman than Trogus', therefore as showing that Roman historians could be both patriotic and critical. Cf. Malaspina (1976), seeing Trogus as "filobarbaro" without this making him anti-Rome.

[40] Cf. Davies (2009, 170–72: "the enactment of the gods' will," 171). On Polybius and Fortune (*Tyche*): F. W. Walbank, *A Historical Commentary on Polybius*, vol. 1 (Oxford, 1957), 16–26; Davidson (2009, 128–30); Hau (2011).

a chance tactical opportunity, detached some cohorts from the more successful Roman right, and attacked the un-protected rear of the winning Macedonian phalanx—a fortune-given stroke. Such details were of no interest to Justin, but the sentiment and its phrase were, and so were kept.[41]

As for the Parthian Empire, it was only the latest ver-sion of the great non-Greek eastern powers that had al-ways dominated their regions apart from the three centu-ries of Seleucid supremacy. Acknowledging its position was hardly to criticize Rome. Moreover, the Parthian pair of books closes with Augustus striking such fear into King Phraates that, without fighting, the emperor both regained the captives and standards that Crassus and Antony had lost, and also extracted Phraates' own children and grand-children as hostages (42.5.10–12). This can only be a sig-nal, one not very subtle either, that even if the two empires are technically matched, we still know which one is supe-rior.[42]

The Critic as Moralist

Pointing out and censuring Roman flaws and vices was not something only Greeks did. Livy found it needful to com-

[41] Polyb. 18.20–27; Walbank, *Commentary on Polybius*, vol. 2 (1967), 575–85.

[42] Similarly, Alidoust (2016, 941), who especially in light of the sarcastic comment (42.4.16) about "Parthia's destiny, where hav-ing parricidal kings is almost the rule," rightly holds (929–41) that the account of the many *parricidia* among Parthian royalty, as earlier among Persian, is a further intentional signal of Rome's continuing (moral) superiority.

plain about Greek art captured from Syracuse in 211 BC giving Romans improper (meaning un-Roman) thoughts, then about the harm wrought by the rich plunder from Asia Minor in 187 (it launched the creeping demoralization of the Roman character).[43] The sacking and looting of Carthage and Corinth forty years later he surely judged equally deplorable, though his narrative of them has been lost. Other Roman writers too wrote strong rhetorical denunciations, often giving them to Rome's opponents. Sallust devised one for Mithridates in his *Histories*, after making trenchant comments in his own monographs; Tacitus would put a ringing invective into the mouth of the Caledonian leader Calgacus just before his battle against Tacitus' revered father-in-law Agricola.[44]

Moreover, readers of the *Historiae Philippicae* would soon find (and of course many already knew) that every one of the critics and mockers of Rome in its pages then suffered utter defeat. Even the Gauls, who have no oration in the work but whom most of the rhetorical critics laud for their victories over Rome, would one day be defeated and conquered too, again as Trogus' Roman readers knew. We cannot assume that Trogus was above dramatic irony.

[43] Livy 25.40.2 (corruptive art from Syracuse), 39.6.3–9 (as with Asiatic *praeda* and *luxuria*). By Augustus' and Livy's day, the damage was total: Livy, *Praef.* 9.

[44] Calgacus' speech: A. J. Woodman, *Tacitus: Agricola* (Cambridge, UK, 2014), 20–25, 236–56. Criticisms of Rome by Greeks and Romans: cf. Balsdon (1979, 161–92); D. Hoyos, *Rome Victorious: The Irresistible Rise of the Roman Empire* (London and New York, 2019), 164–69.

Trogus combines such irony with occasional and fairly conventional moral criticism of Roman imperial flaws. He can present the Romans of past times as morally admirable (18.2.7–10, the Senate of Pyrrhus' time; 31.8.8–9, Scipio Africanus lecturing Antiochus the Great on Roman virtues), and yet, as just mentioned, he too avers—like Sallust, Livy, and others—that the wealth of the Greek east brought vice to Rome. He is pragmatically willing to record how, after 201 BC, the Romans kept looking for pretexts to fight Macedon until they found one (30.2.8–3.6). Pragmatically again, as already mentioned, he tells us of the Romans "readily distributing the property of others" as they began dismantling the Seleucid Empire. In similar fashion, we read how, by 147 BC, Rome was looking for a pretext to confront Greece's over-powerful Achaean League, and none other than *Fortuna* brought them one (34.1.1–5). Like Rome's eminent Greek admirer Polybius, Trogus can be objective when he thinks it appropriate.

His stated views, in Justin's anthology anyway, about his own time are limited. Augustus is properly complimented: through making the Parthians hand over not only Roman captives and standards but also their royal children and grandchildren as hostages, "by the greatness of his name (*magnitudine nominis sui*) Caesar gained more than another general could have by force of arms" (42.5.10–12). And closing the *Historiae* comes mention of Augustus subduing and civilizing Spain after "having conquered the world" by "his victorious arms" (44.5.8). This of course was polite exaggeration by a writer who three books before had divided the world between Rome and Parthia, but Augustus expected such laudation from authors.[45] If there was a more enthusiastic encomium of the emperor somewhere in the *Historiae*, Justin has excluded it.

Virtues and Vices in the Historiae Philippicae

Pompeius Trogus' moral and historical views—with two striking exceptions (as detailed in *"Good and Evil in Philip and Alexander of Macedon,"* below)—were again conventional. Moderation (*moderatio*) is prominent: early on he speaks with unusual warmth about it, contrasting the simplicity of the Scythians with the unhelpful sophistication of the Greeks:

> And would that the rest of mortals had similar moderation and restraint (*moderatio abstinentiaque*) with people's property; for there certainly would not be so many wars going on throughout the ages in every land, nor would more men be taken off by iron and weapons than is naturally determined by fate, making it seem amazing that nature should grant them what Greeks are unable to achieve from the long teachings of sages and precepts of philosophers, and that refined morality is inferior to coarse barbarism. So much more has ignorance of vice benefited them than knowledge of virtue has the Greeks. (2.2.11–15)[46]

[45] Augustus the world's master: e.g., Vit. *De Arch. Praef.* §1; Verg. *Aen.* 6.791–800; Hor. *Epist.* 2.1.1–4; *Carm.* 4.14.41–52; Ov. *Met.* 15.860; *Tr.* 4.4.15; etc.

[46] *Moderatio* in Trogus: Bartlett (2014, 256–60, 262, 279).

This morose comment is matched by another—a perceptive one—at the start of Book 8, with Philip II extending his power across Greece:

> As for the Greek states, while each wanted overall power they all lost power. For rushing wildly into mutual destruction they realized only when overcome that each one's loss meant ruin for them all; for Philip . . . by fostering the various states' disputes and bringing help to the weaker sides made defeated and conquered alike bend to his regal servitude. (8.1.1–3)

An even more bitter outburst, intelligent again even if thoroughly rhetorical, comes only a few pages later (8.4.8–9): "to think that the liberators of the world . . . by their own discord and civil wars they were so reduced as to be fawning on what just recently was one of their paltry client-states," and so on.

In other words, the Greeks failed in both *moderatio* and foresight and paid for it with the loss of freedom. The outcome was the battle of Chaeronea, with Trogus' somber verdict: "This day was for all Greece the end of both her glorious supremacy and her ancient liberty" (9.3.11). Of course the sentiments probably go back to his Greek source (Theopompus quite likely), but to include them in his own work tells us that he shared that judgment.

Leaders with *moderatio* and other virtues—courage (*virtus*), sobriety, justice, and piety—are admired: Cyrus the Great, for instance (1.6.16, 7.6–8, and 8.14); Solon (2.7.4); Pericles in brief remarks (3.6.12, 3.7.7–10); Epaminondas, whose eulogy is the longest in the work

(6.8.1–13); Ptolemy I (13.6.19); Hiero, king of Syracuse (23.4.1–2); and Hannibal, whose virtues of abstemiousness, *moderatio* as a commander, and a chastity so admirable that "one would say he was not a man born in Africa" are fulsomely listed (32.4.9–12). Augustus' bloodless diplomatic success over Parthia must count too.[47]

By contrast, rulers and states who lack virtues bring trouble—often death—on themselves, and very often inflict harm or ruin on their realms too. Such are the effete Assyrian monarchs (1.2.10–3.5; though it took thirteen hundred years for the kingdom to fall!), Athens in the fifth century (5.1.6), Philip II of Macedon and Alexander the Great, Alexander's successors one after another (Books 13–15)—except Lysimachus (15.3.1–2)—and all too many members of the increasingly amoral Seleucid and Ptolemaic dynasties that follow (Books 26–27, 30–32, 38–39). The Parthians are perhaps worst of all (42.4.16). Trogus' history of all these kingdoms thus constitutes, to a great extent, a parade of object lessons in the catastrophic effects of royal immoderation and viciousness.

Good and Evil in Philip and Alexander of Macedon

The prime nonlegendary exhibits of unhinged monarchy are Philip II and his son Alexander the Great—exhibits that possibly his Roman readers would not have expected.

---

[47] Pericles is praised only succinctly (3.6.12, "a man of proven courage"; 3.7.7–10, renown for sacrificing his own property to the public good); his long political career is ignored by the *Prologues* too.

Books 7–9 recount, with seeming dispassion but growing distaste, the opportunistic and ruthless deeds of the father, whose obituary is scathing (9.8.4–10): "compassion and duplicity were qualities he prized equally"; he was "equally charming and treacherous"; and so on. Trogus clearly believes the claim that Philip was murdered through the machinations of his wife, abetted by their son (9.7.1–14)—the first hint that the new empire, the Macedonian and its spinoffs, will be a busy extended saga of violence and treachery.

As for Alexander, he "outdid his father in both virtues and vices" (9.8.11; with father and son then compared in detail, 9.8.12–21). Thereafter his character and deeds (Books 11–12) range across the moral and political spectrum, from moderation, valor, and generosity to arrogance, excess, cruelty, and even savagery.[48] Trogus' narrative virtually alternates between light and darkness; and in Book 12, telling of the final decade of Alexander's life, the shadows darken. The king succumbs to the temptations of Persian luxury and self-indulgence (11.10.1–2, 12.3.8–4.2), begins "to treat his own men savagely, not with the hatred of a king but an enemy" (12.5.1), kills more and more of his friends and followers (12.7.1–2), and spends his last days in drunken revelry before collapsing (12.13.6–9). Trogus then reports in matter-of-fact detail that his death was due not to alcoholism—the official version—but to poison, in a conspiracy hatched by his trusted but increasingly fearful general Antipater (12.14). The

---

[48] On *HP* 11 and 12 see especially Yardley and Heckel (1997), and Horn (2021). On the inaccuracies and errors in 11–12, most or all Justin's work: Yardley and Heckel (1997, 35–41).

book ends, contrarily, with a glowing eulogy of the king's greatness and achievements (12.16)—only for the next book quickly to stress the joy of his fellow-Macedonians at losing him (13.1.7–8).

These depictions of Alexander as an increasingly monstrous even though awesome tyrant, and of his father as a ruthless if impressive one, are the harshest in surviving ancient sources, though other sources too are critical of both at times. Paradoxically, it is Trogus, at any rate through Justin, who alone in ancient accounts of Alexander calls him "the Great" (*Magnus*)—twenty-two times at that, with two more in the *Prologues*.[49]

Trogus, Livy, and Their Contemporaries

Pompeius Trogus was a close contemporary of Rome's premier historian of the Augustan age, Livy. They more than likely knew of each other's existence and writings, and may even have met: Livy was *persona grata* in Augustus' circle well into the early first century AD, and Trogus' paternal link to the emperor's family should have gained him at least intermittent entrée—at any rate until he took an interest in Timagenes, who had fallen out of favor. As noted earlier, Trogus seems to have kept up-to-date with

---

[49] Horn (2021, 282–90) sees Trogus consciously implying parallels between the degenerating Alexander and the un-Roman Antony, and implicitly comparing the king's virtuous and increasingly dismayed Macedonians with the sturdily virtuous Roman People under a regenerative Augustus. These parallels, all the same, can seem more evident to moderns than they likely were to Trogus' Roman readers. On Alexander as "the Great," see Rubincam (2005, esp. 266–71, 273–74).

the books of Livy's *Ab Urbe Condita* as they came out, at least as a source of appealing phraseology.

A current view is that, in a sense, Livy and Trogus partitioned world history between them: Livy undertaking the story of Rome from its foundation, Trogus the rest.[50] By contrast, Livy did the reverse, with seventy-two books (the second half of his *Ab Urbe Condita*) covering just the first century BC. But that they were acquainted and perhaps friends is plausible enough.

There were other "universalist" or near-universalist historians at Rome in the later decades of the final century BC, nearly all Greek: Diodorus Siculus, with a focus chiefly on the Greek and Roman worlds; Nicolaus of Damascus (another imperial favorite, with no fewer than 144 books of *Historia Katholike*, or *General History*, now lost); the geographer-historian Strabo, whose modestly titled *Historical Commentaries* (*Historika Hypomnemata*) were a sequel to Polybius' work; and of course Timagenes, whose patronage from Augustus came to an abrupt end but who then stayed with the independent-minded ex-consul Asinius Pollio (another large-scale modern historian). It is not inconceivable that those whose time and work in Rome overlapped, sometimes over decades, would share acquaintanceship, even friendship—or in some cases rivalry. It is disappointing that the work of not one of them survives in full (of Nicolaus', Strabo's, and Pollio's, noth-

---

[50] Trogus and Livy consciously chose to write foreign and Roman histories, respectively: Yardley and Heckel (1997, 22); Mineo (2016b, 211–15: "l'œuvre de Trogue-Pompée est réellement parallèle à celle de Tite-Live," 212); Borgna (2018, 211–14); Horn (2021, 40–41).

ing at all). We can be grateful that Trogus' *Historiae Philippicae* at least partially does, thanks to his anthologist Justin.

A NOTE ON THE TEXT

The two hundred–odd manuscripts containing Justin's *Epitome* fall into three classes, of which fewer than twenty are systematically reported by editors.[51] In this edition, Seel's revised Teubner text of 1985 is used as a base, adjusted on an eclectic basis in light of recent scholarship. For text-critical details the reader is referred to the critical editions.

ADDENDUM TO EXPLANATORY NOTES

The explanatory notes accompanying the translation are substantially by J. C. Yardley, with additions by D. Hoyos. The abbreviations used in the notes are included with the Bibliography.

Dexter Hoyos
March 27, 2023

[51] For discussion and analysis of the tradition, see Seel (1985, iii–x, xvii); Arnaud-Lindet (2003); and Mineo (2016a, lxx ff.).

ABBREVIATIONS

AO	R. Develin, *Athenian Officials 684–321 B.C.* (New York, 1989)
Barr.	*The Barrington Atlas of the Greek and Roman World,* ed. R. J. A. Talbert and R. S. Bagnall (Princeton, 2000)
Bickerman	*Chronology of the Ancient World* (London, 1968)
BNP	*Brill's New Pauly Online,* ed. H. Cancik, H. Schneider, and C. F. Salazar
CAH	*Cambridge Ancient History,* 2nd ed. (Cambridge, 1970–2005)
CHI	*The Cambridge History of Iran,* vol. 2 (Cambridge, 1985)
CIL	*Corpus Inscriptionum Latinarum*
FGrH	*The Fragments of the Greek Historians. Jacoby Online: Brill's New Jacoby*
Harding	P. Harding, *From the End of the Peloponnesian War to the Battle of Ipsus,* Translated Documents of Greece & Rome, vol. 2 (Cambridge, 1985)
HP	*Historiae Philippicae*
ILS	*Inscriptiones Latinae Selectae*

ABBREVIATIONS

Mineo	B. Mineo, *Justin: Abrégé des Histoires Philippiques de Trogue Pompée*, 2 vols. (Budé, 2016, 2018)
MRR	T. R. S. Broughton, *The Magistrates of the Roman Republic*, 3 vols. (1951–1986)
OCD	*Oxford Classical Dictionary*
OLD	*Oxford Latin Dictionary*
Pease	A. S. Pease, *Publi Vergili Maronis Aeneidos Liber Quartus* (Cambridge, MA, 1935)
RE	*Paulys Real-Encyclopädie der Klassischen Altertumswissenschaft*
Sherk	R. K. Sherk, *Rome and the Greek East to the Death of Augustus*, Translated Documents of Greece & Rome, vol. 4 (New York, 1984)

GENERAL BIBLIOGRAPHY

Adler, E. 2006. "Who's anti-Roman? Sallust and Pompeius Trogus on Mithridates." *Classical Journal* 101:383–407.

Alidoust, F. 2016. "*Parricidia* bei Persern und Parthern in den *Historiae Philippicae*." *Latomus* 75:910–42.

Alonso-Núñez, J. M. 1987. "An Augustan World History: The *Historiae Philippicae* of Pompeius Trogus." *Greece & Rome* 34:56–72.

———. 1995. "Drei Autoren von Geschichtsabrissen der römischen Kaiserzeit: Florus, Iustinus, Orosius." *Latomus* 54:346–60.

———. 2002. "The Augustan Empire and the Historians of the Augustan Epoch: Nicolaus of Damascus, Strabo, Pompeius Trogus, Dionysius of Halicarnassos." Chap. 8 in *The Idea of Universal History in Greece: From Herodotus to the Age of Augustus*, 93–113. Leiden.

Arnaud-Lindet, M.-P., ed. and trans. 2003. *Marcus Iunianus Iustinus, Abrégé des* Histoires Philippiques *de Trogue Pompée*. Corpus Scriptorum Latinorum. Online.

Ballesteros Pastor, L. 2017. "The Speeches in Justin's *Corpusculum Florum*: The Selection and Manipulation of Trogus' *Historiae Philippicae*." In *Anthologies of Historiographical Speeches from Antiquity to Early Modern Times: Rearranging the Tesserae*, edited by J. C. Iglesias

Zoido and Victoria Pineda, 79–94. International Studies in the History of Rhetoric 7. Leiden.

Balsdon, J. P. V. D. 1979. *Romans and Aliens.* London.

Barnes, T. D. 1998. "Two passages of Justin." *Classical Quarterly* 48:589–93.

Bartlett, B. 2014. "Justin's *Epitome*: The Unlikely Adaptation of Trogus' World History." *Histos* 8:246–83.

Baynham, E. 2009. "Barbarians 1: Quintus Curtius' and Other Roman Historians' Reception of Alexander." In Feldherr, 288–300.

Borgna, A. 2018. *Ripensare la storia universale: Giustino e l'Epitome delle* Storie Filippiche *di Pompeo Trogo.* Hildesheim.

———. 2020a. "Couper quoi, comment, pour qui?" In *Epitome: Abréger les textes antiques*, edited by I. Boehm and D. Vallat (nouvelle édition [en ligne]: Lyon): online.

———. 2020b. "Texts and Personalities: Justin and His *Epitoma* of Pompeius Trogus." *Latinitas* N.S. 8:17–40.

Brill's New Jacoby. See *Jacoby Online* (below).

Brunt, P. A. 1980. "On Historical Fragments and Epitomes." *Classical Quarterly* 30:477–94.

Davidson, J. 2009. "Polybius." In Feldherr, 123–36.

Davies, J. 2009. "Religion in Historiography." In Feldherr, 166–80.

Drinkwater, J. F. 1978. "The Rise and Fall of the Gallic Iulii: Aspects of the Development of the Aristocracy of the Three Gauls under the Early Empire." *Latomus* 37:817–50.

Elliott, J. 2018. "Authorship and Authority in the Preface to Justin's *Epitome* of Trogus' *Philippic Histories.*" In *"Animo decipiendi?" Rethinking Fakes and Authorship in Classical, Late Antique, and Early Christian Works*, edited by A. Guzmán and J. Martínez, 109–23. Groningen.

Feldherr, A., ed. 2009. *The Cambridge Companion to the Roman Historians.* Cambridge.

Forni, G., and M. G. Angeli Bertinelli. 1982. "Pompeo Trogo come fonte di storia." In *Aufstieg und Niedergang der römischen Welt. Literatur der augusteischen Zeit*, vol. 30.2, edited by W. Haase, 1298–1362. Berlin and New York.

Gaillard de Semainville, H. 1985. "Circonscription de Bourgogne." *Gallia* 43 no. 2:251–79.

Galimberti, A., and G. Zecchini, eds. 2016. *Studi sull'Epitome di Giustino. III. Il Tardo Ellenismo. I Parti e I Romani.* Milan.

Gutschmid, A. von. 1882. "Trogus und Timagenes." *Rheinisches Museum* 37:548–55.

Hau, L. I. 2011. "*Tychê* in Polybius: Narrative Answers to a Philosophical Question." *Histos* 5:183–207.

Hofmann, D. 2020. Review of A. Borgna (2018). *Klio* 102:748–54.

Horn, N. 2019. "Les *Histoires philippiques* de Trogue Pompée/Justin: une œuvre, deux auteurs, deux époques, deux projets" [review-discussion of A. Borgna (2018)]. *Revue des études anciennes* 121:171–82.

———. 2021. *L'image d'Alexandre le Grand chez Trogue Pompée/Justin. Analyse de la composition historique des* Histoires philippiques *(livres 11 et 12).* Pessac, France.

Jacoby Online. Brill's New Jacoby, pt. 2, ed. Ian Worthington (Leiden): online.

Klotz, A. 1952. "Pompeius (142)." *RE* 21:2300–2313.

Laird, A. 2009. "The Rhetoric of Roman Historiography." In Feldherr, 197–213.

Landucci, F. 2014. "Filippo II e le *Storie Filippiche*: un protagonist storico e storiografico." In *Studi sull'Epitome di Giustino*, vol. 1: *Dagli Assiri a Filippo II di Macedonia*, edited by C. Bearzot and F. Landucci, 233–60. Milan.

Malaspina, E. 1976. "Uno storico filobarbaro, Pompeo Trogo." *Romanobarbarica* 1:135–58.

McInerney, J., and D. W. Roller. 2012. "Timagenes of Alexandria (88)." *FGrH* online.

Mineo, B., ed. 2016a. *Justin: Abrégé des* Histoires Philipiques *de Trogue Pompée.* Vol. 1. Paris.

———. 2016b. "Trogue Pompée et Rome." In Galimberti and Zecchini, 193–219.

Mócsy, A. 1982–1984. "Zu einigen Galliern in der Literatur der Kaiserzeit." *Acta Antiqua Academiae Scientiarum Hungaricae* 30:379–86.

Nixon, C. E. V., and B. S. Rodgers. 1994. *In Praise of Later Roman Emperors. The Panegyrici Latini. Translation, Introduction, and Historical Commentary.* Berkeley, Los Angeles, London.

Raepset-Charlier, M.-T. 2002. "Deux dédicaces religieuses d'Arlon (*ILB* 64 et *ILB* [2] 65) et le culte public des Trévires." *L'Antiquité Classique* 71:103–20.

Rubincam, C. 2005. "A Tale of Two 'Magni': Justin/Trogus on Alexander and Pompey." *Historia* 54:265–74.

Ruehl, F. 1885. *Iustini Epitome Historiarum Philippicarum.* Leipzig.

Seel, O. 1982. "Pompeius Trogus und das Problem der Universalgeschichte." In *Aufstieg und Niedergang der römischen Welt*, vol. 30.2: *Literatur der augusteischen Zeit*, edited by W. Haase, 1363–1423. Berlin.

———. 1985. *M. Iuniani Iustini Epitoma Historiarum Philippicarum Pompei Trogi.* 2nd ed. Bibliotheca Teubneriana. Stutgardia/Stuttgart.

Syme, R. 1988. "The Date of Justin and the Discovery of Trogus." *Historia* 37:358–71.

———. 1992. "Trogus in the H. A.: Some Consequences." In *Institutions, société et vie politique dans l'Empire romain au IVe siècle. Actes de la table ronde uprès l'œuvre d'André Chastagnol (Paris, 20–21 janvier 1989)*, 11–20. Paris.

Urban, R. 1982a. "Gallische Bewusstsein und Romkritik bei Pompeius Trogus." In *Aufstieg und Niedergang der römischen Welt. Literatur der augusteischen Zeit*, vol. 30.2, edited by W. Haase, 1424–43. Berlin and New York.

———. 1982b. "'Historiae Philippicae' bei Pompeius Trogus: Versuch einer Deutung." *Historia* 31:82–96.

Yardley, J. C. 1998. "Justin, Trogus, and the *Aetna*." *Phoenix* 52:103–8.

———. 2000. "Justin on Tribunates and Generalships, *Caesares,* and *Augusti*." *Classical Quarterly* 50:632–34.

———. 2003. *Justin and Pompeius Trogus. A Study of the Language of Justin's* Epitome *of Trogus.* Toronto, Buffalo, London.

Yardley, J. C., and W. Heckel. 1997. *Justin: Epitome of the Philippic History of Pompeius Trogus,* vol. 1: *Books 11–12: Alexander the Great.* Clarendon Ancient History Series: Oxford Scholarship Online. Oxford: online.

Yardley, J. C., P. Wheatley, and W. Heckel. 2011. *Justin:*

GENERAL BIBLIOGRAPHY

Epitome of the Philippic History of Pompeius Trogus,
vol. 2: *Books 13–15: The Successors to Alexander the
Great.* Clarendon Ancient History Series. Oxford.
Zecchini, G. 2016. "Per la datazione di Giustino." In
Galimberti and Zecchini, 221–31.

EPITOME OF
POMPEIUS TROGUS

PRAEFATIO

Cum multi ex Romanis etiam consularis dignitatis viri res
Romanas Graeco peregrinoque sermone in historiam con-
tulissent, seu aemulatione gloriae sive varietate et novitate
operis delectatus vir priscae eloquentiae, Trogus Pompeius, Graecas et totius orbis historias Latino sermone
conposuit, ut, cum nostra Graece, Graeca quoque nostra
lingua legi possent, prorsus rem magni et animi et corpo-
2 ris adgressus. Nam cum plerisque auctoribus singulorum
regum vel populorum res gestas scribentibus opus suum
ardui laboris videatur, nonne nobis Pompeius Herculea
audacia orbem terrarum adgressus videri debet, cuius li-
bris omnium saeculorum, regum, nationum populorum-
3 que res gestae continentur? Et quae historici Graecorum,
prout commodum cuique fuit iter, segregatim occupave-
runt, omissis quae sine fructu erant, ea omnia Pompeius
4 divisa temporibus et serie rerum digesta conposuit. Horum igitur quattuor et quadraginta voluminum (nam toti-
dem edidit) per otium, quo in urbe versabamur, cogniti-
one quaeque dignissima excerpsi et omissis his, quae nec
cognoscendi voluptate iucunda nec exemplo erant necessaria, breve veluti florum corpusculum feci, ut haberent et

---

1 Rome, literary as well as administrative capital.
2 Literally, "little body of flowers."

PREFACE

Although many Romans, even some of consular rank, had written Roman history in Greek, a foreign language, Pompeius Trogus, a man with the eloquence of the ancients, composed his history of Greece and the whole world in the Latin language; and enticed either by a wish to rival these authors' fame or by the originality of such a work, and in order to make Greek history as accessible in our language as ours is in Greek, he certainly undertook something requiring both great intellectual and great physical stamina. For when most authors writing history of individual rulers or peoples find theirs a work requiring intense effort, should we not recognize that Pompeius showed Herculean enterprise in undertaking a universal history, his books covering the annals of all ages, kings, nations and peoples? And what Greek historians treated piecemeal, each following his own interests and omitting what did not serve his purpose, this Pompeius arranged chronologically with items laid out in order. So from these forty-four volumes (for that was the number he published) I, during some free time that we were spending in the City,[1] took excerpts from all his finest work, and, omitting what did not make pleasurable reading or serve to provide a moral, I have produced a brief anthology[2] to refresh the

2

3

4

qui Graece didicissent, quo admonerentur, et qui non
5   didicissent, quo instruerentur. Quod ad te non tam
cognoscendi magis quam emendandi causa transmisi, simul ut et otii mei, cuius et Cato reddendam operam putat,
6   apud te ratio constaret. Sufficit enim mihi in tempore iudicium tuum, apud posteros, cum obtrectationis invidia
decesserit, industriae testimonium habituro.

memory of those who had studied history in Greek, and provide instruction for those who had not. This I have sent 5 to you not so much for your information as for your criticism, and also so you may have some rationale for my leisure time, which Cato also thinks must be accounted for.[3] For I am satisfied to have your opinion just now, and 6 among later generations, once malicious criticism has ceased, to have some witness to my diligence.

[3] See in particular Cic. *Planc.* 66.

LIBER I

1. Principio rerum gentium nationumque imperium penes reges erat, quos ad fastigium huius maiestatis non ambitio popularis, sed spectata inter bonos moderatio provehebat. 2 Populus nullis legibus tenebatur, arbitria principum pro 3 legibus erant. Fines imperii tueri magis quam proferre mos erat; intra suam cuique patriam regna finiebantur. 4 Primus omnium Ninus, rex Assyriorum, veterem et quasi avitum gentibus morem nova imperii cupiditate mutavit. 5 Hic primus intulit bella finitimis et rudes adhuc ad resis- 6 tendum populos terminos usque Libyae perdomuit. Fuere quidem temporibus antiquiores Vezosis Aegyptius et Scy- thiae rex Tanaus, quorum alter in Pontum, alter usque 7 Aegyptum excessit. Sed longinqua, non finitima bella ge- rebant nec imperium sibi, sed populis suis gloriam quae- rebant contentique victoria imperio abstinebant. Ninus magnitudinem quaesitae dominationis continua posses- 8 sione firmavit. Domitis igitur proximis, cum accessione

---

1 See Diod. Sic. 2.1ff., whose source is the same as that of Trogus, Ctesias of Cnidus. See R. Drews, "Assyria in Classical Universal Histories," *Historia* 14 (1965): 129–42. Ninus is prob- ably Tukulti-Ninurta I (1244–1208).

2 The Egyptian king Vezosis is Sesostris in Hdt. 2.102ff., Se- soöstris in Diod. Sic. 1.53ff., and is likely to be Ramses II (1290–

BOOK I

1. In the beginning, authority over peoples and nations lay with kings, who came to this supreme power not through currying favor but through having their good conduct noted among decent men. The people were bound by no 2 laws; the decisions of their leaders were the law. Protect- 3 ing the country's territory rather than advancing it was the norm; kingdoms were limited to each's native land. Ninus,[1] 4 king of the Assyrians, was the very first to change this ancient and almost hereditary custom by his unprece- dented lust for power. He was the first to make war on his 5 neighbors, and he crushed nations still unskilled in self- defense as far as the boundaries of Libya. There were in- 6 deed in earlier days the Egyptian Vezosis and the Scythian king Tanaus,[2] one of whom advanced to Pontus, and the other as far as Egypt. But they were fighting distant, not 7 neighboring, wars and seeking not empire for themselves but glory for their people, and content with victory they eschewed dominion. Ninus secured the wide empire he had won by retaining possession of it. Then subjugating 8 neighbors and strengthened by this acquisition of power

1224), though not all the actions attributed to Sesostris may be- long to Ramses. Tanaus, who does not appear in Justin Book 2, is evidently the eponym of the Tanais River (the modern Don).

virium fortior ad alios transiret et proxima quaeque victoria instrumentum sequentis esset, totius Orientis populos
9 subegit. Postremum bellum illi fuit cum Zoroastre, rege
Bactrianorum, qui primus dicitur artes magicas invenisse
et mundi principia siderumque motus diligentissime spec-
10 tasse. Hoc occiso et ipse decessit, relicto adhuc impubere
filio Ninia et uxore Semiramide.

2. Haec neque inmaturo puero ausa tradere imperium
nec ipsa palam tractare, tot ac tantis gentibus vix patienter
Nino viro, nedum feminae parituris, simulat se pro uxore
2 Nini filium, pro femina puerum. Nam et statura utrique
mediocris et vox pariter gracilis et liniamentorum qualitas
3 matri ac filio similis. Igitur bracchia et crura calciamentis,
caput tiara tegit; et ne novo habitu aliquid occultare videretur, eodem ornatu et populum vestiri iubet, quem mo-
4 rem vestis exinde gens universa tenet. Sic primis initiis
5 sexum mentita puer esse credita est. Magnas deinde res
gessit; quarum amplitudine ubi invidiam superatam putat,
6 quae sit fatetur quemve simulasset. Nec hoc illi dignitatem regni ademit, sed admirationem auxit, quod mulier
7 non feminas modo virtute, sed etiam viros anteiret. Haec
Babyloniam condidit murumque urbi cocto latere circum-

---

3 The name Zoroaster naturally suggests the prophet of Ahura-
Mazda, whose worship was adopted by the Achaemenids of Persia, but Diod. Sic. 2.6.3 calls this man Oxyartes, a name otherwise
borne by the Bactrian-Sogdian chieftain whose daughter Roxane
married Alexander the Great.   4 For the contents of the
following section, see Diod. Sic. 2.4ff., again based on Ctesias and
containing details at variance with the account here. On Semiramis' sexual behavior, see Orosius 4.4ff.

he advanced on others and, with each victory providing
the means for the next, conquered all the peoples of the
East. His final battle was with Zoroaster, king of the Bac- 9
trians, who is reportedly the first to have discovered the
magic arts and made a thorough study of cosmology and
the movement of stars.[3] After killing him, he himself also 10
died, leaving a pubescent son Ninias and a wife Semiramis.[4]

2. She dared not entrust the kingdom to an immature
boy but neither would she openly occupy it herself, for
with so many and such great people barely obeying a man
much less would they obey a woman, and so she pretended
to be Ninus' son, not his wife, a boy not a woman. For both 2
had average height and similarly high-pitched voices and
in features. Mother and son resembled each other. So she 3
kept her arms and legs hidden with coverings, and her
head with a turban; and not to seem to be hiding something by such strange clothing, she ordered the people to
be similarly dressed, a fashion thereafter retained by all
the people.[5] By thus disguising her sex from the start, she 4
was thought to be a boy. She then achieved great things; 5
and when she thought them great enough to have overcome any envy, she revealed who she was and whom she
had pretended to be. Nor did this affect the authority of 6
her rule, but in fact it increased admiration for her, since
she, a woman, was outdoing in courage not only females,
but men as well. It was she who founded Babylon and 7
encircled it with a wall of baked brick, which instead of

---

[5] Hardly true, and Diod. Sic. 2.6.6 indicates that Semiramis
dressed thus only for her journey to Bactria.

dedit, arenae vice bitumine interstrato, quae materia in
8   illis locis passim invenitur e terra exaestuata. Multa et alia
praeclara huius reginae fuere; siquidem, non contenta
adquisitos viro regni terminos tueri, Aethiopiam quoque
9   imperio adiecit. Sed et Indis bellum intulit, quos praeter
10 illam et Alexandrum Magnum nemo intravit. Ad postremum cum concubitum filii petisset, ab eodem interfecta
11 est, duos et XXX annos post Ninum regno potita. Filius
eius Ninias contentus elaborato a parentibus imperio belli
studia deposuit et, veluti sexum cum matre mutasset, raro
12 a viris visus in feminarum turba consenuit. Posteri quoque
eius id exemplum secuti responsa gentibus per internun-
13 tios dabant. Imperium Assyrii, qui postea Syri dicti sunt,
mille trecentis annis tenuere.

3. Postremus apud eos regnavit Sardanapallus, vir mu-
2   liere corruptior. Ad hunc videndum (quod nemini ante
eum permissum fuerat) praefectus ipsius Medis praepositus, nomine Arbactus, cum admitti magna ambitione
aegre obtinuisset, invenit eum inter scortorum greges pur-
puras colo nentem et muliebri habitu, cum mollitia corporis et oculorum lascivia omnes feminas anteiret, pensa
3   inter virgines partientem. Quibus visis indignatus tali feminae tantum virorum subiectum tractantique lanam ferrum et arma habentes parere, progressus ad socios quid
viderit refert; negat se ei parere posse, qui se feminam

---

6 Diod. Sic. 2.28.2 agrees on this figure, but see Drews, "Assyria in Classical Universal Histories," 138ff.

7 Hdt. 2.150; Diod. Sic. 2.23ff., where Arbactus appears as
"Arbaces." Sardanapallus may well be Ashurbanipal (668–629).
From this point, and especially from section 4, the reader should
consult the relevant sections of *CHI* 2.

sand she layered with bitumen, a substance in those areas often found oozing from the ground. Many other famous 8 achievements also belong to this queen; for not content with defending the boundaries achieved by her husband, she also added Ethiopia to her empire. But she even made 9 war on the Indians, whose country no one has entered apart from her and Alexander the Great. Finally, when she 10 sought sexual relations with her son, she was killed by him, thirty-two years after succeeding Ninus on the throne. Her son Ninias, satisfied with the empire built up by his 11 parents, abandoned military activity and, almost as though he had exchanged his sex with his mother's, was rarely seen by men and grew old among a crowd of women. His suc- 12 cessors, following his example, would also relay official responses to their people through intermediaries. His em- 13 pire the Assyrians, who were later called Syrians, ruled for thirteen hundred years.[6]

3. Last to reign among them was Sardanapallus, a man more degenerate than a woman.[7] When his governor of 2 the Medes, Arbactus by name, sought an audience with him (something granted to none before him) and was only with difficulty and after much insistence finally granted admission, he found him among groups of whores spinning purple wool with a distaff and dressed as woman—for he surpassed all women in effeminate appearance and salacious glances—distributing the wool among young girls. Seeing this and furious that so many warriors were 3 subject to such a "woman" and that men with swords and armor were serving someone who worked with wool, he went to his comrades and told them what he had seen; he could not take orders from someone who preferred being

4   malit esse quam virum. Fit igitur coniuratio; bellum Sar-
danapallo infertur. Quo ille audito non ut vir regnum de-
fensurus, sed, ut metu mortis mulieres solent, primo late-
bras circumspicit, mox deinde cum paucis et inconpositis
5   in bellum progreditur. Victus in regiam se recepit, ubi
exstructa incensaque pyra et se et divitias suas in incen-
6   dium mittit, hoc solo imitatus virum. Post hunc rex constituitur interfector eius Arbactus, qui praefectus Medorum fuerat. Is imperium ab Assyriis ad Medos transfert.

    4. Post multos deinde reges per ordinem successionis
2   regnum ad Astyagen descendit. Hic per somnum vidit ex
naturalibus filiae, quam unicam habebat, vitem enatam,
3   cuius palmite omnis Asia obumbraretur. Consulti arioli ex
eadem filia nepotem ei futurum, cuius magnitudo prae-
nuntietur, regnique ei amissionem portendi responderunt.
4   Hoc responso exterritus neque claro viro neque civi filiam
suam, ne paterna maternaque nobilitas nepoti animos
extolleret, sed ex gente obscura tum temporis Persarum
5   Cambysi, mediocri viro, in matrimonium tradidit. Ac ne
sic quidem somnii metu deposito gravidam ad se filiam
arcessit, ut sub avi potissimum oculis partus necaretur.
6   Natus infans datur occidendus Harpago, regis arcanorum
7   participi. Is veritus, si ad filiam mortuo rege venisset imperium, quia nullum Astyages virilis sexus genuerat, ne illa
necati infantis ultionem, quoniam a patre non potuisset, a

---

   8 Whatever is meant by this, Hdt. 1.106 says that the Assyrians
were conquered by Cyaxares the Mede.

   9 For the contents of sections 4 to 6, see Hdt. 1.107ff., where
there are slight differences.

a woman than a man, he said. So a plot was hatched; there 4
was war with Sardanapallus. Hearing of it he, unlike any
man about to defend his kingdom but rather like women
fearing for their lives, first cast about for hiding places, and
then went into battle with a few disorganized men. De- 5
feated he withdrew into his palace, where he built and lit
a funeral pyre and flung both himself and his riches into
the flames, in this alone behaving like a man. After him 6
the man appointed king was his killer Arbactus, who had
been governor of the Medes. He transferred the empire
from the Assyrians to the Medes.[8]

4. After many kings, the throne then came in due succession to Astyages.[9] He saw in a dream a vine sprout from 2
the womb of his only daughter, and by its branches a
shadow was cast over all Asia. When soothsayers were 3
consulted they announced that he would by this same
daughter have a grandson, whose greatness was foretold,
and that loss of his kingdom was also predicted. Terrified 4
by this response he had his daughter marry no prominent
man or any citizen in case parentage on either the father's
or mother's side strengthened the grandson's spirit, but
instead gave her in marriage to Cambyses, a man of hum-
ble birth from the then obscure Persian race. And with 5
fear from his dream not even then removed, he summoned his daughter to him when she was pregnant so the
child should be killed at birth right before the grandfather's eyes. At birth the infant was given to Harpagus, 6
who was privy to the king's secrets, to be killed. He, fear- 7
ing that should the throne come to the daughter on the
king's death, since Astyages had produced no male heir,
and that she, unable to exact vengeance from her father
for the infant's death would do so from his henchman, then

13

8
9
ministro exigeret, pastori regii pecoris puerum exponen-
dum tradit. Forte eodem tempore et ipsi pastori natus filius erat. Eius igitur uxor audita regii infantis expositione
summis precibus rogat sibi perferri ostendique puerum.
10 Cuius precibus fatigatus pastor reversus in silvam invenit
iuxta infantem canem feminam parvulo ubera praebentem
11 et a feris alitibusque defendentem. Motus et ipse misericordia, qua motam etiam canem viderat, puerum defert
12 ad stabula, eadem cane anxie prosequente. Quem ubi in
manum mulier accepit, veluti ad notam adlusit, tantusque
in illo vigor et dulcis quidam blandientis infantis risus
apparuit, ut pastorem ultro rogaret uxor, suum partum pro
illo exponeret permitteretque sibi sive fortunae ipsius sive
13 spei suae puerum nutrire. Atque ita permutata sorte par-
vulorum hic pro filio pastoris educatur, ille pro nepote
14 regis exponitur. Nutrici postea nomen Spargos fuit, quia
canem Persae sic vocant.

5. Puer deinde cum imperiosus inter pastores es-
2 set, Cyri nomen accepit. Mox rex inter ludentes sorte
delectus cum per lasciviam contumaces flagellis cecidis-
set, a parentibus puerorum querela regi delata, in-
dignantibus a servo regio ingenuos homines servilibus
3 verberibus adfectos. Ille arcessito puero et interrogato,
cum nihil mutato vultu fecisse se ut regem respondisset,
admiratum constantiam in memoriam somnii responsique

---

¹⁰ For the story of Astyages and the child, cf. Hdt. 1.110,
where the wife's name is "Spako" and the Greek equivalent
"Cyno." The resemblance to the Roman myth of Romulus and
Remus is striking. See also the story of Habis in Book 44.

¹¹ The Greek *kyrios* means "lord," which, of course, is an ir-
relevant coincidence.

passed him on to the king's cattle herdsman to be exposed.
It so happened that at that same time a son had also been 8
born to the herdsman. So his wife, on hearing of the royal 9
child's exposure, abjectly pleaded with him to have the boy
brought and shown to her. Worn down by her entreaties, 10
the herdsman returned to the wood to find a bitch beside
the infant, offering him her teats and protecting him from
wild animals and birds. Being himself also moved to as 11
much compassion as he had seen also in a dog, he took the
boy to his shed, with that same dog anxiously following
him. When the woman took him in her arms, he snuggled 12
into her as if he knew her, and there seemed such vitality
in him and such sweetness in the affectionate child's smile,
that the wife actually asked the herdsman to expose her
own baby in his place and to allow her (fulfilling either his
destiny or her own hope) to nurse the boy. And so with the 13
youngsters' fates interchanged one was raised as a herdsman's son, the other exposed as the king's grandchild. The 14
child's nurse was later named Spargos because that is Persian for "dog."[10]

5. Then when as a boy he was quite high-handed among
the shepherds, he was given the name "Cyrus."[11] Later 2
when he was chosen as king in a game among his play-
mates and in fun had whipped some who disobeyed him,
a complaint was brought to the king by the boys' parents,
who were outraged that by a slave of the king free people
had been flogged like slaves. When the boy was sum- 3
moned and questioned and with a completely straight face
replied that he had acted as a king, Astyages, admiring his
self-confidence, recalled the dream and the soothsayers'

4 revocatur. Atque ita cum et vultus similitudo et expositio-
   nis tempora et pastoris confessio convenirent, nepotem
5 agnovit. Et quoniam defunctus sibi somnio videretur agi-
   tato inter pastores regno, animum minacem dumtaxat in
6 illo fregit. Ceterum Harpago, amico suo, infestus in ultionem servati nepotis filium eius interfecit epulandum-
7 que patri tradidit. Sed Harpagus ad praesens tempus dissimulato dolore odium regis in vindictae occasionem
8 distulit. Interiecto deinde tempore cum adolevisset Cyrus,
   dolore orbitatis admonitus scribit ei, ut ablegatus ab avo
   in Persas fuerit, ut occidi eum parvulum avus iusserit, ut
   beneficio suo servatus sit, ut regem offenderit, ut filium
9 amiserit. Hortatur exercitum paret et pronam ad regnum
10 viam ingrediatur, Medorum transitionem pollicitus. Epis-
   tula quia palam ferri nequibat regis custodibus omnes
   aditus obsidentibus, exenterato lepori inseritur lepusque
   in Persas Cyro ferendus fido servo traditur; addita retia,
   ut sub specie venatoris dolus lateret.

   6. Lectis ille epistulis eadem somnio adgredi iussus,
   sed praemonitus, ut quem primum postera die obvium
2 habuisset, socium coeptis adsumeret. Igitur antelucano
   tempore ruri iter ingressus obvium habuit servum de er-
3 gastulo cuiusdam Medi, nomine Sybaren. Huius requisita
   origine ut in Persis genitum audivit, demptis conpedibus
4 adsumptoque comite Persepolim regreditur. Ibi convo-
   cato populo iubet omnes praesto cum securibus esse et
5 silvam viae circumdatam excidere. Quod cum strenue fe-

---

   [12] Banishment to Persia has not figured in the story, but
   Herodotus shows Cyrus residing in Persia.

prediction. And so since the facial resemblance, the date 4
of exposure, and a confession from the herdsman all fitted
together, he recognized him as his grandson. And as the 5
dream prophecy appeared fulfilled by the "reign" he had
among the herdsmen, he dropped his threatening atti-
tude, at least toward him But furious with his friend Har- 6
pagus, he killed his son as revenge for saving the grandchild and gave him to his father as a meal. But Harpagus, 7
hiding his grief for the time being, deferred his hatred for
the king and deferred his opportunity for revenge. Then 8
as time passed and Cyrus had matured, he was prompted
by the pain of his loss to write to him about how he had
been banished to Persia by his grandfather,[12] how the
grandfather had ordered him killed as a child, how thanks
to him he had been rescued, and how he had displeased
the king and lost his own son. He urged him to raise an 9
army and embark on an easy road to the throne, assuring
him of defection by the Medes. As it could not be carried 10
openly, with the king's guards blocking all roads, the letter
was put into an eviscerated hare and the hare given to a
trusty slave to be taken to Cyrus in Persia; nets were added
so the plot could be hidden under his disguise as a hunter.

6. After he read the letter, Cyrus was given the same
order in a dream, but was forewarned that the first man
he met the next day he should enlist as an ally in his ventures So setting out before dawn on a country road he met 2
a slave named Sybares from the workhouse of a certain
Mede. Inquiring after his background and hearing he was 3
born in Persia, he removed his fetters and taking him as
companion returned to Persepolis. There, summoning the 4
people, he told everyone to come with axes at the ready to
fell a wood bordering the road. When they vigorously 5

6 cissent, eosdem postera die adparatis epulis invitat; dein
   cum alacriores ipso convivio factos videret, rogat: si condicio ponatur, utrius vitae sortem legant, hesterni laboris
   an praesentium epularum? "Praesentium" ut adclamavere
   omnes, ait hesterno similem labori omnem vitam acturos,
7 quoad Medis pareant; se secutos hodiernis epulis. Laetis
8 omnibus bellum Medis infert. Astyages meriti sui in
9 Harpago oblitus summam belli eidem committit, qui
   exercitum acceptum statim Cyro per deditionem tradidit
10 regisque crudelitatem perfidia defectionis ulciscitur.
   Quod ubi Astyages audivit, contractis undique auxiliis
   ipse in Persas proficiscitur et repetito alacrius certamine
11 pugnantibus suis partem exercitus de tergo ponit et tergi-
   versantes ferro agi in hostes iubet ac denuntiat suis, ni
   vincerent, non minus fortes post terga inventuros, quam a
   frontibus viros; proinde videant, fugientibus haec an illa
12 pugnantibus acies rumpenda sit. Ingens post necessitatem
13 pugnandi animus exercitui eius accessit. Pulsataque cum
   Persarum acies paulatim cederet, matres et uxores eorum
14 obviam occurrunt; orant in proelium revertantur; cunctantibus sublata veste obscena corporis ostendunt rogantes, num in uteros matrum vel uxorum vellent re-
15 fugere. Hac repressi castigatione in proelium redeunt et
16 facta inpressione quos fugiebant fugere conpellunt. In eo
   proelio Astyages capitur, cui Cyrus nihil aliud quam regnum abstulit nepotemque in illo magis quam victorem

complied, he the next day invited the same people to a
feast prepared for them; then when he saw spirits raised   6
just by the feast, he asked what sort of life they would take
if given the choice, yesterday's work or that day's banquet.
When everyone cried out "today's feast," he said all their
life would be like yesterday's labor for as long as they
obeyed the Medes, but like today's feast if they followed   7
him. Everyone pleased, he made war on the Medes. Asty-   8
ages, forgetting his treatment of Harpagus, put the whole
war in his hands, and on accepting the army he promptly   9
surrendered it to Cyrus and by treacherous defection had
his revenge for the king's cruelty. When Astyages heard of   10
it, he gathered fresh forces from all parts, marched into
Persia in person, and returning to the campaign with increased vigor deployed some of his army behind those
already in battle; and he ordered waverers driven back   11
into the enemy at sword point, saying that if they did not
prevail they would find troops to their rear no less formi-
dable than those before them; so they must see whether
the one line must be broken by those fleeing, or the other
by those fighting. Forced into fighting his army saw a huge   12
surge of morale. And when the shaken Persian line was   13
gradually giving way, mothers and wives of the men came
running to meet them; they begged them to return to the
battle; when the men hesitated they lifted their clothes   14
and showed them their private parts, asking if they wanted
to hide in the wombs of their mothers or wives. Checked   15
by this rebuke, they returned to the battle and with a
thrust drove into flight the men from whom they were
fleeing. In that battle Astyages was captured, but Cyrus   16
did no more than deprive him of his kingdom and he
treated him more like his grandson than his conqueror and

egit, eumque maximae genti Hyrcanorum praeposuit.
17 Nam in Medos reverti ipse noluit. Hic finis imperii Medorum fuit. regnaverunt annis CCCL.

7. Initio regni Cyrus Sybaren, coeptorum socium, quem iuxta nocturnum visum ergastulo liberaverat comitemque in omnibus rebus habuerat, Persis praepo-
2 suit sororemque suam ei in matrimonium dedit. Sed civitates, quae Medorum tributariae fuerant, mutato imperio etiam condicionem suam mutatam arbitrantes a Cyro defecerunt, quae res multorum bellorum Cyro causa et origo
3 fuit. Domitis deinde plerisque cum adversus Babylonios bellum gereret, Babyloniis rex Lydorum Croesus, cuius opes divitiaeque insignes ea tempestate erant, in auxilium venit; victusque iam de se sollicitus in regnum refugit.
4 Cyrus quoque post victoriam conpositis in Babylonia re-
5 bus bellum transfert in Lydiam. Ibi fortuna prioris proelii perculsum iam Croesi exercitum nullo negotio fundit;
6 Croesus ipse capitur. Sed quanto bellum minoris periculi,
7 tanto et mitior victoria. Croeso et vita et patrimonii partes et urbs Beroe concessa, in qua etsi non regiam vitam,
8 proximam tamen maiestati regiae degeret. Haec clemen-
9 tia non minus victori quam victo utilis fuit. Quippe ex universa Graecia, cognito quod inlatum Croeso bellum esset, auxilia velut ad commune extinguendum incendium
10 confluebant; tantus Croesi amor apud omnes urbes erat passurusque Cyrus grave bellum Graeciae fuit, si quid in

---

13 See Hdt. 1.71ff., which is not the immediate source here; neither perhaps is Ctesias, who calls Beroe "Barene" (§4 [Photius]). Cyrus' campaign against Croesus dates to 547. The capture of Babylon actually occurred in October 539.

set him over the great Hyrcanian nation. For he himself   17
did not want return to the Medes. This was the end of the
empire of the Medes. They ruled for three hundred and
fifty years.

7. At the beginning of his reign Cyrus appointed as his
governor of Persia Sybares, whom he had freed from the
workhouse after his dream and kept as his companion in
everything, and he gave him his sister in marriage. But   2
states that had been tribute payers to the Medes revolted
from Cyrus, thinking that with the change of government
their status had also changed, and that was the cause and
beginning of many wars for Cyrus. Then after most were   3
defeated and he was at war with the Babylonians, King
Croesus of Lydia, whose power and wealth were famous
at the time, came to their aid;[13] and then defeated and
fearful for his own safety, he fled back into his kingdom.
Cyrus, too, having settled matters in Babylonia after his   4
victory, transferred the war to Lydia. There he routed   5
without difficulty Croesus' army, which was already demoralized by the outcome of the previous battle; Croesus
was himself taken prisoner. But though the campaign was   6
less dangerous the victory more lenient. Croesus was   7
granted both his life and some of his fortune, as well as the
city of Beroe, in which to lead if not a king's life at least
one approaching regal dignity. This clemency served the   8
conqueror no less than the conquered. For from all over   9
Greece, once it was known that Croesus had been attacked, help began pouring as if to extinguish a fire that
threatened everyone; such was the affection felt for   10
Croesus among all the city-states, and Cyrus would have
faced a serious war with Greece had he dealt at all cruelly

11　Croeso crudelius consuluisset. Interiecto deinde tempore
12　occupato in aliis bellis Cyro Lydi rebellavere, quibus ite-
　　rum victis arma et equi adempti iussique cauponas et ludi-
13　cras artes et lenocinia exercere. Ac sic gens industria
　　quondam potens et manu strenua effeminata mollitie
　　luxuriaque virtutem pristinam perdidit et quos ante Cy-
　　rum invictos bella praestiterunt, in luxuriam lapsos otium
　　ac desidia superavit.
14　　　Fuere Lydis multi ante Croesum reges variis casibus
　　memorabiles, nullus tamen fortunae Candauli conparan-
15　dus. Hic uxorem, quam propter formae pulchritudinem
　　deperibat, praedicare omnibus solebat, non contentus
　　voluptatum suarum tacita conscientia, nisi etiam matrimo-
16　nii reticenda publicaret, prorsus quasi silentium damnum
17　pulchritudinis esset. Ad postremum, ut adfirmationi suae
18　fidem faceret, nudam sodali suo Gygi ostendit. Quo facto
　　et amicum in adulterium uxoris sollicitatum hostem sibi
　　fecit et uxorem, veluti tradito alii amore, a se alienavit.
19　Namque brevi tempore caedes Candauli nuptiarum prae-
　　mium fuit et uxor mariti sanguine dotata regnum viri et se
　　pariter adultero tradidit.
　　　　8. Cyrus subacta Asia et universo Oriente in potestatem
　2　redacto Scythis bellum infert. Erat eo tempore regina Scy-
　　tharum Tamyris, quae non muliebriter adventu hostium
　　territa, cum prohibere eos transitu Araxis fluminis posset,
　　transire permisit, et sibi faciliorem pugnam intra regni sui

---

14 Hdt. 1.154ff.　　15 Hdt. 1.8ff.　　16 Hdt. 1.201ff.,
where the objects of Cyrus' ambition are the Massagetae (Der-
bekes in Ctesias 8), whom some said were Scythians, and the
queen is Tomyris. There are other differences of detail.

with Croesus. Then some time later when Cyrus was in- 11
volved in other wars the Lydians revolted,[14] and on being 12
again defeated they were deprived of their weapons and
horses and ordered to keep to innkeeping, stage perfor-
mances and running brothels. And so a people once pow- 13
erful through its energy and brave in battle lost its courage
of old, weakened by easy living and profligacy, and those
who before Cyrus had proved invincible in war, slipped
into extravagant living and were defeated by peace and
lethargy.

The Lydians had many kings before Croesus that were 14
remarkable for vicissitudes in their lives, but none with a
fate like that of Candaules.[15] He had a wife whom he pas- 15
sionately loved for her beauty and whom he was always
praising to everyone, not satisfied with secret awareness
of his sexual delights unless he was also divulging things
to be kept private in marriage, just as if silence were some 16
slight on her beauty. Finally, to confirm what he said, he 17
displayed her naked to his companion Gyges. By doing 18
that he both made an enemy of his friend, who was now
tempted into seducing the wife, and also alienated his wife
by virtually giving her love to another man. For shortly 19
afterward Candaules' murder was the price of her marriage to Gyges and the wife, with her husband's blood as
her dowry, passed both her husband's throne and herself
to her lover.

8. With Asia and the entire East brought under his
power Cyrus invaded Scythia.[16] At that time the queen of 2
the Scythians was Tamyris who, in an unfeminine way, was
not frightened by the enemy's approach, and though able
to prevent them crossing the River Araxes she allowed
them to cross, thinking that for her a battle within the

terminos rata et hostibus obiectu fluminis fugam diffici-
3 liorem. Itaque Cyrus traiectis copiis, cum aliquantisper in
4 Scythiam processisset, castra metatus est. Dein postera
die simulato metu, quasi refugiens castra deseruisset, ita
vini adfatim et ea, quae epulis erant necessaria, reliquit.
5 Quod cum nuntiatum reginae esset, adulescentulum filium ad insequendum eum cum tertia parte copiarum
6 mittit. Cum ventum ad castra Cyri esset, ignarus rei militaris adulescens, veluti ad epulas, non ad proelium venisset, omissis hostibus insuetos barbaros vino se onerare
7 patitur, priusque Scythae ebrietate quam bello vincuntur.
8 Nam cognitis his Cyrus reversus per noctem saucios op-
primit omnesque Scythas cum reginae filio interfecit.
9　　Amisso tanto exercitu et, quod gravius dolendum,
unico filio Tamyris orbitatis dolorem non in lacrimas ef-
fudit, sed in ultionis solacia intendit hostesque recenti
victoria exsultantes pari insidiarum fraude circumvenit;
10 quippe simulata diffidentia propter vulnus acceptum refu-
11 giens Cyrum ad angustias usque perduxit. Ibi conpositis
in montibus insidiis ducenta milia Persarum cum ipso rege
12 trucidavit. In qua victoria etiam illud memorabile fuit,
13 quod ne nuntius quidem tantae cladis superfuit. Caput
Cyri amputatum in utrem humano sanguine repletum
coici regina iubet cum hac exprobratione crudelitatis:
"Satia te" inquit "sanguine, quem sitisti cuiusque insatia-
14 bilis semper fuisti." Cyrus regnavit annis XXX, non initio
tantum regni, sed continuo totius temporis successu ad-
mirabiliter insignis.

bounds of her kingdom would be easier and for an enemy
blocked by a river flight would be more difficult. So Cyrus,   3
after taking his troops over and advancing some distance
into Scythia, marked out his camp. Then the next day,   4
feigning panic and abandoning his camp as if in flight, he
left behind large quantities of wine and things needed for
a feast. When this was reported to the queen, she sent her   5
young son to pursue him with a third of her forces. When   6
they reached Cyrus' camp, the young man, having little
military experience and feeling he had come to a banquet
not a battle, overlooked the enemy and allowed their barbarians, men unused to wine, to load themselves with it,
and the Scythians were defeated by drunkenness rather   7
than battle. For on learning of it Cyrus returned at night,   8
fell upon them when they were still tipsy and killed all the
Scythians along with the queen's son.

After losing such a great army and, even more painful,   9
her only son, Tamyris did not shed tears from the pain of
her loss but rather contemplated revenge to ease her grief
and tricked her enemies with a similar ruse as they gloated
over their recent victory; for feigning loss of confidence   10
after the blow she had received she retreating and lured
Cyrus right into a narrow pass. There with an ambush set   11
in the hills she slaughtered two hundred thousand Persians together with the king himself. In that victory what   12
was also remarkable was that none survived to report the
disaster. The queen ordered Cyrus' head to be cut off and   13
thrust into a wineskin filled with human blood, adding this
rebuke for his ruthlessness: "Glut yourself with blood, for
which you thirsted and of which never had enough." Cyrus   14
reigned for thirty years, and not only at the start of his
reign but throughout it he enjoyed unbroken success.

9. Huic successit filius Cambyses, qui imperio patris
2 Aegyptum adiecit; sed offensus superstitionibus Aegyptio-
3 rum Apis ceterorumque deorum aedes dirui iubet. Ad
Hammonis quoque nobilissimum templum expugnandum
exercitum mittit, qui tempestatibus et harenarum molibus
4 oppressus interiit. Post haec per quietem vidit fratrem
5 suum Mergim regnaturum. Quo somnio exterritus non
6 dubitavit post sacrilegia etiam parricidium facere. Erat
enim difficile, ut parceret suis, qui cum contemptu religionis grassatus etiam adversus deos fuerat.
7 Ad hoc tam crudele ministerium magum quendam ex
8 amicis delegit, nomine Cometen. Interim ipse gladio sua
sponte evaginato in femur graviter vulneratus occubuit
poenasque luit seu imperati parricidii seu perpetrati sa-
9 crilegii. Quo nuntio accepto magus ante famam amissi
regis occupat facinus prostratoque Mergide, cui regnum
10 debebatur, fratrem suum subiecit Oropasten. Erat enim
et oris et corporis liniamentis persimilis, ac nemine subesse dolum arbitrante pro Mergide rex Oropasta constitui-
11 tur. Quae res eo occultior fuit, quod apud Persas persona
12 regis sub specie maiestatis occulitur. Igitur magi ad favorem populi conciliandum tributa et militiae vacationem

---

17 In the sources relevant to section 9, there are discrepancies
as to names, sequence, and more, and it is likely that Cambyses'
name has been unduly blackened. See Hdt. 3.1ff., 61ff.; Ctesias
9ff.; Darius' Behistun inscription (J. M. Baker, *Herodotus and
Bisitun*, Historia Einzelschriften 49 [1987]); the inscription of
Udjahorresnet (A. B. Lloyd, "The Inscription of Udjahorresnet:
A Collaborator's Testament," *Journal of Egyptian Archaeology* 68
[1982], 166ff.); T. C. Young in *CAH*, 4:1–52; M. A. Dandamaev,

9. He was succeeded by his son Cambyses,[17] who added Egypt to his father's empire; but offended by the superstitions of the Egyptians he ordered the temples of Apis and their gods to be destroyed. He also sent an army to plunder the very renowned temple of Hammon, but overtaken by storms and buried in huge sand drifts it was destroyed. After this he saw in his sleep that his brother Mergis would become king. Frightened by the dream he did not after his sacrilege hesitate to commit fratricide. For it was difficult for a man to spare his own family when he had with contempt for religion even vented his rage on the gods!

For such a cruel undertaking he chose from among his friends a certain seer called Cometes. Meanwhile he died himself from a serious thigh wound after his sword was accidentally unsheathed and paid the penalty either for the fratricide he had ordered after his sacrilege or the sacrilege he had committed. At the news and before word spread of the king's death, the seer pushed ahead his crime and murdering Mergis, the rightful heir to the throne, replaced him with his brother Oropastes For in both face and physique he closely resembled him, and as no one suspected trickery Oropastes was appointed king in Mergis' place. The matter was quite easily concealed because among the Persians a king's person is kept out of sight from respect for his royal dignity. So to win support from the people the seers granted remission of taxes and exemption

2 3 4 5 6 7 8 9 10 11 12

A *Political History of the Achaemenid Empire*, trans. W. J. Vogelsang (Leiden, 1989). Trogus, it seems, followed Herodotus' version.

27

13 in triennium permittunt, ut regnum, quod fraude quaesie-
14 rant, indulgentiae largitionibus confirmarent. Quae res
suspecta primo Hostani, viro nobili et in coniectura saga-
15 cissimo, fuit. Itaque per internuntios quaerit de filia, quae
16 inter regias paelices erat, an Cyri filius rex esset. Illa nec
se ipsam scire ait nec ex alia posse cognoscere, quia singu-
17 lae separatim recludantur. Tum pertractare caput dor-
mienti iubet: nam mago Cambyses aures utrasque praeci-
18 derat. Factus dein per filiam certior sine auribus regem
esse, optimatibus Persarum rem indicat et in caedem falsi
19 regis inpulsos sacramenti religione obstringit. Septem tantum conscii fuere huius coniurationis, qui ex continenti,
ne dato in paenitentiam spatio res per quemquam narra-
20 retur, occultato sub veste ferro ad regiam pergunt. Ibi
obviis interfectis ad magos perveniunt, quibus ne ipsis qui-
21 dem animus in auxilium sui defuit, siquidem stricto ferro
22 duos de coniuratis interficiunt. Ipsi tamen corripiuntur a
pluribus, quorum alterum Gobryas medium amplexus,
cunctantibus sociis, ne ipsum pro mago transfoderent,
quia res obscuro loco gerebatur, vel per suum corpus adigi
23 mago ferrum iussit. Fortuna tamen ita regente illo incolumi magus interficitur.

    10. Occisis magis magna quidem gloria recuperati
regni principum fuit, sed multo maior in eo, quod, cum de
2 regno ambigerent, concordare potuerunt. Erant enim virtute et nobilitate ita pares, ut difficilem ex his populo elec-

---

18 Hdt. 3.80ff.

from military service for three years in order to establish 13
by extravagant largesse a reign they had sought by subterfuge. The matter first raised the suspicion of Hostanes, a 14
nobleman and one very astute in reasoning. So through 15
messengers, he asked his daughter, who was among the
royal concubines, whether the king was Cyrus' son. She 16
said she did not personally know and could not find out
from anyone else as they were each confined in separate
quarters. He next told her to feel the king's head while he 17
was asleep; for Cambyses had cut off both of the seer's
ears. Then when assured by his daughter that the king had 18
no ears, he disclosed the matter to some Persian noblemen
and bound them by a solemn religious oath to a plot to
murder the false king. Only seven were party to this con- 19
spiracy; and for the plot not to be revealed by anyone if
given time for a change of heart they went immediately to
the palace with swords hidden under their clothes. There, 20
killing those in their way, they reached the seers, who did
not themselves lack the spirit for self-defense, since they 21
drew their swords and killed two of the conspirators. They 22
were themselves overpowered by superior numbers, however, one of whom Gobryas seized around the waist, and
while his companions hesitated, fearing they might stab
him instead of the seer since this was happening in the
dark, he told them to stab the seer even through his own
body. Fortune so willing, however, he was unharmed and 23
the seer killed.

10. By killing the seers they achieved great renown for
recovering the throne, but they won much more for being
able to agree when it came to discussing the kingdom.[18]
For so evenly matched in courage and noble birth were 2
they that their equality made choosing from among them

3 tionem aequalitas faceret. Ipsi igitur viam invenerunt, qua
4 de se iudicium religioni et fortunae committerent, pac-
tique inter se sunt, ut die statuta omnes equos ante regiam
primo mane perducerent, et cuius equus inter solis ortum
5 hinnitum primus edidisset, is rex esset. Nam et solem Persae unum deum esse credunt et equos eidem deo sacratos
6 ferunt. Et erat inter coniuratos Darius, Hystaspis filius, cui
de regno sollicito equi custos ait, si ea res victoriam mora-
7 retur, nihil negotii superesse. Per noctem deinde equum
pridie constitutam diem ad eundem locum ducit ibique
equae admittit, ratus ex voluptate Veneris futurum quod
8 evenit. Postera die itaque, cum ad statutam horam omnes
convenissent, Darii equus cognito loco ex desiderio feminae hinnitum statim edidit et segnibus aliis felix auspicium
9 domino primus emisit. Tanta moderatio ceteris fuit, ut
audito auspicio confestim equis desilierint et Darium re-
10 gem salutaverint. Populus quoque universus secutus iudi-
11 cium principum eundem regem constituit. Sic regnum
Persarum septem nobilissimorum virorum virtute quaesi-
12 tum tam levi momento in unum conlatum est. Incredibile
prorsus tanta patientia gessisse eos, quod ut eriperent magis, mori non recusaverint.

13 Quamquam praeter formam virtutemque hoc imperio
dignam etiam cognatio Dario iuncta cum pristinis regibus
14 fuit. Principio igitur regni Cyri filiam in matrimonium
recepit, regalibus nuptiis regnum firmaturus, ut non tam
in extraneum translatum, quam in familiam Cyri reversum
videretur.

---

[19] Darius was, as he himself says in the Behistun inscription, one of the Achaemenids. He in fact married two daughters of Cyrus, Atossa and Artystone (Hdt. 3.88).

difficult for the people. They therefore themselves found 3
a way to leave the decision about them to religion and
fortune, and agreed among themselves that early in the 4
morning of a an appointed day they would all lead their
horses before the palace, and he whose horse neighed first
at sunrise would be king. For Persians believe the sun to 5
be the only god and they also regard horses as sacred to
the same god. Now among the conspirators was Darius, 6
son of Hystaspes, who being concerned about the impending kingship was told by his groom that if that was all that
impeded his victory there really was no problem. Then in 7
the night before the appointed day he took his horse to the
appointed place and coupled it with a mare, thinking that
the horse's sensual pleasure would yield a certain result,
as indeed it did. So the next day, when all the noblemen 8
met at the specified hour, Darius' horse, recognizing the
spot and feeling desire for the mare, immediately neighed,
and while the other animals did nothing it was the first to
emit the happy omen for its master. Such was the others' 9
moderation that on hearing the omen they jumped from
their horses and hailed Darius as king. Their people also 10
all accepted the nobles' decision and made him king. Thus 11
the kingdom of Persia that was sought by seven courageous men of the highest rank was conferred on the one
for such a flimsy reason. It was certainly beyond belief that 12
they behaved so calmly over what they did not refuse
death to take from the seers!

Yet his good looks and courage apart, Darius was also 13
worthy of this power through his family ties with earlier
kings. So at the beginning of his rule he took Cyrus' 14
daughter in marriage to strengthen the rule with royal
nuptials so that it might appear that rather than being
turned over to a stranger it had returned to Cyrus' family.[19]

15   Interiecto deinde tempore cum Assyrii descivissent et Babyloniam occupassent difficilisque urbis expugnatio esset, aestuante rege unus de interfectoribus magorum, Zopyrus, domi se verberibus lacerari toto corpore iubet, nasum, aures et labia sibi praecidi, atque ita regi inopi-

16 nanti se offert. Attonitum et quaerentem Darium causas auctoremque tam foedae lacerationis tacitus quo proposito fecerit edocet, formatoque in futura consilio trans-

17 fugae titulo Babyloniam proficiscitur. Ibi ostendit populo laniatum corpus, queritur crudelitatem regis, a quo in regni petitione non virtute, sed auspicio, non iudicio ho-

18 minum, sed hinnitu equi superatus sit; iubet illos ex amicis

19 exemplum capere, quid hostibus cavendum sit; hortatur, non moenibus magis quam armis confidant, patianturque

20 se commune bellum recentiore ira gerere. Nota nobilitas viri pariter et virtus omnibus erat, nec de fide timebant, cuius veluti pignora vulnera corporis et iniuriae notas

21 habebant. Constituitur ergo dux omnium suffragio, et accepta parva manu semel atque iterum cedentibus ex

22 consulto Persis secunda proelia facit. Ac postremo universum sibi creditum exercitum Dario prodit urbemque ip-

23 sam in potestatem eius redigit. Post haec Darius bellum Scythis infert, quod sequenti volumine referetur.

Then some time later when the Assyrians revolted and 15
seized Babylon[20] and assaulting the city proved difficult
and Darius was furious, one of the killers of the seers,
Zopyrus, ordered that he should at home be lashed all over
his body and have his nose, ears and lips cut off; and in
that state he presented himself to the unsuspecting king.
When Darius in astonishment asked the reasons for it, the 16
person responsible for such hideous disfigurement and
the culprit's name, he quietly explained his motive and
with a plan fixed for the future set off for Babylon, seemingly as a fugitive. There he showed the people his muti- 17
lated body and complained about the cruelty of a king
whose candidacy for the throne lay not in merit but an
omen, not in men's judgment but the neighing of a horse;
he told them to see from this example of his treatment of 18
friends what his enemies must guard against; he urged 19
them not to rely on walls but on weapons, and allow him
in his more recent anger to direct a combined operation
against Darius. The man's nobility and his courage were 20
both known to everybody, and they had no concern about
his integrity, for which they had as guarantee his wounds
and disfigurement. So he was made general by everyone's 21
vote, and given a small detachment he, with the Persians
making a prearranged retreat before him, fought one or
two successful battles. And finally, when the whole army 22
was entrusted to him, he betrayed it to Darius, and brought
the city itself under his power. After this Darius made war 23
on the Scythians, to be recounted in the following volume.

[20] Hdt. 3.150ff. Zopyrus was in fact the son of Megabyzus, the
one who had been among the killers (Hdt. 3.70).

LIBER II

1. In relatione rerum ab Scythis gestarum, quae satis am-
plae magnificaeque fuerunt, principium ab origine re-
2 petendum est. Non enim minus inlustria initia quam imperium habuere, nec virorum magis quam feminarum
3 virtutibus claruere, quippe cum ipsi Parthos Bactrianos-
que, feminae autem eorum Amazonum regna condiderint,
4 prorsus ut res gestas virorum mulierumque considerant-
ibus incertum sit, uter apud eos sexus inlustrior fuerit.
5 Scytharum gens antiquissima semper habita, quamquam inter Scythas et Aegyptios diu contentio de generis
6 vetustate fuerit Aegyptiis praedicantibus, initio rerum,
cum aliae terrae nimio fervore solis arderent, aliae ri-
gerent frigoris inmanitate, ita ut non modo primae generare homines, sed ne advenas quidem recipere ac tueri
possent, priusquam adversus calorem vel frigus velamenta
corporis invenirentur vel locorum vitia quaesitis arte re-
7 mediis mollirentur, Aegyptum ita temperatam semper
fuisse, ut neque hiberna frigora nec aestivi solis ardores

---

1 Hdt. 4 begins with a long treatment of the Scythians, but this
was certainly not the direct source of Trogus. At Hdt. 4.5.1 we
find the Scythian claim to be the *youngest* of peoples, and at 2.2
the Egyptians concede the issue of antiquity to the Phrygians.

34

BOOK II

1. In an account of the achievements of the Scythians, which were quite rich and munificent, one must return to their beginnings. For their earliest times were no less illustrious than their empire, and they were not more famous for their men's than for their women's achievements, since while they themselves founded the Parthian and Bactrian empires, it was the women who founded the Amazon Kingdom, so that in judging the achievements of males and females one is uncertain which sex's history was the more illustrious among them.[1]

The Scythian race has always been thought the most ancient although between Scythians and Egyptians there was a long-standing dispute over their age, the Egyptians claiming that at the start of things, when some lands burned in the sun's excessive heat and others froze in brutally cold climates, these could not have been the lands that first produced men since they could not even receive and maintain immigrants until body clothing could be devised to counter heat and cold and inhospitable conditions be mitigated by skillful advances, whereas Egypt had always been so temperate that neither winter cold nor the

The Scythians are dealt with by T. Sulimirski in chapter 4 of *CHI* 2.

8 incolas eius premerent, solum ita fecundum, ut alimen-
9 torum in usum hominum nulla terra feracior fuerit. Iure
igitur ibi primum homines natos videri debere, ubi edu-
cari facillime possent.

10 Contra Scythae caeli temperamentum nullum esse
11 vetustatis argumentum putabant. Quippe naturam, cum
primum incrementa caloris ac frigoris regionibus distinxit,
statim ad locorum patientiam animalia quoque generasse;
12 sed et arborum ac frugum pro regionum condicione apte
13 genera variata. Et quanto Scythis sit caelum asperius
quam Aegyptiis, tanto et corpora et ingenia esse duriora.
14 Ceterum si mundi, quae nunc partes sunt, aliquando uni-
tas fuit, sive inluvies aquarum principio rerum terras
obrutas tenuit, sive ignis, qui et mundum genuit, cuncta
possedit, utriusque primordii Scythas origine praestare.
15 Nam si ignis prima possessio rerum fuit, qui paulatim
extinctus sedem terris dedit, nullam prius quam sep-
temtrionalem partem hiemis rigore ab igne secretam,
16 adeo ut nunc quoque nulla magis rigeat frigoribus; Aegyptum vero et totum Orientem tardissime temperatum,
quippe qui etiam nunc torrenti calore solis exaestuet.
17 Quodsi omnes quondam terrae submersae profundo fuerunt, profecto editissimam quamque partem decurrenti-
bus aquis primum detectam, humillimo autem solo ean-
18 dem aquam diutissime inmoratam; et quanto prior
quaeque pars terrarum siccata sit, tanto prius animalia
19 generare coepisse. Porro Scythiam adeo editiorem omnibus terris esse, ut cuncta flumina ibi nata in Maeotim,
tum deinde in Ponticum et Aegyptium mare decurrant;

---

2 The Sea of Azov.

heat of the summer sun oppressed its inhabitants, and so 8
fertile was its soil that no land was more productive in food
for human consumption. So one would be right to accept 9
that men were first born where they could be most easily
nurtured.

The Scythians, however, thought a temperate climate 10
no proof of antiquity. For Nature, they said, in first giving 11
different regions varying degrees of heat and cold had
immediately produced animals capable of adapting to
their environment; but it had also diversified species of 12
trees and crops suited to regional conditions. And the 13
Scythian climate being harsher than the Egyptian made
Scythians physically and mentally more robust than Egyptians. Besides, if the world, which is now in parts, was once 14
undivided, then whether the earth was submerged in
floodwater or engulfed in a fire that also gave birth to the
universe, the Scythians prevail on either cosmic theory.
For if the fire first covering the earth gradually died down 15
and gave place to land, no region can have been detached
from the fire by the severity of winter before the north,
where it is so harsh that even now nowhere is more ice-
bound. Egypt certainly and all the East was the latest 16
cooling, for even now it blazes in the sun's torrid heat. But 17
if all lands were once submerged in deep water, the higher
ground was surely the first uncovered by the retreating
flood, while that same water would have remained longest
on the lowest soil; and the sooner any part of the world 18
dried out, the sooner it would have started producing
living creatures. In fact Scythia is so much higher than 19
all other lands that all rivers rising in it flow into Lake
Maeotis,[2] and then into the Pontus and the Egyptian

20 Aegyptum autem, quae tot regum, tot saeculorum cura
inpensaque munita sit et adversum vim incurrentium
aquarum tantis structa molibus, tot fossis concisa, ut, cum
his arceantur, illis recipiantur aquae, nihilo minus coli nisi
refuso Nilo non potuerit, nec possit videri hominum vetustate ultima, quae aggerationibus regum sive Nili tra-
21 hentis limum terrarum recentissima videatur. His igitur
argumentis superatis Aegyptiis antiquiores semper Scythae visi.

2. Scythia autem in orientem porrecta includitur ab
uno latere Ponto, ab altero montibus Riphaeis, a tergo
2 Asia et Phasi flumine. Multum in longitudinem et latitu-
3 dinem patet. Hominibus inter se nulli fines. Neque enim
agrum exercent, nec domus illis ulla aut tectum aut sedes
est, armenta et pecora semper pascentibus et per incultas
4 solitudines errare solitis. Vxores liberosque secum in
plaustris vehunt, quibus coriis imbrium hiemisque causa
5 tectis pro domibus utuntur. Iustitia gentis ingeniis culta,
6 non legibus. Nullum scelus apud eos furto gravius: quippe
sine tecti munimento pecora et armenta habentibus quid
7 inter silvas superesset, si furari liceret? Aurum et argen-
8 tum non perinde ac reliqui mortales adpetunt. Lacte et
9 melle vescuntur. Lanae his usus ac vestium ignotus et
quamquam continuis frigoribus urantur, pellibus tamen

---

3 So the text, but unless Trogus made some comparison with
the low, inundated areas of Egypt, "Egyptian Sea" is perhaps an
error (on the part of Justin or a scribe) for "Aegean Sea," given
the proximity of "Egypt." The Pontus is the Black Sea.

4 Latin *refuso*. An emendation suggested by D. R. Shackleton

Sea.[3] Egypt, however, was built up with care and expense   20
by so many kings over so many ages, and with such huge
structures built to combat the violence of its inundations
and with so many canals dug, some for holding back water
and others for bringing it in—but even then land could not
be cultivated without the receding of the Nile.[4] It could
not be thought as having the most ancient population,
either, since its barrages, whether constructed by its kings
or formed by the silting of the Nile, suggest it the most
recent of countries. So with the Egyptians bested by such   21
arguments the Scythians have always been seen as older.

2. Now Scythia, stretching eastward, is bordered on its
one side by the Pontus, on the other by the Riphaean
Mountains, and to the rear by Asia and the River Phasis.[5]   2
It is great both in length and latitude. Its people have no   3
fixed boundaries. For they neither work the soil or have
any house, building or fixed abode, being always pasturing
cattle and sheep and living nomadic lives in desolate wilds.
Their wives and children they take along with them in   4
wagons which, covered with hides as protection against
rain and winter, they use as homes. Justice for their people   5
rests in their nature, not laws. No crime is more serious   6
among them than theft; for without buildings to guard
sheep and cattle, what would be left in the forests if rob-
bery were condoned? Silver and gold they do not hanker   7
after like other mortals. Their diet is milk and honey. The   8
                                                             9
use of wool and clothing is unknown to them, and although
always facing blistering cold they use hides and rodent

Bailey in *Phoenix* 34 (1980): 227–28, referring to the annual retreat of the floodwaters.

[5] Now the Rioni, in Georgia.

10 ferinis ac murinis utuntur. Haec continentia illis morum
quoque iustitiam edidit, nihil alienum concupiscentibus;
11 quippe ibidem divitiarum cupido est, ubi et usus. Atque
utinam reliquis mortalibus similis moderatio abstinen-
12 tiaque alieni foret; profecto non tantum bellorum per om-
13 nia saecula terris omnibus continuaretur, neque plus hominum ferrum et arma quam naturalis fatorum condicio
raperet, prorsus ut admirabile videatur, hoc illis naturam
14 dare, quod Graeci longa sapientium doctrina praeceptis-
que philosophorum consequi nequeunt, cultosque mores
15 incultae barbariae conlatione superari. Tanto plus in illis
proficit vitiorum ignoratio quam in his cognitio virtutis.

3. Imperium Asiae ter quaesivere; ipsi perpetuo ab
2 alieno imperio aut intacti aut invicti mansere. Darium,
regem Persarum, turpi ab Scythia submoverunt fuga,
3
4 Cyrum cum omni exercitu trucidaverunt, Alexandri Magni
ducem Zopyriona pari ratione cum copiis universis dele-
5
6 verunt. Romanorum audivere, non sensere arma. Parthi-
7 cum et Bactrianum imperium ipsi condiderunt. Gens laboribus et bellis aspera, vires corporum inmensae; nihil
parare, quod amittere timeant, nihil victores praeter glo-
8 riam concupiscunt. Primus Scythis bellum indixit Vezosis,
rex Aegyptius, missis prius legationibus, qui hostibus pa-
9 rendi legem dicerent. Sed Scythae iam ante de adventu
10 regis a finitimis certiores facti legatis respondent: tam
opulenti populi ducem stolide adversus inopes occupasse
11 bellum, quod magis domi fuerit illi timendum, quod belli

---

⁶ These events are chronologically reversed: see above, 1.8,
and below, 2.6.9–11.   ⁷ See 12.1.4–5, 16–17.
⁸ See 41.1.1–2, 2.3–4.   ⁹ See 1.1.6 and note.

skins. This simple lifestyle of theirs has also given them a   10
just character, coveting no one else's belongings; for lust
for riches is found only where they are in use. And would   11
that the rest of mortals had similar moderation and restraint with people's property; for there certainly would   12
not be so many wars going on throughout the ages in every
land, nor would more men be taken off by iron and weap-   13
ons than is naturally determined by fate, making it seem
amazing that nature should grant them what Greeks are   14
unable to achieve from the long teachings of sages and
precepts of philosophers, and that refined morality is inferior to coarse barbarism. So much more has ignorance   15
of vice benefited them than knowledge of virtue has the
Greeks.

3. Domination of Asia they sought three times; they
themselves always remained untouched or undefeated by
any foreign power. The Persian king Darius they drove   2
from Scythia in humiliating flight, Cyrus they massacred[6]   3
with his entire army, and Alexander the Great's general   4
Zopyrion they also killed with all his troops.[7] Roman arms   5
they have heard about but not faced. The Parthian and   6
Bactrian empires they themselves founded.[8] They are a   7
people savage after hardships and wars and they have
enormous physical strength; they hanker after nothing
they would fear to lose, and when victorious they want
nothing but glory. The first to declare war on Scythians was   8
Vezosis, the Egyptian king,[9] who sent forward delegations
to dictate terms of surrender to his enemy. But being ear-   9
lier informed of the king's coming by their neighbors, the
Scythians replied to the legates that the leader of such a   10
rich people would be foolish to have made war on a poor
people, because he had more to fear at home as the out-   11

41

certamen anceps, praemia victoriae nulla, damna mani-
12   festa sint. Igitur non exspectaturos Scythas, dum ad se
veniatur, cum tanto sibi plura in hoste concupiscenda sint,
13   ultroque praedae ituros obviam. Nec dicta res morata.
14   Quos cum tanta celeritate advenire rex didicisset, in fugam vertitur exercituque cum omni apparatu belli relicto
15   in regnum trepidus se recepit. Scythas ab Aegypto paludes
prohibuere.

Inde reversi Asiam perdomitam vectigalem fecere,
modico tributo magis in titulum imperii quam in victoriae
16   praemium inposito. XV annis pacandae Asiae inmorati
uxorum flagitatione revocantur, per legatos denuntianti-
bus, ni redeant, subolem se ex finitimis quaesituras nec
passuras, ut in posteritatem Scytharum genus per feminas
17   intercidat. His igitur Asia per mille quingentos annos vec-
18   tigalis fuit. Pendendi tributi finem Ninus, rex Assyriorum,
inposuit.

4. Sed apud Scythas medio tempore duo regii iuvenes,
Plynos et Scolopitus, per factionem optimatum domo pulsi
2   ingentem iuventutem secum traxere et in Cappadociae
ora iuxta amnem Thermodonta consederunt subiectosque
3   Themiscyrios campos occupavere. Ibi per multos annos
spoliare finitimos adsueti conspiratione populorum per
4   insidias trucidantur. Horum uxores cum viderent exilio
additam orbitatem, arma sumunt finesque suos submo-
5   ventes primo, mox etiam inferentes bella defendunt. Nu-

---

[10] By the Euxine Sea in modern Turkey: *Barr.* 87 B3.

come of a battle was uncertain, the rewards of a victory
nothing, and the losses clear. So the Scythians would not   12
wait for him to come to them since for themselves there
were far more desirable things among their enemy, and
they would just come for their spoils! That said, action was   13
not delayed. When the king was told that they were ap-   14
proaching at great speed, he turned to flight, and abandoning the army with all its military equipment he withdrew
in panic into his kingdom. The Scythians were kept out of   15
Egypt by the marshlands.

On their return from there they conquered Asia and
made it pay taxes, but at a modest rate and more to signify
their authority than as a prize of victory. When they had   16
remained there fifteen years to pacify Asia they were recalled by insistent pleas from their wives, who told them
through envoys that if they failed to return they would
seek to have children by neighboring peoples and not have
the women responsible for the later extinction of the
Scythian race. So Asia remained tax-paying to them for   17
fifteen hundred years. An end to tribute payment was im-   18
posed by Ninus, king of the Assyrians.

4. But meanwhile, in Scythia, two young princes, Plynos and Scolopitus, who were driven from home by an
aristocratic faction, took large numbers of young men with
them, settled on the coast of Cappadocia near the River   2
Thermodon, and conquered and occupied the Themiscyra
plain.[10] There, after many years of regularly plundering   3
their neighbors, they were killed in an ambush during
a conspiracy of the people. When their wives saw   4
widowhood added to their exile, they took up weapons
and driving off aggressors first, and then soon even starting wars, they managed to defend their lands. They also   5

bendi quoque finitimis animum omisere, servitutem, non
6 matrimonium appellantes. Singulare omnium saeculorum
exemplum, ausae rem publicam augere sine viris; iam
7 etiam cum contemptu virorum tuentur. Et ne feliciores
aliae aliis viderentur, viros, qui domi remanserant, inter-
8 ficiunt. Vltionem quoque caesorum coniugum excidio fini-
9 timorum consequuntur. Tum pace armis quaesita, ne ge-
10 nus interiret, concubitus finitimorum ineunt. Si qui mares
nascerentur, interficiebant. Virgines in eundem ipsis mo-
11 rem, non otio neque lanificio, sed armis, equis, venationi-
bus exercebant, inustis infantum dexterioribus mammis,
ne sagittarum iactus impediantur; unde dictae Amazones.
12   Duae his reginae fuere, Martesia et Lampeto, quae in
duas partes agmine diviso, inclitae iam opibus, vicibus
13 gerebant bella, soli terminos alternis defendentes, et ne
successibus deesset auctoritas, genitas se Marte praedica-
14 bant. Itaque maiore parte Europae subacta Asiae quoque
15 nonnullas civitates occupavere. Ibi Epheso multisque aliis
urbibus conditis partem exercitus cum ingenti praeda
16 domum dimittunt. Reliquae, quae ad tuendum Asiae imperium remanserant, concursu barbarorum cum Martesia
regina interficiuntur.
17   In huius locum filia eius Orithyia regno succedit, cui
praeter singularem belli scientiam eximia servatae in
18 omne aevum virginitatis admiratio fuit. Huius virtute tantum additum gloriae et famae Amazonum est, ut Herculi
rex, cui duodecim stipendia debebat, quasi inpossibile

---

11 Literally, "breastless" (Greek *mazon* = "breast"), though the
left was retained for nursing children.

abandoned the idea of marrying their neighbors, calling it
slavery, not marriage. Setting a precedent unparalleled in   6
history they dared to build a society without men; then
with contempt for men they also defended it. And for   7
some not to appear more fortunate than others, they killed
men who had remained at home. They also took revenge   8
for their murdered husbands by wiping out their neighbors. Then peace was settled with weapons and for their   9
line not to die out they had sexual relations with their
neighbors. Any males that were born they would put to   10
death. Girls they trained after their own lifestyle, not in
idleness or wool working but in armed combat, horse rid-   11
ing and hunting, and their right breasts were cauterized in
infancy so their archery not be hindered (hence their
name "Amazons"[11]).

They had two queens, Martesia and Lampeto, who di-   12
vided their army in two—they were already famous for
their power—and waged war in turns, alternating the defense of their boundaries, and so their successes should   13
not lack fame they would claim to be daughters of Mars.
So after conquering most of Europe they also seized a   14
number of the city-states of Asia. After there founding   15
Ephesus and many other cities they sent some of the army
home with huge amounts of plunder. The others, who had   16
remained to protect their Asian empire, were killed, in an
attack by barbarians, together with their queen Martesia.

Replacing her in the kingdom was her daughter Ori-   17
thyia, who beside having remarkable military skills also
won great admiration for preserving her virginity throughout her life. From her valor so much more glory and fame   18
accrued to the Amazons that Hercules was ordered by the
king to whom he owed his twelve labors to bring him, as

imperaverit, ut arma reginae Amazonum sibi adferret.
19 Eo igitur profectus longis novem navibus comitante prin-
20 cipum Graeciae iuventute inopinantes adgreditur. Duae
tum sorores Amazonum regna tractabant, Antiope et Ori-
21 thyia; sed Orithyia foris bellum gerebat. Igitur cum Hercules ad litus Amazonum adplicuit, infrequens multitudo
22 cum Antiope regina nihil hostile metuente erat. Qua re
effectum est, ut paucae repentino tumultu excitae arma
23 sumerent facilemque victoriam hostibus darent. Multae
itaque caesae captaeque, in his duae Antiopae sorores,
24 Melanippe ab Hercule, Hippolyte a Theseo. Sed Theseus
obtenta in praemium captiva eandem in matrimonium
25 adsumpsit et ex ea genuit Hippolytum. Hercules post victoriam Melanippen captivam sorori reddidit et pretium
arma reginae accepit. Atque ita functus imperio ad regem
revertitur.
26   Sed Orithyia, ubi conperit bellum sororibus inlatum ac
raptorem esse Atheniensium principem, hortatur comites
in ultionem frustraque et Ponti sinum et Asiam edomitam
esse dicit, si Graecorum non tam bellis quam rapinis pa-
27 teant. Auxilium deinde a Sagylo, rege Scythiae, petit: genus Scytharum esse, cladem virorum, necessitatem armorum, belli causas ostendit, adsecutasque virtute, ne
28 segniores viris feminas habere Scythae viderentur. Motus
ille domestica gloria mittit cum ingenti equitatu filium
29 Panasagorum in auxilium. Et ante proelium dissensione
orta ab auxiliis desertae bello ab Atheniensibus vincuntur.
30 Receptaculum tamen habuere castra sociorum, quorum

---

12 That is, the Amazons.

if it were an impossible assignment, the weapons of the
Amazon queen. So setting off with nine warships and ac-   19
companied by the leading young men of Greece, he took
the Amazons by surprise. Two Amazon sisters then ruled   20
the kingdom, Antiope and Orithyia; but Orithyia was fighting a campaign abroad. Now when Hercules landed on the   21
Amazons' shore, a small retinue was there with queen
Antiope, who feared no attack. So it transpired that few   22
took up arms in the surprise attack and gave their enemy
an easy victory. Many were then killed or captured, includ-   23
ing two of Antiope's sisters—Menalippe taken by Hercules, and Hippolyte by Theseus. But Theseus when awarded   24
the captive as his prize married her and by her had his son
Hippolytus. After the victory Hercules restored his cap-   25
tive Menalippe to her sister and as a reward received the
arms of the queen. And so after fulfilling his mission he
returned to the king.

But when Orithyia learned of the war made on her   26
sisters and their abductor being the Athenian leader, she
urged her companions to seek revenge and said that conquering the Gulf of Pontus and Asia had been for nothing
if they faced not so much wars with the Greeks as plundering. She then sought help from Sagylus, king of Scythia;   27
they were of Scythian descent,[12] she said, their husbands
had been massacred and they had been forced to take up
arms, and she presented the reasons for war, adding that
in valor Scythian women seemed no less enterprising than
men. Stirred by national pride he sent his son Panasagorus   28
with a large contingent of cavalry to aid them. And when   29
dissension arose before the battle they were deserted by
their allies and defeated in the war by the Athenians. They   30
found shelter in their allies' camp, however, and with their

auxilio intactae ab aliis gentibus in regnum revertuntur.

31 Post Orithyiam Penthesilea regno potita est, cuius Troiano bello inter fortissimos viros, cum auxilium adversus Grae-

32 cos ferret, magna virtutis documenta exstitere. Interfecta deinde Penthesilea exercituque eius absumpto paucae, quae in regno remanserant, aegre se adversus finitimos defendentes usque tempora Alexandri Magni duraverunt.

33 Harum Minithyia sive Thalestris regina, concubitu Alexandri per dies tredecim ad subolem ex eo generandum obtento, reversa in regnum brevi tempore cum omni Amazonum nomine intercidit.

5. Scythae autem tertia expeditione Asiana cum annis octo a coniugibus ac liberis afuissent, servili bello domi

2 excipiuntur. Quippe coniuges eorum longa exspectatione virorum fessae nec iam teneri bello, sed deletos ratae ser-

3 vis ad custodiam pecorum relictis nubunt, qui reversos cum victoria dominos velut advenas armati finibus pro-

4 hibent. Quibus cum varia victoria fuisset, admonentur Scythae mutare genus pugnae, memores non cum hostibus, sed cum servis proeliandum, nec armorum, sed dominorum iure vincendos, verbera in aciem, non tela adferenda, omissoque ferro virgas et flagella ceteraque servilis

5 metus paranda instrumenta. Probato omnes consilio instructi, sicut praeceptum erat, postquam ad hostem accessere, inopinantibus verbera intenta; adeoque illos perculerunt, ut quos ferro non poterant, metu verberum

---

13 See 12.3.5–7.

14 The following story is told in Hdt. 4.2ff., though without the details in section 6 and 7 here.

help returned to their kingdom untouched by other peoples. After Orithyia Penthesilea took over the kingdom; 31 and to her valor in the Trojan War great testimonials survive of when she fought among the bravest heroes and brought the Trojans aid against the Greeks. Then when 32 Penthesilea was killed and her army destroyed, the few Amazons that remained in the kingdom continued to survive, despite the difficulty of defending themselves against neighbors, down to the time of Alexander the Great. One 33 of them, the queen Minithyia or Thalestris, was permitted to sleep with Alexander for thirteen days to have a child by him,[13] and returning to her kingdom she shortly afterward died along with the entire Amazon name.

5. Now on their third Asian expedition the Scythians had been separated from their wives and children for eight years and were facing a slave war at home.[14] For tired of 2 the long wait for their husbands and assuming they had been killed in battle rather than just detained by the war, their wives married the slaves that were left in charge of their cattle, and when their masters returned victorious 3 they armed themselves and barred them entry to the land as if they were foreigners. While victory over them remained in doubt, the Scythians were prompted to change their battle strategy, remembering that it was not with enemies that they had to fight but with slaves, men to be overcome not by weapons but their authority as masters, and that into battle they should carry whips, not weapons, and forgetting their swords take up canes, lashes and the other instruments for intimidating slaves. Since everyone 5 approved the plan, they equipped themselves as instructed, and on reaching their enemy rained lashes on unsuspecting men; and they so overpowered them that by fear of the lash they defeated men they could not with the

vincerent, fugamque non ut hostes victi, sed ut fugitivi
6 servi capesserent. Quicumque capi potuerunt, supplicia
7 crucibus luerunt. Mulieres quoque male sibi consciae par-
8 tim ferro, partim suspendio vitam finierunt. Post haec pax
9 apud Scythas fuit usque tempora Ianthyri regis. Huic
Darius, rex Persarum, sicut supra dictum est, cum filiae
10 eius nuptias non obtinuisset, bellum intulit et armatis sep-
tingentis milibus hominum Scythiam ingressus, non facientibus hostibus pugnae potestatem metuens, ne inter-
rupto ponte Histri reditus sibi intercluderetur, amissis
11 LXXX milibus hominum trepidus refugit; quae iactura
abundante multitudine inter damna numerata non est.
12 Inde Asiam et Macedoniam domuit; Ionas quoque navali
13 proelio superat. Dein cognito quod Athenienses Ionis contra se auxilium tulissent, omnem impetum belli in eos convertit.

6. Nunc quoniam ad bella Atheniensium ventum est,
quae non modo ultra spem gerendi, verum etiam ultra
gesti fidem peracta sunt, operaque Atheniensium effectu
maiora quam voto fuere, paucis urbis origo repetenda est,
2 et quia non, ut ceterae gentes, a sordidis initiis ad summa
3 crevere. Soli enim praeterquam incremento etiam origine

---

15 In 1.10.23.   16 The text refers to Asia, but we might
rather expect mention of Thrace, subdued with Macedonia by
Darius in 513. The naval battle would seem to be that at Lade,
which preceded the fall of Miletus in 493, signaling the end of
the Ionian revolt in the early chapters of Hdt. 6. The Athenians
had withdrawn their aid earlier.

17 The notion of Athenian autochthony is commonplace (see,
e.g., Thuc. 1.2). Early Athenian history, with all its variants, was
the subject of reconstruction, especially by the series of Atthidog-
raphers, which really began in the mid-fourth century with

sword, men who now ran not like defeated enemies but
runaway slaves. Any able to be caught were punished with   6
crucifixion. Women, too, conscious of their guilt put an   7
end to their lives, some with the sword, some by hanging.
After this there was peace among the Scythians down to   8
the time of King Ianthyrus. On him Darius, king of the   9
Persians, declared war when, as noted above,[15] he failed
to obtain his daughter's hand in marriage, and with an   10
armed force of seven hundred thousand men he invaded
Scythia, but since his enemy allowed no opportunity for
pitched battle and he feared his return might be cut off if
the Ister bridge were broken down, he retreated in panic
losing eighty thousand men, a loss that given the huge   11
Persian numbers was not considered disastrous. Next he   12
overcame Asia and Macedonia; and he also defeated the
Ionians in a naval battle.[16] Then on learning that the Athe-   13
nians had brought the Ionians help against him, he turned
the whole thrust of the war on them.

6. Now since we have come to the Athenian wars,
which ended not only exceeding their hopes but even
straining belief after the event, and since the achievements of the Athenians proved greater than they could
have prayed for, we must briefly return to the city's origins,   2
and do it also because they did not, like other peoples,
rise to greatness from lowly beginnings.[17] For they   3
alone take pride in their origins as well as their growth;

Cleidemus (though earlier, Hellanicus of Lesbos had produced a
short treatment) and led to the most compendious and later most
consulted of them, Philochorus, in the third century. The fragments are collected in *FGrH*, beginning at no. 323. See also
C. Hignett, *A History of the Athenian Constitution* (Oxford,
1952), ch. 2.

4 gloriantur; quippe non advenae neque passim collecta
populi conluvies originem urbi dedit, sed eodem innati
solo, quod incolunt, et quae illis sedes, eadem origo est.
5 Primi lanificii et olei et vini usum docuere. Arare quoque
ac serere frumenta glandem vescentibus monstrarunt.
6 Litterae certe ac facundia et hic civilis disciplinae ordo
veluti templum Athenas habent.
7   Ante Deucalionis tempora regem habuere Cecropem,
quem, ut omnis antiquitas fabulosa est, biformem tradi-
dere, quia primus marem feminae matrimonio iunxit.
8 Huic successit Cranaus, cuius filia Atthis nomen regioni
9 dedit. Post hunc Amphictyonides regnavit, qui primus
Minervae urbem sacravit et nomen civitati Athenas dedit.
10 Huius temporibus aquarum inluvies maiorem partem po-
11 pulorum Graeciae absumpsit. Superfuerunt, quos refugia
montium receperunt, aut ad regem Thessaliae Deuca-
lionem ratibus evecti sunt, a quo propterea genus homi-
12 num conditum dicitur. Per ordinem deinde successionis
regnum ad Erechtheum descendit, sub quo frumenti satio
13 est Eleusinae a Triptolemo reperta, in cuius muneris ho-
14 norem noctes initiorum sacratae. Tenuit et Aegeus, Thesei
pater, Athenis regnum, a quo per divortium discedens
Medea propter adultam privigni aetatem Colchos cum
15 Medo filio ex Aegeo suscepto concessit. Post Aegeum
Theseus ac deinceps Thesei filius Demophoon, qui auxilium Graecis adversus Troianos tulit, regnum possedit.

---

18 That is, in the early history of the world. Deucalion and his
wife, Pyrra, alone survived the flood sent by Zeus to destroy
earth's wicked inhabitants.   19 Cecrops is elsewhere described
as part man, part snake and is credited with the introduction
of monogamy, the division of Attica into twelve communities

for it was neither immigrants nor a randomly gathered 4
rabble that founded their city, but they were born from
the same soil that they inhabit, and where they live is also
where they began. They were the first to teach the use of 5
wool, olive oil and wine. Plowing and crop planting they
also demonstrated to people feeding on acorns. Literature 6
for sure and eloquence and this ordered civilization of
ours have Athens as their temple.

Before Deucalion's time[18] they had Cecrops as their 7
king who, they claimed (since all antiquity has mythology)
was of both sexes, because first he joined male and female
in marriage.[19] He was succeeded by Cranaus, whose 8
daughter Atthis gave the region its name. After him 9
reigned Amphictyonides, who first dedicated the city to
Minerva and gave the state its name of Athens. During his 10
time a flood destroyed the greater part of Greece's population. The survivors were those who found refuge in the 11
mountains or escaped on boats to the king of Thessaly
Deucalion, to whom the founding of the human race is
therefore attributed. In due order of succession the throne 12
then came down to Erechtheus, under whom the planting
of grain was discovered at Eleusis by Triptolemus, in 13
honor of whose gift the nocturnal rites were instituted.
Aegeus too, Theseus' father, reigned at Athens, whom Me- 14
dea divorced after her stepson reached adulthood (and she
then returned to Colchis with Medus, the son she had
borne to Aegeus). After Aegeus Theseus held the throne, 15
and then his son, Demophoön, who brought the Greeks
aid against the Trojans.

(Athens was previously called Cecropia), and much else. He himself is said to have married a daughter of Actaeus, Attica's first
king. Justin has possibly misunderstood what he found in Trogus.

16   Erant inter Athenienses et Dorienses simultatium veteres offensae, quas vindicaturi bello Dorienses de eventu
17 proelii oracula consuluerunt. Responsum superiores fore,
18 ni regem Atheniensium occidissent. Cum ventum esset in
bellum, militibus ante omnia custodia regis praecipitur.
19 Atheniensibus eo tempore rex Codrus erat, qui et responso dei et praeceptis hostium cognitis permutato regis
habitu pannosus, sarmenta collo gerens castra hostium
20 ingreditur. Ibi in turba obsistentium a milite, quem falce
astu convulneraverat, interficitur. Cognito regis corpore
21 Dorienses sine proelio discedunt. Atque ita Athenienses
virtute ducis pro salute patriae morti se offerentis bello
liberantur.

7. Post Codrum nemo Athenis regnavit, quod memo-
2   riae nominis eius tributum est. Administratio rei publicae
3   annua magistratibus permissa. Sed civitati nullae tunc le-
4   ges erant, quia libido regum pro legibus habebatur. Legi-
tur itaque Solon, vir iustitiae insignis, qui velut novam
5   civitatem legibus conderet. Qui tanto temperamento inter
plebem senatumque egit (cum, si quid pro altero ordine
tulisset, alteri displiciturum videretur), ut ab utrisque
6   parem gratiam traheret. Huius viri inter multa egregia il-
7   lud memorabile fuit. Inter Athenienses et Megarenses de

---

[20] The three major divisions of the Greek peoples were the
Ionians (including the Athenians), the Dorians (including the
Spartans and the Megarians, mentioned below), and the Aeolians.

[21] Athenian tradition held that between the end of the kingship and the beginning of the annual archonship there were seven
ten-year archons. Developments are summarily treated in *Ath.
Pol.* 3. The first annual archon dates to the end of the 680s. There

There were longstanding grievances between Athe- 16
nians and Dorians,[20] and to settle them by war the Dorians
consulted the oracle about the outcome of a battle. The 17
response was they would prevail if they did not kill the
king of the Athenians. When it came to the battle, the 18
Dorian soldiers were told that above all else they must
keep the king protected. The king of the Athenians at the 19
time was Codrus, who on hearing both of the god's oracle
and the enemy's orders exchanged his royal robes for rags,
and carrying a bundle of sticks on his back entered the
enemy camp. There in a crowd that was blocking his path 20
he was killed by a soldier, whom he had cunningly wounded
with a sickle. Recognizing the king's body, the Dorians left
the field without a fight. And so through the valor of a 21
leader sacrificing himself for his country's safety the Athenians were freed from the war.

7. After Codrus no one reigned in Athens, which is a
tribute to his memory.[21] State government was left to an- 2
nually elected magistrates. But the city then had no laws 3
because the will of the kings was thought the law. So Solon, 4
a man of outstanding integrity, was chosen virtually to
found a new state with codified laws. With such evenness 5
did he deal with the plebs and senate (for it seemed that
any measure adopted in favor of one order would dis-
please the other) that he won the support of both. Among 6
this man's many fine achievements the following was remarkable. Between the Athenians and Megarians there 7

was in fact a codification of sorts by Draco, but the full code came
with Solon, who was archon in 594/3 (*AO* 37f.). Solon's moderation is a commonplace derived from his own poetry.

proprietate Salaminae insulae prope usque interitum ar-
8 mis dimicatum fuerat. Post multas clades capital esse apud
Athenienses coepit, si quis legem de vindicanda insula
9 tulisset. Sollicitus igitur Solon, ne aut tacendo parum rei
publicae consuleret aut censendo sibi, subitam dementiam simulat, cuius venia non dicturus modo prohibita, sed
10 et facturus erat. Deformis habitu more vaecordium in
11 publicum evolatfactoque concursu hominum, quo magis
consilium dissimulet, insolitis sibi versibus suadere populo
12 coepit, quod vetabatur, omniumque animos ita cepit, ut
extemplo bellum adversus Megarenses decerneretur insu-
laque devictis hostibus Atheniensium fieret.

8. Interea Megarenses memores inlati Atheniensibus
belli et deserti, ne frustra arma movisse viderentur, matro-
nas Atheniensium in Eleusinis sacris noctu oppressuri
2 naves conscendunt. Qua re cognita dux Atheniensium
Pisistratus iuventutem in insidiis locat, iussis matronis
solito clamore ac strepitu etiam in accessu hostium, ne
3 intellectos se sentiant, sacra celebrare; egressosque navibus Megarenses inopinantes adgressus delevit ac protinus
classe captiva intermixtis <inter milites> muliebribus, ut
speciem captarum matronarum praeberent, Megara con-
4 tendit. Illi cum et navium formam et petitam praedam
cognoscerent, obvii ad portum procedunt, quibus caesis

---

22 Pisistratus became tyrant for the first time in 561/0.

had been almost deadly armed clashes over possession of
the island of Salamis. After many defeats it began to be a   8
capital offense at Athens for anyone to propose legislation
about laying claim to the island. So Solon, concerned that   9
by remaining silent he might be acting contrary to the
state's interests but that by giving his opinion he might be
acting against his own interest, he feigned a sudden attack
of insanity, by which he could be excused for not only
making an illegal proposal but even carrying it through. In   10
slovenly clothing he rushed into the streets like the insane,
and attracting a crowd of men, he (the better to hide his   11
plan) proceeded to exhort the people, in verses that were
strange for him, to accept advice that was forbidden by   12
law; and so successfully did he persuade everyone that war
was immediately declared on the Megarians, the enemy
was defeated, and the island fell to the Athenians.

8. The Megarians meanwhile remembered the war
they had brought on the Athenians and then abandoned,
and not wishing to appear to have taken up arms in vain[22]
they boarded ships for a night attack on the Athenian la-
dies at the Eleusinian Mysteries. On learning of this the   2
Athenian general Pisistratus set young men in ambush and
ordered matrons to practice their rites with their usual
cries and hubbub even while the enemy was approaching
so they should not realize they had been found out; and   3
when the Megarians disembarked he, taking them by surprise, wiped them out and, placing women in the captured
ships among the soldiers so they would seem to be captured matrons, he then made for Megara. Since the Mega-   4
rians recognized both the shape of the vessels and their
prospective prey, they came to meet them at the harbor,

5 Pisistratus paulum a capienda urbe afuit. Ita Dorienses suis dolis hosti victoriam dedere.

6 Sed Pisistratus, quasi sibi, non patriae vicisset, tyranni-
7 dem per dolum occupat. Quippe voluntariis verberibus domi adfectus laceratoque corpore in publicum degre-
8 ditur, advocata contione vulnera populo ostendit, de cru-delitate principum, a quibus haec se passum simulabat,
9 queritur; adduntur vocibus lacrimae et invidiosa oratione multitudo credula accenditur: amore plebis invisum se
10 senatui simulat. Obtinet ad custodiam corporis sui satel-litum auxilium, per quos occupata tyrannide per annos XXXIII regnavit.

9. Post huius mortem Diocles, alter ex filiis, per vim
2 stuprata virgine a fratre puellae interficitur. Alter, Hippias nomine, cum imperium paternum teneret, interfectorem
3 fratris conprehendi iubet, qui cum per tormenta conscios caedis nominare cogeretur, omnes amicos tyranni nomi-
4 navit, quibus interfectis quaerenti tyranno, an adhuc ali-qui conscii essent, neminem ait superesse, quem amplius
5 mori gestiat quam ipsum tyrannum. Qua voce eiusdem se tyranni victorem post vindictam pudicitiae sororis osten-
6 dit. Huius virtute cum admonita civitas libertatis esset,
7 tandem Hippias regno pulsus in exsilium agitur, qui pro-fectus in Persas ducem se Dario inferenti Atheniensibus bellum, sicut supra significatum est, adversus patriam suam offert.

---

23 In fact, Pisistratus ruled from 561/0 to 557/6, then again from 546 to 527.   24 There is no consistency in the versions of the immediately following events; Justin's has affinities with *Ath. Pol.* 18 (see also Hdt. 5.55ff.; Thuc. 6.54ff.). Hippias' brother was Hipparchus, who was killed in 514 by Harmodius and Aristogeiton; Hippias was ousted in 511/10.

and cutting them down Pisistratus was not far off captur- 5
ing the city. So, caught in their own trap, the Dorians
ceded victory to their enemy.

But Pisistratus, as if it had been for himself and not his 6
country that he had prevailed, craftily seized the tyranny.
For being voluntarily beaten at home he went down into 7
the streets with his body lacerated, and calling an assembly 8
showed the people his wounds and deplored the savagery
of the aristocrats from whom he pretended he had received them; tears were added to his allegations and the 9
gullible crowd was inflamed by a frenzied oration; from
love for his people, he said, he was hated by the senate.
He received a train of attendants as a bodyguard, and seiz- 10
ing the tyranny with them he ruled for thirty-three years.[23]

9. After his death Diocles, one of his two sons, raped a
girl and was killed by her brother.[24] When the other son, 2
whose name was Hippias, succeeded to his father's power,
he ordered his brother's killer to be arrested, and when 3
forced under torture to name his accomplices in the murder he named all the friends of the tyrant; and when these 4
were put to death and the tyrant asked if there were still
more accomplices, he replied that there remained nobody
he wished to see die more than the tyrant himself. By say- 5
ing that he showed that he had got the better of the tyrant
by avenging his sister's honor. When the state was re- 6
minded of its lost liberty by his courage, Hippias was finally deposed and driven into exile; and setting off for 7
Persia where, as noted above, Darius was launching a war
on the Athenians, he offered himself as a guide against his
own country.

59

8   Igitur Athenienses audito Darii adventu auxilium a
9   Lacedaemoniis, socia tum civitate, petiverunt, quos ubi
viderunt quadridui teneri religione, non exspectato auxilio
instructis decem milibus civium et Plataeensibus auxilia-
ribus mille adversus sexcenta milia hostium in campis
10   Marathoniis in proelium egrediuntur. Miltiades et dux
belli erat et auctor non exspectandi auxilii; quem tanta
fiducia ceperat, ut plus praesidii in celeritate quam in so-
11   ciis duceret. Magna igitur in pugnam euntibus animorum
alacritas fuit, adeo ut, cum mille passus inter duas acies
essent, citato cursu ante iactum sagittarum ad hostem
12   venerint. Nec audaciae eius eventus defuit. Pugnatum est
enim tanta virtute, ut hinc viros, inde pecudes putares.
13   Victi Persae in naves confugerunt, ex quibus multae sup-
pressae, multae captae sunt.
14   In eo proelio tanta virtus singulorum fuit, ut, cuius laus
15   prima esset, difficile iudicium videretur. Inter ceteros tamen Themistoclis adulescentis gloria emicuit, in quo iam
16   tum indoles futurae imperatoriae dignitatis apparuit. Cy-
negiri quoque, militis Atheniensis, gloria magnis scriptorum laudibus celebrata est, qui post proelii innumeras
17   caedes, cum fugientes hostes ad naves egisset, onustam
navem dextra manu tenuit nec prius dimisit, quam manum
18   amitteret; tum quoque amputata dextera navem sinistra
conprehendit, quam et ipsam cum amisisset, ad postre-
19   mum morsu navem detinuit. Tantam in eo virtutem fuisse,
ut non tot caedibus fatigatus, non duabus manibus amissis

So the Athenians on hearing of Darius' approach   8
sought help from the Spartans, then an allied state, but   9
when they saw that they would be delayed four days by
religious observances, they did not wait for help and mar-
shaling ten thousand citizens and a thousand Plataean
auxiliaries went forth into battle against six hundred thousand of the enemy on the plains of Marathon. Miltiades   10
was both the commander and also one advising against
waiting for support; and such confidence had come to him
that he saw more protection in swift action than in his
allies. So going into battle they had fire in their hearts, so   11
much that despite a mile separating the two battle lines
they breaking into a run, reached their enemy before arrows were shot. Nor was his bravado unsuccessful. For   12
they fought with such courage that you might think there
were men on one side and cattle on the other. Defeated,   13
the Persians fled to their ships, many of which were sunk,
and many captured.

In that battle such was the valor of various fighters that   14
who deserved the most praise seems difficult to judge.
Among them, however, the young Themistocles' glory was   15
conspicuous, his qualities even then evident, suggesting
great leadership ahead. The Athenian soldier Cynegirus'   16
glorious deed has also won accolades from historians: after
killing countless numbers in the battle and driving the   17
enemy fleeing to their ships, he with his right hand held
onto a ship loaded with men and would not release it until
he lost the hand, and then even after his right hand was   18
severed he gripped the vessel with his left and finally, after
losing that one as well, he held on to the ship with his
teeth. Such was his courage that, not exhausted from kill-   19
ing so many and not beaten by the loss of both hands, he

victus, truncus ad postremum et velut rabida fera dentibus
20 dimicaverit. Ducenta milia Persae eo proelio sive naufra-
21 gio amisere. Cecidit et Hippias, tyrannus Atheniensis,
autor et concitor eius belli, diis patriae ultoribus poenas
repetentibus.

10. Interea et Darius, cum bellum restauraret, in ipso
apparatu decedit, relictis multis filiis et in regno et ante
2 regnum susceptis. Ex his Ariamenes maximus natu aetatis
privilegio regnum sibi vindicabat, quod ius· et ordo
3 nascendi et natura ipsa gentibus dedit. Porro Xerxes con-
troversiam non de ordine, sed de nascendi felicitate refe-
4 rebat; nam Ariamenen primum quidem Dario, sed privato
5 provenisse; se regi primum natum. Fratres itaque suos,
qui ante geniti essent, privatum patrimonium, quod eo
tempore Darius habuisset, non regnum vindicare sibi
posse; se esse, quem primum in regno iam rex pater sus-
6 tulerit. Huc accedere, quod Ariamenes non patre tantum,
sed et matre privatae adhuc fortunae, avo quoque materno
7 privato procreatus sit; se vero et matre regina natum et
patrem non nisi regem vidisse, avum quoque maternum
Cyrum se regem habuisse, non heredem, sed conditorem
8 tanti regni. Ita etsi in aequo iure utrumque fratrem pater
9 reliquisset, materno tamen se iure et avito vincere. Hoc
certamen concordi animo ad patruum suum Artaphernen
10 veluti ad domesticum iudicem deferunt, qui domi cognita
causa Xerxen praeposuit; adeoque fraterna contentio fuit,

---

25 These Persian losses are much exaggerated, nor did Hippias die there.   26 Darius died in November 486. The following story is also told in Hdt. 7.2f., though with differences of
detail and personnel, and with Darius still alive.

fought to the end despite the mutilation, using his teeth
like a wild animal. two hundred thousand Persians were   20
lost in that battle or from shipwreck. Hippias the Athenian 21
tyrant, and that war's author and fomenter, was also killed,
his country's avenging deities demanding punishment.[25]

10. Meanwhile Darius also died when he was reviving
the war and in the midst of preparations, leaving many
sons that were born to him both during and before his
reign.[26] The eldest of them, Ariamenes, asserted his claim   2
to the throne by virtue of his age, a right established for
peoples both by priority of birth and nature itself. Now   3
Xerxes favored having the matter decided not on primo-
geniture but appropriate circumstances at birth; for al-   4
though Ariamenes was the one first born to Darius it was
when he was still a private citizen; he himself was the first
child born to him after he became king. So his brothers   5
who had been born earlier could lay claim to property that
Darius had possessed at that time, but not the throne; *he*
was the first child that his father had recognized when
king. In addition to that Ariamenes was born when not   6
only his father but also his mother were plain citizens, as
had been his maternal grandfather; he himself, however,   7
was born when his mother was queen and he had also seen
his father only as king, and he had had as grandfather on
his mother's side King Cyrus, who was not the heir to, but
the founder of, such a great empire. So, even if their father 8
had left both brothers on equal terms, he still had the better claim by virtue of his mother and grandfather. This   9
dispute they by mutual agreement referred to their uncle
Artaphernes as a family judge, and after examining the   10
case within the home he decided in Xerxes' favor; and so

ut nec victor insultaverit nec victus doluerit ipsoque litis
tempore munera invicem miserint, iucunda quoque inter
se, non solum credula convivia habuerint, iudicium quo-
11 que ipsum sine arbitris, sine convicio fuerit. Tanto mode-
ratius tum fratres inter se maxima regna dividebant, quam
nunc exigua patrimonia partiuntur.

12 Igitur Xerxes bellum a patre coeptum adversus Grae-
13 ciam quinquennium instruxit. Quod ubi primum didicit
Demaratus, rex Lacedaemoniorum, qui apud Xerxen exulabat, amicior patriae post fugam, quam regi post beneficia, ne inopinato bello opprimerentur, omnia in tabellis
ligneis magistratibus perscribit easdemque cera superin-
14 ducta delet, ne aut scriptura sine tegmine indicium daret
aut recens cera dolum proderet, fido deinde servo per-
ferendas tradit iusso magistratibus Spartanorum tradere.
15 Quibus perlatis Lacedaemone quaestioni res diu fuit,
quod neque scriptum aliquid viderent nec frustra missas
suspicarentur, tantoque rem maiorem, quanto esset occul-
16 tior putabant. Haerentibus in coniectura viris soror regis
17 Leonidae consilium scribentis invenit. Erasa igitur cera
belli consilia deteguntur.

18 Iam Xerxes septingenta milia de regno armaverat et
trecenta milia de auxiliis, ut non inmerito proditum sit,
19 flumina ab exercitu eius siccata Graeciamque omnem vix

---

27 The essential account of Xerxes' invasion, beginning 481/0,
is Hdt. 7–9, which, however, could hardly have been Trogus' direct source. The story of Demaratus is not in Hdt.; the numbers
given at section 18 to 20 are at best confused when compared with
Hdt. 7.60, 89, 97; similarly, 11.2 compared with Hdt. 7.202. The
story of Leonidas' attack on the Persian camp is not in Hdt.; but
see Diod. Sic. 11.9f., which may point to Ephorus as the source.

fraternal was the disagreement that there was neither
taunting from the winner nor hard feelings on the part of
the loser, and at the very time of the dispute they sent each
other gifts and invited each other to dinner, where the
atmosphere was one not only of trust but also conviviality;
and the decision was itself also reached without witnesses
and without acrimony. So much more reasonable were 11
brothers at that time in dividing huge empires between
them than they are now in apportioning paltry estates.

So for five years Xerxes prepared for the war against 12
Greece that was started by his father.[27] Demaratus, king 13
of the Lacedaemonians, was then in exile at Xerxes' court
but had remained more loyal to his native city after his
banishment than to the king after his benefactions; and as
soon as he learned of it, and so the Spartans should not be
crushed by an unexpected war, he gave their magistrates
a message written on wooden tablets, which he then rendered unreadable by pouring wax over them so that no 14
uncovered piece of writing would leave any clue, or fresh
wax betray his stratagem; and he then gave the tablets to
a loyal slave, ordering him to pass them on to the Spartan
magistrates. When they were delivered the matter was 15
long discussed at Sparta, because the magistrates could
see no writing but also suspected they had not been sent
without some purpose; and they thought the it all the more
important for being so strange. While his men remained 16
stuck in guesswork, the sister of King Leonidas hit on the
writer's intent. So when the wax was scraped off the plans 17
came to light.

Xerxes had already put seven hundred thousand men 18
from his kingdom under arms as well as three hundred
thousand auxiliaries, so the story of rivers drained by his 19

20 capere exercitum eius potuisse. Naves quoque rostratas
mille ducentas, onerarias autem tria milia numero ha-
21 buisse dicitur. Huic tanto agmini dux defuit. Ceterum si
22 regem spectes, divitias, non ducem laudes; quarum tanta
copia in regno eius fuit, ut, cum flumina multitudine
23 consumerentur, opes tamen regiae superessent. Ipse autem primus in fuga, postremus in proelio semper visus est,
24 in periculis timidus, sicubi metus abesset, inflatus; denique ante experimentum belli fiducia virium veluti naturae
ipsius dominus et montes in planum deducebat et convexa
vallium aequabat et quaedam maria pontibus sternebat,
quaedam ad navigationis commodum per conpendium
ducebat.

    11. Cuius introitus in Graeciam quam terribilis, tam
2 turpis ac foedus discessus fuit. Namque cum Leonida, rex
Spartanorum, cum IV milibus militum angustias Thermopylarum occupasset, Xerxes contemptu paucitatis eos pugnam capessere iubet, quorum cognati Marathonia pugna
3 interfecti fuerant. Qui dum ulcisci suos quaerunt, principium cladis fuere; succedente dein inutili turba maior
4 caedes editur. Triduo ibi cum dolore et indignatione Per-
5 sarum dimicatum. Quarta die cum nuntiatum esset Leonidae a XX milibus hostium summum cacumen teneri,
tum hortatur socios, recedant et se ad meliora patriae
tempora reservent, sibi cum Spartanis fortunam experien-
6 dam; plura patriae quam vitae debere, ceteros ad praesidia
7 Graeciae servandos. Audito regis imperio discessere ceteri, soli Lacedaemonii remanserunt.

army and all Greece scarcely capable of containing the
force is not without merit. He also, it is said, had twelve   20
hundred men-of-war and three thousand transport vessels. What this huge army lacked was a leader. If you saw   21
the king, you would praise his wealth, not his leadership;
such were resources in his kingdom that even though riv-   22
ers were being drained by his hordes there still remained
the wealth of a king. However, he was himself always seen   23
to be first in flight and last in battle, in danger cowardly,
arrogant once fear was gone; in fact, before experience of   24
war, he would through confidence in his strength behave
like the lord of nature itself and would be leveling mountains, filling in valleys, spanning some seas with bridges,
and making others more navigable by shortcuts.

11. His entry into Greece was just as terrifying as his
disgraceful retreat was humiliating. For when Leonidas,   2
king of the Spartans, took possession of the pass at Thermopylae with four thousand men, Xerxes, contemptuous
of his small numbers, ordered into battle men whose relatives had been killed in the battle of Marathon. In trying   3
to avenge their kinsmen, these were the start of the disaster; then with a useless rabble replacing them the slaughter only mounted. There for three days the fight went on,   4
to the Persians' distress and indignation. On the fourth   5
day, when it was reported to Leonidas that a hill top was
being held by an enemy force of twenty thousand men, he
urged his allies to retreat and hold themselves in reserve
for their country's better times, while he and his Spartans   6
must put fortune to the test; they owed more to their
country than to their lives, he said but the others must be
kept safe for the defense of Greece. On receiving the   7
king's order the others left, and only the Spartans remained.

8 Initio huius belli sciscitantibus Delphis oracula respon-
9 sum fuerat, aut regi Spartanorum aut urbi cadendum. Et
   idcirco rex Leonidas, cum in bellum proficisceretur, ita
   suos firmaverat, ut ire se parato ad moriendum animo
10 scirent angustiasque propterea occupaverat, ut cum paucis aut maiore gloria vinceret aut minore damno rei publi-
11 cae caderet. Dimissis igitur sociis hortatur Spartanos,
   meminerint qualitercumque proeliatis cadendum esse;
   caverent, ne fortius mansisse quam dimicasse videantur;
12 nec exspectandum, ut ab hoste circumvenirentur, sed dum
   nox occasionem daret, securis et laetis superveniendum;
13 nusquam victores honestius quam in castris hostium peri-
14 turos. Nihil erat difficile persuadere persuasis mori: statim
15 arma capiunt et sexcenti viri castra quingentorum milium
   inrumpunt statimque regis praetorium petunt, aut cum
   illo aut, si ipsi oppressi essent, in ipsius potissimum sede
16 morituri. Tumultus totis castris oritur. Spartani, postquam
   regem non inveniunt, per omnia castra victores vagantur;
   caedunt sternuntque omnia, ut qui sciunt se pugnare
17 non spe victoriae, sed in mortis ultionem. Proelium a
18 principiio noctis in maiorem partem diei tractum. Ad postremum non victi, sed vincendo fatigati inter ingentes
19 stratorum hostium catervas occiderunt. Xerxes duobus
   vulneribus terrestri proelio acceptis experiri maris fortunam statuit.

---

28 The conventional number of Spartans at Thermopylae is
three hundred.

At the start of this war the Delphic oracle had been 8
consulted, and the response had been that either the king
of the Spartans or their city must fall. And for that reason 9
King Leonidas, when he was setting out for the war, had
so strengthened his men's resolve as to make them aware
that they were going into battle ready for death; and he
had occupied the pass so that with only a few men they 10
would either prevail with greater glory or die with less
harm to the state. So dismissing their allies he urged the 11
Spartans to remember that, no matter how they fought,
die they must; they should not appear to have been braver
remaining than in fighting; they must not wait to be sur- 12
rounded by their enemy, but, while night granted an opportunity, they must catch them when they were confident
and in high spirits; for nowhere will victors die more hon- 13
orably than in their enemy's camp. There was no difficulty 14
in persuading men who were already persuaded to die;
they immediately took up their weapons and six hundred 15
men burst into a camp of five hundred thousand and
headed straight for the king's tent, either to die together
with him or, if overpowered themselves, to die right where
he stood.[28] Uproar arose throughout the camp. The Spar- 16
tans, when they did not find their king, wandered victorious throughout the camp; they wreaked wholesale slaughter and havoc, knowing they were fighting not in hope of
victory but to avenge their own deaths. The battle went on 17
from the start of night into most of the day. In the end not 18
defeated but tired from inflicting defeat, they collapsed
amid huge mounds of their dead enemies. Having re- 19
ceived two blows in land battles, Xerxes decided to put
fortune to the test at sea.

12. Sed Atheniensium dux Themistocles cum animadvertisset Ionas, propter quos bellum Persarum suscepe-
runt, in auxilium regis classe venisse, sollicitare eos in par-
2   tes suas statuit, et cum conloquendi copiam non haberet,
quo applicituri erant, symbolos proponi et saxis proscribi
3   curat: "Quae vos, Iones, dementia tenet? Quod facinus
agitatis? Bellum inferre olim conditoribus vestris, nuper
4   etiam vindicibus cogitatis? An ideo moenia vestra condi-
5   dimus, ut essent qui nostra delerent? Quid si non haec et
Dario prius et nunc Xerxi belli causa nobiscum foret, quod
6   vos rebellantes non destituimus? Quin vos in haec castra
7   vestra ex ista obsidione transitis? Aut si hoc parum tutum
est, at vos commisso proelio ite cessim, inhibite remis et a
bello discedite."
8   Ante navalis proelii congressionem miserat Xerxes IV
milia armatorum Delphos ad templum Apollinis diripien-
9   dum, prorsus quasi non cum Graecis tantum, sed et cum
10   diis inmortalibus bellum gereret; quae manus tota imbri-
bus et fulminibus deleta est, ut intellegeret, quam nullae
11   essent hominum adversum deos vires. Post haec Thes-
piades et Plataeas et Athenas vacuas hominibus incendit,
et quoniam ferro in homines non poterat, in aedificia igne
12   grassatur. Namque Athenienses post pugnam Maratho-
niam praemonente Themistocle, victoriam illam de Persis
non finem, sed causam maioris belli fore, CC naves fabri-

---

29 Cf. Hdt. 8, though again Trogus shows other influences.
This section begins after Artemisium, which is omitted by Justin.
For the basis of Themistocles' appeal, cf. 2.9.15. There is also a
reference to the aid Athens sent to the Ionians when they at-
tempted to revolt from Persian control between 499 and 494,
something also passed over by Justin.

BOOK II

12. But when the Athenian leader Themistocles saw that the Ionians, for whom they undertook war with the Persians, had come to support the king with a fleet, he decided to tempt them over to his side,[29] and since he had no opportunity to parley with them, he had signs erected and written on rocks where they would put in: "What idiocy is possessing you, Ionians? What crime are you cooking up? Are you considering making war on people who were once your founders and recently also your defenders? Was that why we established your city walls—to have others destroying *ours*? What about our earlier war with Darius and the one now with Xerxes, caused by our not abandoning you in your rebellion? Why not come over to this, *your* camp, from that siege you are under? Or if this is too unsafe, at least give way at the start of the fighting starts, row astern and leave the war."

Before any sea engagement Xerxes had sent four thousand soldiers to Delphi to plunder the temple of Apollo, as if he were fighting a war not only with the Greeks but even with the immortal gods; and that entire force was destroyed by rain and bolts of lightning for him to understand how powerless human strength is against the gods. After this he burned Thespiae, Plataea and Athens, which had been left without people, and since he could not wreak havoc on humans with the sword he did so on buildings with fire. For after the battle of Marathon Themistocles warned the Athenians that victory over the Persians would not mean the end of the war but was cause for a greater one, and so they constructed two hundred ships.[30]

[30] See Hdt. 7.140ff. and *AO* 58 (the year 483/2).

13 caverunt. Adventante igitur Xerxe consulentibus Delphis
oraculum responsum fuerat, salutem muris ligneis tueren-
14 tur. Themistocles navium praesidium demonstratum ratus
persuadet omnibus, patriam municipes esse, non moenia,
civitatemque non in aedificiis, sed in civibus positam;
15 melius itaque salutem navibus quam urbi commissuros;
16 huius sententiae etiam deum auctorem esse. Probato consilio coniuges liberosque cum pretiosissimis rebus abditis
insulis relicta urbe demandant; ipsi naves armati conscen-
17 dunt. Exemplum Atheniensium et aliae urbes imitatae.
18 Itaque cum adunata omnis sociorum classis et intenta
in bellum navale esset angustiasque Salaminii freti, ne
circumveniri a multitudine posset, occupassent, dissensio
19 inter civitatum principes oritur. Qui cum deserto bello ad
sua tuenda dilabi vellent, timens Themistocles, ne dis-
cessu sociorum vires minuerentur, per servum fidum Xerxi
nuntiat, uno in loco eum contractam Graeciam capere
20 facillime posse. Quodsi civitates, quae iam abire vellent,
21 dissipentur, maiore labore ei singulas consectandas. Hoc
dolo inpellit regem signum pugnae dare. Graeci quoque
adventu hostium occupati proelium conlatis viribus capes-
22 sunt. Interea rex velut spectator pugnae cum parte navium
in litore remanet.
23 Artemisia autem, regina Halicarnasi, quae in auxilium
Xerxi venerat, inter primos duces bellum acerrime ciebat,
24 quippe ut in viro muliebrem timorem, ita in muliere
25 virilem audaciam cerneres. Cum anceps proelium esset,

Then when on Xerxes' approach they consulted the Del-   13
phic oracle the response had been that they should ensure
their safety with wooden walls. Themistocles, believing   14
that meant naval protection, persuaded everyone that
their country was its people, not its walls, that the state lay
not its buildings but its people; so it was better to entrust   15
their safety to their ships than their city, and this was also
the advice of the god, he said. The plan approved, they set   16
their wives and children along with their most precious
possessions on some remote islands and abandoned the
city; they themselves boarded the ships with weapons. The   17
Athenian example was also followed by other cities.

So when the whole allied fleet was brought together   18
and ready for the sea battle and they had occupied the
strait of Salamis to prevent any encirclement by superior
numbers, dissension arose among leaders of their states.
Since these wished to abandon the war and slip away to   19
protect their own lands, Themistocles, for the Greeks'
strength not to be weakened by the departure of the allies,
sent Xerxes a message through a trusty slave that being
concentrated in one place Greece could be easily taken.
But if the states that were now wishing to retreat dis-   20
persed, he would have more difficulty pursuing them one
by one. With this ruse he forced the king to give the signal   21
for battle. The Greeks, caught by their enemy's approach,
also went into battle with their forces united. Meanwhile   22
the king, like a spectator of a fight, remained on the shore
with part of his fleet.

Now Artemisia, queen of Halicarnassus, had come to   23
assist Xerxes and was fighting among his best commanders, so one could see in a man a woman's fear and in a   24
woman a man's bravado. When the battle remained still   25

73

Iones iuxta praeceptum Themistoclis pugnae se paulatim subtrahere coeperunt; quorum defectio animos cetero-
26 rum fregit. Itaque circumspicientes fugam pelluntur Per-
27 sae et mox proelio victi in fugam vertuntur. In qua trepidatione multae captae naves, multae mersae; plures tamen non minus saevitiam regis, quam hostem timentes domum dilabuntur.

13. Hac clade perculsum et dubium consilii Xerxen
2 Mardonius adgreditur. Hortatur ut in regnum abeat, ne quid seditionis moveat fama adversi belli et in maius, sicuti
3 mos est, omnia extollens; sibi CCC milia armatorum lecta ex omnibus copiis relinquat, qua manu aut cum gloria eius perdomiturum se Graeciam aut, si aliter eventus ferat,
4 sine eiusdem infamia hostibus cessurum. Probato consilio Mardonio exercitus traditur; reliquas copias rex ipse de-
5 ducere in regnum parat. Sed Graeci audita regis fuga consilium ineunt pontis interrumpendi, quem ille Abydo veluti victor maris fecerat, ut intercluso reditu aut cum exercitu deleretur aut desperatione rerum pacem victus
6 petere cogeretur. Sed Themistocles timens, ne interclusi hostes desperationem in virtutem verterent et iter, quod aliter non pateret, ferro patefacerent (satis multos hostes in Graecia remanere dictitans, nec augeri numerum reti-
7 nendo oportere) cum vincere consilio ceteros non posset, eundem servum ad Xerxen mittit certioremque consilii
8 facit et occupare transitum maturata fuga iubet. Ille per-

---

[31] This is quite garbled compared with Hdt. 8.107ff.

undecided, the Ionians, following an order from Themistocles, began gradually withdrawing from the fight; and their defection broke the spirit of the others. So while 26 looking around for an escape route the Persians were driven back and soon after, defeated in the battle, they turned to flight. In the chaos many ships were captured, 27 and many more sunk; more, however, fearing the king's severity no less than their enemy slipped away home.

13. Shattered by this defeat and wondering what to do, Xerxes was approached by Mardonius. He urged him to 2 go back to his kingdom so no insurrection should arise from reports of a failed campaign, exaggerating everything as usual; and he asked to be left three hundred thousand 3 soldiers, picked from all his troops, a force with which he would either conquer Greece with glory for him or, if things turn out differently, he could without dishonoring him yield to the enemy. His advice accepted, Mardonius 4 was assigned an army; and the other troops the king himself prepared to lead back to his kingdom. But when the 5 Greeks heard about of the king's flight they got the idea of breaking down the bridge that he had built at Abydus as "lord of the sea," so that with his retreat cut off he would either be destroyed with his army or from despair[31] be forced to sue for peace. But Themistocles feared that, if 6 cut off, the enemy might turn from despair to courage, and open up with the sword a path that would not otherwise be open (they had enough enemies left in Greece, he kept saying, and their number should not be increased by holding them back); and when he could not convince the 7 others with the plan, he sent the same slave to Xerxes, apprised him of the plan and told him to secure his crossing with a swift retreat. He, smitten by the news, gave his 8

culsus nuntio tradit ducibus milites perducendos; ipse
9 cum paucis Abydum contendit. Vbi cum solutum pontem
hibernis tempestatibus offendisset, piscatoria scapha tre-
10 pidus traiecit. Erat res spectaculo digna et aestimatione
sortis humanae, rerum varietate miranda in exiguo latentem videre navigio, quem paulo ante vix aequor omne
capiebat, carentem omni etiam servorum ministerio, cuius
11 exercitus propter multitudinem terris graves erant. Nec
pedestribus copiis, quas ducibus adsignaverat, felicius iter
fuit, siquidem cotidiano labori (neque enim ulla est me-
12 tuentibus quies) etiam fames accesserat. Multorum deinde dierum inopia contraxerat et pestem, tantaque foe-
ditas morientium fuit, ut viae cadaveribus implerentur
alitesque et bestiae escae inlecebris sollicitae exercitum
sequerentur.

14. Interim Mardonius in Graecia Olynthum expugnat.
2 Athenienses quoque in spem pacis amicitiamque regis
sollicitat, spondens incensae eorum urbis etiam in maius
3 restitutionem. Postquam nullo pretio libertatem his vena-
lem videt, incensis quae aedificare coeperat, copias in
4 Boeotiam transfert. Eo et Graecorum exercitus, qui cen-
5 tum milium fuit, secutus est ibique proelium commissum.
Sed fortuna regis cum duce mutata non est. Nam victus
6 Mardonius veluti ex naufragio cum paucis profugit. Castra
referta regalis opulentiae capta. Vnde primum Graecos
diviso inter se auro Persico divitiarum luxuria cepit.

---

32 Hdt. 8.127 has Artabazus, not Mardonius. After this we
move into Hdt. 9 and the end of the war. The distinctions at the
end of section 11 could represent a confused version of what is
found in Diod. Sic. 11.27.

commanders the task of leading over the troops; and he himself hurried to Abydus with a few men. When he there found the bridge broken down by winter storms, he crossed in panic in a fishing boat. That was a sight worth watching for the light it shed son the human condition: by an amazing reversal of fortune to see, hiding in a tiny boat, a man whom the entire ocean could recently barely contain and, deprived even of assistance from slaves, one whose armies had burdened the earth with their numbers. Nor was the return journey happier for the infantry troops that he had assigned to his commanders, since in addition to their daily hardships—for there is no rest for men in fear—there was also starvation. Many days without food had then also brought disease, and such was the ghastly state of dying men that roads became filled with corpses and birds and animals, lured by the carrion, kept following the army.

14. Meanwhile Mardonius captured Olynthus in Greece,[32] and he also tried to entice the Athenians into hopes of a peace treaty and alliance with the king, pledging to rebuild their burned-down city on an even grander scale. When he saw their freedom not for sale at any price, he burned down what he had started to rebuild and moved his troops into Boeotia. The Greek army, which was a hundred thousand strong, also followed him and there battle was joined. But the fortunes of the king did not change with the general. For a defeated Mardonius fled as if from a shipwreck with a few men.[33] His camp, full of royal treasure, was captured. So when Persian gold was divided among them, the Greeks were for first time taken with a taste for extravagant riches.

[33] In reality, Mardonius perished in the battle.

7   Eodem forte die, quo Mardonii copiae deletae sunt, etiam navali proelio in Asia sub monte Mycale adversus
8 Persas dimicatum est. Ibi ante congressionem, cum classes ex adverso starent, fama ad utrumque exercitum venit, vicisse Graecos et Mardonii copias occidione cecidisse.
9 Tantam famae velocitatem fuisse, ut, cum matutino tempore proelium in Boeotia commissum sit, meridianis horis in Asiam per tot maria et tantum spatii tam brevi horarum
10 momento de victoria nuntiatum sit. Confecto bello, cum de praemiis civitatium ageretur, omnium iudicio Atheni-
11 ensium virtus ceteris praelata. Inter duces quoque Themistocles princeps civitatum testimonio iudicatus gloriam patriae suae auxit.

    15. Igitur Athenienses aucti et praemiis belli et gloria
2 urbem ex integro condere moliuntur. Cum moenia maiora conplexi fuissent, suspecti esse Lacedaemoniis coepere reputantibus, quibus ruina urbis tantum incrementi dedis-
3 set, quantum sit datura munita civitas. Mittunt ergo legatos, qui monerent, ne munimenta hostibus et receptacula
4 futuri belli exstruant. Themistocles ut vidit spei urbis invideri, non existimans abrupte agendum, respondit legatis, ituros Lacedaemonem, qui de ea re pariter cum illis con-
5 sulant. Sic dimissis Spartanis hortatur suos, opus maturent.
6 Dein ipse interiecto tempore in legatione proficiscitur, et nunc in itinere infirmitate simulata, nunc tarditatem collegarum accusans, sine quibus agi iure nihil posset, diem

---

34 *Barr.* 61 E2.

It so happened that on that same day that Mardonius' 7
forces were destroyed a sea battle was also fought in
Asia against the Persians off the promontory of Mycale.[34]
There, before the engagement and as the fleets faced each 8
other, a rumor reached both sides that the Greeks had
prevailed and Mardonius' troops had been wiped out.
Such was the speed of the report, they say, that although 9
the battle was fought in Boeotia in the morning news of
the victory reached Asia about noon, crossing so many seas
and so much land in such a short time. When the war 10
ended and awarding prizes to various states was discussed,
the Athenians' valor was ranked above everyone else's.
Among generals Themistocles, being judged the greatest 11
among the city-states, further increased the glory of his
country.

15. So with their might strengthened by the spoils of
war and their renown, the Athenians set about rebuilding
their city. Since they surrounded it with stronger walls, 2
they began to be eyed suspiciously by the Spartans, who
wondered how much the city's fortifications would add
when it had been so much enhanced by its destruction. So 3
they sent delegates to advise them against building what
could be fortresses and places of refuge for enemies in a
later war. When Themistocles saw the city's aspirations 4
arousing envy, he, thinking he should not react impul-
sively, replied to the delegates that men would come to
Sparta to discuss that matter together with them. After 5
thus sending of the Spartans, he urged his people to ac-
celerate the work. Then he later himself set off on an 6
embassy, and on one occasion feigning illness en route and
on another blaming delay by colleagues without whom
nothing could be fairly discussed, he kept prevaricating

de die proferendo spatium consummando operi quaere-
7 bat; cum interim nuntiatur Spartanis opus Athenis matu-
rari, propter quod denuo legatos mittunt ad inspiciendam
8 rem. Tum Themistocles per servum magistratibus scribit
Atheniensium, legatos vinciant pignusque teneant, ne in
9 se gravius consulatur. Adiit deinde contionem Lacedaemoniorum, indicat permunitas Athenas esse et posse iam
inlatum bellum non armis tantum, sed etiam muris susti-
10 nere; si quid ob eam rem de se crudelius statuerent, lega-
11 tos eorum in hoc pignus Athenis retentos. Graviter deinde
castigavit eos, quod non virtute, sed inbecillitate sociorum
12 potentiam quaererent. Sic dimissus veluti triumphatis
Spartanis a civibus excipitur.
13   Post haec Spartani, ne vires otio corrumperent et ut bis
inlatum a Persis Graeciae bellum ulciscerentur, ultro fines
14 eorum populantur. Ducem suo sociorumque exercitui
deligunt Pausaniam, qui pro ducatu regnum Graeciae
adfectans proditionis praemium cum Xerxe nuptias filiae
eius paciscitur redditis captivis, ut fides regis aliquo bene-
15 ficio obstringeretur. Scribit praeterea Xerxi, quoscumque
ad se nuntios misisset, interficeret, ne res loquacitate ho-
16 minum proderetur. Sed dux Atheniensium Aristides, belli
socius, collegae conatibus obviam eundo, simul et in rem
sapienter consulendo proditionis consilia discussit. Nec
multo post accusatus Pausanias damnatur.

---

35 For Themistocles' embassy see *AO* 65f. (the year 479/8).

36 That is, Persian territory. Again, the following is closer to
Diod. Sic. 11.44f. than anything else (cf. Thuc. 1.128ff.). For
Aristides see *AO* 66f. (the year 478/7).

and wasting time for the work to be completed; and mean-   7
while the Spartans were told that the work at Athens was
being hurried along, at which they immediately sent ambassadors to investigate the matter. Then Themistocles,   8
using a slave, wrote to the Athenian magistrates telling
them to imprison the legates and hold them as security for
any reprisals against him. He next went to the Spartan   9
assembly and reported that Athens was well fortified and
now able to withstand attack not only with weapons but
also with walls; and should they because of it consider   10
harsh reprisals against them, their delegates were held in
Athens as security against it. He then severely repri-   11
manded them for seeking power not through their courage but the weakness of their allies. So after being re-   12
leased he was welcomed by his citizens as having triumphed
over Sparta.[35]

After this the Spartans, not to impair their strength by   13
inactivity and also to avenge the two wars brought on
Greece by the Persians, went so far as plundering their
territory.[36] As commander for their own and their allies'   14
army they chose Pausanias who, aspiring to rule all Greece
rather than just lead it, bargained with Xerxes to grant him
his daughter in marriage as the price of his treason, returning to him his prisoners of war so the king could be bound
by some favor. He also wrote a letter to Xerxes telling him   15
to kill any messengers he might send so the matter should
not be betrayed by people's gossip. But the Athenian gen-   16
eral Aristides, his ally in the war, by blocking his colleague's maneuvers and also taking appropriately astute
measures, thwarted his plans for betrayal. Not much later
Pausanias was tried and convicted.

17   Igitur Xerxes, cum proditionis dolum publicatum vide-
18   ret, ex integro bellum instituit. Graeci quoque ducem constituunt Cimona Atheniensium, filium Miltiadis, quo duce
apud Marathonem pugnatum est, iuvenem, cuius magni-
19   tudinem futuram pietatis documenta prodiderunt; quippe
patrem ob crimen peculatus in carcerem coniectum ibique defunctum translatis in se vinculis ad sepulturam re-
20   demit. Nec in bello iudicium deligentium fefellit, siquidem non inferior virtutibus patris Xerxen, terrestri
navalique bello superatum, trepidum recipere se in regnum coegit.

So when Xerxes saw the treacherous plot had been revealed, he restarted the war.[37] The Greeks also appointed a leader, Cimon of Athens, son of Miltiades, under whose leadership the battle of Marathon had been fought, a young man whose future greatness was augured by instances of his filial piety; for when his father was thrown in prison charged with embezzlement and died there, he, taking his fetters on himself, redeemed the dead man's body for burial. Nor in the war did he disappoint the judgment of those who chose him, for no less than his father in merit he defeated Xerxes on land and sea, and made him withdraw in panic into his kingdom.

[37] Cf. Diod. Sic. 11.60ff. The references to Cimon are very general, but see *AO* 67 (the year 478/7) and under subsequent years; also Plutarch's biography. For Miltiades see *AO* 56 (the year 490/89).

LIBER III

1. Xerxes, rex Persarum, terror antea gentium, bello in
Graecia infeliciter gesto etiam suis contemptui esse coe-
2 pit. Quippe Artabanus, praefectus eius, deficiente cotidie
regis maiestate in spem regni adductus cum septem ro-
bustissimis filiis regiam vesperi ingreditur (nam amicitiae
iure semper illi patebat), trucidatoque rege voto suo ob-
3 sistentes filios eius dolo adgreditur. Securior de Artaxerxe,
puero admodum, fingit regem a Dario, qui erat adulescens, quo maturius regno potiretur, occisum; inpellit Ar-
4 taxerxen parricidium parricidio vindicare. Cum ventum
ad domum Darii esset, dormiens inventus, quasi somnum
5 fingeret, interficitur. Dein cum unum ex regis filiis sceleri
suo superesse Artabanus videret metueretque de regno
certamina principum, adsumit in societatem consilii Bac-
6 cabasum, qui praesenti statu contentus rem prodit Artaxerxi: ut pater eius occisus sit, ut frater falsa parricidii
suspicione oppressus, ut denique ipsi pararentur insidiae.
7 His cognitis Artaxerxes, verens Artabani numerum filiorum, in posterum diem paratum esse armatum exercitum
iubet, recogniturus et numerum militum et in armis

---

1 For the following cf. Ctesias 33ff.; Diod. Sic. 11.69. The
Baccabasus mentioned below is Megabyzus.

2 That is, Artaxerxes.

84

BOOK III

1. Xerxes, king of the Persians, earlier the terror of nations, after his failed war in Greece was starting to be despised even by his subjects.[1] So Artabanus, his prefect, with the 2 king's sovereignty being daily on the decline, was led to hope for the throne, and with seven very strong sons he entered the palace one evening (for from their friendship it always remained open to him), and after murdering the king, craftily began trying to remove the sons obstructing his wish. Less concerned about Artaxerxes, who was just a 3 boy, he falsely claimed the king had been killed by Darius, who was a young man, so he could sooner gain the throne; and he pushed Artaxerxes into avenging one murder with another murder. On arrival at Darius' home he was found 4 asleep but was killed as if he were pretending to be sleeping. Then when Artabanus saw one of the king's sons had 5 survived his villainy and he feared competition for the throne among the nobility, he enlisted in his scheme Baccabasus, who, satisfied with the status quo, divulged the 6 matter to Artaxerxes, telling him how his father was murdered, how his brother had been disposed of with a trumped-up suspicion of parricide, and finally how a plot was being hatched against him.[2] Hearing this Artaxerxes, 7 fearing the number of Artabanus' sons, ordered the army to be put under arms the following day for a review both

8   industriam singulorum. Itaque cum inter ceteros ipse
Artabanus armatus adsisteret, rex simulat se breviorem
loricam habere, iubet Artabanum secum commutare,
exuentem se ac nudatum gladio traicit; tum et filios eius
9   corripi iubet. Atque ita egregius adulescens et caedem
patris et necem fratris et se ab insidiis Artabani vindicavit.

2. Dum haec in Persis geruntur, interea Graecia omnis
ducibus Lacedaemoniis et Atheniensibus in duas divisa
partes ab externis bellis velut in viscera sua arma convertit.
2   Fiunt igitur de uno populo duo corpora, et eorundem castrorum homines in duos hostiles exercitus dividuntur.
3   Hinc Lacedaemonii communia quondam civitatum auxilia
ad vires suas trahere, inde Athenienses, et vetustate gentis
et gestis rebus inlustres propriis viribus confidebant.
4   Atque ita duo potentissimi Graeciae populi institutis Solo-
nis et Lycurgi legibus pares ex aemulatione virium in bellum ruebant.
5   Namque Lycurgus cum fratri suo Polydectae, Spartanorum regi, successisset regnumque sibi vindicare potuisset, Charillo, filio eius, qui natus postumus erat, cum

---

3 This is very schematic and inaccurate. The Greeks had
formed an alliance against Xerxes, but after the war the Athenians
became leaders of its naval arm, conventionally described by the
modern term "Delian League," an organization that became in
effect an Athenian Empire; see R. Meiggs, *The Athenian Empire*
(Oxford, 1972); P. Low, *The Athenian Empire* (Edinburgh, 2008).
The Spartans remained associated with other states in mainland
Greece and in particular dominated the Peloponnese.

4 On Lycurgus and the Spartan system, to which we are taken
back, there are a number of sources, including Plut. *Vit. Lyc.* See
in general P. Cartledge, *Sparta and Laconia. A Regional History*

of his soldiers' numbers and each man's proficiency in combat. So when among the others Artabanus himself was also himself standing in armor, the king pretended that his own cuirass was too short and ordered Artabanus to exchange his with him, and as he was removing it and was unprotected, he ran him through with his sword; then he also ordered the arrest of his sons. And so the fine young man both avenged the assassination of his father and the murder of his brother and also saved himself from the machinations of Artabanus. 8 9

2. As this was happening in Persia, in the meantime all of Greece, led by the Spartans and the Athenians, split into two alliances, and after their foreign wars turned its weapons on its own vitals. So from one people two separate entities emerged, and men of the same camp became divided into two opposing forces. On the one side the Spartans added to their strength what had earlier been the joint forces of the city-states; and on the other the Athenians, renowned both for the antiquity of their people and for their achievements, had confidence in their own strength.[3] And so two most powerful peoples in Greece, equally great from Solon's institutions and Lycurgus' laws, were rushing into war in a trial of strength.[4] 2 3 4

For although Lycurgus might have succeeded his brother Polydectes, king of the Spartans, and claimed the throne for himself, he with total honor restored it to the 5

1300–362 B.C. (London, 1979), with a discussion of the king lists in Appendix 3 (see also Bickerman 156). As sources for Trogus on Sparta, Phylarchus, Ephorus, Antiochus, and Timaeus have all been proposed.

ad aetatem adultam pervenisset, regnum summa fide re-
6 stituit, ut intellegerent omnes, quanto plus apud bonos
7 pietatis iura quam omnes opes valerent. Medio igitur tempore, dum infans convalescit tutelamque eius administrat,
non habentibus Spartanis leges instituit, non inventione
8 earum magis, quam exemplo clarior: siquidem nihil lege
ulla in alios sanxit, cuius non ipse primus in se documen-
9 tum daret. Populum in obsequia principum, principes ad
10 iustitiam imperiorum firmavit. Parsimoniam omnibus sua-
sit, existimans laborem militiae adsidua frugalitatis con-
11 suetudine faciliorem fore. Emi singula non pecunia, sed
12 conpensatione mercium iussit. Auri argentique usum velut omnium scelerum materiam sustulit.

3. Administrationem rei publicae per ordines divisit:
2 regibus potestatem bellorum, magistratibus iudicia et
annuos successores, senatui custodiam legum, populo
sublegendi senatum vel creandi quos vellet magistratus
3 potestatem permisit. Fundos omnium aequaliter inter
omnes divisit, ut aequata patrimonia neminem poten-
4 tiorem altero redderent. Convivari omnes publice iussit,
5 ne cuius divitiae vel luxuria in occulto essent. Iuvenibus
non amplius una veste uti toto anno permissum, nec
quemquam cultius quam alterum progredi ne epulari
6 opulentius, ne imitatio in luxuriam verteretur. Pueros
puberes non in forum, sed in agrum deduci praecepit, ut
primos annos non in luxuria, sed in opere et in laboribus
7 agerent. Nihil eos somni causa substernere et vitam sine
pulmento degere neque prius in urbem redire, quam viri

---

5 Sparta had two kings, the magistrates are the ephors, and
the senate is the gerousia.

man's posthumous son Charillus when the boy came of age, so all should understand how much more important 6 claims of duty were for good men than full power. So in 7 the meantime, as the child grew and he was supervising his tutelage, he established laws for the Spartans, who had none, earning no greater renown for drafting them than for the precedent he set; for he legislated for others noth- 8 ing he did not himself first illustrate by his own example. He reinforced the people's deference to their leaders, and 9 the authorities' justice in the exercise of their powers He 10 urged thrift on everyone, thinking the hardship of military service would be made easier by continually practicing frugality. He ordered all transactions to be based not on 11 money but barter. Use of gold and silver he suppressed as 12 being the source of all crime.

3. The government of the state he divided among the classes: to kings he granted the right to conduct war, to the 2 magistrates judicial administration with annual replace- ments, to the senate custody of the laws, and to the people the right to choose the senate and elect the magistrates as they wanted.[5] Farmland he divided equally among all of 3 them for a leveling of possessions to leave no one better off than another. They were all ordered to eat together in 4 public so a person's riches or high living should not remain hidden. Young men were allowed no more than one gar- 5 ment all year, and no one could go out better dressed than others or eat more expensive meals lest imitation lead to extravagance. Boys at puberty should not be taken into the 6 forum, he advised, but into the country, to spend their early years not in luxury but in work and manual labor. They should have no bedding to sleep on, he decreed, 7 their diet must be plain food, and they must not return to

8 facti essent, statuit. Virgines sine dote nubere iussit, ut uxores eligerentur, non pecuniae, severiusque matrimonia sua viri coercerent, cum nullis frenis dotis tenerentur.

9 Maximum honorem non divitum et potentium, sed pro gradu aetatis senum esse voluit, nec sane usquam terrarum locum honoratiorem senectus habet.

10 Haec quoniam primo solutis antea moribus dura videbat esse, auctorem eorum Apollinem Delphicum fingit et inde se ea ex praecepto numinis detulisse, ut consuescendi

11 taedium metus religionis vincat. Dein ut aeternitatem legibus suis daret, iure iurando obligat civitatem, nihil eos de eius legibus mutaturos priusque reverteretur, et simulat se ad oraculum Delphicum proficisci, consulturum

12 quid addendum mutandumque legibus videretur. Proficiscitur autem Cretam ibique perpetuum exsilium egit abicique in mare ossa sua moriens iussit, ne relatis Lacedaemonem solutos se Spartani religione iuris iurandi in dissolvendis legibus arbitrarentur.

4. His igitur moribus ita brevi civitas convaluit, ut, cum Messeniis propter stupratas virgines suas in sollemni Messeniorum sacrificio bellum intulissent, gravissima se exsecratione obstrinxerint, non prius quam Messeniam expugnassent reversuros, tantum sibi vel de viribus suis

2 vel de fortuna spondentes. Quae res initium dissensionis

3 Graeciae et intestini belli causa et origo fuit. Itaque cum

---

6 The fullest source for the Messenian Wars is Pausanias Book 4, where the named sources are Rhianus of Bene and Myron of Priene. Trogus may have followed Ephorus (cf. *FGrH* 70 F 216), and there is a summary treatment at Diod. Sic. 15.66, but the only contemporary source was the seventh-century poet Tyrtaeus (see below). The first war with Messenia took place from about 735 to

town before they became young men. Virgins he ordered 8
to be married without dowry so wives would be chosen,
not money, and husbands would more strictly control
spouses when held by no bonds of dowry. The greatest 9
honor he wished to be shown not to the rich and powerful,
but according to seniority to the aged, and certainly nowhere on earth is age more highly respected than there.

Since he at first saw these restrictions as being harsh 10
after the earlier loose morality, he pretended their author
was Delphic Apollo and that he had brought them from
there on divine instructions, so religious fear should overcome reluctance to accept something new. Then to give 11
his laws eternal validity, he bound the state on oath to
make no changes in his laws before his return and pretended he was going to Delphi to consult the oracle on
appropriate additions and modifications to the laws. He 12
actually left for Crete and lived there in permanent exile,
and when dying he ordered his bones thrown into the sea
so if they were brought back the Spartans would not feel
released from the sacred bond of their oath not to repeal
his legislation.

4. So thanks to such morality their state soon grew so
strong[6] that when they made war on the Messenians over
the rape of some Spartan girls at a Messenian religious
festival, they bound themselves by the most solemn oath
not to return before defeating Messenia, an oath they took
from confidence in either their strength or fortune. This 2
was the beginning of Greek dissension and the cause and
start of internal warfare. Thus when the Spartans became 3

715; the second, which Pausanias dates from 685 to 668, was in
fact slightly later.

contra praesumptionem suam annis X in obsidione urbis
tenerentur et querelis uxorum post tam longam viduita-
4 tem revocarentur, veriti ne hac perseverantia belli gravius
sibi quam Messeniis nocerent. Quippe illis quantum
iuventutis bello intercidat, mulierum fecunditate suppleri,
sibi et bellis damna adsidua et fecunditatem uxorum abs-
5 tinentibus viris nullam esse; itaque legunt iuvenes ex eo
genere militum, qui post ius iurandum in supplementum
venerant, quibus Spartam remissis promiscuos omnium
6 feminarum concubitus permisere, maturiorem futuram
conceptionem rati, si eam singulae per plures viros expe-
7 rirentur. Ex his nati ob notam materni pudoris Partheniae
vocati.

8 Qui cum ad annos XXX pervenissent, metu inopiae
(nulli enim pater existebat, cuius in patrimonium succes-
sio speraretur) ducem Phalantum adsumunt, filium Arati,
qui auctor Spartanis fuerat iuventutis ad generandam
9 subolem domum remittendae, ut, sicuti dudum patrem
eius nascendi auctorem habuissent, sic ipsum spei ac dig-
10 nitatis suae haberent. Itaque nec salutatis matribus, e quarum adulterio infamiam collegisse videbantur, ad sedes
11 inquirendas proficiscuntur; diuque et per varios casus
iactati tandem in Italiam deferuntur et occupata arce Tarentinorum, expugnatis veteribus incolis, sedes ibi consti-
12 tuunt. Sed post annos plurimos dux eorum Phalantus per
seditionem in exsilium proturbatus Brundisium se contu-

---

7 "Partheniae" means something like "virgin births" or "births
produced by women who should have been virgins."

8 The traditional date is 706, which is roughly consistent with
the archaeological remains.

unexpectedly held in a ten-year siege of their city and were
being called home by complaints from their wives about
their long widowhood, they feared that in thus prolonging 4
the war they might be harming themselves more than they
were the Messenians. For in the enemy's case casualties
among younger men were replaced by their wives' fertility,
but for them there was constant attrition in battle and in
their husbands' absence the wives' fertility meant nothing;
and so they selected some young men from a group of 5
soldiers who had arrived as reinforcements after the taking of the oath, and sending them back to Sparta they allowed them promiscuous sexual relations with all their
women, thinking that conception would come earlier if all 6
the women tried with several men. Those born of such 7
parents were called, in memory of their mothers' shame,
Partheniae.[7]

When they reached the age of thirty and they feared 8
being left indigent (for none had a father whose estate he
could hope to inherit) they chose as their leader Phalantus, the son of Aratus, as their leader, the man who had
urged the Spartans to send the young men home to pro-
create so that, just as they had earlier had the father re- 9
sponsible for their births, so also would they have the son
responsible for their hopes and social standing. Therefore 10
with no farewell to the mothers by whose adultery they
felt they had incurred disgrace, they set off in search of a
home; and after a long time and many adventures they 11
finally landed in Italy, and seizing the citadel of the Tarentines and defeating the earlier inhabitants, they made their
home there.[8] But many years later their leader Phalantus, 12
driven into exile during political upheaval, made his way

lit, quo expulsi sedibus suis veteres Tarentini concesse-
13 rant. His moriens persuadet, ut ossa sua postremasque
reliquias conterant et tacite spargi in foro Tarentinorum
14 curent; hoc enim modo recuperare illos patriam suam
15 posse Apollinem Delphis cecinisse. Illi arbitrantes eum in
ultionem sui civium fata prodidisse praeceptis paruere.
16 Sed oraculi diversa sententia fuerat. Perpetuitatem enim
17 urbis, non amissionem hoc facto promiserat. Ita ducis
exsulis consilio et hostium ministerio possessio Tarentina
18 Partheniis in aeternum fundata, ob cuius beneficii memoriam Phalanto divinos honores decrevere.

5. Interea Messenii, cum virtute non possent, per insi-
2 dias expugnantur. Dein cum per annos octoginta gravia
servitutis verbera, plerumque et vincula ceteraque captae
civitatis mala perpessi essent, post longam poenarum
3 patientiam bellum restaurant. Lacedaemonii quoque eo
conspiratius ad arma concurrunt, quod adversus servos
4 dimicaturi videbantur. Itaque cum hinc iniuria, inde in-
dignitas animos acueret, Lacedaemonii de belli eventu
oraculo Delphis consulto iubentur ducem belli ab Athe-
5 niensibus petere. Porro Athenienses, cum responsum
cognovissent, in contemptum Spartanorum Tyrtaeum,
6 poetam claudo pede, misere, qui tribus proeliis fusos eo
usque desperationis Spartanos adduxit, ut servos suos ad
supplementum exercitus manumitterent hisque interfectorum matrimonia pollicerentur, ut non numero tantum

---

9 Tyrtaeus' Athenian origin (also found at Paus. 4.15.6) is a
later invention as lame as the poet was supposed to be. See M. R.
Lefkowitz, *The Lives of the Greek Poets* (London, 1981), 35, 38ff.

10 In Seel's text *fusus* refers to Tyrtaeus, but the variant *fusos*
(adopted by Ruehl), referring to the Spartans, makes better
sense.

to Brundisium, where the earlier citizens of Tarentum had
withdrawn after being chased from their homes. When   13
dying he persuaded them to grind his bones and the rest
of his remains and have them secretly scattered in the
forum of Tarentum; for in this way, he said, Apollo at   14
Delphi had foretold they could recover their homeland.
They, thinking it was for his own revenge that he had re-   15
vealed the destiny of his citizens, obeyed his instructions.
But the oracle's meaning had been different. For it was   16
continued possession of the city not loss of it that had been
promised if it were done. So with an exiled leader's advice   17
and their enemies' help their occupation of Tarentum was
forever established for the Partheniae, and in memory of   18
his benefaction they decreed Phalantus divine honors.

5. Meanwhile the Messenians, although they could not
be taken by valor, were taken by treachery. Then when   2
they had for eighty years suffered brutal beatings like
slaves, and often also imprisonment and the other misfortunes of a captured city, they finally after long enduring
these punitive measures renewed the war. The Lacedae-   3
monians also rushed to arms with greater unity because it
looked as if they would be fighting slaves. So since spirits   4
were inflamed by feelings of injustice on the one side and
humiliation on the other, the Spartans after consulting the
Delphic oracle about the war's outcome were told to ask
the Athenians for a war commander. With that, when the   5
Athenians learned of the oracle's response, they as an in-
sult sent to the Spartans the lame poet Tyrtaeus;[9] three   6
defeats had driven the Spartans[10] to such despair that Tyrtaeus could convince them to free their slaves to supplement their forces and promised them the wives of men

7 amissorum civium, sed et dignitati succederent. Sed reges
8 Lacedaemoniorum, ne contra fortunam pugnando maiora
   detrimenta civitati infunderent, reducere exercitum vo-
9 luerunt, ni intervenisset Tyrtaeus, qui conposita carmina
   exercitui pro contione recitavit, in quibus hortamenta
   virtutis, damnorum solacia, belli consilia conscripserat.
10 Itaque tantum ardorem militibus iniecit, ut non de salute,
   sed de sepultura solliciti tesseras insculptis suis et patrum
11 nominibus dextro bracchio deligarent, ut, si omnes adversum proelium consumpsissent et temporis spatio confusa
   corporum liniamenta essent, ex indicio titulorum tradi
12 sepulturae possent. Cum sic animatum reges exercitum
13 viderent, curant rem hostibus nuntiare; Messeniis autem
   non timorem res, sed aemulationem mutuam dedit.
14 Itaque tantis animis concursum est, ut raro umquam
15 cruentius proelium fuerit. Ad postremum tamen victoria
   Lacedaemoniorum fuit.

   6. Interiecto tempore tertium quoque bellum Messenii
2 reparavere, in cuius auxilium Lacedaemonii inter reliquos
3 socios etiam Athenienses adhibuere; quorum fidem cum
   suspectam haberent, supervacaneos simulantes a bello
4 eosdem dimiserunt. Hanc rem Athenienses graviter ferentes pecuniam, quae erat in stipendium Persici belli ab
   universa Graecia conlata, a Delo Athenas transferunt, ne
   deficientibus a fide societatis Lacedaemoniis praedae ac
5 rapinae esset. Sed nec Lacedaemonii quievere, qui cum
   Messeniorum bello occupati essent, Peloponnenses in-
6 misere, qui bellum Atheniensibus facerent. Parvae tunc
   temporis classe in Aegyptum missa vires Atheniensibus
   erant. Itaque navali proelio dimicantes facile superantur.

killed in action, saying they would not only replace all their
fallen citizens but also inherit their social standing. But 7
the Spartan kings, to avoid further damaging their state by 8
tempting fortune, wanted to withdraw the army, had it not 9
been for Tyrtaeus, who at a gathering recited to the army
his own poetry in which he had composed exhortations to
courage, consolations for their losses, and plans for the
war. And with that such fervor did he inspire in the men 10
that, being no longer concerned about saving themselves
but only about their burial, they fastened tags to their right
arms inscribed with their own and their fathers' names, so 11
that if they all fell in a losing battle and their features were
disfigured by the passage of time, they could given a burial
from the information on the tags. When the kings saw 12
their army so invigorated they had it reported to the enemy; but to the Messenians that brought not fear but mu- 13
tual rivalry. So with such fervor was battle joined that 14
rarely was there ever a more bloody clash. Finally however 15
victory went to the Spartans.

6. After some time the Messenians also started a third
war, and to support them the Spartans called on all their 2
allies, including even the Athenians; but since they sus- 3
pected their loyalty, they dismissed them from the war
with the excuse that they were unessential. Offended by 4
this slight the Athenians transferred from Delos to Athens
the money that had been contributed by all Greece for
financing the Persian War, so that if they seceded from the
alliance, it would not be pillaged and looted by the Spartans. But neither did the Spartans remain idle, and being 5
themselves embroiled in war with Messenia they sent
other Peloponnesians to fight the war with the Athenians.
At that time the Athenian strength was low after a fleet 6
had been into Egypt. So they were easily defeated when

7 Interiecto deinde tempore post reditum suorum aucti et
8 classis et militum robore proelium reparant. Iam et Lacedaemonii omissis Messeniis adversus Athenienses arma
9 verterant. Diu varia victoria fuit; ad postremum aequo
Marte utrimque discessum.

10   Inde revocati Lacedaemonii ad Messeniorum bellum,
ne medium tempus otiosum Atheniensibus relinquerent,
cum Thebanis paciscuntur, ut Boeotiorum imperium his
restituerent, quod temporibus belli Persici amiserant, ut
11 illi Atheniensium bella susciperent. Tantus furor Spartanorum erat, ut duobus bellis inplicti suscipere tertium
non recusarent, dummodo inimicis suis hostes adqui-
12 rerent. Igitur Athenienses adversus tantam tempestatem
belli duos duces deligunt, Periclen, spectatae virtutis vi-
13 rum, et Sophoclen, scriptorem tragoediarum, qui diviso
exercitu et Spartanorum agros vastaverunt et multas Asiae
civitates Atheniensium imperio adiecerunt.

7. His malis fracti Lacedaemonii in annos XXX pepige-
runt pacem, sed tam longum otium inimicitiae non tule-
2 runt. Itaque extra XV annos rupto foedere cum contemptu
3 deorum hominumque fines Atticos populantur et, ne
praedam potius quam pugnam expetisse viderentur,
4 hostes ad proelium provocant. Sed Athenienses consilio
Periclis ducis populationis iniuriam differunt in tempus
ultionis, supervacuam pugnam existimantes, cum ulcisci
5 hostem sine periculo possent. Dein interiectis diebus
naves conscendunt et nihil sentientibus Lacedaemoniis

---

11 This is the height of confusion: Pericles and Sophocles were
generals together, but in 441/0 in another theater (*AO* 80f.); what
seems to be meant here is the activity of Tolmides and Pericles
in 456/5 and 455/4 (*AO* 76f.) and developments of subsequent
years.

they fought a sea battle. Then, sometime later, when after   7
the return of their men they had grown in both naval and
infantry strength, they resumed the war. By now the Spar-   8
tans, having abandoned the Messenian campaign, had also
turned their arms on the Athenians. Victory long hung in   9
the balance; finally, the two parted on equal terms.

Recalled from there to the Messenian War the Spar-   10
tans, in order meanwhile not to leave the Athenians at
peace, negotiated with the Thebans to restore to them the
power over the Boeotians that they had lost in the time the
Persian War, if they agreed to undertake wars against the
Athenians. Such was the rage of the Spartans that, al-   11
though entangled in two wars, they did not refuse to undertake a third provided they could gain adversaries for
their enemy. So the Athenians, facing such a storm of   12
warfare, appointed two generals: Pericles, a man of proven
courage, and Sophocles, the writer of tragedies,[11] and   13
these, dividing the army, both ravaged Spartan lands and
also added many Asian city-states to the Athenian Empire.

7. Dejected by these setbacks the Spartans settled a
thirty-year peace, but their enmity toward Athens would
not bear such long inaction.[12] So after fifteen years they   2
broke the treaty and with contempt for gods and men ravaged the territory of Attica, and not to appear to have   3
come for plunder rather than a fight, they tried to provoke
their enemy into battle. But on the advice of their leader   4
Pericles the Athenians postponed revenge for the unjust
pillaging, thinking pitched battle superfluous when they
could take revenge on the enemy without risk. Then some   5
days later they boarded ships and with the Lacedaemoni-

---

[12] The peace was made in 446/5, and war broke out in 432/1.

totam Spartam depraedantur multoque plura auferunt
6 quam amiserant, prorsus ut in conparatione damnorum
longe pluris fuerit ultio quam iniuria.

7 Clara quidem haec Periclis expeditio habita, sed multo
8 clarior privati patrimonii contemptus fuit. Huius agros in
populatione ceterorum intactos hostes reliquerant, spe-
rantes adquirere se illi posse aut periculum ex invidia aut
9 ex suspicione proditionis infamiam. Quod ante prospiciens
Pericles et futurum populo praedixerat et ad invidiae
impetum declinandum agros ipsos dono rei publicae de-
10 derat, atque ita, unde periculum quaesitum fuerat, ibi
maximam gloriam invenit.

11 Post haec interiectis diebus navali proelio dimicatum
12 est; victi Lacedaemonii fugerunt. Nec cessatum deinceps
est, quin aut terra aut mari varia proeliorum fortuna invi-
13 cem se trucidarent. Denique fessi tot malis pacem in an-
14 nos L fecere, quam non nisi sex annis servaverunt. Nam
indutias, quas proprio nomine condixerant, ex sociorum
15 persona rumpebant, quippe quasi minus periurii con-
traherent, si ferentes sociis auxilia potius quam si aperto
16 proelio dimicassent. Hinc bellum in Siciliam translatum,
quod priusquam expono, de Siciliae situ pauca dicenda
sun.

---

13 The following story seems to be an embellishment on Pericles' promise to give his lands to the state; they remained untouched (Thuc. 2.13.1).   14 The Peace of Nicias in 421.

15 The epitome rushes through the period covered by Thuc.
1–5 and Diod. Sic. 11–12; Ephorus may have been the source. On
the date of Athenian assistance to Sparta, see *AO* under 463/2 and
462/1. The transfer of the treasury to Athens is traditionally dated
to 454, but a date in the 460s is supported by what little literary
evidence we have (N. D. Robertson, "The True Nature of the

ans suspecting nothing pillaged all Sparta and carried off much more than they had lost, so much in fact that in a comparison of losses the retaliation far surpassed the injury. 6

This raid of Pericles became famous, but far more famous was his indifference toward his own property.[13] His own lands, although everyone else's were plundered, the enemy had left untouched in their raids, hoping to expose him to danger from jealousy or disgrace through suspicion of treason. Anticipating this Pericles had both forewarned the people of what was ahead, and to avoid an onset of jealousy had also gifted those very lands to the state, and so from what was meant to bring him danger he won the greatest glory. 7 8 9 10

Some days after this a sea battle was fought; the Spartans fled in defeat. Nor was there then any pause, since on land and sea both sides kept slaughtering each other on land or on sea in battles that were intermittently successful. Finally exhausted by so many misfortunes they concluded a fifty-year peace that they kept for no more than six years.[14] For the truce, which they had made in their own names, they would keep breaking with their allies as a front, as if they were committing less perjury by assisting their allies than if they had been fighting in open warfare. From there the war was transferred to Sicily, and before I give an account of it, a little needs to be said about Sicilian geography.[15] 11 12 13 14 15 16

'Delian League' 478–461 B.C.," *American Journal of Ancient History* 5 [1982]: 112ff.). The so-called First Peloponnesian War began in 459. Athens' involvement in Egypt is usually dated from 460 to 454, but the six-year commitment could have begun a year or two earlier.

LIBER IV

1. Siciliam ferunt angustis quondam faucibus Italiae ad-
haesisse direptamque velut a corpore maiore impetu su-
2 peri maris, quod toto undarum onere illuc vehitur. Est
autem terra ipsa tenuis ac fragilis et cavernis quibusdam
fistulisque ita penetrabilis, ut ventorum tota ferme flatibus
3 pateat; nec non et ignibus generandis nutriendisque soli
ipsius naturalis materia. Quippe intrinsecus stratum sul-
4 phure et bitumine traditur, quae res facit, ut spiritu cum
igne in terra interiore luctante frequenter et conpluribus
locis nunc flammas, nunc vaporem, nunc fumum eructet.
5 Inde denique Aetnae montis per tot saecula durat incen-
6 dium. Et ubi acrior per spiramenta cavernarum ventus
7 incubuit, harenarum moles egeruntur. Proximum Italiae
promuntorium Regium dicitur, ideo quia Graece abrupta
8 hoc nomine pronuntiantur. Nec mirum, si fabulosa est loci
9 huius antiquitas, in quem res tot coiere mirae. Primum
quod nusquam alias torrens fretum, nec solum citato im-

---

1 The Upper Sea should be the Adriatic, but the Tyrrhenian
is meant here. Thuc. 6–7 deals with the Sicilian expedition, including remarks on the nature of Sicily, but this is not the direct
source of the present account. Again one thinks of Ephorus, especially with the expedition of 427/6 (below), and Philistus has
been detected behind details of the later expedition.

BOOK IV

1. They say that Sicily was once attached to Italy by a narrow isthmus and wass torn from the main body of the land by the buffeting of the Upper Sea, which pounds that region with the full weight of its waves.[1] But the land there is fine and crumbly and so perforated with caverns and grottos as to be almost entirely exposed to the wind's blasts and the composition of its soil is also naturally suited to generating and supporting fire. For it is said to have an inner layer of sulfur and bitumen, which means that when the wind and the subterranean fire battle each other the earth in several places often belches forth now flames, now vapor, and now smoke. That is actually why Mount Aetna's fire has lasted for so many centuries. And when wind sweeps more forcefully through air passages in its caverns, sand is thrown up in piles. The promontory of Italy closest to Sicily is called Rhegium, because that is how "things fractured" is said in Greek.[2] Nor is it surprising if this area's ancient history is legendary, when so many wonders have accumulated in it. This is primarily because such stormy straits exist nowhere else,[3] with a current not only

[2] From the Greek verb *rhegnumi*, "to break."
[3] The Straits of Messina.

petu, verum etiam saevo, neque experientibus modo ter-
10 ribile, verum etiam procul visentibus. Vndarum porro in
se concurrentium tanta pugna est, ut alias veluti terga
dantes in imum desidere, alias quasi victrices in sublime
ferri videas; nunc hic fremitum ferventis aestus, nunc illic
gemitum in voraginem desidentis exaudias.

11   Accedunt vicini et perpetui Aetnae montis ignes et
insularum Aeolidum, velut ipsis undis alatur incendium;
12 neque enim in tam angustis terminis aliter durare tot saeculis tantus ignis potuisset, nisi humoris nutrimentis ale-
13 retur. Hinc igitur fabulae Scyllam et Charybdin peperere,
hinc latratus auditus, hinc monstri credita simulacra, dum
navigantes magnis verticibus pelagi desidentis exterriti
latrare putant undas, quas sorbentis aestus vorago conlidit.
14 Eadem causa etiam Aetnae montis perpetuos ignes facit.
15 Nam aquarum ille concursus raptum secum spiritum in
imum fundum trahit atque ibi suffocatum tam diu tenet,
donec per spiramenta terrae diffusus nutrimenta ignis
incendat.
16   Iam ipsa Italiae Siciliaeque vicinitas, iam promuntorio-
rum altitudo ipsa ita similis est, ut quantum nunc admira-
tionis, tantum antiquis terroris dederit, credentibus,
coeuntibus in se promuntoriis ac rursum discedentibus
17 solida intercipi absumique navigia. Neque hoc ab antiquis
in dulcedinem fabulae conpositum, sed metu et admirati-
18 one transeuntium. Ea est enim procul inspicientibus natura loci, ut sinum maris, non transitum putes, quo cum

swift but violent, terrifying not only for those experiencing
it, but even for those viewing it at distance. Furthermore   10
waves crash against each other in such conflict that you see
some sinking to the depths as if fleeing and others as if
victorious raised into the air; and now you can hear the
roar of the boiling surf, and now its groaning as it sinks into
a whirlpool.

Its close neighbors are the perennial fires of both   11
Mount Aetna and the Aeolian Islands, their combustion
seemingly fueled by those very waters; for so great a fire   12
could not have lasted so many centuries and within such
narrow confines were it not fed by some fuel derived from
moisture. Hence the myths that produced Scylla and Cha-   13
rybdis, hence the barking sound, and hence the monster-
like shapes when sailors, terrified by the great whirlpools
formed by the sinking sea, thought waves were barking as
they clashed in the maelstrom and the current was sucking
them down. The same phenomenon also produces Mount   14
Aetna's perpetual fires. For that clash of currents takes air   15
along with it, draws it down to the seabed, and there holds
it compressed until, seeping through vents in the soil, it
ignites flammable materials.

Now Italy's very proximity to Sicily, and their promon-   16
tories also being so similar in height, make our wonder like
that of the terror of the ancients, who believed that with
the promontories clashing and again separating entire
ships were caught and swallowed up. Nor was this fabri-   17
cated by the ancients as an entertaining tale but came
rather from the terror and awe of travelers. For when seen   18
from afar such are the natural features of the area that you
would think it a gulf in the coastline, not a strait, but when
you approach, you would think that what had earlier been

accesseris, discedere ac seiungi promuntoria, quae ante iuncta fuerant, arbitrere.

2. Siciliae primo Trinacriae nomen fuit, postea Sicania
2 cognominata est. Haec a principio patria Cyclopum fuit,
3 quibus exstinctis Cocalus regnum insulae occupavit. Post
quem singulae civitates in tyrannorum imperium concesse-
4 runt, quorum nulla terra feracior fuit. Horum ex numero
Anaxilaus iustitia cum ceterorum crudelitate certabat,
5 cuius moderationis haud mediocrem fructum tulit; quippe
decedens cum filios parvulos reliquisset tutelamque eorum Micalo, spectatae fidei servo, commisisset, tantus
amor memoriae eius apud omnes fuit, ut parere servo
quam deserere regis filios mallent principesque civitatis
obliti dignitatis suae regni maiestatem administrari per
6 servum paterentur. Imperium Siciliae etiam Karthaginienses temptavere, diuque varia victoria cum tyrannis di-
7 micatum. Ad postremum amisso Hamilcare imperatore
cum exercitu aliquantisper quievere victi.

3. Medio tempore, cum Regini discordia laborarent
civitasque per dissensionem divisa in duas partes esset,
veterani ex altera parte ab Himera in auxilium vocati, pulsis civitate contra quos inplorati fuerant et mox caesis quibus tulerant auxilium, urbem cum coniugibus et liberis
2 sociorum occupavere, ausi facinus nulli tyranno conparan-

---

4 Meaning "three-cornered."

5 A mythical king of Sicily who welcomed Daedalus after he
fled from Crete (Diod. Sic. 4. 78–9).   6 Anaxilaus of Rhegium died in 476/5; Diod. Sic. 11.48.2, where the regent is Micy-
thus. For the Carthaginians see below, Book 19.

7 This story seems to have escaped Diodorus, unless it is al-

promontories joined together are now separating and pulling apart.

2. Sicily's first name was Trinacria;[4] later it was renamed Sicania. This was originally the home of the Cyclopes, and after they died out Cocalus[5] ruled the island. After him their cities fell one by one under the power of tyrants, in which no land has been more fertile. One of these, Anaxilaus, rivaled in his justice the ruthlessness of all the others and earned no small return for his restraint;[6] for when dying he left infant sons behind and entrusted their guardianship to Micalus, a slave of proven loyalty, and such was the affection with which he was remembered by everyone that they preferred to be ruled by a slave than to abandon the king's children, and the state's most prominent citizens, with no thought for their own status, allowed the kingdom to be ruled by a slave. The Carthaginians also tried to seize power over Sicily, and a long struggle with its tyrants followed, with intermittent success. Finally they lost their general Hamilcar together with his army and stood down for a time, defeated.

3. Meanwhile, when the people of Rhegium were experiencing discord and in the dissension the state split into two factions,[7] some veterans of one side were called to their aid from Himera; and driving out those they had been called on to fight, and later killing those to whom they had brought the aid, they took possession of the city together with the wives and children of their allies, committing a crime comparable with no tyrant's since for the

luded to at 11.76.5 (the year 461/0). More likely it is a garbled retrojection of Rhegium's takeover, in 280 BC, by a garrison installed there by Rome.

dum, quippe ut Reginis melius fuerit vinci quam vicisse.
3 Nam sive victoribus captivitatis iure servissent sive amissa
patria exsulare necesse habuissent, non tamen inter aras
et patrios lares trucidati crudelissimis tyrannis patriam
cum coniugibus ac liberis praedam reliquissent.
4 Catinienses quoque cum Syracusanos graves paterentur, diffisi viribus suis auxilium ab Atheniensibus petivere;
5 qui seu studio maioris imperii, quod Asiam Graeciamque
penitus occupaverant, seu metu factae pridem a Syracusanis classis, ne Lacedaemoniis illae vires accederent,
Lamponium ducem cum classe in Siciliam misere, ut sub
specie ferendi Catinensibus auxilii temptarent Siciliae
6 imperium. Et quoniam prima initia frequenter caesis hostibus prospera fuerant, maiore denuo classe et robustiore
exercitu Lachete et Chariade ducibus Siciliam petivere;
7 sed Catinienses sive metu Atheniensium sive taedio belli
pacem cum Syracusanis remissis Atheniensium auxiliis
fecerant.

4. Interiecto deinde tempore, cum fides pacis a Syracusanis non servaretur, denuo legatos Athenas mittunt, qui
sordida veste, capillo barbaque promissis et omni squaloris
habitu ad misericordiam commovendam adquisito con-

---

8 This version is nearer to that at Diod. Sic. 12.53ff. than to
that in Thucydides, even to the spelling of Charoiades' name as
"Chariades." The latter and Laches were generals in 427/6 (*AO*
124f.); Charoiades died, and Laches was succeeded in the next
year by Pythodorus. Justin's Lamponius is a mystery, unless he
represents a Lampon and an otherwise unattested generalship for
(perhaps) *AO* no. 1772. A further mystery is why the people of
Catania, who in the later expedition had to be forced to side with

people of Rhegium defeat would have been better than victory. For had they been either duly enslaved by their 3 victors or driven into exile after losing their country, they would at least not have been butchered amid their altars and ancestral gods and have left their country to the most vicious tyrants, together with their wives and children as plunder.

The people of Catania, when they were enduring harsh 4 Syracusan domination and had no confidence in their strength, also sought aid from the Athenians;[8] and being 5 either eager for a greater empire, since they had already advanced deep into Asia and Greece, or alarmed by a fleet earlier constructed by the Syracusans (who feared any increase in Spartan strength), these sent their general Lamponius to Sicily with a fleet to try to gain control of Sicily on a pretext of bringing aid to the Catanians. And since 6 the early stages had proved successful, with heavy enemy losses, they mounted another expedition, this time with a larger fleet and stronger army under the leadership of Laches and Chariades, and headed for Sicily; but the Ca- 7 tanians, either fearing the Athenians or weary of war, had made peace with the Syracusans, sending back the Athenian reinforcements.

4. Then some time later, when their peace terms were not respected by the Syracusans, they again sent delegates to Athens, and these approached their assembly in a terrible state, with dirty clothes, unkempt hair and beards, and a thoroughly wretched appearance designed

Athens, have replaced those of Leontini here and the Egestans in section 4.

2 tionem deformes adeunt; adduntur precibus lacrimae et
ita misericordem populum supplices movent, ut damna-
3 rentur duces, qui ab his auxilia deduxerant. Igitur classis
ingens decernitur; creantur duces Nicias et Alcibiades et
Lamachos, tantisque viribus Sicilia repetitur, ut ipsis ter-
4 rori essent, in quorum auxilia mittebantur. Brevi post tempore revocato ad reatum Alcibiade duo proelia pedestria
5 secunda Nicias et Lamachos faciunt; munitionibus deinde
circumdatis hostes etiam marinis commeatibus in urbe
6 clausos intercludunt. Quibus rebus fracti Syracusani aux-
7 ilium a Lacedaemoniis petiverunt. Ab his mittitur Gylip-
8 pus solus, sed in quo instar omnium auxiliorum erat. Is
audito in itinere belli iam inclinato statu auxiliis partim in
Graecia, partim in Sicilia contractis opportuna bello loca
9 occupat. Duobus deinde proeliis victus, congressus tertio
occiso Lamacho et hostes in fugam conpulit et socios obsi-
10 dione liberavit. Sed cum Athenienses a bello terrestri in
navale se transtulissent, Gylippus classem Lacedaemone
11 cum auxiliis arcessit. Quo cognito et ipsi Athenienses in
locum amissi ducis Demosthenen et Eurymedonta cum
12 supplemento copiarum mittunt. Peloponnesii quoque
communi civitatum decreto ingentia Syracusanis auxilia
misere, et quasi Graeciae bellum in Siciliam translatum
esset, ita ex utraque parte summis viribus dimicabatur.

5. Prima igitur congressione navalis certaminis Athenienses vincuntur; castra quoque cum omni publica ac
2 privata pecunia amittunt. Super haec mala cum etiam ter-

---

9 While "Lamachos" is a deviation from Latinate versions of
names, it reflects the manuscripts.

to excite pity; tears were added to their appeals, and so 2
far did their entreaties move the people that the generals
who had withdrawn reinforcements from them were condemned. A huge fleet was therefore decreed; Nicias, Al- 3
cibiades and Lamachos were appointed its commanders,[9]
and they returned to Sicily with such massive forces that
they brought fear on the very people they were being sent
to help. Shortly afterward when Alcibiades was recalled to 4
face trial, two successful land battles were fought by
Nicias and Lamachos; then encircling them with siege 5
works these kept their enemy confined in the city cut off
even from seaborne supplies. Demoralized by the situa- 6
tion, the Syracusans sought help from the Spartans. By 7
them they were sent only Gylippus, but in him was power
equal to all reinforcements. He, hearing en route that the 8
war had already been going poorly, raised auxiliary troops
partly in Greece and partly in Sicily and seized some
ground favorable for the war. Then after being defeated 9
in two battles, he engaged in a third, killed Lamachos, and
both routed his enemy and also raised the siege of his allies. But since the Athenians had now moved from land to 10
naval warfare, Gylippus sent for a fleet from Lacedaemon
with reinforcements. On learning of it the Athenians, to 11
replace their fallen general, also sent out Demosthenes
and Eurymedon with supplementary troops. The Pelo- 12
ponnesians, under a joint decree of their states, also sent
huge reinforcements to the Syracusans, and as if the war
in Greece had been moved to Sicily it was being fought by
both sides with all their might.

5. So in the first battle at sea the Athenians were defeated; they also lost their camp together with all their
state and privately owned money. When they were after 2

restri proelio victi essent, tunc Demosthenes censere coepit, ut abirent Sicilia, dum res quamvis adflictae nondum
3 tamen perditae forent. Neque in bello male auspicato amplius perseverandum; esse domi graviora et forsitan infeliciora bella, in quae servare hos urbis apparatus oporteat.
4 Nicias seu pudore male actae rei, seu metu destitutae spei
5 civium, seu inpellente fato manere contendit. Reparatur igitur navale bellum et animi a prioris fortunae procella ad
6 spem certaminis revocantur; sed inscitia ducum, qui inter angustias maris tuentes se Syracusanos adgressi, facile vin-
7 cuntur. Eurymedon dux in prima acie fortissime dimicans primus cadit, XXX naves, quibus praefuerat, incenduntur.
8 Demosthenes et Nicias et ipsi victi exercitum in terram
9 deponunt, tutiorem fugam rati itinere terrestri. Ab his relictas CXXX naves Gylippus invasit, ipsos deinde inse-
10 quitur; fugientes partim capit, partim caedit. Demosthenes amisso exercitu a captivitate gladio et voluntaria
11 morte se vindicat, Nicias autem ne Demosthenis quidem exemplo ut sibi consuleret admonitus cladem suorum auxit dedecore captivitatis.

these failures also defeated in a land battle, Demosthenes began to think they should leave Sicily while their situation, though poor, was still not completely lost. They 3 should not persevere with a war that started inauspiciously, he said; there were at home more serious and perhaps even less successful wars for which they should reserve these resources of their city. Nicias, either ashamed of 4 their failure or afraid to abandon the hopes of his countrymen, or else simply driven on by fate, insisted on their remaining. The war at sea was thus resumed and after 5 fortune's earlier storm they were restored to optimism for the fight; but through the incompetence of the command- 6 ers, who attacked the Syracusans when they were defending themselves in a narrow strait, they were easily defeated. Eurymedon their commander, fighting valiantly in 7 the front line, fell first, and thirty ships under his command were burned. Demosthenes and Nicias, also them- 8 selves defeated, put their armies ashore, thinking that flight overland was safer. The hundred and thirty ships 9 abandoned by them Gylippus commandeered, and then he set off after the men themselves; some of the fugitives he captured, some he killed. Demosthenes, with his army 10 lost, redeemed himself from captivity by suicide with his sword, but Nicias, prompted to self-respect not even by 11 Demosthenes' example, heightened his men's defeat with the ignominy of capture.[10]

[10] This detail is unique to this account; in both Thucydides and Diodorus, Demosthenes, like Nicias, is also captured and put to death.

LIBER V

1. Dum Athenienses in Sicilia bellum per biennium cupidius quam felicius gerunt, interim concitor et dux eius Alcibiades absens Athenis insimulatur mysteria Cereris initiorum sacra, nullo magis quam silentio sollemnia, en-
2 untiavisse, revocatusque a bello ad iudicium, sive conscientia sive indignitatem rei non ferens, tacitus in exilium
3 Elidem profectus est. Inde, ubi non damnatum se tantum, verum etiam diris per omnium sacerdotum religiones
4 devotum cognovit, Lacedaemona se contulit ibique regem Lacedaemoniorum inpellit turbatis Atheniensibus adverso
5 Siciliae proelio ultro bellum inferre. Quo facto omnia Graeciae regna velut ad extinguendum commune incen-
6 dium concurrunt; tantum odium Athenienses inmoderati
7 imperii crudelitate contraxerant. Darius quoque, rex Persarum, memor paterni avitique in hanc urbem odii facta cum Lacedaemoniis per Tisaphernen, praefectum Lydiae,

---

[1] This is a carryover from the last book in terms of sources. From 1.11 on, cf. Thuc. 8 and Diod. Sic. 13.36ff. See also Plut. *Vit. Alc.*, and for the profanation of the mysteries, Andocides' *On the Mysteries*. A recent treatment of Alcibiades is W. M. Ellis, *Alcibiades* (London and New York, 1989); see also P. J. Rhodes, *Alcibiades* (Barnsley, UK, 2011). We know that Alcibiades went

BOOK V

1. While the Athenians were for two years fighting the war in Sicily with more energy than success,[1] its prime mover and leader Alcibiades was then being charged at Athens in his absence with having divulged the sacred mysteries of Ceres, whose sanctity lies more than anything in their secrecy; and when recalled from the war to face trial he, 2 either from guilt or being unable to bear the indignity of it, slipped quietly into exile in Elis. When he then learned 3 that he had not only been condemned but also solemnly consigned to hell by the sacred oaths of all the priests, he left for Sparta and there pushed the king of the Spartans 4 into war with the Athenians, then in disarray after their defeat in Sicily. After that all the Greek states[2] came to- 5 gether as if to put out a fire that threatened them all; such 6 was the hatred that the Athenians had incurred by the cruelty of their oppressive empire. Furthermore Darius, 7 king of the Persians, mindful of his father's and grandfather's enmity toward this city, made a pact with the Spartans through Tissaphernes, his satrap of Lydia, and prom-

from Argos to Sparta, but since Nep. *Alc.* 4.4 says he went from Elis to Thebes, we may be dealing with the variant account of Ephorus. The defeat in Sicily dates to 413.

[2] Strangely, Justin has "regna," literally, "kingdoms."

8 societate omnem sumptum belli pollicetur. Et erat hic quidem titulus cum Graecis coeundi; re autem vera timebat, ne victis Atheniensibus ad se Lacedaemonii arma transfer-

9 rent. Quis igitur miretur tam florentes Atheniensium opes ruisse, cum ad opprimendam unam urbem totius Orientis

10 vires concurrerent? Non tamen inerti neque incruento cecidere bello, sed proeliati ad ultimum, victores etiam interdum consumpti magis fortunae varietate quam victi

11 sunt. Principio belli omnes ab his etiam socii desciverant, ut fit: quo se fortuna, eodem etiam favor hominum inclinat.

    2. Alcibiades quoque motum adversus patriam bellum non gregarii militis opera, sed imperatoris virtutibus adiu-

2 vat; quippe acceptis V navibus in Asiam contendit et tributarias Atheniensium civitates auctoritate nominis sui ad

3 defectionem conpellit. Sciebant enim domi clarum, nec exilio videbant factum minorem, nec tam ablatum Atheniensibus ducem quam Lacedaemoniis traditum, parta

4 qui cum amissis imperia pensaret. Sed apud Lacedaemonios virtus Alcibiadis plus invidiae quam gratiae contraxit.

5 Itaque cum principes velut aemulum gloriae suae interficiendum insidiis mandassent, cognita re Alcibiades per uxorem Agidis regis, quam adulterio cognoverat, ad Tisaphernen, praefectum Darii regis, profugit, cui se celeriter

---

3 This king is Darius II, who ruled from 424 to 404. Darius' father, Artaxerxes II, had in fact concluded at least one peace with Athens, so perhaps Trogus had meant Darius' grandfather Xerxes and great-grandfather Darius I.

4 "The start of the war" presumably relates to the new circumstances of 412/11.

ised to cover all the costs of the war.[3] While this was the   8
pretext for cooperating with the Greeks, in fact he was
afraid that if the Athenians were defeated the Spartans
would turn their weapons on him. Who, then, should be   9
surprised that the flourishing power of Athens collapsed,
when the forces of the entire East united to overthrow a
single city? They did not, fall without a struggle, however,   10
or without drawing blood, but fighting to the end, and
sometimes even victorious, they were overwhelmed by
fortune's fickleness rather than defeated. At the start of the   11
war even their allies had all deserted them, as happens:
wherever fortune leans, so also does the favor of men.[4]

2. Alcibiades also helped in the war that he had fomented against his own country, not as a common soldier
but with his qualities as a general; for taking command of   2
five ships he swiftly moved into Asia and by the authority
of his name incited the tribute-paying states of Athens to
defection. For they knew of his fame at home, and they   3
did not see him diminished by exile; and it was less a case
of a leader being taken from the Athenians than of the
Spartans being handed one, and his new powers compen-
sated for those he had lost. But among the Spartans Al-   4
cibiades' qualities aroused more jealousy than goodwill.
So some of their leaders, seeing him a rival for their status,   5
had ordered his assassination, and when Alcibiades
learned of it through King Agis' wife, with whom he had
been having an adulterous affair,[5] he fled to Tissaphernes,
satrap of King Darius, with whom he quickly ingratiated

[5] A notorious affair, which, genuine or not, resulted in Agis'
son Leotychidas being regarded as illegitimate, which gave Agis'
brother Agesilaus the succession.

117

6 officii comitate et obsequendi gratia insinuavit. Erat enim
   et aetatis flore et formae veneratione nec minus eloquen-
7 tia etiam inter Athenienses insignis, sed in conciliandis
   amicitiarum studiis quam in retinendis vir melior, quia
8 morum vitia sub umbra eloquentiae primo latebant. Igitur
   persuadet Tisapherni, ne tanta stipendia classi Lacedae-
9 moniorum praeberet; vocandos enim in portionem muneris Ionios, quorum pro libertate, cum tributa Atheniensi-
10 bus penderent, bellum susceptum sit. Sed nec auxiliis
   nimis enixe Lacedaemonios iuvandos; quippe memorem
   esse debere alienam se victoriam, non suam instruere, et
11 eatenus bellum sustinendum, ne inopia deseratur. Nam
   regem Persarum dissentientibus Graecis arbitrum pacis
   ac belli fore, et quos suis non possit, ipsorum armis victu-
   rum; perfecto autem bello statim ei cum victoribus dimi-
12 candum. Domesticis itaque bellis Graeciam obterendam,
   ne externis vacet, exaequandasque vires partium et infe-
13 riores auxilio levandos. Non enim quieturos post hanc
   victoriam Spartanos, quia vindices se libertatis Graeciae
14 professi sint. Grata oratio Tisapherni fuit. Itaque commea-
   tus maligne praebere, classem regiam non totam mittere,
   ne aut victoriam daret aut necessitatem deponendi belli
   inponeret.
   3. Interea Alcibiades hanc operam civibus venditabat.
2 Ad quem cum legati Atheniensium venissent, pollicetur

---

⁶ See above, 5.1.7. Channeled through the satrap Tissaphernes the help went mainly for a fleet to challenge Athenian naval
superiority. The freeing of the Ionians and other Aegean states
under Athenian domination had been Spartan propaganda from
the start of the Peloponnesian War, though part of the under-
standing with Sparta was that these states should again come into

himself by his courteous ways and obsequious charm. For 6
he was both in the prime of life and strikingly handsome
and no less renowned for his oratory, even among the
Athenians, but he was also a man better at starting friend- 7
ships than keeping them, because his character flaws
would at first lie hidden under the shadow of his eloquence. So he persuaded Tissaphernes not to provide so 8
much money to the Spartan fleet; for the Ionians should 9
be called on to share the costs, he said, since it was for
their freedom, since they were paying tribute to the Athenians,[6] that the war had been undertaken. But neither 10
must he give the Spartans too much help; for he should
remember that he was preparing another's victory, not his
own, and the war should be subsidized only as far as not
being abandoned through lack of funds. For it was the king 11
of the Persians who would be the arbiter of peace and war
while the Greeks were quarreling, and those he could not
defeat with his own weapons he would defeat with theirs;
but once the war was over he must immediately fight the
victors. So Greece must be worn down by internal wars so 12
that she should not be free for foreign ones, and both
sides' strength must kept even and the weaker given
help. For the Spartans would not relax after victory in this 13
war since they had professed themselves the champions of
Greek liberty. What he said pleased Tissaphernes. So he 14
provided supplies sparingly, and did not send the entire
royal fleet, in order neither to hand them victory nor have
them forced to abandon the war.

3. Meanwhile Alcibiades was promoting this service
among the citizens. When ambassadors came to him from 2

Persian possession, freedom from which had brought them into
Athens' sphere after 479.

his amicitiam regis, si res publica a populo translata ad
3 senatum foret, sperans ut aut concordante civitate dux
belli ab omnibus legeretur aut discordia inter ordines facta
4 ab altera parte in auxilium vocaretur. Sed Atheniensibus
inminente periculo belli maior salutis quam dignitatis cura
5 fuit. Itaque permittente populo imperium ad senatum
6 transfertur. Qui cum insita genti superbia crudeliter in
plebem consuleret, singulis tyrannidis sibi inpotentiam
vindicantibus, ab exercitu Alcibiades exsul revocatur dux-
7 que classi constituitur. Statim igitur Athenas scribit, ex
continenti se cum exercitu venturum recepturumque a
8 quadringentis iura populi, ni ipsi redderent. Hac denun-
tiatione optimates territi primo urbem prodere Lacedaemoniis temptavere, dein, cum id nequissent, in exilium
9 profecti sunt. Igitur Alcibiades intestino malo patria libe-
rata summa cura classem instruit atque ita in bellum adversus Lacedaemonios pergit.

4. Iam Sesto Mindarus et Pharnabazus, Lacedaemo-
2 niorum duces, instructis navibus expectabant. Proelio
commisso victoria penes Athenienses fuit. In eo bello

---

[7] In Athenian terms, a (or the) "senate" can mean only the
boule, which was to be of four hundred, with citizen rights confined to the five thousand, who eventually became the essential
body after the demise of the closer oligarchy; though they are still
in control at the end of Thucydides, they soon gave way to the
resurgent democracy. On these complicated events, see A. W.
Gomme, A. Andrewes, and K. J. Dover, *A Historical Commentary
on Thucydides*, vol. 5 (Oxford, 1981), 184ff.; P. J. Rhodes, *A Commentary on the Aristotelian Athenaion Politeia* (Oxford, 1981),
362ff.

[8] Evidently, the battle of Cyzicus. Pharnabazus was not a
Spartan general, but the Persian satrap of Hellespontine Phrygia.

the Athenians, he promised them an alliance with the king
if the government were transferred from the popular assembly to the senate;[7] hoping that either the factions in 3
the state would come together and he be unanimously
chosen to lead the war, or, should there be conflict between the classes that he would be invited to help by one
of the sides. But for the Athenians, with the threat of war 4
hanging over them, self-preservation was of greater concern than honor. So, with the acquiescence of the people 5
power was transferred to the senate. When these, with the 6
ingrained arrogance of their class, treated the commons
savagely, some individuals seizing unbridled tyrannical
power, Alcibiades was recalled from exile by the army and
put in charge of the fleet. He therefore wrote immediately 7
to Athens that he would come at once with the army and
take the rights of the people back from the Four Hundred
if they themselves did not restore them. Terrified by this 8
threat, the aristocrats first tried to betray the city to the
Spartans, and then, when unable to do so, went into exile.
So Alcibiades, his homeland freed from internal problems, 9
fitted out a fleet with the utmost care and proceeded into
war against the Spartans.

4. By now Mindarus and Pharnabazus, the Spartan
generals, were waiting at Sestus with their ships drawn
up. When battle was joined victory went to the Athenians.[8] 2

Though Xenophon's *Hellenica* takes up where Thucydides leaves
off, the account in Justin does not come close to that in Xenophon
until section 6, leaving Ephorus as the likely source at least until
that point; see Diod. Sic. 13.42ff. There is a biography of Lysander by Plutarch. The Carthaginian attack on Sicily dates to
410/9 and Alcibiades' return to Athens to 407/6.

maior pars exercitus et omnes ferme hostium duces caesi,
3 naves LXXX captae. Interiectis quoque diebus, cum bellum Lacedaemonii a mari in terram transtulissent, iterato
4 vincuntur. His malis fracti pacem petiere, quam ne acciperent opera eorum effectum est, a quibus ea res quaestum praebebat. Interea et Syracusanorum auxilia inlatum
5 tum praebebat. Interea et Syracusanorum auxilia inlatum a Karthaginiensibus Siciliae bellum domum revocavit.
6 Quibus rebus destitutis Lacedaemoniis Alcibiades cum classe victrici Asiam vastat, multis locis proelia facit, ubique victor recipit civitates, quae defecerant, nonnullas
7 capit et imperio Atheniensium adicit, atque ita prisca navali gloria vindicata, adiecta etiam laude terrestris belli,
8 desideratus civibus suis Athenas revertitur. His omnibus proeliis ducentae naves hostium et praeda ingens capta.
9 Ad hunc redeuntis exercitus triumphum effusa omnis multitudo obviam procedit et universos quidem milites,
10 praecipue tamen Alcibiaden miratur; in hunc oculos civitas universa, in hunc suspensa ora convertit, hunc quasi de
11 caelo missum et ut ipsam Victoriam contuentur; laudant quae pro patria, nec minus admirantur quae exsul contra gesserit, excusantes ipsi, iratum provocatumque fecisse.
12 Enimvero tantum in uno viro fuisse momenti, ut maximi imperii subversi et rursum recepti auctor esset, et unde stetisset eo se victoria transferret, fieretque cum eo mira
13 quaedam fortunae inclinatio. Igitur omnibus non humanis tantum, verum et divinis eum honoribus onerant; certant

In that war most of the enemy force and almost all its senior officers were killed, and eighty ships were captured. Some days later, when the Spartans had moved from sea to land operations, they were again defeated. Broken by these reverses they sued for peace, which through the efforts of those for whom the war was profitable they failed to achieve. Meanwhile the Syracusan auxiliary forces were also brought home by an attack on Sicily by the Carthaginians. While the Spartans were left helpless by these events, Alcibiades devastated Asia with his victorious fleet, fought battles in many places, and victorious everywhere retook cities that had defected, and captured several others, annexing them to the empire of the Athenians; and so, with their naval glory of old reaffirmed and the land operations also added to it, he, sorely missed by his citizens returned to Athens. In all these battles two hundred enemy vessels and huge amounts of booty were taken.

For this triumphal return of the army a whole crowd came streaming out to meet them and showed their admiration for all the soldiers, but particularly for Alcibiades; toward him the whole state turned its eyes, toward him their anxious faces, him people contemplated as though heaven-sent and Victory itself; they praised what he had done for his country, but admired no less what he had done against it in exile, themselves defending him as having acted in anger and from provocation. In fact, they said, in this one man had been such dynamism as to be the cause of the greatest empire's collapse and then its recovery; and wherever he stood victory would come to him, and with him would come some amazing reversal of fortune. So they loaded him with all the honors, not only mortal but divine ones as well; and they bickered among

secum ipsi, utrum contumeliosius eum expulerint an re-
14 vocaverint honoratius. Ipsos illi deos gratulantes tulere
15 obviam, quorum execrationibus erat devotus, et cui
paulo ante omnem humanam opem interdixerant, eum, si
queant, in caelo posuisse cupiunt. Explent contumelias
16 honoribus, detrimenta muneribus, execrationes precibus.
17 Non Siciliae illis adversa pugna in ore est, sed Graeciae
victoria; non classes per illum amissae, sed adquisitae; nec
18 Syracusarum, sed Ioniae Hellespontique meminerunt. Sic
Alcibiades numquam mediocribus nec in offensam nec in
favorem studiis suorum exceptus est.

5. Dum haec aguntur, et a Lacedaemoniis Lysander
classi belloque praeficitur et in locum Tisaphernis Darius,
rex Persarum, filium suum Cyrum Ioniae Lydiaeque praeposuit, qui Lacedaemonios auxiliis opibusque ad spem
2 fortunae prioris erexit. Aucti igitur viribus Alcibiaden cum
centum navibus in Asiam profectum, dum agros longa
pace divites securus populatur et praedae dulcedine sine
insidiarum metu sparsos milites habet, repentino adventu
3 oppressere; tantaque caedes palantium fuit, ut plus vulneris eo proelio Athenienses acciperent, quam superioribus
4 dederant, et tanta desperatio apud Athenienses erat, ut ex
continenti Alcibiaden ducem Conone mutarent, arbi-
5 trantes victos se non fortuna belli, sed fraude imperatoris,
apud quem plus prior offensa valuisset quam recentia

---

themselves over what meant more, their disgraceful ex-
pulsion of him or his honorable recall. They carried to   14
meet him in congratulation the very gods by whom they
had cursed him, and one to whom they had shortly before   15
refused all human aid they now wished, if they only could,
to set in heaven.[9] They were remedying their insults with 16
honors, their damage with gifts, their curses with prayers.
It was not about defeat in Sicily that they talked, but   17
victory in Greece; not fleets lost by him, but the ones he
had taken; not Syracuse that they remembered, but Ionia
and the Hellespont. Such was Alcibiades' welcome, his   18
people's feelings either of resentment or approval never
lukewarm.

5. While this was happening Lysander was put in
charge of the fleet and the war by the Spartans, and in
place of Tissaphernes Darius, king of the Persians, also set
his own son Cyrus over Ionia and Lydia; and he by supply-
ing the Spartans with reinforcements and resources rallied
them to hopes of their earlier success. While their strength 2
was thus augmented Alcibiades had now set off for Asia
with a hundred ships, and while, heedless of danger, he
had his men plundering territory that was rich after a long
peace, his men were dispersed enjoying looting with no
fear of ambush when the Spartans suddenly appeared and
overwhelmed them; and such was the slaughter of his scat- 3
tered troops that the Athenians suffered more damage
in that battle than they had inflicted in their earlier ones,   4
and such was the despair among the Athenians that they
immediately replaced Alcibiades as commander with
Conon,[10] thinking themselves defeated not by the fortunes of war but the treachery of a commander for whom   5
earlier rejection had meant more than recent benefits;

6 beneficia; vicisse autem eum priore bello ideo tantum, ut
ostenderet hostibus, quem ducem sprevissent, et ut carius
7 eis ipsam victoriam venderet. Omnia enim credibilia in
8 Alcibiade vigor ingenii et morum luxuria faciebat. Veritus
itaque multitudinis impetum denuo in voluntarium exsilium proficiscitur.

6. Itaque Conon Alcibiadi suffectus, habens ante oculos cui duci successisset, classem maxima industria exor-
2 nat; sed navibus exercitus deerat, fortissimis quibusque in
3 Asiae populatione amissis. Armantur tamen senes aut
inpuberes pueri, et numerus militum sine exercitus ro-
4 bore expletur. Sed non magnam bello moram aetas fecit
inbellis; caeduntur passim aut fugientes capiuntur; tantaque strages aut occisorum aut captivorum fuit, ut Atheniensium deletum non imperium tantum, verum etiam
5 nomen videretur. Quo proelio perditis et desperatis rebus
ad tantam inopiam rediguntur, ut consumpta militari aetate peregrinis civitatem, servis libertatem, damnatis in-
6 punitatem darent. Eaque conluvione hominum domini
antea Graeciae conscripto exercitu vix libertatem tueban-
7 tur. Iterum tamen fortunam maris experiundam decer-
8 nunt. Tanta virtus animorum fuit, ut, cum paulo ante sa-
9 lutem desperaverint, nunc non desperent victoriam. Sed
neque is miles erat, qui nomen Atheniensium tueretur,
neque eae vires, quibus vincere consuerant, neque ea scientia militaris in his, quos vincula, non castra continue-
10 rant. Itaque omnes aut capti aut occisi. Cum dux Conon

---

11 This is the battle of Aegospotami in 405/4; see *AO* 180f.

he had prevailed in the previous campaign, they thought, 6
only to show the enemy what a commander they had rejected, and to sell them victory at a higher price. For in 7
Alcibiades' case everything was made plausible by his
quick intelligence and moral depravity. And so, fearing a 8
violent reaction of the mob, he again set off into voluntary
exile.

6. So Conon, Alcibiades' replacement, bearing in mind
the man he had succeeded as commander, took great pains
in equipping the fleet; but the ships lacked fighting men, 2
all the best having been lost in the marauding in Asia. Old 3
men or young boys were put under arms, however and a
complement of soldiers was reached without strengthen-
ing the army. But war was not long delayed by men of an 4
age unready for combat; they were massacred everywhere
or captured in flight; and so heavy were losses either
through casualties or men taken captive that it seemed that
not only the power of Athens had been destroyed but even
its name. Brought to ruin and despair by that battle they 5
were reduced to such straits that, depleted of men of military age, they were granting foreigners citizenship, slaves
emancipation, and condemned criminals pardon. And with 6
these dregs of humanity the former lords of Greece could
barely raise an army and protect their liberty. They never- 7
theless again decided to try their fortunes at sea. Such 8
courage was there in their hearts that, although they had
recently despaired for their lives, they did not now despair
of victory. But this was neither the caliber of soldier to 9
defend the Athenian name, nor a force accustomed to
achieving victory, nor did men have the required military
skill who had been kept in chains, not a camp. So all of
them were either taken prisoner or killed.[11] Since only 10

proelio superfuisset solus, crudelitatem civium metuens cum octo navibus ad regem Cyprium concedit Euagoram.

7. ‹Lysander› autem, dux Lacedaemoniorum, rebus
2 feliciter gestis fortunae hostium insultat. Captivas naves cum praeda bellica in triumphi modum ornatas mittit
3 Lacedaemona ac tributarias Atheniensium civitates, quas metus dubiae belli fortunae in fide tenuerat, voluntarias recipit, nec aliud dicionis Atheniensium praeter urbem ipsam relinquit.
4 Quae cuncta cum Athenis nuntiata essent, omnes relictis domibus per urbem discurrere pavidi, alius alium scis-
5 citari, auctorem nuntii requirere; non pueros inprudentia, non senes debilitas, non mulieres sexus inbecillitas domi tenet: adeo ad omnem aetatem tanti mali sensus penetra-
6 verat. In foro deinde coeunt atque ibi perpeti nocte fortu-
7 nam publicam questibus iterant. Alii fratres aut filios aut parentes deflent; cognatos alii, alii amicos cognatis cari- ores, et cum privatis casibus querelam publicam miscent:
8 iam se ipsos, iam ipsam patriam perituram miserioremque
9 incolumium quam amissorum fortunam iudicantes; sibi quisque ante oculos obsidionem, famem et superbum
10 victoremque hostem proponentes; iam ruinam urbis et incendia, iam omnium captivitatem et miserrimam ser-
11 vitutem recordantes; feliciores prorsus priores urbis rui- nas ducentes, quae incolumibus filiis parentibusque tecto-
12 rum tantum ruinae taxatae sint. Nunc autem non classem, in quam sicuti pridem confugiant, superesse, non exer-

their leader Conon had survived the battle, he fearing rough treatment from his citizens withdrew with eight ships to the Cypriot king Evagoras.

7. Now Lysander, leader of the Spartans, was after his success scoffing at his enemies' misfortune. The captured 2 ships together with the spoils of war he sent to Sparta decorated as for a triumph, and he accepted the voluntary 3 surrender of tributary states that fear of the war's vacillating fortunes had kept loyal to Athens; and of Athenian power he left nothing but the city itself.

When this was all reported at Athens, everyone left 4 their homes and rushed panic-stricken through the streets, questioning each other and trying to ascertain he source of the news; boys were not kept at home by inexperience, 5 nor old men by infirmity, nor women by the weakness of their sex—so much had awareness of the calamity touched every age. They then gathered in the forum and there kept 6 lamenting the state's misfortune throughout the night. Some were weeping for brothers, sons or parents, others 7 for relatives, yet others for friends dearer to them than relatives; and they mingled public mourning with their private misfortunes, now judging their own end to be near, 8 now their fatherland's, and thinking the plight of the survivors worse than that of the fallen; and they were all 9 picturing to themselves siege, starvation and an arrogant, victorious enemy; now it was the city's destruction and 10 burning that they were thinking about, now the captivity facing everyone and their pitiful enslavement; happier in- 11 deed had been the city's earlier destruction, they mused, which, with children and parents left unharmed, had cost them only the destruction of buildings. But now there 12 remained no fleet to which they could run for refuge as citum, cuius virtute servati pulchriora possent moenia exstruere.

8. Sic defletae ac prope perditae urbi hostes superveniunt et obsidione circumdata obsessos fame urgent.
2 Sciebant enim neque ex advectis copiis multum superesse,
3 et ne novae advehi possent providerant. Quibus malis Athenienses fracti post longam famem et adsidua suorum funera pacem petivere, quae an dari deberet, diu inter
4 Spartanos sociosque deliberatum. Cum multi delendum Atheniensium nomen urbemque incendio consumendam censerent, negarunt se Spartani ex duobus Graeciae oculis
5 alterum eruturos, pacem polliciti, si demissa Piraeum versus muri bracchia deicerent navesque, quae reliquae forent, traderent, reique publicae ex semet ipsis XXX
6 rectores acciperent. In has leges traditam sibi urbem
7 Lacedaemonii formandam Lysandro tradiderunt. Insignis hic annus et expugnatione Athenarum et morte Darii, regis Persarum, et exsilio Dionysii, Siciliae tyranni, fuit.

8 Mutato statu Athenarum etiam civium condicio mutatur. XXX rectores rei publicae constituuntur, qui fiunt XXX
9 tur. XXX rectores rei publicae constituuntur, qui fiunt XXX
10 tyranni. Quippe a principio tria milia sibi satellitum statuunt, quantum ex tot cladibus prope nec civium superfuerat, et quasi parvus hic ad continendam civitatem exer-
11 fuerat, et quasi parvus hic ad continendam civitatem exer-

---

12 Literally, "arms of the wall."   13 The year is 405/4. Diod. Sic. 14.8f. details the problems and virtual exile of Dionysius, on whom see below, Book 20.   14 To the continuing sources add, for Athenian affairs, primary and secondary references found in *AO* under the years 404/3 to 401/0.

15 The parenthesis translates what the Latin (albeit strange) seems to say, but in fact elsewhere we hear of three hundred armed attendants; the Thirty conceived the idea of limiting citi-

before, no army by whose courage they could be rescued
to build finer walls.

8. It was on a city so distressed and almost lost that
their enemies fell, and laying siege to it they started starv-
ing out its beleaguered people. For they knew that not   2
much remained of supplies that had been brought in, and
they had ensured that no fresh ones could be brought in.
The Athenians, broken by such misfortunes, after pro-   3
longed starvation and unending deaths among their people sued for peace, but whether it should be granted was
long debated among the Spartans and their allies. While   4
many advocated eliminating the Athenian name and destroying the city by fire, the Spartans said they would not
gouge out one of Greece's two eyes, promising peace if the   5
Athenians demolished the twin walls[12] going down to Pi-
raeus, surrendered any remaining ships, and accepted
from among themselves thirty men as governors of their
state. The city surrendered to them on these terms, the   6
Spartans assigned its organization to Lysander. This year   7
was notable for the capture of Athens as well as the death
of Darius, king of Persia, and the exile of Dionysius, tyrant
of Sicily.[13]

With the change in the Athenian constitution came also   8
a change in its citizen structure.[14] Thirty governors for the   9
state were appointed, who became thirty tyrants. For from   10
the start they assigned themselves three thousand bodyguards (almost all the citizens to have survived its many
disasters),[15] and as if this were a small army for suppress-   11

zenship to a body of three thousand, later gaining discretionary
authority to put to death anyone not on this list. These facts seem
to have been confused.

131

12 citus esset, septingentos milites a victoribus accipiunt.
Caedes deinde civium ab Alcibiade auspicantur, ne iterum
13 rem publicam sub obtentu liberationis invaderet. Quem
cum profectum ad Artaxerxen, Persarum regem, conpe-
14 rissent, citato itinere miserunt, qui eum interciperent; a
quibus occupatus, cum occidi aperte non posset, vivus in
cubiculo, in quo dormiebat, crematus est.

9. Liberati hoc ultoris metu tyranni miseras urbis reli-
2 quias caedibus et rapinis exhauriunt. Quod cum displicere
uni ex numero suo, Theramen, didicissent, ipsum quoque
3 ad terrorem omnium interficiunt. Fit igitur ex urbe passim
omnium fuga, repleturque Graecia Atheniensium exuli-
4 bus. Quod etiam ipsum auxilium cum miseris eriperetur
(nam Lacedaemoniorum edicto civitates exules recipere
5 prohibebantur), omnes se Argos et Thebas contulere; ibi
non solum tutum exilium egerunt, verum etiam spem reciperandae patriae receperunt.
6 Erat inter exules Thrasybulus, vir strenuus et domi
nobilis, qui audendum aliquid pro patria et pro salute
communi etiam cum periculo ratus, adunatis exulibus cas-
7 tellum Phylen Atticorum finium occupat. Nec deerat qua-
rundam civitatum tam crudelis casus miserantium favor.
8 Itaque et Ismenias, Thebanorum princeps, etsi publicis
9 non poterat, privatis tamen viribus adiuvabat, et Lysias,

---

16 The Spartan garrison under Callibius.

17 There are various versions of Alcibiades' death, of which
Val. Max. 1.7 ext. 9 perhaps follows Trogus; also Nep. *Alc.* 10;
Diod. Sic. 14.11; Plut. *Vit. Alc.* 38ff. The ultimate source of Tro-
gus' account could well have been Theopompus.

18 Xen. *Hell.* 2.4.1 has Megara and Thebes.

ing the state, they were also given a further seven hundred soldiers by the victors.[16] The murder of citizens then began with Alcibiades, lest he should seize government again on a pretext of freeing the state. When they discovered he had left for the court of Artaxerxes, the Persian king, they swiftly sent assassins to intercept him; and when he was overtaken by them and could not be murdered openly, he was burned alive in the bedroom in which he was sleeping.[17]

9. Freed of this fear of an avenger the tyrants started destroying the sad remnants of the city with murders and looting. When they learned that one of their own number, Theramenes, disapproved of this, they killed him as well to intimidate everybody else. There was thus total flight from the city everywhere, and Greece became filled with Athenian exiles. When even exile itself was suddenly snatched from the unfortunates (for by a Spartan edict, city-states were barred from accepting exiles), they all made for Argos and Thebes; and there they not only spent exile in safety but even regained hope of recovering their country.[18]

Among the exiles was Thrasybulus, who was an enterprising man and in his homeland a noble, and he, thinking something had to be done for their country and everybody's safety even if it involved risk, united the exiles and seized the stronghold of Phyle in Attic territory. Nor was there lack of support from the numerous states sympathizing with the poor people's cruel plight. Thus even Ismenias, the Theban leader,[19] although unable to do so officially, nevertheless assisted with his private resources, and

[19] An anti-Spartan fourth-century Theban politician.

Syracusanus orator, exul tunc, quingentos milites stipendio suo instructos in auxilium patriae communis eloquen-
10 tiae misit. Fit itaque asperum proelium. Sed cum hinc pro
patria summis viribus, inde pro aliena dominatione secu-
11 rius pugnaretur, tyranni vincuntur. Victi in urbem refuge-
runt, quam exhaustam caedibus suis etiam armis spoliant.
12 Deinde cum omnes Athenienses proditionis suspectos
haberent, demigrare eos ex urbe iubent et in bracchiis
muri, quae diruta fuerant, habitare, extraneis militibus
13 imperium tuentes. Post haec Thrasybulum corrumpere
14 imperii societatem pollicentes conantur. Quod cum non
contigisset, auxilia a Lacedaemoniis petivere, quibus acci-
15 tis iterato proeliantur. In eo bello Critias et Hippolochus,
omnium tyrannorum saevissimi, cadunt.

10. Ceteris victis cum exercitus eorum, ex quibus
maior pars Atheniensium erat, fugeret, magna voce Thrasybulus exclamat: cur se victorem fugiant potius quam ut
2 vindicem communis libertatis adiuvent? Civium illam
meminerint aciem, non hostium esse; nec se ideo arma
cepisse, ut aliqua victis adimat, sed ut adempta restituat;
3 XXX se dominis, non civitati bellum inferre. Admonet deinde cognationis, legum, sacrorum, tum vetusti per tot
bella commilitii, orat misereantur exsulum civium, si tam
patienter ipsi serviant; reddant sibi patriam, accipiant

---

[20] Xen. *Hell.* 2.4.19 has Hippomachus.

[21] These were, of course, those Athenian citizens who from
choice or under duress were on the side of the tyrants, a point
made here mainly to create the context for Thrasybulus' remarks,
but also perhaps to emphasize the fact that foreign troops were
in a minority and this was essentially a civil war.

Lysias, the Syracusan orator, who was then in exile, equipped five hundred soldiers at his own expense and sent them to aid the communal home of oratory. So there 10 was a fierce battle. But since on one side it was all-out fighting for one's own country, and on the other quite a careless attempt at seizing someone else's, the tyrants were defeated. Defeated they fled into a city that was al- 11 ready exhausted from bloodshed and they also stripped it of its weapons. Then, since they suspected all Athenian 12 citizens of treachery, they ordered them to leave the city and live within the double walls, which had been demolished, guarding their power with foreign troops. After this 13 they tried bribing Thrasybulus with a promise of joint rulership. When that did not work, they sought help from the 14 Spartans, and when that arrived they fought again. In that 15 battle Critias and Hippolochus,[20] the most ruthless of all tyrants, were killed.

10. When the rest were defeated and their army, which made up mostly of Athenians,[21] was in flight, Thrasybulus shouted after them in a loud voice; why were they fleeing from him as though from a conqueror, he asked, rather than vindicating their shared liberty? They should remem- 2 ber that this was a battle line of citizens, he said, not of enemies; he had not taken up arms to deprive them of anything after their defeat, but to restore what had been taken from them; it was their thirty masters not their state that he was attacking. He then reminded them of their 3 shared ancestry, laws and sacred rites, and next of their long comradeship in so many wars and begged them at least to commiserate with their exiled compatriots even if they could so passively submit to slavery themselves; let them restore his fatherland to him and take their own

4 libertatem. His vocibus tantum promotum est, ut reversus
in urbem exercitus XXX tyrannos emigrare Eleusinam
5 iuberet, substitutis decem, qui rem publicam regerent;
qui nihil exemplo prioris dominationis territi eandem
6 viam crudelitatis adgressi sunt. Dum haec aguntur, nuntiatur Lacedaemone in bellum Athenienses exarsisse; ad
7 quod comprimendum Pausanias rex mittitur. Qui misericordia exulis populi permotus patriam miseris civibus restituit et decem tyrannos ex urbe Eleusinam emigrare ad
8 ceteros iubet. Quibus rebus cum pax statuta esset, interiectis diebus repente tyranni non minus restitutos exules
quam se in exilium actos indignantur, quasi vero aliorum
libertas sua servitus esset, et bellum Atheniensibus infe-
9 runt. Sed ad conloquium veluti dominationem recepturi
progressi per insidias conprehensi ut pacis victimae trucidantur. Populus, quem emigrare iusserant, in urbem revo-
10 catur. Atque ita per multa membra civitas dissipata in
11 unum tandem corpus redigitur, et ne qua dissensio ex ante
actis nasceretur, omnes iure iurando obstringuntur, discordiarum oblivionem fore.
12   Interea Thebani Corinthiique legatos ad Lacedaemonios mittunt, qui ex manubiis portionem praedae com-
13 munis belli periculique peterent. Quibus negatis non quidem aperte bellum adversus Lacedaemonios decernunt,
sed tacitis animis tantam iram concipiunt, ut subesse bellum intellegi posset.

---

22 While the Thebans had been on the Spartan side in the war,
their disagreements had begun immediately after. Thwarted in
their motion for Athens' destruction, they had even harbored
Athenian fugitives; see above, 5.8.4 (without naming the Thebans) and 5.9.4ff.

liberty! With these words he so moved them that the army   4
returned to the city and ordered the thirty tyrants to de-
camp to Eleusis, replacing them with ten men who would   5
govern the state; but undeterred by the example of the
earlier repression, these embarked on the same ruthless
path. In the course of this it was reported in Sparta that   6
war had flared up among the Athenians; and King Pausanias was sent to suppress it. He, being moved to compas-   7
sion for an exiled people, restored their homeland to the
unfortunate citizens and ordered the ten tyrants to leave
the city for Eleusis to join the others. When peace was   8
restored by these measures, the tyrants were suddenly
filled with no less anger by the recall of exiles than by their
own banishment (as if other peoples' freedom was slavery
for them) and they made war on the Athenians. But when   9
coming forward to parley in the belief they would regain
their authority, they were ambushed and slaughtered as
sacrificial victims to the peace. The people they had ordered to leave were recalled to the city. And so a state   10
fragmented into many parts was finally reconstituted as
one body, and so no dissension should arise from the ear-   11
lier incidents they all swore an oath to an amnesty over the
discord.

Meanwhile, the Thebans[22] and Corinthians sent leg-   12
ates to the Spartans to claim a share of profits from the
sale of plunder from a war in which everyone had faced
danger. This was refused, and while they did not openly   13
declare war on the Spartans it could be clearly seen that
they were silently becoming so angry that a war was
coming.

11. Eodem forte tempore Darius, rex Persarum, mori-
2 tur, Artaxerxe et Cyro filiis relictis. Regnum Artaxerxi,
Cyro civitates, quarum praefectus erat, testamento lega-
3 vit. Sed Cyro iudicium patris iniuria videbatur; itaque
4 occulte adversus fratrem bellum parabat. Quod cum nuntiatum Artaxerxi esset, arcessitum ad se fratrem et in-
nocentiam dissimulatione belli simulantem conpedibus
aureis vinxit interfecissetque, ni mater prohibuisset.
5 Dimissus igitur Cyrus iam non occulte bellum, sed palam,
nec per dissimulationem, sed aperta professione parare
6 coepit; auxilia undique contrahit. Lacedaemonii memores
Atheniensi bello enixa eius opera adiutos, velut ignoran-
tes, contra quem bellum pararetur, decernunt auxilia Cyro
7 mittenda, ubi res eius exegisset, quaerentes apud Cyrum
gratiam et apud Artaxerxen, si vicisset, veniae patrocinia,
8 cum nihil adversus eum aperte decrevissent. Sed cum in
bello fors proelii utrumque fratrem pugnae obtulisset,
9 prior Artaxerxes a fratre vulneratur; quem cum equi fuga
periculo subtraxisset, Cyrus a cohorte regia oppressus
interficitur. Sic victor Artaxerxes et praeda fraterni belli et
exercitu potitur.
10 In eo proelio decem milia Graecorum in auxilio Cyri
fuere, quae et in cornu, in quo steterant, vicerunt et post
mortem Cyri neque armis a tanto exercitu vinci neque
11 dolo capi potuerunt; revertentesque inter tot indomitas
nationes et barbaras gentes per tanta itineris spatia virtute
se usque terminos patriae defenderunt.

---

[23] See above, 5.8.7, for Darius' death. For the Greek involvement in the following events and especially the return of the ten
thousand, see Xenophon's *Anabasis*; also Xen. *Hell.* 3.1; Ctesias
19–20; Diod. Sic. 14.19ff., with which the present text shows
some affinity.

11. By chance, at that same time, the Persian king Darius died, leaving two sons, Artaxerxes and Cyrus.[23] He bequeathed his kingdom to Artaxerxes in his will, and to Cyrus the provinces of which he was governor. But to Cyrus his father's decision seemed unfair; and so he began secretly preparing for war against his brother. When this was reported to Artaxerxes, he had his brother summoned and although he feigned innocence, he kept him in fetters of gold and would have killed if their mother had not stopped him. So when released Cyrus began preparing for war, no longer secretly but openly, and not hiding it, but declaring it; and he assembled forces from all around. The Spartans, remembering his strong support for them in their war with Athens, and feigning ignorance of the identity of the intended foe, decreed that Cyrus should be sent help when his circumstances required it, thus currying favor with Cyrus and also having a chance of pardon from Artaxerxes should he prove victorious, since they had made no open declaration against him. But when in the war the fortunes of battle brought the brothers face to face, Artaxerxes was wounded first by his brother; and when his horse bolted and whisked him out of danger, Cyrus was caught and killed by the royal bodyguard. Thus a victorious Artaxerxes took possession of both the plunder from the war of the brothers and of his army.

In that battle ten thousand Greeks supported Cyrus; they were victorious on the wing on which they were posted and after Cyrus' death could neither be conquered by so great an army nor caught; and returning through so many savage tribes and barbarous peoples while covering such huge distances, they valiantly defended themselves right to the borders of their country.

LIBER VI

1. Lacedaemonii, more ingenii humani quo plura habent eo ampliora cupientes, non contenti accessione Atheniensium opum vires sibi duplicatas totius Asiae imperium adfectare coeperunt. Sed maior pars sub regno Persarum
2 erat. Itaque Hercylides dux in hanc militiam electus cum videret sibi adversus duos praefectos Artaxerxis regis, Pharnabazum et Tisaphernen, maximarum gentium viribus succinctos dimicandum, pacificandum cum altero sta-
3 tuit. Aptior visus Tisaphernes, vir et industria potior et militibus Cyri quondam regis instructior, in conloquium
4 vocatur et statutis condicionibus ab armis dimittitur. Hanc rem Pharnabazus apud communem regem criminatur: ut
5 Lacedaemonios Asiam ingressos non reppulerit armis, sed inpensis regis aluerit merceturque ab his, ut differant bella quam gerant, tamquam non ad unius summam impe-
6 rii detrimentum omne perveniat. Indignum ait bella non perfici, sed redimi, hostem pretio, non armis submoveri.
7 His vocibus regem Tisapherni alienatum hortatur, ut in locum eius navalis belli ducem eligat Conona Athenien-

---

[1] Dercylidas, correctly given in the prologue of Trogus. We are in 399/8, and the following events are covered by Xen. *Hell.* 3.1.8ff. and into Book 4; Diod. Sic. 14.38ff.

BOOK VI

1. Human nature being what it is, the more the Spartans had the more they coveted, and not satisfied with having doubled their strength by acquiring the resources of Athens they began to aim at dominating all Asia. But most of it was under Persian rule. So when Hercylides[1] was chosen 2 as leader for this campaign and he saw that he must fight against two satraps of King Artaxerxes, Pharnabazus and Tissaphernes, who had under them the strength of powerful nations, he decided he must make peace with one or the other. Since Tissaphernes appeared the better choice, 3 being a man both more energetic and also, with the troops of the late prince Cyrus, better equipped, he was called to parley and on terms being negotiated he was removed from the war. About this matter Pharnabazus complained 4 to their king: when the Spartans entered Asia, he said, Tissaphernes did not repel them by armed force but maintained them at the king's expense and was buying a post- 5 ponement of hostilities from them rather than fighting them, as if each loss did not affect the whole empire. It 6 was disgraceful for wars not to be fought but bought off, he said, an enemy removed by payment not repelled by arms. Alienating the king from Tissaphernes with such 7 talk, he urged him to replace him as commander of the war at sea with Conon the Athenian, who after losing his

141

8 sem, qui amissa bello patria Cypri exulabat; quippe Atheniensibus, etsi fractae sint opes, manere tamen navalem
usum, nec, si eligendus sit ex universis, meliorem alium
9 esse. Acceptis igitur quingentis talentis iussus est Conona
classi praeficere.

2. His cognitis Lacedaemonii et ipsi a rege Aegypti
2 Hercynione auxilia navalis belli per legatos petunt, a quo
centum triremes et sexcenta milia modium frumenti
missa; a ceteris quoque sociis ingentia auxilia contracta
3 sunt. Sed tanto exercitui et contra tantum ducem deerat
4 dignus imperator. Itaque postulantibus sociis Agesilaum,
regem tunc Lacedaemoniorum, propter responsa oraculi
Delphici diu Lacedaemonii an eum summae rei praepo-
5 nerent deliberaverunt, quibus futurus imperii finis denun-
tiabatur, cum regium claudicasset imperium; erat enim
6 pede claudus. Ad postremum statuerunt melius esse in-
7 cessu regem quam imperio regnum claudicare. Postquam
Agesilaum cum ingentibus copiis in Asiam misere, non
facile dixerim quod aliud par ducum tam bene conpara-
8 tum fuerit. Quippe aetas, virtus, consilium, sapientia
utrique prope una, gloria quoque rerum gestarum eadem.
9 Quibus cum paria omnia fortuna dederit, invictum tamen
10 ab altero utrumque servavit. Magnus igitur amborum
11 apparatus belli, magnae res gestae fuerunt. Sed Cononem
seditio militum invadit, quos praefecti regis fraudare sti-

---

2 Tissaphernes met his end in 395/4, but it cannot be said that
he was replaced by Conon.

3 See Diod. Sic. 14.79ff., where the Egyptian king is called
Nephereus, i.e., Nefaarud I (399–393). Xenophon and Plutarch
both wrote biographies of Agesilaus, who ruled in Sparta from

country in the war was in exile in Cyprus;[2] for the Athe- 8
nians, although their power was broken, still had naval
strength, and even if they had unlimited choice there was
no better man. So given five hundred talents he was or- 9
dered to put Conon in command of the fleet.

2. On learning of it the Spartans for their part also
sought assistance from King Hercynio of Egypt by means
of legates, and by him they were sent a hundred triremes 2
and six hundred thousand bushels of wheat;[3] from their
other allies they also acquired massive auxiliary forces.
But what such a great army and one facing such a great 3
leader was lacking was a worthy commander. Then when 4
the allies asked for Agesilaus, king of the Spartans at that
time, the Spartans long debated whether to give him supreme command because of prophecies from the Delphic
Oracle in which an end of their empire was foretold when 5
the royal power became lame; for Agesilaus was lame. In 6
the end they decided it better to have a king who was lame
in walking than a kingdom lame in wielding its power.
After they sent Agesilaus with huge forces into Asia I 7
would not find it easy to cite another pair of generals that
were so well matched. For in age, courage, strategic acu- 8
men, and intelligence they were almost the same, and
their military records were equally distinguished. While 9
fortune gave them qualities similar in all respects she nevertheless kept each undefeated by the other. So both 10
men's war preparations were great, and great their exploits. But Conon was overtaken by a revolt of his soldiers, 11

399 to 360. He had been in Asia for some time and was recalled
because of the Corinthian War in 394.

143

pendio soliti erant, eo instantius debita poscentibus, quo
12 graviorem sub magno duce militiam praesumebant. Itaque Conon diu rege per epistulas frustra fatigato ad
13 postremum ipse ad eum pergit, a cuius aspectu et con-
loquio prohibitus est, quod eum more Persarum adorare
14 nollet. Agit tamen cum eo per internuntios et queritur
opulentissimi regis bella inopia dilabi, et qui exercitum
parem hostibus habeat, pecunia vinci, qua praestet, infe-
rioremque eum ea parte virium inveniri, qua longe supe-
15 rior sit. Postulat dari sibi ministrum inpensae, quia pluri-
16 bus id mandare perniciosum sit. Dato stipendio ad classem
remittitur, nec moram agendis rebus facit; multa fortiter,
multa feliciter agit, agros hostiles vastat, urbes expugnat
17 et quasi tempestas quaedam cuncta prosternit. Quibus
rebus territi Lacedaemonii ad patriae subsidium revocan-
dum ab Asia Agesilaum decernunt.

3. Interim Pisandrus ab Agesilao proficiscente dux
patriae relictus ingentem classem summis viribus instruit,
2 fortunam belli temptaturus. Nec non et Conon tunc primum cum hostium exercitu concursurus magna cura suos
3 ordinat. Summa igitur non ducum tantum in eo proelio
4 quam vulgi aemulatio fuit. Nam et ipse dux Conon non
5 tam Persis quam patriae studebat, et sicuti adflictis Atheni-

---

4 Xen. *Hell.* 4.3.10ff.; Diod. Sic. 14.83. Pisander was Agesilaus' brother-in-law. The battle is that of Cnidus in 394. If Justin
is placing the restoration of democracy in this year, he is obviously
mistaken, but perhaps the impression comes from condensation
of a longer summary in Trogus.

whom the king's officers had been regularly defrauding of
their pay, his troops becoming all the more urgent in demanding arrears since they reckoned that under a great
leader a campaign would be all the more difficult. So 12
Conon, after long but fruitless appeals in dispatches to the
king, finally approached him in person, but he was not 13
permitted to see and talk to him because he would not do
obeisance before him in the Persian manner. He did how- 14
ever discuss matters with him through intermediaries and
complained that wars now being fought by the wealthiest
king were flagging for want of funds, and that although he
had an army equal to the enemy's the king was being defeated through failure to spend money, in which he had
the advantage, and was found wanting in the area where
he was far superior. He demanded he be given a finance 15
officer, because to assign that function to a number of
people would be ruinous. Given money he was sent back 16
to the fleet, and he lost no time in going into action; he
brought off many brave and many successful operations,
plundered enemy countryside, stormed cities, and destroyed everything like some tornado. Alarmed by all this, 17
the Spartans decided that to support the homeland Agesilaus must be recalled from Asia.

3. Meanwhile Pisander, left leader of the country when
Agesilaus set off, devoted all his energy to equipping a
massive fleet to try the fortunes of war.[4] Furthermore 2
Conon, then about to face his first encounter with the
enemy, deployed his troops with great care. There was 3
thus intense rivalry in that battle, not only among the leaders but also among their men. For even their commander 4
Conon was not himself as committed to Persia as to his
own country, and just as with the fall of Athens he had 5

145

ensium rebus auctor amissae dominationis fuerat, sic volebat idem haberi redditae patriamque vincendo recipere,
6 quam victus amiserat; eo speciosius, quod ne ipsorum quidem Atheniensium, sed alieni proelii viribus dimicet,
pugnaturus periculo regis, victurus praemio patriae, glo-
riamque diversis artibus quam priores civitatis suae duces
7 consecuturus: quippe illos vincendo Persas patriam defen-
disse, se Persas victores faciendo restituturum patriam
esse.
8 Porro Pisandrus pro coniunctione Agesilai etiam virtutum aemulator erat contendebatque, ne a rebus gestis eius
et gloriae splendore decederet, neu tot bellis ac saeculis
quaesitum imperium brevis momenti culpa subverteret.
9 Eadem militum et omnium remigum cura erat, quos
maior sollicitudo cruciabat, non tam ne ipsi quaesitas opes
amitterent, quam ne pristinas Athenienses reciperent.
10 Sed quanto maius proelium fuit, tanto et clarior victoria
11 Cononis. Victi Lacedaemonii fugam capesserunt, praesi-
12 dia hostium Athenis deducuntur, populo restituta dignitate condicio servilis eripitur, multae quoque civitates
recipiuntur.
4. Hoc initium Atheniensibus resumendae potentiae et
2 Lacedaemoniis habendae finis fuit. Namque veluti cum
imperio etiam virtutem perdidissent, contemni a finitimis
3 coepere. Primi igitur Thebani Atheniensibus auxiliantibus
4 bellum his intulere, quae civitas ex finitimis incrementis

---

[5] We have for the following period the continuing accounts of
Xenophon and Diodorus. Justin is condensed and confused. Lysander died at Haliartus in 395/4, a battle that Justin has evidently
confused with that of Leuctra in 371.

been responsible for the loss of the empire so now he wished to be seen as its restorer and to recover with a victory the country he had lost in defeat, and do it all the 6 more impressively by not even fighting with the strength of Athens, but that of a foreign nation; and he would fight with the king risking defeat and victory benefitting his own country to achieve glory by means different from his city's earlier leaders: for they had defended the country by de- 7 feating Persians while he would be renewing the country by making Persians victors.

Then there was Pisander, whose kinship made him em- 8 ulate Agesilaus' virtues, and he was trying not to fall short of his relative's achievements and illustrious reputation, or to ruin by a moment's failure an empire built up by so many wars and over so many centuries. That same concern 9 was felt by his soldiers and all the oarsmen, who were tormented with worry less about themselves losing their recent gains than the Athenians recovering their earlier possessions. But the harder the battle, the more brilliant 10 became Conon's victory. In defeat the Spartans fled, the 11 enemy garrison was withdrawn from Athens, the people 12 of Athens had their former standing restored, their subject status was removed, and many of their cities were recovered.

4. This was the start of the Athenian recovery of power and the end of Spartan hold on theirs. For as though they 2 had lost their valor together with their empire, they began to be despised by their neighbors.[5] So first Thebes, with 3 Athenian support, made war on them, a city state that 4

147

virtute Epaminondae ducis ad spem imperii Graeciae
5 erecta est. Fit itaque terrestre proelium eadem Lacedaemoniorum fortuna, qua pugnatum adversus Conona navali
6 proelio fuerat. In eo bello Lysander, quo duce Athenienses
7 victi a Lacedaemoniis fuerant, interficitur. Pausanias quoque, alter dux Lacedaemoniorum, proditionis accusatus in
8 exilium abiit. Igitur Thebani potiti victoriam universum
exercitum ad urbem Lacedaemoniorum ducunt, facilem
expugnationem rati, quoniam deserti a sociis omnibus
9 erant. Quod metuentes Lacedaemonii regem suum Agesilaum ex Asia, qui ibi magnas res gerebat, ad defensionem
10 patriae arcessunt. Occiso enim Lysandro nullius alterius
11 fiduciam ducis habebant. Cuius quoniam serus adventus
12 erat, conscripto exercitu obviam hosti procedunt. Sed victis adversus paulo ante victores nec animus neque vires
13 pares fuere; prima itaque congressione funduntur. Deletis
iam suorum copiis supervenit rex Agesilaus, qui restituto
proelio non difficulter recenti et multis expeditionibus
indurato milite hostibus victoriam eripuit; ipse tamen graviter sauciatur.

5. Quibus rebus cognitis Athenienses verentes, ne iterum Lacedaemoniis victoribus in pristinam sortem ser-
2 vitutis redigerentur, exercitum contrahunt eumque in
auxilium Boeotiorum per Iphicraten, XX quidem annos
3 natum, sed magnae indolis iuvenem, duci iubent. Huius
4 adulescentis supra aetatem virtus admirabilis fuit, nec
umquam ante eum Athenienses inter tot tantosque duces
aut spei maioris aut indolis maturioris imperatorem ha-
5 buerunt, in quo non imperatoriae tantum, verum et ora-
toriae artes fuere.

---

6 The date is 393/2; see *AO* 211.

from small beginnings rose through the courage of its leader Epaminondas, to hopes of dominating Greece. So there was a land battle in which Spartan fortunes were just as they had been in the naval battle against Conon. In that battle Lysander, under whom the Athenians had been defeated by the Spartans, was killed. Pausanias, the other Spartan general, was also charged with treason and went into exile. So after their victory the Thebans led their entire army to the city of the Spartans, thinking that storming it would be easy since they had been deserted by all their allies. In fear of that the Spartans recalled their king Agesilaus from Asia—he was there campaigning very successfully—to defend their country. For after Lysander was killed, they had confidence in no other leader. Since he was late in coming, they raised an army and went out to face the enemy. But defeated men had neither the same spirit nor the strength to face their recent conquerors; and so they were scattered in the first engagement. His people's forces were already destroyed when King Agesilaus arrived, but renewing the fight with fresh troops hardened by many campaigns he had no difficulty in snatching victory from the enemy; he himself, however, was seriously wounded.

5. Learning of this the Athenians were afraid that they could be reduced to their former state of serfdom if the Spartans were again victorious; so they put an army together and ordered it to be taken to assist the Boeotians by Iphicrates, only twenty years old but a youth of great talent. This young man had admirable qualities beyond his years, and never before him did the Athenians, among all their many great leaders, have a general of greater promise or more precocious genius, since in him there were not only military but also rhetorical abilities.[6]

6   Conon quoque audito reditu Agesilai et ipse ex Asia ad
7 depopulandos Lacedaemoniorum agros revertitur, atque
   ita undique belli formidine circumstrepente clausi Spar-
8 tani ad summam desperationem rediguntur. Sed Conon
   vastatis hostium terris Athenas pergit, ubi magno civium
   gaudio exceptus plus tamen tristitiae ipse ex incensa et
   diruta a Lacedaemoniis patria quam laetitiae ex recupe-
9 rata post tantum temporis cepit. Itaque quae incensa fuerant, praedarum sumptu et exercitu Persarum restituit;
10 quae diruta, refecit. Fatum illud Athenarum fuit, ut ante
   a Persis crematae manibus eorum, et nunc a Lacedaemoniis dirutae ex spoliis Lacedaemoniorum restituerentur
11 versaque vice haberent nunc socios, quos tunc hostes habuerant, et hostes nunc paterentur, cum quibus iunctae
   tunc artissimis societatis vinculis fuerant.
       6. Dum haec geruntur, Artaxerxes, rex Persarum, lega-
   tos in Graeciam mittit, per quos iubet omnes ab armis
   discedere; qui aliter fecisset, eum se pro hoste habiturum;
2 civitatibus libertatem suaque omnia restituit. Quod non
   Graeciae laboribus adsiduisque bellorum internecivis
3 odiis consulens fecit, sed ne occupato sibi Aegyptio bello,
   quod propter auxilia adversus praefectos suos Lacedaemoniis missa susceperat, exercitus sui in Graecia detine-
4 rentur. Fessi igitur tot bellis Graeci cupide paruere. Hic
5 annus non eo tantum insignis fuit, quod repente pax tota
   Graecia facta est, sed etiam eo, quod eodem tempore urbs
   Romana a Gallis capta est.

---

[7] A Persian embassy did come to Greece in 392/1, but peace
was made later, in 387/6 (the probable date for the Gallic sack of
Rome).

Conon, too, on hearing of Agesilaus' return, himself 6
came back from Asia to lay waste Lacedaemonian lands,
and so, enclosed on all sides with the fear of war echoing 7
around them, the Spartans were reduced to utter despair.
But after plundering his enemy's lands Conon made for 8
Athens where, although welcomed with great joy by his
fellow citizens, he nevertheless felt more dejection over
the burning and destruction of his country by the Spartans
than joy at its recovery after such a long time. So what had 9
been burned he restored, from the proceeds of his booty
and by using the Persian army; and what had been demolished he rebuilt. Such was the fate of Athens: earlier 10
burned by the Persians it was rebuilt by their hands, and
now destroyed by the Spartans it was being restored from
Spartan spoils; and, with the tables turned they now had 11
as allies their former foes, and faced as enemies people
with whom they had earlier been linked by the closest ties.

6. While this was taking place, Artaxerxes, king of the
Persians, sent legates to Greece with orders for everyone
to lay down arms;[7] any failing to comply he would consider
enemies; and to the city-states he restored freedom and
all their property. This he did not out of concern for 2
Greece's troubles and wars arising from its incessant ani-
mosities, but so that, while he was himself preoccupied 3
with an Egyptian war that he had undertaken over assistance sent to the Spartans against his satraps, his armies
would not be held back in Greece. So being weary of so 4
many wars the Greeks readily complied. This year was 5
notable not only for there suddenly being peace throughout Greece, but also because at that same time the city of
Rome was captured by the Gauls.

6   Sed Lacedaemonii securi insidiantes, absentiam Arca-
dum speculati castellum eorum expugnant occupatoque
7 praesidium inponunt. Itaque armato instructoque exercitu Arcades adhibitis in auxilium Thebanis amissa bello
8 repetunt. In eo proelio Archidamus, dux Lacedaemonio-
9 rum, vulneratus; qui cum caedi suos iam ut victos videret,
per praeconem corpora interfectorum ad sepulturam
10 poscit (hoc est enim signum apud Graecos victoriae tradi-
tae), qua confessione contenti Thebani signum parcendi
dedere.

    7. Paucis deinde post diebus neutris quicquam hostile
facientibus, cum quasi tacito consensu indutiae essent
Lacedaemoniis alia bella adversus finitimos gerentibus,
Thebani Epaminonda duce occupandae urbis eorum
2 spem ceperunt. Igitur principio noctis taciti Lacedaemona
proficiscuntur, non tamen adgredi incautos potuerunt.
3 Quippe senes et cetera inbellis aetas, cum adventum hostium praesensissent, in ipsis portarum angustiis armati
4 occurrunt; et adversus XV milia militum non amplius cen-
5 tum iam effetae aetatis viri pugnae se offerunt. Tantum
animorum viriumque patriae et penatium conspectus sub-
ministrabat, tantoque praesentia quam recordatione sui
6 maiores spiritus largiuntur. Nam ut videre, inter quae et
pro quibus starent, aut vincendum sibi aut moriendum
7 censuerunt. Pauci igitur sustinuere senes aciem, cui par
8 ante dies universa iuventus esse non potuit. In eo proelio

---

8 We have now leaped to 365/4 and events covered (but with
no mention of the Thebans) by Xen. *Hell.* 7.4.19ff. The confusion
continues through section 7, where we are into 363/2 and the
battle of Mantinea; Xen. *Hell.* 7.5; Diod. Sic. 15.82ff.

The Spartans, however, lying safely in ambush and tak- 6
ing note of when the Arcadians were away, stormed one
of their strongholds and, occupying it, imposed a garrison
there.[8] So equipping and mobilizing an army, the Arcadi- 7
ans enlisted the aid of the Thebans and recovered by war
what they had lost. In that battle Archidamus, leader of 8
the Spartans, was wounded; and when he saw his men 9
being cut down and clearly defeated, he through a herald
reclaimed the bodies of the dead for burial (for this is a 10
sign of conceding victory among the Greeks) and satisfied
with this acknowledgment the Thebans gave the sign for
showing mercy.

7. Then a few days later when neither side took any
hostile action and, as if by tacit agreement, there was a
truce as the Lacedaemonians were engaged in other wars
against neighbors, the Thebans, led by Epaminondas, en-
tertained the hope of taking their city. So at nightfall they 2
set quietly off to Lacedaemon, but they were unable to
mount a surprise attack. For the older men and the others 3
not of fighting age. since they had some presentiment of
their enemy's approach, met them under arms right in the
narrow passageway of their city gates; and facing fifteen 4
thousand soldiers no more than a hundred men of advanced age committed to battle. Such was the spirit and 5
fortitude that the sight of their homeland and hearths inspired in them, and so much more were their spirits raised
by their presence there than by any memories of them!
For when they saw amid what and for whom they were 6
fighting, they saw they must either conquer or die. Thus a 7
few old men held off a battle line that some days earlier a
whole force of young men could not withstand. In that 8

9 duo duces hostium cecidere, cum interim Agesilai adventu
10 nuntiato Thebani recessere. Nec bellum diu dilatum,
   siquidem Spartanorum iuventus senum virtute et gloria
   incensa teneri non potuit, quin ex continenti acie decer-
11 neret. Cum victoria Thebanorum esset, Epaminonda,
   dum non ducis tantum, verum et fortissimi militis officio
12 fungitur, graviter vulneratur. Quo audito his ex dolore
   metus et illis ex gaudio stupor inicitur atque ita velut ex
   placito consensu a proelio disceditur.

   8. Post paucos deinde dies Epaminonda decedit, cum
2 quo vires quoque rei publicae ceciderunt. Nam sicuti telo
   si primam aciem praefregeris, reliquo ferro vim nocendi
   sustuleris, sic illo, velut mucrone teli, ablato duce Thebanorum rei quoque publicae vires hebetatae sunt, ut non
   tam illum amisisse quam cum illo interisse omnes videren-
3 tur. Nam neque hunc ante ducem ullum memorabile bellum gessere, nec postea virtutibus, sed cladibus insignes
   fuere, ut manifestum sit patriae gloriam et natam et ex-
4 tinctam cum eo fuisse. Fuit autem incertum, vir melior an
5 dux esset. Nam et imperium non sibi semper, sed patriae
6 quaesivit, et pecuniae adeo parcus fuit, ut sumptus funeri
7 defuerit. Gloriae quoque non cupidior quam pecuniae;
8 quippe recusanti omnia imperia ingesta sunt, honoresque
   ita gessit, ut ornatum non accipere, sed dare ipsi dignitati
9 videretur. Iam litterarum studium, iam philosophiae
   doctrina tanta, ut mirabile videretur, unde tam insignis
10 militiae scientia homini inter litteras nato. Neque ab hoc

---

9 This was the battle of Mantineia (362 BC), won by the Thebans and their allies against Sparta and an Athenian contingent.
Justin is wrong to imply it was a drawn battle.

battle two of their enemy's generals fell and meanwhile   9
when news came of Agesilaus' arrival the Thebans withdrew. Nor was the war long postponed, for the younger   10
Spartans, fired by the old men's courage and glorious action, could not be restrained from immediately deciding
the issue in battle. When victory lay in the Thebans' grasp,   11
Epaminondas, while doing his duty both as brave soldier
as well as general, was seriously wounded. At the news one   12
side was struck with grief and fear and the other with joy,
and as if by common consent they left the battle.[9]

8. A few days later Epaminondas died, and with him
the power of his state also perished. For just as by breaking   2
off the sharp point a javelin you have removed the rest of
the weapon's ability to inflict damage, so too by the re-
moval of the Theban general, who was the weapon's point,
the state's power was also blunted, so that it seemed not
so much to have lost him as entirely disappeared with him.
For before he was their leader the Thebans fought no   3
notable war, and after him were known not for military
prowess but for defeats, making it clear that his country's
glorious period was both born with him and died with him.
It was uncertain, however, whether he was a better man   4
or leader. For he always sought power not for himself but   5
for his country, and to money he was also so indifferent   6
that funds were lacking for his funeral. For fame he was   7
also no more eager than he was for money; indeed, all his
powers were heaped on him against his will, and his honors   8
he accepted in such a way as to appear not to be winning
approval but actually adding to the distinction. So great   9
was his literary culture, so great his philosophical learning
that it seemed extraordinary to find such a man with such
military knowledge was also steeped in literature. Nor was   10

155

11 vitae proposito mortis ratio dissensit. Nam ut relatus in
castra semianimis vocem spiritumque collegit, id unum a
circumstantibus requisivit, num cadenti sibi scutum ade-
12 misset hostis. Quod ut servatum audivit adlatumque veluti
laborum gloriaeque socium osculatus est, iterum quaesi-
13 vit, utri vicissent. Ut audivit Thebanos, bene habere se
rem dixit atque ita velut gratulabundus patriae exspiravit.

9. Huius morte etiam Atheniensium virtus intercidit;
2 siquidem amisso, cui aemulari consueverant, in segnitiam
3 torporemque resoluti non ut olim in classem et exercitus,
sed in dies festos apparatuque ludorum reditus publicos
4 effundunt et cum auctoribus nobilissimis poetisque thea-
tra celebrant, frequentius scenam quam castra visentes
5 versificatoresque meliores quam duces laudantes. Tunc
vectigal publicum, quo antea milites et remiges alebantur,
cum urbano populo dividi coeptum.

6 Quibus rebus effectum est, ut inter otia Graecorum
sordidum et obscurum antea Macedonum nomen emer-
7 geret, et Philippus obses triennio Thebis habitus, Epaminondae et Pelopidae virtutibus eruditus, regnum Macedoniae Graeciae et Asiae cervicibus veluti iugum servitutis
inponeret.

---

10 Epaminondas' death here is apparently much swifter than
at 6.8.1.

11 We may detect here the moralizing tone of Theopompus.
In the wake of a debilitating war with some of their allies, the
Athenians instituted economies through a budget system wherein
the theoric fund, technically meant to provide the cost of theater
attendance to citizens, became the repository of excess revenues.
See *AO* 7.

how he died at variance with how he lived. For when car-   11
ried half-dead back to camp he regained consciousness
and the ability to speak, he asked only one question of
those standing around him, whether when he fell the enemy had taken his shield. When he heard that it had been   12
recovered and it was then brought to him, he kissed it as
being his ally in toil and glory and asked another question,
namely which side had been successful. When he heard it   13
was the Thebans, he said that all was well and congratulating his native land took his final breath.[10]

9. With his death Athenian valor also died, for with   2
their traditional rival gone they slipped into lethargy and   3
torpor and, rather than spending state revenues on their
fleet and armies as they did before, they poured them into
festivals and staging public games,[11] and with their most   4
famous authors and poets flocked to theaters, visiting a
stage more often than a camp, and praising versifiers as
being better than generals. It was a that point that state   5
revenues, by which soldiers and oarsmen were earlier
maintained, began to be disbursed among the urban pop-
ulace.

So it was that while the Greeks were at leisure the lowly   6
and little-known name of Macedon was starting to emerge,
and Philip, three years held hostage in Thebes and there   7
trained in those qualities possessed by Epaminondas and
Pelopidas, was imposing the kingdom of Macedonia on
the shoulders of Greece and Asia as a yoke of slavery.[12]

[12] Philip's sojourn in Thebes is noted also by Diod. Sic. 15.67.4
(under the year 369/8) and Plut. *Vit. Pel.* 26.4ff.

LIBER VII

1. Macedonia ante a nomine Emathionis regis, cuius prima virtutis experimenta in illis locis exstant, Emathia
2 cognominata est. Huius sicuti incrementa modica, ita ter-
3 mini perangusti fuere. Populus Pelasgi, regio Bottia dice-
4 batur. Sed postea virtute regum et gentis industria subac-
tis primo finitimis, mox populis nationibusque, imperium
5 usque extremos Orientis terminos prolatum. In regione
Paeonia, quae nunc portio est Macedoniae, regnasse fertur Pelegonus, pater Asteropaei, cuius Troiano bello inter
6 clarissimos vindices urbis nomen accipimus. Ex alio latere
in Europa regnum Europus nomine tenuit.
7 Sed et Caranus cum magna multitudine Graecorum
sedes in Macedonia responso oraculi iussus quaerere, cum
Emathiam venisset, urbem Edessam non sentientibus
oppidanis propter imbrium et nebulae magnitudinem
gregem caprarum imbrem fugientium secutus occupavit;
8 revocatusque in memoriam oraculi, quo iussus erat duci-
9 bus capris imperium quaerere, regni sedem statuit; reli-

---

1 It is as likely as can be that Trogus' source for Macedonian affairs was Theopompus. The history of Macedon to the death of Philip may conveniently be followed in *A History of Macedonia*, vol. 1, to 550, by N. G. L. Hammond (Oxford, 1972); vol. 2, 550–336, by Hammond and G. T. Griffith (Oxford, 1979).

BOOK VII

1. Macedonia was earlier called Emathia, named after King Emathion, whose early courageous exploits live on in the lore of those regions.[1] Its beginnings were modest and 2 its territory also very small. The people were called Pelas- 3 gians, the region Bottia.[2] But later through the valor of its 4 kings and its people's industry it first subjugated neigh- bors, and soon after peoples and tribes, extending its em- pire to the furthest limits of the East. In the region of 5 Paeonia, which now forms part of Macedonia, Pelegonus, father of Asteropaeus, is said to have reigned, and we are told that in the Trojan War his name ranks among the city's most famous defenders. In another area of Europe a man 6 named Europus had a kingdom.

But Caranus,[3] ordered by an oracle to seek a home in 7 Macedonia, had also come to Emathia with a large band of Greeks, and following a herd of goats running from a downpour he seized the city of Edessa, its inhabitants being taken unawares because of heavy rain and dense fog; and recalling the oracle by which he had been told to seek 8 his empire led by she-goats, made it his capital, and scru- 9

[2] Usually Latinized as Bottiaea.
[3] The legendary founder of the Macedonian dynasty.

gioseque postea observavit, quocumque agmen moveret,
ante signa easdem capras habere, coeptorum duces habi-
10 turus, quas regni habuerat auctores. Urbem Edessam ob
memoriam muneris Aegaeas, populum Aegeadas vocavit.
11 Pulso deinde Mida (nam is quoque portionem Macedoniae tenuit) aliisque regibus pulsis in locum omnium solus
12 successit primusque adunatis gentibus variorum populorum veluti unum corpus Macedoniae fecit, crescentique
regno valida incrementorum fundamenta constituit.

2. Post hunc Perdicca regnavit, cuius et vita inlustris et
mortis postrema, veluti ex oraculo, praecepta memorabilia
2 fuere. Siquidem senex moriens Argeo filio monstravit
locum, quo condi vellet; ibique non sua tantum, sed et
succedentium sibi in regnum ossa poni iussit, praefatus,
3 quoad ibi conditae posterorum reliquiae forent, regnum
4 in familia mansurum; creduntque hac superstitione ex-
tinctam in Alexandro stirpem, quia locum sepulturae
5 mutaverit. Argeus moderate et cum amore popularium
administrato regno successorem filium Philippum reliquit, qui inmatura morte raptus Aëropum, parvulum ad-
6 modum, instituit heredem. Sed Macedonibus adsidua
certamina cum Thracibus et Illyriis fuere, quorum armis
veluti cotidiano exercitio indurati gloria bellicae laudis
7 finitimos terrebant. Igitur Illyrii infantiam regis pupilli

---

4 So the Latin, but surely the truth was that goats were repre-
sented *on* the standards.

5 The Greek for goat was *aix*, in the genitive case *aigos*; the
latter would be Latinized as "aegus."

6 Cf. Hdt. 8.137ff., where the succession is as here, except that
Alcetas is between Aëropus and Amyntas.

pulously thereafter, wherever he took his army, he would keep those same goats before his standards[4] to have as leaders in his ventures the animals he had had as his kingdom's founders. The city of Edessa he in remembrance 10
of this gift called Aegaea, and its people Aegeads.[5] Then 11
driving out Midas (for he too ruled part of Macedonia) and other kings, he replaced them all as sole ruler, and being 12
the first to bring together the tribes of its various peoples he made a unified body of Macedonia and provided a firm basis for the growth of his expanding kingdom.

2. After him Perdiccas was king,[6] a man whose famous life and almost oracular final instructions at death were both memorable. For when he was dying in old age he 2
showed his son Argeus the spot where he wanted to be buried; and there he ordered not only his own bones but also those of his successors to the throne to be laid, saying that as long as their descendants' remains were buried 3
there the kingdom would remain in the family; and from 4
such superstition people think his line died out with Alexander because he changed the place of burial.[7] Argeus 5
after ruling the kingdom with moderation and love for his people left as his successor his son Philip and he, taken by an early death, appointed as his heir Aëropus, who was still very young. But the Macedonians faced incessant wars 6
with Thracians and Illyrians, who toughened with campaigns as their regular training would intimidate their neighbors by their famed military reputation. So the Illyr- 7
ians, contemptuous of the infant royal ward, attacked the

---

[7] Alexander the Great, that is, who purportedly asked to be buried at the oracle of Ammon in Libya, but was finally entombed at Alexandria in Egypt.

8 contemnentes bello Macedonas adgrediuntur. Qui proelio
pulsi rege suo in cunis prolato et pone aciem posito acrius
9 certamen repetivere, tamquam ideo victi antea fuissent,
10 quod bellantibus sibi regis sui auspicia defuissent, futuri
vel propterea victores, quod ex superstitione animum
11 vincendi ceperant; simul et miseratio eos infantis tenebat,
quem, si victi forent, captivum de rege facturi videbantur.
12 Conserto itaque proelio magna caede Illyrios fudere,
ostenderuntque hostibus suis priore bello regem Macedo-
13 nibus, non virtutem defuisse. Huic Amyntas succedit et
propria virtute et Alexandri filii egregia indole insigniter
14 clarus; cui Alexandro tanta omnium virtutum natura ornamenta extitere ut etiam Olympio certamine vario ludicro-
rum genere contenderit.

    3. Cum interim Darius, rex Persarum, turpi ab Scythia
fuga submotus, ne ubique deformis militiae damnis haberetur, mittit cum parte copiarum Magabasum ad subigenda
Thraciam ceteraque eius tractus regna, quibus pro ignobili
2 momento erat accessura Macedonia. Qui brevi tempore
executo regis imperio legatis ad Amyntam, regem Macedoniae, missis obsides in pignus futurae pacis dari sibi
3 postulabat. Sed legati benigne excepti inter epulas ebrietate crescente rogant Amyntam, ut apparatui epularum
adiciat ius familiaritatis adhibitis in convivium suum filiis
et uxoribus; id apud Persas haberi pignus et foedus hospi-
4 tii. Quae ut venerunt ⟨Persis⟩ petulantius contrectantibus

---

8 This is Alexander I Philhellene (Hdt. 5.22), who ruled ca.
495 to 452.

9 See Hdt. 5.14ff. "Magabasus" is Megabazus. For Darius and
the Scythians, see above, 2.5.10ff.

Macedonians. These, defeated in the battle, then carried 8
their king forward in his cradle, set him behind their battle line, and renewed the fight more fiercely, thinking that 9
they were earlier defeated because they had fought without their king's auspices, but now they would be victors 10
because from that superstition they had gained determi-
nation to be so, and they were also taken with pity for the 11
child, whom they would, if defeated, evidently be making
a captive after being a king. So when battle was joined, 12
they routed the Illyrians with great slaughter, and they
showed their enemies that in the earlier engagement what
the Macedonians lacked was their king, not courage. He 13
was succeeded by Amyntas, a man very well renowned
both for his own courage and his son Alexander's sterling
character; this Alexander was so endowed by nature with 14
all manner of superb abilities that he even competed in
various events in the Olympic games.[8]

3. Meanwhile Darius, king of the Persians, after being
driven from Scythia in ignominious flight, and now fearing
that he might everywhere be discredited for his military
losses,[9] sent Magabasus with part of his troops to conquer
Thrace and the other kingdoms of that area, to which
would be added—it being of little importance—Macedonia. He, promptly obeying the king's order and sending 2
envoys to Amyntas, king of Macedonia, insisted on being
given hostages as a guarantee of future peace. But after 3
being given a cordial reception the envoys, becoming increasingly drunk throughout the dinner, asked Amyntas to
add intimate friendship to his magnificent feast by inviting
his daughters and wives to the feast; among Persians, they
said, this was seen as a binding pledge of hospitality. When 4
they came and the Persians began fondling them in too

filius Amyntae Alexander rogat patrem, respectu aetatis ac
gravitatis suae abiret convivio, pollicitus se hospitum tem-
5 peraturum iocos. Quo digresso mulieres quoque paululum e convivio evocat, cultius exornaturus gratioresque
6 reducturus. In quarum locum matronali habitu exornatos
iuvenes opponit, eosque petulantiam legatorum ferro,
7 quod sub veste gerebant, conpescere iubet. Atque ita
interfectis omnibus ignarus rei Magabasus, cum legati
non redirent, mittit eo cum exercitus parte Bubarem, ut
8 in bellum facile et mediocre, dedignatus ipse ire, ne de-
9 honestaretur proelio tam foedae gentis. Sed Bubares ante
bellum amore filiae Amyntae captus omisso bello nuptias
facit depositisque hostilibus animis in adfinitatis iura succedit.

4. Post discessum a Macedonia Bubaris Amyntas rex
decedit, cuius filio et successori Alexandro cognatio Bubaris non Darii tantum temporibus pacem praestitit, verum
etiam Xerxen adeo conciliavit, ut, cum Graeciam veluti
tempestas quaedam occupasset, inter Olympum Haemu-
mque montes totius regionis eum imperio donaverit.
2 Sed nec virtute minus quam Persarum liberalitate regnum
ampliavit.

3 Per ordinem deinde successionis regnum Macedoniae
4 ad Amyntam, fratris eius Menelai filium, pervenit. Hic
quoque insignis industria et omnibus imperatoriis virtuti-

---

10 Alexander was succeeded by his son Perdiccas II (ca. 452–
413), and Perdiccas was succeeded by Archelaus (413–399). Four
brief and turbulent reigns preceded that of Amyntas III (392–
370), father of Philip. Alexander II lasted until his murder in 368,

familiar a manner, Amyntas' son Alexander asked his father to consider his age and dignity and leave the banquet, promising he would temper the exuberance of their guests. After he left Alexander also briefly called the 5 women away from the banquet, to have them more attractively made up and brought back more desirable. In 6 their place he set some young men in women's clothing, and he ordered them to use swords that they carried beneath their clothes to curb the lechery of the envoys. So 7 when all were killed and his envoys did not return, Magabasus, unaware of it, sent Bubares there with part of his army on what he expected would be an easy campaign of little significance, not deigning to go himself so as not to 8 lose face by fighting such a contemptible people. But be- 9 fore any war started Bubares fell in love with the daughter of Amyntas, married her and renouncing hostilities entered into a formal family relationship.

4. After Bubares' departure from Macedonia King Amyntas died, and the family tie that his son and successor Alexander had with Bubares not only ensured peace in Darius' time but also put him on such good terms with Xerxes that, when he swept through Greece like some whirlwind, he put him in charge of the whole area between Mount Olympus and Mount Haemus. But it was no 2 less through valor than Persian generosity that Alexander expanded his kingdom.

In order of succession, the kingdom of Macedonia then 3 came down to Amyntas, son of Alexander's brother Menelaus.[10] He, too, was remarkable for his energy and had all 4

Ptolemy until 365, when he was killed by Perdiccas III, who ruled until 359, when in fact he fell in battle against the Illyrians.

5 bus instructus fuit, qui ex Eurydice tres filios sustulit,
Alexandrum, Perdiccam et Philippum, Alexandri Magni
Macedonis patrem, et filiam Euryonen, ex Gygaea autem
6 Archelaum, Arridaeum, Menelaum. Cum Illyriis deinde
7 et cum Olynthiis gravia bella gessit. Insidiis etiam Eurydices uxoris, quae nuptias generi pacta occidendum virum
regnumque adultero tradendum susceperat, occupatus
fuisset, ni filia paelicatum matris et sceleris consilia prodi-
8 disset. Functus itaque tot periculis senex decessit, regno
maximo ex filiis Alexandro tradito.

5. Igitur Alexander inter prima initia regni bellum ab
Illyriis pacta mercede et Philippo fratre dato obside rede-
2 mit. Interiecto quoque tempore per eundem obsidem
cum Thebanis gratiam pacis reconciliat. Quae res Philippo
3 maxima incrementa egregiae indolis dedit, siquidem Thebis triennio obses habitus prima pueritiae rudimenta in
urbe severitatis antiquae et in domo Epaminondae, summi
4 et philosophi et imperatoris, deposuit. Nec multo post
Alexander insidiis Eurydices matris adpetitus occumbit,
5 cui Amyntas in scelere deprehensae propter communes
liberos, ignarus eisdem quandoque exitiosam fore, peper-
6 cerat. Frater quoque eius Perdicca pari insidiarum fraude
7 decipitur. Indignum prorsus libidinis causa liberos a matre
vita privatos, quam scelerum suorum suppliciis liberorum
8 contemplatio vindicaverat. Perdiccae hoc indignior caedes
videbatur, quod ei apud matrem misericordiam ne parvu-
9 lus quidem filius conciliaverat. Itaque Philippus diu non

---

11 See above, 6.9.7.
12 He would have been Amyntas IV; it is debatable whether
or not Philip II (359–336) began as regent for the latter.

the qualities of a general; by Eurydice he had three sons, 5
Alexander, Perdiccas, and Philip, the father of Alexander
the Great of Macedon, and a daughter Euryone, and by
Gygaea he had Archelaus, Arridaeus, and Menelaus. He 6
then fought difficult wars with the Illyrians and the Olynthians. He might also have fallen victim to the treachery 7
of his wife Eurydice, who after negotiating a marriage with
her son-in-law had undertaken to kill her husband and
transfer the kingdom to her lover, but their daughter betrayed her mother's liaison and criminal plans. So having 8
survived so many dangers he died an old man, passing the
throne to the eldest of his sons, Alexander.

5. Now in the early days of his reign Alexander averted
war by negotiating with the Illyrians and giving them his
brother Philip as a hostage. Some time later, by using the 2
same hostage, he reestablished peace with the Thebans.
It was this that most served to develop Philip's exceptional
genius,[11] for kept hostage at Thebes for three years he 3
spent the earliest stages of adolescence in a city of old-
fashioned austerity and in the home of Epaminondas, an
exceptional philosopher and general. Not much later Al- 4
exander succumbed to treachery, a victim of his mother
Eurydice; although she had once been caught red-handed 5
Amyntas had nevertheless spared her life for the sake of
the children they shared, unaware that she would one day
prove their undoing. His brother Perdiccas also fell victim 6
to one of her treacherous plots. Dreadful indeed was it for 7
children to be murdered by their mother from lust, when
consideration for these children had saved her from punishment for her own crimes! The murder of Perdiccas 8
seemed all the more scandalous for the mother's pity being aroused not even by his having an infant son.[12] Thus 9

167

10 regem, sed tutorem pupilli egit. At ubi graviora bella in-
minebant serumque auxilium in expectatione infantis erat,
conpulsus a populo regnum suscepit.

6. Ut est ingressus imperium, magna de illo spes omnibus fuit et propter ipsius ingenium, quod magnum spon-
debat virum, et propter vetera Macedoniae fata, quae

2 cecinerant, uno ex Amyntae filiis regnante florentissimum
fore Macedoniae statum, cui spei scelus matris hunc resi-

3 duum fecerat. Principio rerum cum hinc caedes fratrum
indigne peremptorum, inde hostium multitudo, hinc insidiarum metus, inde inopia continui belli et exhausti

4 regni inmaturam aetatem tironis urgerent: bella, quae
velut conspiratione quadam ad opprimendam Macedoniam multarum gentium ex diversis locis uno tempore

5 confluebant, quoniam omnibus par esse non poterat, dis-
pensanda ratus alia interposita pactione conponit, alia
redimit facillimis quibusque adgressis, quorum victoria et
militum trepidos animos firmaret et contemptum sibi ho-

6 stium demeret. Primum illi cum Atheniensibus certamen
fuit; quibus per insidias victis metu belli gravioris, cum

7 interficere omnes posset, incolumes sine pretio dimisit.
Post hos bello in Illyrios translato multa milia hostium

8 caedit; hinc Thessaliam non praedae cupiditate, sed quod
exercitui suo robur Thessalorum equitum adiungere ges-

---

13 The narrative account of the period of Philip's reign is Diod.
Sic. 16 (with interspersed attention to Sicily in particular). For
treatments of the Macedonian, cf. J. R. Ellis, *Philip II and Mace-
donian Imperialism* (London, 1976); G. Cawkwell, *Philip of
Macedon* (London 1978); I. Worthington, *Philip II of Macedonia*
(New Haven, 2010).

Philip for a long time acted not as king but as the minor's guardian. But when more serious wars threatened and any 10 assistance to be expected from the child lay too far ahead, he, pressed by the people, took over the kingdom.

6. When he came to power, everyone had great expectations of him, both for his character, which held promise of a great man, and also because of ancient Macedonian prophecies that had foretold that when one of Amyntas' 2 sons became king Macedonia would see great prosperity,[13] a hope that his mother's evildoing had left only him to fulfill. Right from the start the newcomer's years were 3 beset with problems: here his brothers foully murdered, there hordes of enemies; here fear of treason, there his kingdom exhausted by an ongoing war; and as if by some 4 conspiracy to crush Macedonia there were wars with many peoples accumulating in various places at the same time. He could not face all of them together, and so, thinking 5 they must be dealt with separately, he settled some by negotiation, bought off others, and attacked all the easiest ones, victory over whom would both bolster his men's resolve and also remove his enemies' contempt for him. His 6 first battle was with the Athenians; these he defeated by ambush, and although he could have killed them all he from fear of a more serious war released them unharmed and without ransom.[14] After these he transferred the war 7 to the Illyrians and killed many thousands of his enemies; he then took Thessaly with a surprise attack since this was the last thing anyone feared, and this was not for plunder but because he was eager to add the strong Thessalian 8

[14] This supposed early war with Athens is fiction, source unknown. Philip's early relations with Athens were cordial.

tiebat, nihil minus quam bellum metuentem inprovisus
9 expugnat, unumque corpus equitum pedestriumque copiarum invicti exercitus fecit; urbem nobilissimam Larissam
10 capit. Quibus rebus feliciter provenientibus Olympiadam,
Neoptolemi, regis Molossorum, filiam, uxorem ducit, con-
11 ciliante nuptias fratre patrueli, auctore virginis, Arryba,
rege Molossorum, qui sororem Olympiadis Troada in
matrimonio habebat; quae causa illi exitii malorumque
12 omnium fuit. Nam dum regni incrementa adfinitate Philippi adquisiturum sperat, proprio regno ab eodem privatus in exilio consenuit.
13 His ita gestis Philippus iam non contentus submovere
14 bella ultro etiam quietos lacessit. Cum Mothonam urbem
oppugnaret, in praetereuntem de muris sagitta iacta dex-
15 trum oculum regis effodit. Quo vulnere nec segnior in
16 bellum nec iracundior adversus hostes factus est, adeo ut
interiectis diebus pacem deprecantibus dederit, nec mo-
deratus tantum, verum etiam mitis adversus victos fuerit.

cavalry to his own army, and by amalgamating his cavalry 9
and infantry he created an invincible army. He also captured the famous city of Larissa. While these operations 10
were proceeding successfully he married Olympias,[15]
daughter of Neoptolemus, king of the Molossians, a match 11
arranged by Arrybas, king of the Molossians, who was the
girl's cousin and guardian and married to her sister, Troas;
and this caused that man's downfall and all his troubles.
For while hoping to increase his kingdom by a family tie 12
with Philip, he was stripped of his own kingdom by that
same man and grew old in exile.[16]

After these achievements Philip was no longer content 13
with just warding off attacks and even started challenging
peaceful nations. When he was attacking the city of 14
Methone, an arrow shot from the defenses as he was passing before its walls struck out the right eye of the king. By 15
the wound he was rendered neither less effective in combat nor more savage in dealing with enemies, so much so 16
that when some days later they sued for peace he granted
it, and was not only restrained but even merciful toward
the defeated.[17]

[15] In 357. Arrybas was the brother of Neoptolemus, who was
king before him, and so Olympias' uncle.

[16] This came in 342; below, 8.6.7.

[17] The attack on Methone was in 355/4. If Diod. Sic. 16.34.4f.
is to be believed, Philip was hardly so lenient.

LIBER VIII

1. Graeciae civitates, dum imperare singulae cupiunt,
2 imperium omnes perdiderunt. Quippe in mutuum exitium sine modo ruentes omnibus perire, quod singulae
3 amitterent, non nisi oppressae senserunt; siquidem Philippus, rex Macedoniae, velut e specula quadam libertati omnium insidiatus, dum contentiones civitatum alit auxilium inferioribus ferendo, victos pariter victoresque subire regiam servitutem coegit.
4 Causa et origo huius mali Thebani fuere, qui cum rerum potirentur, secundam fortunam inbecillo animo ferentes victos armis Lacedaemonios et Phocenses, quasi Parva supplicia caedibus et rapinis luissent, apud commune Graeciae concilium superbe accusaverunt. Lace-
5 daemoniis crimini datum, quod arcem Thebanam indutiarum tempore occupassent, Phocensibus, quod Boeotiam depopulati essent: prorsus quasi post arma et bellum lo-
6
7 cum legibus reliquissent. Cum iudicium arbitrio victorum exerceretur, tanta pecunia damnantur, quanta exsolvi non

---

1 For other accounts and Trogus' probable source, see above at 7.6.

2 The council is that of the Amphictyons of Delphi, the year 355/4. Diod. Sic. 16.14.3 names Demophilus, Ephorus' son, and

172

BOOK VIII

1. As for the Greek states, while each wanted overall power they all lost power.[1] For rushing wildly into mutual 2 destruction they realized only when overcome that each one's loss meant ruin for them all; for Philip, king of Mace- 3 donia, preying on everyone's liberty as if from some look-out post, by fostering the various states' disputes and bringing help to the weaker sides made defeated and conquered alike bend to his regal servitude.

The root cause of this problem was the Thebans, who 4 when they gained power, used their success foolishly; they defeated the Spartans and Phocians in battle but as if these had suffered too little pain in slaughter and pillage, they arrogantly indicted them before the combined council of Greece.[2] The accusation against the Spartans was that 5 they had seized the Theban citadel during a truce, against the Phocians that they had plundered Boeotia—as if after 6 armed warfare they had left room for legalities. Since ar- 7 bitration lay with the victors, fines were so high that paying

other sources. The charge against Sparta relates to the seizure of the Cadmeia in 382 (Xen. *Hell.* 5.2.25ff.), but the charge had been laid after Leuctra in 371 (Diod. Sic. 16.23.2). The major sin of the Phocians was to have cultivated the sacred plain of Cirrha (Diod. Sic. 16.23.3). Philomelus' death came in 354/3.

8 posset. Igitur Phocenses cum agris, liberis coniugibusque privarentur, desperatis rebus Philomelo quodam duce veluti deo irascentes templum Apollinis Delphis occupa-
9 vere. Inde auro et pecunia divites conducto mercenario
10 milite bellum Thebanis intulerunt. Factum Phocensium, tametsi omnes execrarentur propter sacrilegium, plus tamen invidiae Thebanis, a quibus ad hanc necessitatem
11 conpulsi fuerant, quam ipsis intulit. Itaque auxilia his et
12 ab Atheniensibus et a Lacedaemoniis missa. Prima igitur
13 congressione Philomelus Thebanos castris exuit. Sequenti proelio primus inter confertissimos dimicans cecidit et
14 sacrilegii poenas impio sanguine luit. In huius locum dux Onomarchus creatur.

2. Adversus quem Thebani Thessalique non ex civibus
2 suis, ne victoris potentiam ferre non possent, sed Philippum, Macedoniae regem, ducem eligunt et externae dominationi, quam in suis timuerunt, sponte succedunt.
3 Igitur Philippus, quasi sacrilegii, non Thebanorum ultor esset, omnes milites coronas laureas sumere iubet, atque
4 ita veluti deo duce in proelium pergit. Phocenses insignibus dei conspectis conscientia delictorum territi abiectis armis fugam capessunt, poenasque violatae reli-
5 gionis sanguine et caedibus suis pendunt. Incredibile quantum ea res apud omnes nationes Philippo gloriae
6 dedit; illum vindicem sacrilegii, illum ultorem religionum; quod orbis viribus expiari debuit, solum qui piacula exige-
7 ret extitisse. Dignum itaque qui a diis proximus habeatur,

---

3 This is the battle of the Crocus Field in 352.

them was impossible. So when the Phocians had their 8
lands, children and wives taken from them, they became
desperate and, led by a certain Philomelus, they as though
in anger with the god seized the temple of Apollo at Delphi. Enriched with the gold and money from there, they 9
hired mercenaries and attacked the Thebans. The action 10
of the Phocians, although cursed by everyone for the sacrilege, raised greater hostility against the Thebans, by
whom they had been driven to such desperate measures,
than it did against the Phocians themselves. So they were 11
sent reinforcements by both the Athenians and the Spartans. In the first engagement Philomelus robbed the The- 12
bans of their camp. In the next battle he, fighting in the 13
thick of it, was the first to fall and paid the price of his
sacrilege with his impious blood. In his place Onomarchus 14
was made general.

2. To face him the Thebans and the Thessalians, fearing the power victory might give him, chose as leader not
one of their own citizens, but Philip, king of Macedonia, 2
and willingly yielded to foreigners power they feared in
their own people. So Philip, as if he were punishing sacri- 3
lege, not the Thebans, ordered all his soldiers to put on
laurel crowns and like that marched into battle as if led by
the god. The Phocians, sighting the god's emblems and 4
being conscious of their misdeeds, flung down their weapons in terror and started to flee, and they paid for their
desecration with their own blood and slaughter.[3] It is in- 5
credible how much glory this incident brought Philip
among all nations: he was the avenger of sacrilege, he was 6
the champion of religion; for a crime that the world's
forces should have united to avenge only he had come
to demand atonement! So, worthy of being considered 7

8 per quem deorum maiestas vindicata sit. Sed Athenienses audito belli eventu, ne in Graeciam Philippus transiret, angustias Thermopylarum pari ratione sicuti antea advenientibus Persis occupavere, sed nequaquam simili aut
9 virtute aut causa: siquidem tunc pro libertate Graeciae, nunc pro sacrilegio publico, tunc a rapina hostium templa vindicaturi, nunc adversus vindices templorum raptores
10 defensuri; aguntque propugnatores sceleris, cuius turpe
11 erat alios vindices fuisse, inmemores prorsus, quod in dubiis rebus suis illo deo etiam consiliorum auctore usi fuerant, quod illo duce tot bella victores inierant, tot urbes auspicato condiderant, tantum imperium terra marique quaesierant, quod nihil sine maiestate numinis eius aut
12 privatae umquam aut publicae rei gesserant. Tantum facinus admisisse ingenia omni doctrina exculta, pulcherrimis legibus institutisque formata, ut quid posthac suscenseri iure barbaris possit non haberent.

3. Sed nec Philippus melioris fidei adversus socios fuit.
2 Quippe veluti timens, ne ab hostibus sacrilegii scelere vinceretur, civitates, quarum paulo ante dux fuerat, quae sub auspiciis eius militaverant, quae gratulatae illi sibique vic-
3 toriam fuerant, hostiliter occupatas diripuit; coniuges li-
4 berosque omnium sub corona vendidit; non deorum inmortalium templis, non aedibus sacris, non diis penatibus publicis privatisque, ad quos paulo ante ingressus hospita-
5 liter fuerat, pepercit: prorsus ut non tam sacrilegii ultor extitisse quam sacrilegiorum licentiam quaesisse videre-
6 tur. Inde veluti rebus egregie gestis in Thraciam traicit,

---

4 That is, Apollo.

second to the gods was the man who had championed the
gods! But the Athenians on hearing of the outcome of the   8
battle occupied the pass at Thermopylae to stop Philip
from entering Greece, just as they had done earlier when
the Persians were coming, but now not with the same
courage or purpose; for then it was for the liberty of   9
Greece, now over state sacrilege; then to protect temples
from enemy pillaging, now to defend temple pillagers
against an avenging army; and they were acting as defend-   10
ers of a crime, vindicating which would have been disgraceful for others, evidently forgetting that in their own   11
difficult times it was that god[4] whose advice they had followed, that under his leadership they had marched successfully into so many wars, founded so many cities with
favorable auspices, and won so great an empire on land
and sea; and that they had never embarked on any enterprise either privately or publicly without his divine sanction. That such a crime had been committed by intellects   12
steeped in all manner of learning and shaped by the most
enlightened laws and institutions meant that they thereafter had no right to rage against barbarians!

3. But Philip was no more loyal to his allies. Indeed as   2
if fearing to be outdone by his enemies in the crime of
sacrilege, he overran and pillaged states of which he had
shortly before been the leader, which had fought under his
command and been congratulating him and themselves on
victory; wives and children in all of them he sold off; nei-   3
4
ther temples of the immortal gods did he spare nor holy
shrines nor public and private guardian deities whose
presence he had recently entered as a guest, so that he   5
actually seemed less an avenger of sacrilege than one who
had sought license for sacrilege. Then as if he had achieved   6

177

ubi bello pari perfidia gesto captisque per dolum et occisis finitimis regibus universam provinciam imperio Macedo-
7 niae adiungit. Deinde ad abolendam invidiae famam, qua insignis praeter ceteros tunc temporis habebatur, per
8 regna mittit et opulentissimas civitates, qui opinionem sererent regem Philippum magna pecunia locare et muros per civitates et fana ac templa facienda, et ut per prae-
9 cones susceptores sollicitarent. Qui cum in Macedoniam venissent, variis dilationibus frustrati, vim regiae maiesta-tis timentes taciti proficiscebantur.

10 Post haec Olynthios adgreditur; receperant enim per misericordiam post caedem unius duos fratres eius, quos Philippus ex noverca genitos veluti participes regni inter-
11 ficere gestiebat. Ob hanc igitur causam urbem antiquam et nobilem exscindit et fratres olim destinato supplicio tradit praedaque ingenti pariter et parricidii voto fruitur.
12 Inde, quasi omnia quae agitasset animo ei licerent, auraria
13 in Thessalia, argenti metalla in Thracia occupat, et ne quod ius vel fas inviolatum praetermitteret, piraticam quoque exercere instituit.

14 His ita gestis forte evenit, ut eum fratres duo, reges Thraciae, non contemplatione iustitiae eius, sed invicem metuentes, ne alterius viribus accederet, disceptationum

---

5 Seel's emendation of the MSS' "Cappadocia," which makes no sense; the Thracian Chersonese may be presumed ("Chal-cidiam" Bongars).

6 The serious campaign against the Olynthians began in 349/8. Demosthenes, particularly in his Olynthiac orations, is a major, if hardly dispassionate, source. Philip's immediate aim in Thrace was the kingdom of Cersebleptes.

glorious successes he went over into Thrace,[5] where, in an equally treacherous war, capturing by subterfuge and killing neighboring kings, he annexed all its territory to the Macedonian Empire. Then, to remove the ill repute he 7 had earned, being now more infamous than anyone of that time, he sent men through kingdoms and richest city-states to spread the word that King Philip was spending 8 large amounts of money on building walls, shrines, and temples throughout the various states, and that by using heralds they should seek out contractors. When these 9 reached Macedonia they were put off with various excuses and, fearing the violence of his rule, quietly slipped away.

After this he attacked the Olynthians; for they had from 10 pity given refuge to two of his half brothers,[6] his step-mother's sons[7]—having already murdered one he was eager to kill them as possible claimants to the throne. So for 11 this reason he destroyed their famous old city, consigned the brothers to their preordained fate, and enjoyed the massive plunder and the fratricide he wished for. Then, as 12 if allowed anything he could envisage he seized gold mines in Thessaly and silver mines in Thrace, and to leave no 13 human or holy law unbroken he also turned his hand to piracy.[8]

After that it so happened that two brothers, kings of 14 Thrace, chose him as arbitrator of their disagreements, not with his justice in mind but each simply fearing that

[7] Gygaea: above, 7.4.5.

[8] The gold mines of Pangaeum were in Thrace, not Thessaly; nor had Thessaly any silver mines. The accusation of piracy is also false.

15 suarum iudicem eligerent. Sed Philippus more ingenii sui ad iudicium veluti ad bellum inopinantibus fratribus instructo exercitu supervenit regnoque utrumque non iudicis more, sed fraude latronis ac scelere spoliavit.

4. Dum haec aguntur, legati Atheniensium petentes
2 pacem ad eum venerunt. Quibus auditis et ipse legatos Athenas cum pacis condicionibus misit; ibique ex com-
3 modo utrorumque pax facta. Ex ceteris quoque Graeciae civitatibus non pacis amore, sed belli metu legationes ve-
4 nere; siquidem crudescente ira Thessali Boeotiique orant, ut professum adversus Phocenses ducem Graeciae exhi-
5 beat; tanto odio Phocensium ardentes, ut obliti cladium suarum perire ipsi quam non perdere eos praeoptarent, expertamque Philippi crudelitatem pati quam parcere ho-
6 stibus suis mallent. Contra Phocensium legati adhibitis Lacedaemoniis et Atheniensibus bellum deprecabantur,
7 cuius ab eo dilationem ter iam emerant. Foedum prorsus miserandumque spectaculum, Graeciam etiamnunc et viribus et dignitate orbis terrarum principem, regum certe gentiumque semper victricem et multarum adhuc urbium dominam alienis excubare sedibus aut rogantem bellum
8 aut deprecantem; in alterius ope spem omnem posuisse orbis terrarum vindices, eoque discordia sua civilibusque bellis redactos, ut adulentur ultro sordidam paulo ante
9 clientelae suae partem, et haec potissimum facere Thebanos Lacedaemoniosque, antea inter se imperii, nunc gratiae imperantis aemulos.

---

9 For their various accounts of the embassies of 347 and 346, see Dem. 19 and Aeschin. 2, and from shortly after the Peace of Philocrates, Dem. 5. See also *AO* 318ff.

the other might outdo him. But true to his nature Philip   15
appeared for the case as if for a war with an army in battle
order, taking the brothers by surprise and, not as an arbiter but with a thief's duplicity robbed them both of the
kingdom.

4. While this was happening Athenian delegates came
to him suing for peace.[9] After hearing them he in turn sent   2
ambassadors to Athens with peace conditions; and there a
peace was concluded satisfactory to both parties. From   3
the other Greek city-states delegations also arrived, not
from love of peace but fear of war; for as their anger in-   4
creased the Thessalians and Boeotians were begging him
to show himself the leader of Greece against the Phocians
that he had professed to be; such was their burning hatred   5
for the Phocians that, forgetting their own defeats, they
preferred to die themselves rather than not destroy them,
and to face Philip's cruelty, which they had already experienced, rather than spare their enemies. However, dele-   6
gates from the Phocians, supported by the Spartans and
Athenians, were begging him to avoid war, having already
on three occasions bought a postponement from him. A   7
truly terrible and wretched sight this was: Greece, even
now the world's leader in strength and reputation, a country ever the conqueror of kings and nations and still mistress of many cities, keeping watch at foreign courts and
either calling for war or begging to avoid it; to think that   8
the liberators of the world had all their hopes placed in
another's aid, and that by their own discord and civil wars
they were so reduced as to be fawning on what just recently was one of their paltry client-states, and especially   9
to see Thebans and Spartans doing so, men earlier rivals
for supreme power but now only for a despot's favor!

181

10   Philippus inter haec venditatione gloriae suae tantarum urbium fastidium agitat atque utros potius dignetur
11 aestimat. Secreto igitur auditis utrisque legationibus his
veniam belli pollicetur, iure iurando adactis responsum
nemini prodituros; illis contra venturum se auxiliumque
12 laturum; utrosque vetat parare bellum aut metuere. Sic
variato responso securis omnibus Thermopylarum angustias occupat.

    5. Tunc primum Phocenses captos se fraude Philippi
2 animadvertentes trepidi ad arma confugiunt. Sed neque
spatium erat instruendi belli nec tempus ad contrahenda
auxilia; et Philippus excidium minabatur, ni fieret deditio.
$\frac{3}{4}$ Victi igitur necessitate pacta salute se dediderunt. Sed
pactio eius fidei fuit, cuius antea fuerat deprecati belli
5 promissio. Igitur caeduntur passim rapiunturque; non liberi parentibus, non coniuges maritis, non deorum simu-
6 lacra templis suis relinquuntur. Vnum tantum miseris solacium fuit, quod, cum Philippus portione praedae socios
fraudasset, nihil rerum suarum apud inimicos viderunt.

7   Reversus in regnum, ut pecora pastores nunc in hiber-
nos, nunc in aestivos saltus traiciunt, sic ille populos et
urbes, ut illi vel replenda vel derelinquenda quaeque loca
8 videbantur, ad libidinem suam transfert. Miseranda ubi-
9 que facies et excidio similis erat. Non quidem pavor ille
hostilis nec discursus per urbem militum erat, non tumul-
10 tus armorum, non bonorum atque hominum rapina, sed
tacitus maeror et luctus, verentibus, ne ipsae lacrimae pro

Philip, meanwhile, flaunting his supremacy, affected 10
disdain for such great cities and pondered which of the
two he should favor. So holding private audiences with 11
each embassy he promised one he would not go to war,
binding them on oath not to divulge his reply to anyone,
and the other he promised to join and bring aid; and both
he told not to prepare for war or have any fear. Everyone 12
thus feeling secure with his different replies he seized the
pass at Thermopylae.

5. Then the Phocians, aware for the first time that they
had been caught in Philip's trap, rushed to arms in panic.
But there was neither opportunity to prepare for war nor 2
time to gather support; and Philip was threatening destruction if they did not surrender. So from sheer necessity 3
they bargained for their lives and surrendered. But his 4
commitment was as trustworthy as his earlier promise of
avoiding war. So they were slaughtered and plundered 5
everywhere; parents were not left their children, nor husbands their wives, nor temples their statues of the gods.
There was only one consolation for the pitiful survivors: 6
since Philip had cheated his allies of their share of the
plunder, they saw none of their property in their enemies'
hands.

Returning to his kingdom, Philip was just like shep- 7
herds driving flocks now into winter and now into summer
pastures: he indiscriminately transplanted peoples and cities as he felt regions needed populating or depopulating.
Everywhere it was a wretched sight and like total destruc- 8
tion. While there was not the panic an enemy inspires, no 9
troops running around in a city, no armed melee, no plundering of property and no abduction of people, there was 10
a silent, forlorn dejection, with people afraid that their

11 contumacia haberentur. Crescit dissimulatione ipsa dolor,
12 hoc altius demissus, quo minus profiteri licet. Nunc sepulcra maiorum, nunc veteres penates, nunc tecta, in quibus
13 geniti erant quibusque genuerant, considerabant, miserantes nunc vicem suam, quod in eam diem vixissent, nunc
filiorum, quod non post eam diem nati essent.

6. Alios populos in finibus ipsis hostibus opponit; alios
in extremis regni terminis statuit; quosdam bello captos in
2 supplementis urbium dividit. Atque ita ex multis gentibus
nationibusque unum regnum populumque constituit.

3 Conpositis ordinatisque Macedoniae rebus Dardanos
4 ceterosque finitimos fraude captos expugnat. Sed nec a
proximis manus abstinet; siquidem Arrybam, regem Epiri,
uxori suae Olympiadi artissima cognatione iunctum, pel-
5 lere regno statuit atque Alexandrum, privignum eius, uxoris Olympiadis fratrem, puerum honestae pulchritudinis,
6 in Macedoniam nomine sororis arcessit, omnique studio
sollicitatum spe regni simulato amore ad stupri consuetu-
dinem perpulit, maiora in eo obsequia habiturus sive con-
7 scientiae pudore sive regni beneficio. Cum igitur ad XX
annos pervenisset, ereptum Arrybae regnum puero admo-
8 dum tradit, scelestus in utroque. Nam nec in eo ius cognationis servavit, cui ademit regnum, et eum, cui dedit, inpu-
dicum fecit ante quam regem.

---

10 We are in 344/3. On Arrybas cf. above, 7.6.10ff.; he was
expelled in 342 (Dem. 7.32; Diod. Sic. 16.72.1).

very tears could be seen as opposition. Grief is itself in- 11
creased by dissimulation; the less expression it is given the
deeper it goes. Now they would wistfully contemplate the 12
tombs of their forefathers, now their ancient family deities, now the houses in which they were born and had
produced children, and they thought ruefully now of their 13
own fate in living to that day, now their children's in not
being born after that day.

6. Some of these peoples he placed right on their borders to face his enemies; others he settled on his frontiers;
and some prisoners of war he distributed to increase city
populations. And so from a multitude of peoples and tribes 2
he made one kingdom and one people.

With Macedonian affairs organized and settled he then 3
took the Dardanians and his other neighbors by surprise
and overwhelmed them.[10] But he did not even keep his 4
hands off his closest relatives; for he decided to drive Arrybas, king of Epirus, from his throne, a man who was a
very close blood relation of his wife Olympias, and he also 5
summoned to Macedonia in his sister's name Arrybas'
stepson Alexander, a handsome and virtuous young boy
and brother of his own wife Olympias; and after doing 6
everything to seduce him by promising him his step-
father's throne and feigning love for him, he drove him
into a homosexual liaison so as to have him more submis-
sive either from a guilty conscience or by the prospect of
the kingdom. So when he reached the age of twenty, he 7
gave him, just a boy, the throne he had taken from Arrybas,
thus being a villain to both. For he did not respect kinship 8
rights for the one from whom he took the kingdom, and
the one to whom he gave it he made a catamite and then
a king.

LIBER IX

1. In Graeciam Philippus cum venisset, sollicitatus pauca-
rum civitatium direptione et ex praeda modicarum urbium quantae opes universarum essent animo prospiciens,
2 bellum toti Graeciae inferre statuit. In cuius emolumen-
tum egregie pertinere ratus, si Byzantium, nobilem et
maritimam urbem, receptaculum terra marique copiis
suis futurum, in potestatem redegisset, eandem clauden-
3 tem sibi portas obsidione cinxit. Haec namque urbs condita primo a Pausania, rege Spartanorum, et per septem
annos possessa fuit; dein variante victoria nunc Lacedae-
4 moniorum, nunc Atheniensium iuris habita est, quae
incerta possessio effecit, ut nemine quasi suam auxiliis
5 iuvante libertatem constantius tueretur. Igitur Philippus
longa obsidionis mora exhaustus pecuniae conmercium de
6 piratica mutuatur. Captis itaque CLXX navibus mercium
et distractis anhelantem inopiam paululum recreavit.
7 Deinde, ne unius urbis obpugnatione tantus exercitus te-
neretur, profectus cum fortissimis multas Chersonensi ur-
8 bes expugnat, filiumque Alexandrum, decem et octo annos

---

1 The year is 340 (Diod. Sic. 16.74); Philip's assault began with
Perinthus, near Byzantium. For Pausanias see above, 2.15.14ff.,
and *AO* 67f. But Byzantium was founded in the seventh century
BC, not by Pausanias two centuries later.

BOOK IX

1. When Philip came into Greece, lured by the prospect of looting a few states, and then assessed from the plunder taken from some quite small cities the collective wealth of all of them, he decided to make war on all of Greece.[1] To 2 help that along he felt it might be very useful if he brought under his power the famous maritime city of Byzantium as a safe base for his land and sea forces, and when it closed its gates on him he laid siege to it. Now this city was 3 first founded by Pausanias, king of the Spartans, and for seven years it had remained under him; then as victory fluctuated it was at one time under the Spartans and at another under the Athenians, and the uncertainty of pos- 4 session meant that with no one claiming it as its own it retained its independence all the more firmly. Philip, ex- 5 hausted by a long-protracted siege, now turned to piracy to raise money. So capturing a hundred and seventy mer- 6 chant ships and selling off their cargoes, he briefly relieved his acute financial problems. Then, for such a huge force 7 not to be held up in the siege of one city, he setting off with his strongest troops stormed many cities in the Cher- sonese, and he summoned his son Alexander, who was 8

natum, ut sub militia patris tirocinii rudimenta deponeret,
9 ad se arcessit. In Scythiam quoque praedandi causa profectus est, more negotiantium inpensas belli alio bello
refecturus.

2. Erat eo tempore rex Scytharum Atheas, qui cum
bello Histrianorum premeretur, auxilium a Philippo per
Apollonienses petit, in successionem eum regni Scythiae
2 adoptaturus; cum interim Histrianorum rex decedens et
3 metu belli et auxiliorum necessitate Scythas solvit. Itaque
Atheas remissis Macedonibus nuntiari Philippo iubet, neque auxilium eius se petisse neque adoptionem mandasse;
4 nam neque vindicta Macedonum egere Scythas, quibus
meliores forent, neque heredem sibi incolumi filio deesse.
5 His auditis Philippus legatos ad Atheam mittit inpensae
obsidionis portionem petentes, ne inopia deserere bellum
6 cogatur; quod eo promptius eum facere debere, quod missis a se in auxilium eius militibus ne sumptum quidem
7 viae, non modo officii pretia dederit. Atheas inclementiam
caeli et terrae sterilitatem causatus, quae non patrimoniis
ditet Scythas, sed vix alimentis exhibeat, respondit nullas
8 sibi opes esse, quibus tantum regem expleat; et turpius
9 putare parvo defungi quam totum abnuere; Scythas autem
virtute animi et duritia corporis, non opibus censeri.

---

2 Alexander was in fact some sixteen years old and according
to Plut. *Vit. Alex.* 9 was left in charge in Macedonia.

3 Diodorus Siculus (16.1.5) obviously knew of the following
episode, but Justin is the only extant source. See in general T. S.
Brown, "Herodotus and Justin 9.2," *The Ancient History Bulletin*
2 (1988): 1ff. The Histriani were presumably a people dwelling
by the Danube (Ister).

eighteen years old, for him to have his early training under
his father's command.[2] He also set off into Scythia on a   9
marauding expedition, to recoup like the merchants one
war's expenses with profits from another.

2. At that time the king of the Scythians was Atheas,
who since he was in difficulty in a war with the Histriani
sought support from Philip through the people of Apollonia, agreeing to accept him as heir to the kingdom of
Scythia;[3] but when the king of the Histriani died in the   2
meantime he freed the Scythians from both fear of war
and need of any auxiliaries. So Atheas sent back the Mace-   3
donians and had a message taken to Philip that he had
neither requested his help nor ordered his adoption; for   4
Scythians had no need of Macedonians to defend them,
he said, since they were their superiors, and still having a
living son he did not lack an heir. On hearing that Philip   5
sent envoys to Atheas asking for some of the expenses of
the siege[4] so he would not be forced to abandon the campaign through lack of funds; and he should the more read-   6
ily supply them, he said, because when troops had been
sent to his assistance by him, he had not even paid for their
journey, much less their service. Atheas proffered the ex-   7
cuse of his kingdom's harsh climate and poor soil, which
so far from enriching the Scythians barely kept them fed,
and said that he had not the resources to meet such a great
king's needs; and he felt discharging part of his debt more   8
insulting than completely defaulting; The Scythians were   9
known for their courage and physical strength, not wealth,
he said.

4 That is, of Byzantium.

10 Quibus inrisus Philippus soluta obsidione Byzantii Scythica bella adgreditur, praemissis legatis, quo securiores
faceret, qui nuntient Atheae: dum Byzantium obsidet,
11 vovisse se statuam Herculi, ad quam in ostio Histri po-
nendam se venire, pacatum accessum ad religionem dei
12 petens, amicus ipse Scythis venturus. Ille, si voto fungi
vellet, statuam sibi mitti iubet; non modo ut ponatur, verum etiam ut inviolata maneat pollicetur; exercitum autem
13 fines ingredi negat se passurum. Ac si invitis Scythis statuam ponat, eo digresso sublaturum versurumque aes sta-
14 tuae in aculeos sagittarum. His utrimque inritatis animis
proelium committitur. Cum virtute et animo praestarent
15 Scythae, astu Philippi vincuntur. XX milia puerorum ac
feminarum capta, pecoris magna vis, auri argentique nihil.
16 Ea primum fides inopiae Scythicae fuit. XX milia nobilium
equarum ad genus faciendum in Macedoniam missa.

3. Sed revertenti ab Scythia Triballi Philippo occurrunt; negant se transitum daturos, ni portionem praedae
2 accipiant. Hinc iurgium et mox proelium; in quo ita in
femore vulneratus est Philippus, ut per corpus eius equus
3 interficeretur. Cum omnes occisum putarent, praeda
amissa est. Ita Scythica velut devota spolia paene luctuosa
Macedonibus fuere.

4 Vbi vero ex vulnere primum convaluit, diu dissimula-
5 tum bellum Atheniensibus infert, quorum causae Thebani

---

5 The Danube.

6 Cf. Marsyas of Pella, *FGrH* 135/6 F 17, without comment
on the horse's fate.

7 For events leading up to the battle of Chaeronea in 338, see
also Dem. 18.

Mocked in this way Philip raised the siege of Byzan- 10
tium and began his Scythian wars, sending envoys ahead
to make his enemy feel more secure and to inform Atheas
that, during his siege of Byzantium, he had vowed a statue
to Hercules, that he was now coming to erect it at the 11
mouth of the Ister,[5] and that he requested safe passage
to discharge his religious obligations to the god since he
would come in person as the Scythians' friend. Atheas told 12
him that, if he wished to discharge his vow, the statue must
be sent to him, and he promised that it would not only be
erected but also remain inviolate; but he would not allow
the army into his territory. And if he erected the statue 13
against the will of the Scythians, he would remove it after
he left and turn the statue's bronze into arrowheads. With 14
such squabbling between the two they clashed in battle.
Although the Scythians were superior in valor and spirit,
they were defeated by Philip's cunning. Twenty thousand 15
children and women were captured, and a large number of cattle, but no gold or silver. That was the first confirmation of the poverty of the Scythians. Twenty thousand 16
thoroughbred mares were sent to Macedonia for breed-
ing.

3. But when returning from Scythia, Philip encountered the Triballians, who said they would refuse him passage unless given part of his plunder. There was a dispute 2
and soon a battle; and in it Philip received a wound to the
thigh such that the weapon passed through him and killed
his horse.[6] Since everyone thought him dead, the plunder 3
was lost. So as if under a curse the Scythian spoils almost
brought the Macedonians grief.

But as soon as he recovered from his wound he brought 4
on the Athenians a war that he had long been hiding,[7] and 5

se iunxere, metuentes, ne victis Atheniensibus veluti vici-
6 num incendium belli ad se transiret. Facta igitur inter
duas paulo ante infestissimas civitates societate legationibus Graeciam fatigant; communem hostem putant com-
7 munibus viribus submovendum; neque enim cessaturum
Philippum, si prospere prima successerint, nisi omnem
8 Graeciam domuerit. Motae quaedam civitates Atheniensibus se iungunt; quasdam autem ad Philippum belli me-
9 tus traxit. Proelio commisso, cum Athenienses longe maiore militum numero praestarent, adsiduis bellis indurata
10 virtute Macedonum vincuntur. Non tamen inmemores
pristinae gloriae cecidere; quippe adversis vulneribus omnes loca, quae tuenda a ducibus acceperant, morientes
11 corporibus texerunt. Hic dies universae Graeciae et gloriam dominationis et vetustissimam libertatem finivit.

4. Huius victoriae callide dissimulata laetitia. Denique
non solita sacra Philippus illa die fecit, non in convivio
risit, non ludos inter epulas adhibuit, non coronas aut
unguenta sumpsit, et quantum in illo fuit, ita vicit, ut vic-
2 torem nemo sentiret. Sed nec regem se Graeciae, sed
3 ducem appellari iussit. Atque ita inter tacitam laetitiam et
dolorem hostium temperavit, ut neque apud suos exul-
4 tasse neque apud victos insultasse videretur. Atheniensibus, quos passus infestissimos fuerat, et captivos gratis
remisit et bello consumptorum corpora sepulturae reddi-

---

[8] The Athenian side.   [9] In fact, the Athenians and their
allies probably outnumbered Philip's forces only slightly (about
35,000 to 32,000).   [10] Philip's reaction as here portrayed
contrasts markedly with Diod. Sic. 16.87 (though there Demades
changes the king's demeanor) and Plut. *Vit. Dem.* 20.3.

the Thebans joined their side,[8] fearing that if they were defeated the war could spread to them like a neighbor's fire. An alliance was therefore arranged between two city- 6 states that shortly before were mortal enemies, and they plied Greece with deputations; their common enemy they thought should be repelled by their joint forces for Philip 7 would not let up, if he had success at the start, without subjugating all of Greece. Some of the states were per- 8 suaded and joined the Athenians; others, however, were drawn to Philip by fear of war. When battle was joined, 9 although the Athenians had far superior numbers they were defeated by a Macedonian valor honed by incessant warfare.[9] But they did not fall forgetting their glory of old; 10 for with frontal wounds they all with their dying bodies covered the posts they been given to defend by their gen- erals. This day was for all Greece the end of both her 11 glorious supremacy and her ancient liberty.

4. Joy over this victory was shrewdly concealed.[10] In fact Philip did not offer his usual sacrifices that day, did not laugh at dinner, allowed no games during the feasting, and did not put on garlands or perfume; and as much as he could he conquered with no one feeling him a con- queror. He insisted on being addressed not as "king of 2 Greece" but as "general." And between his silent joy and 3 the distress of his enemies he was so restrained as to ap- pear neither to have gloated among his own men or been insulting toward the defeated. To the Athenians, whom he 4 had seen as his bitterest foes, he both released prisoners ransom free and also returned bodies of the dead for

dit, reliquiasque funerum ut ad sepulcra maiorum defer-
5 rent ultro hortatus est. Super haec Alexandrum filium cum
amico Antipatro, qui pacem cum his amicitiamque iunge-
6 ret, Athenas misit. Thebanorum porro non solum captivos,
7 verum etiam interfectorum sepulturam vendidit. Principes civitatis alios securi percussit, alios in exilium redegit,
8 bonaque omnium occupavit. Pulsos deinde per iniuriam
in patriam restituit. Ex horum numero trecentos exules
9 iudices rectoresque civitati dedit. Apud quos cum potentissimi quique rei eius ipsius criminis postularentur, quod
per iniuriam se in exilium egissent, huius constantiae fuerant, ut omnes se auctores faterentur meliusque cum re
publica actum, cum damnati essent quam cum restituti,
10 contenderent. Mira prorsus audacia: de iudicibus vitae
necisque suae, quemadmodum possunt, sententiam ferunt contemnuntque absolutionem, quam dare inimici
possunt, et quoniam rebus nequeunt ulcisci, verbis usur-
pant libertatem.

5. Conpositis in Graecia rebus Philippus omnium civitatum legatos ad firmandum rerum praesentium statum
2 evocari Corinthum iubet. Ibi pacis legem universae Graeciae pro meritis singularum civitatum statuit, consilium-
que omnium veluti unum senatum ex omnibus legit.
3 Soli Lacedaemonii et regem et leges contempserunt, servitutem, non pacem rati, quae non ipsis civitatibus con-
4 veniret, sed a victore ferretur. Auxilia deinde singularum
civitatum describuntur, sive adiuvandus ea manu rex op-
pugnante aliquo foret seu duce illo bellum inferendum.

---

[11] On the agreement made at Corinth, see also Dem. 17 and
the inscription translated as Harding no. 99.

burial, and he actually encouraged them to carry the remains to the tombs of their forefathers. In addition he sent 5 his son Alexander, together with his friend Antipater, to Athens to conclude a peace treaty and alliance with them. For Thebans, however, he put a price not only on prison- 6 ers but even on burial of their dead. In the case of their 7 state's leading citizens he had some beheaded, others he drove into exile, and he seized everybody's property. He 8 then repatriated those unjustly driven out. Three hundred of them he made state judges and governors. When all 9 the most powerful citizens were arraigned before these charged with unlawfully driving them into exile, they remained so unrelenting that they all declared themselves guilty and insisted the state had been better served by their exile than by their restoration. This was certainly 10 audacious: they were, as far as they could, delivering a verdict on judges who had power of life and death over them and they rejected any acquittal their enemies could grant them; and since they could not take revenge by action, they asserted their freedom in words.

5. Matters now settled in Greece, Philip had delegates summoned to Corinth from all the states to ratify the present situation.[11] There he stipulated peace conditions for 2 all Greece based on the merits of its various states, and chose a common council, like one senate, from all of them. Only the Spartans showed contempt both for the king and 3 his terms, thinking that whatever was not agreed on by the city-states themselves but imposed by a conqueror was not peace. A list was then drawn up of auxiliary forces from 4 each state either for assisting the king if he were attacked or for conducting offensive war under his leadership.

5 Neque enim dubium erat imperium Persarum his appara-
6 tibus peti. Summa auxiliorum CC milia peditum fuere et
7 equitum XV milia. Extra hanc summam et Macedoniae
exercitus erant et confinis domitarum gentium barbaria.
8 Initio veris tres duces in Asiam Persarum iuris praemittit,
9 Parmenionem, Amyntam et Attalum, cuius sororem nuper
expulsa Alexandri matre Olympiade propter stupri suspi-
tionem in matrimonium receperat.

6. Interea, dum auxilia a Graecia coeunt, nuptias Cleopatrae filiae et Alexandri, quem regem Epiri fecerat, cele-
2 brat. Dies erat pro magnitudine duorum regum, et con-
locantis filiam et uxorem ducentis, apparatibus insignis.
3 Sed nec ludorum magnificentia deerat; ad quorum spectaculum Philippus cum sine custodibus corporis medius
inter duos Alexandros, filium generumque, contenderet,
4 Pausanias, nobilis ex Macedonibus adulescens, nemini
suspectus, occupatis angustiis Philippum in transitu ob-
truncat diemque laetitiae destinatum foedum luctu fune-
5 ris facit. His primis pubertatis annis stuprum per iniuriam
passus ab Attalo fuerat, cuius indignitati haec etiam foedi-
6 tas accesserat. Nam perductum in convivium solutumque

---

12 Diod. Sic. 16.91 does not include Amyntas. Philip had no
need to divorce Olympias to marry another wife, who was Cleopatra, Attalus' *niece* (whom Arr. *Anab.* 3.6.5 calls Eurydice).

13 Alexander I of Epirus, Olympias' brother; cf. 8.6.4ff. On the
problem of Philip's murder in 336, see the diametrically opposed
views of R. Develin, "The Murder of Philip II," *Antichthon* 15
(1981): 86ff.; J. R. Ellis, "The Assassination of Philip II," in *Ancient Macedonian Studies in Honor of Charles F. Edson* (Thes-
saloniki, 1981), 99ff.; also W. Heckel, "Philip and Olympias (337/6

For there was no doubt that the Persian Empire was the 5
object of these preparations. In total the auxiliary troops 6
came to two hundred thousand infantry and fifteen thousand cavalry. Beside this total there were also the Mace- 7
donian armies and, on their borders, the subject barbarian
tribes. At the start of spring he sent three generals ahead 8
into the area of Asia that was under Persian rule: Parme- 9
nion, Amyntas, and Attalus, whose sister he had recently
taken in marriage, having divorced Alexander's mother
Olympias on suspicion of adultery.[12]

6. Meanwhile, as the auxiliary troops from Greece were
assembling, he celebrated the marriage of his daughter
Cleopatra to the Alexander whom he had made king of
Epirus.[13] The day was remarkable for sumptuous prepara- 2
tions in line with the greatness the two kings, one giving
away a daughter, the other taking a wife. But there was no 3
lack of magnificent games, either. As Philip, flanked by the
two Alexanders, his son and son-in-law, and without bodyguards, hurried to see them, Pausanias, a young Macedo- 4
nian nobleman, whom no one suspected, stood in a narrow
alley way and cut Philip down as he passed by, and ruined
with funerary sorrow a day earmarked for merriment. In 5
his early years of puberty he had been sexually abused by
Attalus, and to that indignity this further outrage had also
been added. For taking him into a banquet and getting 6

B.C.)," in *Classical Contributions. Studies in Honour of M. F. McGregor* (Locust Valley, NY, 1981), 51ff.; W. Heckel et al., "'The Giver of the Bride, the Bridegroom, and the Bride'": A Study of the Murder of Philip II and Its Aftermath," in T. Howe et al., *Ancient Historiography on War and Empire* (Oxford, 2017), 92–124.

mero Attalus non suae tantum, verum et convivarum libi-
dini velut scortorum iure subiecerat ludibriumque om-
7 nium inter aequales reddiderat. Hanc rem aegre ferens
8 Pausanias querelam Philippo saepe detulerat. Cum variis
frustrationibus non sine risu differretur et honoratum insuper ducatu adversarium cerneret, iram in ipsum Philippum vertit ultionemque, quam ab adversario non poterat,
ab iniquo iudice exegit.

7. Creditum est etiam inmissum ab Olympiade, matre
Alexandri, fuisse, nec ipsum Alexandrum ignarum pater-
2 nae caedis extitisset; quippe non minus Olympiada re-
pudium et praelatam sibi Cleopatram quam stuprum
3 Pausaniam doluisse. Alexandrum quoque regni aemulum
fratrem ex noverca susceptum timuisse; eoque factum, ut
in convivio antea primum cum Attalo, mox cum ipso patre
4 iurgaret, adeo ut etiam stricto gladio eum Philippus con-
sectatus sit aegreque a filii caede amicorum precibus exo-
5 ratus. Quamobrem Alexander ad avunculum se in Epirum
6 cum matre, inde ad reges Illyriorum contulerat; vixque
revocanti mitigatus est patri precibusque cognatorum
7 aegre redire conpulsus. Olympias quoque fratrem suum
Alexandrum, Epiri regem, in bellum subornabat pervicis-
8 setque, ni filiae nuptiis pater generum occupasset. His
stimulis irarum utrique Pausaniam de inpunitate stupri
sui querentem ad tantum facinus inpulisse creduntur.

him drunk with wine, Attalus had subjected him not only to his own carnal desires but also to his fellow diners', like a prostitute, and made him a laughingstock among his peers. Bitterly aggrieved over this incident, Pausanias had 7 often complained to Philip. When he was fobbed off with 8 various excuses, and not without ridicule, and could also see his enemy honored with the rank of general, he vented his rage on Philip himself and from an unfair judge took the revenge that he could not from his enemy.

7. It is also thought that Pausanias was set on him by Alexander's mother Olympias, and that Alexander himself had not been unaware of a plot to murder his father; for 2 Olympias was believed to have been no less aggrieved over her repudiation and Cleopatra being preferred to her than Pausanias was over his sexual abuse. It was also thought 3 that Alexander had feared rivalry for the throne with a brother born of his stepmother, and that this had led to his quarreling at a banquet, first with Attalus and then with Philip himself, and so acrimoniously that Philip even 4 lunged at him with sword drawn and was only with difficulty prevented from killing his son by entreaties from his friends. Because of this Alexander had gone with his 5 mother to his uncle in Epirus, and then on to the kings of Illyria; and when he was recalled by Philip he could barely 6 be reconciled with him and was only with difficulty made to return by entreaties from his relatives. Olympias was 7 also trying to induce her brother Alexander, king of Epirus, to go to war and would have succeeded had not the father anticipated her by offering this prospective son-in-law his daughter in marriage. Goaded by all this both men 8 are thought to have pushed Pausanias into a heinous crime when he complained about his abuse going unpunished.

9 Olympias certe fugienti percussori etiam equos habuit
10 praeparatos. Ipsa deinde audita regis nece cum titulo officii ad exequias cucurrisset, in cruce pendentis Pausaniae
capiti eadem nocte, qua venit, coronam auream inposuit,
quod nemo alius audere nisi haec superstite Philippi filio
11 potuisset. Paucos deinde post dies refixum corpus inter-
fectoris super reliquias mariti cremavit et tumulum ei
eodem fecit in loco parentarique eidem quotannis incussa
12 populo superstitione curavit. Post haec Cleopatram, a qua
pulsa Philippi matrimonio fuerat, in gremio eius prius filia
interfecta, finire vitam suspendio coegit, spectaculoque
pendentis ultionem potita est, ad quam per parricidium
13 festinaverat. Novissime gladium illum, quo rex percussus
est, Apollini sub nomine Myrtales consecravit, hoc enim
14 nomen ante Olympiadis parvulae fuit. Quae omnia ita palam facta sunt, ut timuisse videatur, ne facinus ab ea commissum non probaretur.

8. Decessit Philippus XL et septem annorum, cum
2 annis XXV regnasset. Genuit ex Larissaea saltatrice filium
3 Arridaeum, qui post Alexandrum regnavit. Habuit et multos alios filios ex variis matrimoniis regio more susceptos,
4 qui partim fato, partim ferro periere. Fuit rex armorum
5 quam conviviorum apparatibus studiosior, cui maximae
opes erant instrumenta bellorum; divitiarum quaestu
6 quam custodia sollertior. Itaque inter cotidianas rapinas

---

14 The crucifixion of Pausanias was either execution itself or
his corpse was crucified, which would be in line with Diodorus
Siculus' report that he was killed immediately after the murder.

15 She was also known under two other names, Polyxena and
Stratonice (Plut. *Mor.* 401a–b). The dedication of the sword also
appears at Val. Max. 1.8. ext. 9, possibly derived from Trogus.

Olympias at all events even had horses ready for the assas- 9
sin's getaway. She herself, on hearing of the king's assas- 10
sination, then hastened, seemingly out of duty, to the funeral, and on the very night she arrived she set a golden
wreath on Pausanias' head while he still hung on the
cross,[14] something that no one but she could done while
Philip's son was still alive. Then some days later when the 11
assassin's body was taken down she cremated it over her
husband's remains and erected a tomb for him in the same
place and inspiring superstition in the people had annual
funerary offerings made to him. After this she forced 12
Cleopatra, for whom Philip had divorced her, to hang herself, after first murdering her daughter in the mother's
arms; and with the sight of her rival hanging there she
achieved the revenge to which she had rushed by parricide. Finally she consecrated to Apollo the sword with 13
which the king was stabbed, doing it under the name Myr-
tale (for this was Olympias' name as a little girl[15]) All this 14
was so overtly done that she seems to have feared that the
crime might not be clearly seen to have been committed
by her.

8. Philip died at the age of forty-seven after reigning
for twenty-five years. By a dancer from Larissa he fathered 2
a son, Arridaeus, who reigned after Alexander. He also had 3
many other children from various marriages, as kings do,
some of whom died of natural causes, some by the sword.
He was a king with military rather than convivial interests, 4
one whose greatest treasures were the instruments of war; 5
and he was better at acquiring wealth than keeping it.
Thus despite his daily pillaging he always lacked funds. 6

7   semper inops erat. Misericordia in eo et perfidia pari iure
8   dilectae. Nulla apud eum turpis ratio vincendi. Blandus
    pariter et insidiosus, adloquio qui plura promitteret quam
9   praestaret; in seria et iocos artifex. Amicitias utilitate, non
    fide colebat. Gratiam fingere in odio, instruere inter con-
    cordantes odia, apud utrumque gratiam quaerere sollem-
10 nis illi consuetudo. Inter haec eloquentia et insignis oratio,
    acuminis et sollertiae plena, ut nec ornatui facilitas nec
    facilitati inventionum deesset ornatus.
11   Huic Alexander filius successit et virtute et vitiis patre
12 maior. Itaque vincendi ratio utrique diversa. Hic aperta,
    ille artibus bella tractabat. Deceptis ille gaudere hostibus,
13 hic palam fusis. Prudentior ille consilio, hic animo
14 magnificentior. Iram pater dissimulare, plerumque etiam
    vincere; hic ubi exarsisset, nec dilatio ultionis nec modus
15 erat. Vini nimis uterque avidus, sed ebrietatis diversa vitia.
    Patri mos erat etiam de convivio in hostem procurrere,
    manum conserere, periculis se temere offerre; Alexander
16 non in hostem, sed in suos saeviebat. Quam ob rem saepe
    Philippum vulneratum proelia remisere, hic amicorum
17 interfector convivio frequenter excessit. Regnare ille cum
    amicis nolebat, hic in amicos regna exercebat. Amari pater
18 malle, hic metui. Litterarum cultus utrique similis. Soller-
19 tiae pater maioris, hic fidei. Verbis atque oratione Philip-

---

16 Probably a rhetorical plural referring to the killing of Clei-
tus in 328 (below, 12.6).

Compassion and duplicity were qualities he prized equally.   7
For him no path to victory was dishonorable. Equally   8
charming and treacherous, he would promise more in talk
than he would deliver; in conversation both serious and
jovial he was a master. Friendships he cultivated for ad-   9
vantage, not with integrity. Feigning goodwill while feeling hatred, sowing discord between parties already agreeing and then trying to win the favor of both, that for him
was normal practice. In addition to this was eloquence and   10
brilliant oratory, full of shrewdness and insight, so that his
elegant style did not lack fluency nor his fluency stylistic
elegance.

He was succeeded by his son Alexander, who outdid his   11
father in both virtue and vices. Thus each had his own way   12
of winning. Alexander fought openly, Philip with trickery.
One took pleasure in duping his enemies, the other in
openly putting them to flight. One was more prudent in   13
strategy, the other had greater vision. The father could   14
hide his anger, and usually even suppress it; when Alexander's had flared up, there was no delaying vengeance and
no restraint. Both were over fond of wine, but their drunk-   15
enness brought out different deficiencies. The father's way
was to rush at the enemy from dinner, engage him in
combat and recklessly expose himself to danger; Alexander would vent his rage not on his enemy but his own men.
Thus Philip's battles often saw him brought back wounded;   16
the other often left dinner as murderer of his friends.[16]
The one refused to share royal power with his friends; the   17
other wielded his power over his. The father preferred
being loved, the son being feared. Both had similar literary   18
interests. The father had greater cunning, the son greater
loyalty. In language and discourse Philip was more tem-   19

20 pus, hic rebus moderatior. Parcendi victis filio animus et
promptior et honestior. Frugalitati pater, luxuriae filius
21 magis deditus erat. Quibus artibus orbis imperii fundamenta pater iecit, operis totius gloriam filius consum-
mavit.

perate, Alexander more so in his actions. In sparing the   20
defeated the son was readier and more magnanimous. The
father was more inclined to thrift, the son to extravagance.
With such qualities the father laid the foundations of a   21
worldwide empire; the son brought the whole glorious
work to completion.

LIBER X

1. Artaxerxi, regi Persarum, ex paelicibus centum quindecim filii fuere, sed tres tantum iusto matrimonio suscepti,
2 Darius, Ariaratus et Ochus. Ex his Darium contra morem
Persarum, apud quos rex non nisi morte mutatur, per in-
dulgentiam pater regem vivus fecit, nihil sibi ablatum exis-
3 timans, quod in filium contulisset, sinceriusque gaudium
ex procreatione capturus, si insignia maiestatis suae vivus
4 in filio conspexisset. Sed Darius post nova paternae pieta-
5 tis exempla interficiendi patris consilium cepit, sceleratus,
si solus parricidium cogitasset, tanto sceleratior, quod in
societatem facinoris adsumptos L fratres fecit parricidas.
6 Ostenti prorsus genus, ubi in tanto populo non solum so-
ciari, verum etiam sileri parricidium potuit, ut ex L liberis
nemo inventus sit, quem aut paterna maiestas aut veneratio senis aut indulgentia patris a tanta inmanitate revoca-
7 ret. Adeone vile paternum nomen apud tot numero filios
fuit, ut, quorum praesidio tutus etiam adversus hostes esse

---

1 Book 10 was lengthier than Justin's précis here, as its separate *Prologue* shows; perhaps he thought the bulk of it too unin-
teresting for his readers.

2 Artaxerxes II Mnemon (405–359), whose biography was
composed by Plutarch. Cf. Diod. Sic. 15.93.1 (the year 362/1).

BOOK X

1.[1] Artaxerxes,[2] king of the Persians, had one hundred and fifteen sons born from concubines, but only three from legitimate marriage, Darius, Ariaratus and Ochus. One of 2 them, Darius, was through the kindness of his father made king contrary the custom of the Persians, among whom the king is replaced only after death; Artaxerxes thought that nothing conferred on a son was taken from him, and 3 that he would have fuller joy from fatherhood if he saw the royal insignia on his son while still alive himself. But Dar- 4 ius after the novel display of paternal devotion decided on a plan for murdering his father, heinous enough, had he 5 plotted the parricide alone, but even more evil because by also bringing fifty of his brothers to join the crime he made them parricides as well. It is truly amazing that among so 6 many people a communal murder could not only be committed but also kept secret, and that not one of his fifty children could be found whom a father's dignity, respect for an old man, or consideration of a father's kindness could deter from such a heinous crime. Can the word 7 "father" have been so reviled among so many sons that one who should have been protected by them even against

debuerit, eorum insidiis circumventus tutior ab hostibus quam a filiis fuerit?

2 2. Causa parricidii sceleratior ipso parricidio fuit. Occiso quippe Cyro fraterno bello, cuius mentio supra habita est, Aspasian, paelicem eius, rex Artaxerxes in matrimo- 3 nium receperat. Hanc patrem cedere sibi sicuti regnum Darius postulaverat; qui pro indulgentia sua in liberos 4 primo facturum se dixerat, mox paenitentia ductus, ut honeste negaret quod temere promiserat, solis eam sacerdotio praefecit, quo perpetua illi ab omnibus viris pudici- 5 tia imperabatur. Hinc exacerbatus iuvenis in iurgia primo patris erupit, mox facta cum fratribus coniuratione, dum patri insidias parat, deprehensus cum sociis poenas parri- 6 cidii diis paternae maiestatis ultoribus dedit. Coniuges quoque omnium cum liberis, ne quod vestigium tanti sce- 7 leris extaret, interfectae. Post haec Artaxerxes morbo ex dolore contracto decedit, rex quam pater felicior.

3. Hereditas regni Ocho tradita, qui timens parem coniurationem regiam cognatorum caede et strage principum replet, nulla, non sanguinis, non sexus, non aetatis, misericordia permotus, scilicet ne innocentior fratribus parri- 2 cidis haberetur. Atque ita veluti purificato regno bellum 3 Cadusiis infert. In eo adversus provocatorem hostium

---

3 5.11.1ff. On Aspasia see Xen. *Anab.* 1.10.2; Plut. *Vit. Artax.* 26.3ff.—at 27.3 she is priestess of Artemis [Anaitis] at Ecbatana.
4 Artaxerxes III Ochus (359–338). See Diod. Sic. 17.5.3ff. Ochus was poisoned and his youngest son, Arses, placed on the throne; he too was murdered, just before the death of Philip in 336. Darius III then eliminated the dual murderer Bagoas. Darius ruled until 330; see Books 11 and 12.

enemies was instead engulfed by their treachery, safer from his enemies than from his sons?

2. The motive for the murder was more wicked than the murder itself. When Cyrus died in the war between 2 brothers, which was mentioned above, King Artaxerxes had taken Aspasia, his mistress, to be his wife.[3] Darius had 3 then insisted that his father cede her to him just as he had the kingdom; and he with his usual indulgence toward his children had at first agreed that he would, but soon regret- 4 ting it he, in order to withhold with honor what he had rashly promised, appointed her to the priesthood of the sun, in which lifelong abstinence from sex with all men was enforced on her. Enraged by this the young man first 5 broke into quarrels with his father, then hatched a conspiracy with his brothers, and when caught, together with his accomplices conspiring to prepare a coup against the father, he paid the penalty for murder to the gods who avenge disrespect for a father's dignity. The wives of all of 6 them, together with their children, were also put to death for no trace of such a heinous crime to survive. After this 7 Artaxerxes died of an illness brought on by grief, a happier king than father.

3. The kingdom was inherited by Ochus, who from fear of a similar conspiracy filled the palace with his kinsmen's blood and the slaughter of leading citizens,[4] being moved to pity by nothing, not family ties, not sex, not age, in order of course to appear no more innocent than his murderous brothers. And so after thus purifying the kingdom, as it 2 were, he attacked the Cadusians. When in that war an 3

Codomannus quidam cum omnium favore processisset,
hoste caeso victoriam suis pariter et prope amissam glo-
4 riam restituit. Ob haec decora idem Codomannus prae-
5 ficitur Armeniis. Interiecto deinde tempore post mortem
Ochi regis ob memoriam pristinae virtutis rex a populo
constituitur, Darii nomine, ne quid regiae maiestati de-
6 esset, honoratus; bellumque cum Alexandro Magno diu
7 variante fortuna magna virtute gessit. Postremo victus ab
Alexandro et a cognatis occisus vitam pariter cum Persarum regno finivit.

enemy soldier issued a challenge to single combat, a certain Codomannus came forward, cheered on by everyone, and killing his adversary he restored to his companions both victory and the glory they had almost lost. For these 4 glorious feats that same Codomannus was made prefect of Armenia. Then some time later, after King Ochus' death, 5 he was made king by his people from memory of his earlier courage and was honored with the name Darius so he not lack royal status; and he fought a long war with Alexander 6 the Great with intermittent success and great courage. Finally defeated by Alexander and killed by his relatives 7 he brought both his life and the Persian Empire to an end.

LIBER XI

1. In exercitu Philippi sicuti variae gentes erant, ita eo
2 occiso diversi motus animorum fuere. Alii quippe iniusta
3 servitute oppressi ad spem se libertatis erigebant, alii taedio longinquae militiae remissam sibi expeditionem gau-
4 debant, nonnulli facem nuptiis filiae accensam rogo patris
5 subditam dolebant. Amicos quoque tam subita mutatione
rerum haud mediocris metus ceperat, reputantes nunc
provocatam Asiam, nunc Europam nondum perdomitam,
6 nunc Illyrios, Thracas et Dardanos ceterasque barbaras
gentes fidei dubiae et mentis infidae; qui omnes populi si
7 pariter deficiant, sisti nullo modo posse. Quis rebus veluti
8 medela quaedam interventus Alexandri fuit, qui pro contione ita vulgus omne consolatus hortatusque pro tempore
est, ut et metum timentibus demeret et in spem omnes
9 inpelleret. Erat hic annos XX natus, in qua aetate ita mo-

---

[1] The translation of Books 11–15 is published separately in the
Clarendon Ancient History Series with a full commentary by
Waldemar Heckel, which I have consulted for these more modest
notes, and to which I direct the interested reader's attention. For
the period to 301, see *A History of Macedonia* vol. III, Part One
(Oxford, 1988) by N. G. L. Hammond.

[2] For Philip's death, see 9.6ff.

[3] This probably has a technical reference. The prominent

BOOK XI

1.[1] In Philip's army just as there were different nationalities, so with his death there were varied reactions.[2] Some 2
feeling oppressed in unjust servitude were roused to hope
of freedom; others from weariness of long campaigns were 3
happy to be spared the mission; and a number were sad- 4
dened that a torch lit for a daughter's marriage had been
put to her father's funeral pyre. His friends[3] had also been 5
taken with no slight fear by the sudden change in the situation, thinking now about Asia, which had been challenged, now about Europe, still not wholly subdued, and 6
now about the Illyrians, Thracians, Dardanians and other
barbarian tribes of dubious loyalty and fickle temperament; if all these peoples revolted, stopping them would
certainly be impossible.[4] To all this came, like some anti- 7
dote, the arrival of Alexander, who before an assembly 8
offered the whole crowd such timely consolation and encouragement that he removed anxiety from the fearful and
inspired hope in everybody. He was twenty years old, and 9

nobles of the king's entourage were known as *hetairoi*, "companions," but "friends" became another, semi-official term for them.
   [4] The major parallel narratives are Diod. Sic. 17, Curtius Rufus and Arrian, to which we can add Plutarch's biography. The
question of Trogus' immediate source is a vexed one.

derate de se multa pollicitus est, ut appareret plura eum
10   experimentis reservare. Macedonibus inmunitatem cunc-
tarum rerum praeter militiae vacationem dedit; quo facto
tantum sibi favorem omnium conciliavit, ut corpus homi-
nis, non virtutem regis mutasse se dicerent.

    2. Prima illi cura paternarum exequiarum fuit, in qui-
bus ante omnia caedis conscios ad tumulum patris occidi
2   iussit. Soli Alexandro Lyncestae ⟨parricidarum⟩ fratri
pepercit, servans in eo auspicium dignitatis suae; nam
3   regem eum primus salutaverat. Aemulum quoque imperii,
Caranum, fratrem ex noverca susceptum, interfici curavit.
4   Inter initia multas gentes rebellantes conpescuit, orientes
5   nonnullas seditiones extinxit. Quibus rebus erectus citato
gradu in Graeciam contendit, ubi exemplo patris Corinthum evocatis civitatibus dux in locum eius substituitur.
6   Inchoatum deinde a patre Persicum bellum adgreditur.
7   In cuius apparatu occupato nuntiatur Athenienses et Lacedaemonios ab eo ad Persas defecisse auctoremque eius
defectionis magno auri pondere a Persis corruptum De-
8   mosthenem oratorem extitisse, qui Macedonum deletas
omnes cum rege copias a Triballis adfirmaverit producto

---

    5 For what this might mean and individuals involved, see the
works cited in the note to 9.6. Alexander of Lyncestis was Antipater's son-in-law and was executed for treason in 329 after being
kept in chains for three years (see 11.7.1 and 12.14.1). Caranus is
widely held to be a fiction.

    6 Justin here reflects claims other than that Pausanias had
been a lone assassin; see the works referred to in the note to 9.6,
above. The text, however, is difficult, and the presence of "assassins" is conjectural.

at that age he showed great promise, with such restraint
that he seemed to have more in reserve for the future. To   10
the Macedonians he granted exemption from everything
but military service; and by this he won such support that
they said they had had a change in a man's body, not in
their king's valor.

2. His first concern was for his father's funeral, and
before all else he ordered those guilty of his killing to be
executed at his father's tomb.[5] Only Alexander of Lynces-   2
tis, the brother of the assassins,[6] did he spare, preserving
in him a good omen for his reign; for it was he who had
first saluted him as king. A rival for power, Caranus, his   3
half brother and his stepmother's son, he also had executed. Among his first actions was suppressing many in-   4
surgent peoples, and wiping out some incipient rebellions.
Emboldened by his success he swiftly marched into   5
Greece, where following his father's example he called the
city-states to Corinth and replaced him as their leader. He   6
then embarked on the Persian War started by his father.
While occupied with the preparations news arrived that   7
the Athenians and Spartans[7] had defected from him to the
Persians and that the instigator of that defection, bribed
with a large amount of gold by the Persians, had been the
orator Demosthenes, who, he was told, had claimed that   8
all the Macedonian forces, together with their king, had
been wiped out by the Triballians, and he had brought a

---

[7] The Spartans in fact had not joined the alliance nor did they
take action until later. Perhaps the Thebans belong here. For
Demosthenes and Athens, see *AO* 364f., 373ff. (the years 336/5
and 335/4).

in contionem auctore, qui in eo proelio, in quo rex cecide-
9   rit, se quoque vulneratum diceret. Qua opinione mutatos
omnium ferme civitatium animos esse; praesidia Macedo-
10 num obsideri. Quibus motibus occursurus tanta celeritate
instructo paratoque exercitu Graeciam oppressit, ut,
quem venire non senserant, videre se vix crederent.

3. In transitu hortatus Thessalos fuerat beneficiorum-
que Philippi patris maternaeque suae cum his ab Aeaci-
2 darum gente necessitudinis admonuerat. Cupide haec
Thessalis audientibus exemplo patris dux universae gentis
creatus erat et vectigalia omnia reditusque suos ei tradi-
3 derant. Sed Athenienses, sicuti primi defecerant, ita primi
4 paenitere coeperunt, contemptum hostis in admirationem
vertentes pueritiamque Alexandri spretam antea supra
5 virtutem veterum ducum extollentes. Missis itaque legatis
bellum deprecantur, quibus auditis et graviter increpatis
Alexander bellum remisit.

6   Inde Thebas exercitum convertit, eadem indulgentia
7 usurus, si parem paenitentiam invenisset. Sed Thebani
armis, non precibus nec deprecatione usi sunt. Itaque victi
gravissima quaeque supplicia miserrimae captivitatis ex-
8 perti sunt. Cum in concilio de excidio urbis deliberaretur,
Phocenses et Plataeenses et Thespienses et Orchomenii,
Alexandri socii victoriaeque participes, excidia urbium
9 suarum crudelitatemque Thebanorum referebant, studia
in Persas non praesentia tantum, verum et vetera adversus

---

8 There is no other evidence for Demosthenes taking Persian
bribes or for his supposed informant.

9 The Molossian royal house, of which Olympias was a mem-
ber, claimed descent from Neoptolemus, son of Achilles, and
Achilles came from Phthia, probably Pharsalus in Thessaly.

witness into the meeting to testify that in the battle in which the king fell he had also been wounded himself.[8] Believing this almost all city-states had a change of mind, 9 he said, and the Macedonian garrisons were under siege. To meet the uprisings, Alexander raised and equipped an 10 army and overran Greece with such speed that they could hardly believe they were seeing an army they had not realized was coming.

3. On his journey he had offered encouragement to the Thessalians and reminded them of his father Philip's services and his mother's connection with them from the Aeacids.[9] The Thessalians listening eagerly to this, he had, like 2 his father, been made commander of the whole people, and they had transferred all their taxes and revenues to him. But the Athenians, just as they had been the first to 3 defect, were also the first to have regrets, turning their 4 contempt for their enemy into admiration, and praising Alexander's youth, earlier scorned by them, more than the courage of their earlier leaders. So sending legates 5 they begged to be spared war, and after hearing them and sternly reprimanding them Alexander renounced war.

From there he turned his army toward Thebes intend- 6 ing to show the same mercy if he found similar regret. But 7 the Thebans resorted to arms, not appeals or entreaty. So after being defeated they suffered all the worst punishments of the most wretched captivity. When destruction 8 of their city was discussed in council, the Phocians, Plataeans, Thespians and Orchomenians, allies of Alexander and men who had shared his victory, kept referring to the destruction of their own cities and the ruthlessness of the Thebans, taunting them not only with their present but 9 also their earlier support of Persia against the freedom of

217

10 Graeciae libertatem increpantes, quam ob rem odium eos omnium populorum esse; quod vel ex eo manifestari, quod iure iurando se omnes obstrinxerint, ut victis Persis The-
11 bas diruerent. Adiciunt et scelerum priorum fabulas, quibus omnes scaenas repleverint, ut non praesenti tantum perfidia, verum et vetere infamia invisi forent.

4. Tunc Cleadas, unus ex captivis, data potestate dicendi: non a rege se defecisse, quem interfectum audie-
2 rint, sed a regis heredibus; quicquid in eo sit admissum, credulitatis, non perfidiae culpam esse, cuius tamen iam
3 magna se supplicia pependisse deleta iuventute. Nunc senum feminarumque sicuti infirmum, ita innoxium restare vulgus, quod ipsum stupris contumeliisque ita vexa-
4 tum esse, ut nihil amarius umquam sint passi; nec iam pro civibus se, qui tam pauci remanserint, orare, sed pro innoxio patriae solo et pro urbe, quae non viros tantum,
5 verum et deos genuerit. Privata etiam regem superstitione deprecatur geniti apud ipsos Herculis, unde originem gens Aeacidarum trahat, actaeque Thebis a patre eius Phi-
6 lippo pueritiae; rogat urbi parcat, quae maiores eius partim apud se genitos deos adoret, partim educatos summae
7 maiestatis reges viderit. Sed potentior fuit ira quam preces. Itaque urbs diruitur; agri inter victores dividuntur;

---

10 Most recently Plataea, Thespiae, and Orchomenus had been destroyed by Thebes in the 370s and 360s. Thebes had gone over to the Persians in 481, and in the aftermath the city was threatened (Hdt. 9.86ff.).   11 This character appears in no other source and may have been invented for the purpose of the speech (by Cleitarchus?).   12 Hercules (Heracles) was the mythical ancestor of the Macedonian royal house, which was in

Greece.[10] Because of this, they said, they were hated by everyone, which was clear from the fact that all had bound themselves with a solemn oath to destroy Thebes once the Persians were defeated. They also added tales of their earlier crimes, with which they filled all their plays, so they should be hated not only for their current treachery but also for their past infamy.

4. Then Cleadas, one of the prisoners,[11] was given permission to speak. The Thebans, he said, had defected not from the king, whom they heard had been killed, but from the king's heirs; and whatever wrong he had done must be blamed on credulity, not disloyalty, and for it they had already paid a heavy price with the loss of their young men. Now what remained was a crowd of old men and women, both enfeebled and harmless, themselves, having themselves been maltreated with violence and outrage more distressing than anything they had ever experienced; and now their entreaties were not for their citizens, so few of whom remained, but for the innocent soil of their country and a city that had given birth not only men but also to gods. He even appealed to him through his personal devotion to Hercules, who was born among them and from whom the Aeacid people traced its descent, and also through his father Philip's boyhood in Thebes;[12] and he asked him to spare a city that had worshipped his ancestors as gods, men who either had been born there or seen kings of the greatest majesty brought up there. But anger had more force than their entreaties. So the city was destroyed;

10

11

2

3

4

5

6

7

fact the Argeadae. Alexander's emulation of Hercules is constantly attested. For Philip in Thebes, see above, 7.5.1ff.

8 captivi sub corona venduntur, quorum pretium non ex
ementium commodo, sed ex inimicorum odio extenditur.
9 Miseranda res Atheniensibus visa; itaque portas refugis
10 profugorum contra interdictum regis aperuere. Quam
rem ita graviter tulit Alexander, ut secunda legatione denuo bellum deprecantibus ita demum remiserit, ut ora-
tores et duces, quorum fiducia totiens rebellent, sibi
11 dedantur; paratisque Atheniensibus, ne cogantur, subire
bellum, eo res deducta est, ut retentis oratoribus duces in
12 exilium agerentur, qui ex continenti ad Darium profecti
non mediocre momentum Persarum viribus accessere.

5. Proficiscens ad Persicum bellum omnes novercae
suae cognatos, quos Philippus in excelsiorem dignitatis
2 locum provehens imperiis praefecerat, interfecit. Sed nec
suis, qui apti regno videbantur, pepercit, ne qua materia
3 seditionis procul se agente in Macedonia remaneret et
reges stipendiarios conspectioris ingenii ad conmilitium
4 secum trahit, segniores ad tutelam regni relinquit. Adunato
deinde exercitu naves onerat, unde conspecta Asia incre-
dibili ardore mentis accensus duodecim aras deorum in
5 belli vota statuit. Patrimonium omne suum, quod in Macedonia Europaque habebat, amicis dividit, sibi Asiam suf-
6 ficere praefatus. Priusquam ulla navis litore excederet,
hostias caedit, petens victoriam bello, quo totiens a Persis
7 petitae Graeciae ultor electus sit, quibus longa iam satis et

---

13 Cf. *AO* 373ff. (the year 335/4).   14 "His stepmother's
relatives" in fact refers only to Cleopatra's uncle Attalus. Other
than Amyntas, son of Perdiccas, it is hard to imagine any potential
rivals for the throne. The kings mentioned are the Thracian
prince Sitalces and Ariston of Paeonia.

its lands were divided among the victors; captives were   8
sold at auction, prices rising not from buyers' wish for a
bargain but from hatred of their enemies. It seemed pitiful   9
to the Athenians; and so they opened their gates to the
refugees despite an interdiction by the king. Alexander   10
took this so seriously that, when they sent a second embassy to avert war, he finally let the envoys depart only on
condition that he have the orators and generals from confidence in whom they so often rebelled surrendered to
him;[13] and since the Athenians, in order not to be forced   11
into that, were ready to face war, the issue reached a point
where the orators were retained and the generals driven
into exile (and these immediately joined Darius and were   12
no small addition to the Persian forces).

5. Setting off for the Persian War Alexander executed
all his stepmother's relatives whom Philip had promoted
to higher office and given military commands. But neither   2
did he spare any of his own people who appeared fit for
ruling, so there should be no chance of sedition in Macedonia while he was on campaign far away.[14] and any   3
tribute-paying kings of exceptional ability he took with
him as comrades in arms, leaving the more listless in
charge of the kingdom. Then after assembling an army he   4
loaded the ships, and incredibly elated with the sight of
Asia from them he erected twelve altars to the gods as
votive offerings for the war. All ancestral possessions of his   5
in Macedonia and Europe he distributed among his
friends, saying that Asia sufficed for him. Before any ship   6
left shore he sacrificed animal victims, requesting victory
in a war for which he was chosen to avenge all those Persian assaults on Greece; their empire had already lasted   7

matura imperia contigisse quorumque tempus esse vices
8 excipere melius acturos. Sed nec exercitus eius alia quam
9 regis animorum praesumptio fuit; quippe obliti omnes
coniugum liberorumque et longinquae a domo militiae
Persicum aurum et totius Orientis opes iam quasi suam
praedam ducebant, nec belli periculorumque, sed divitia-
10 rum meminerant. Cum delati in continentem essent, primus Alexander iaculum velut in hostilem terram iecit
11 armatusque de navi tripudianti similis prosiluit atque ita
hostias caedit, precatus, ne se regem illae terrae invitae
12 accipiant. In Ilio quoque ad tumulos eorum, qui Troiano
bello ceciderant, parentavit.

6. Inde hostem petens militem a populatione Asiae
prohibuit, parcendum suis rebus praefatus, nec perdenda
2 ea, quae possessuri venerint. In exercitu eius fuere peditum XXXII milia, equitum IV milia quingenti, naves cen-
3 tum octoginta duae. Hac tam parva manu universum terrarum orbem utrum sit admirabilius vicerit an adgredi
4 ausus fuerit, incertum est. Cum ad tam periculosum bellum exercitum legeret, non iuvenes robustos nec primum
florem aetatis, sed veteranos, plerosque etiam emeritae
5 militiae, qui cum patre patruisque militaverant, elegit, ut
non tam milites quam magistros militiae electos putares.
6 Ordines quoque nemo nisi sexagenarius duxit, ut, si principia castrorum cerneres, senatum te priscae alicuius rei
7 publicae videre diceres. Itaque nemo in proelio fugam,

---

15 There were some Macedonian forces already in Asia Minor,
so that Alexander opened his campaigns with almost fifty thousand foot and horse.   16 A clear exaggeration. Of the generals only Parmenion (born around 400) is demonstrably over sixty.

long enough and was ready for the taking, he said, and the
time had come for their replacement by others who would
do better. Nor did his army's confidence differ from the 8
king's: for forgetting wives and children and a campaign 9
far from home, they all already had minds fixed on Persian
gold and the wealth of the entire East as being their personal plunder and were thinking not of war and its perils
but riches. When they had been carried to the mainland, 10
Alexander first hurled a spear into what he considered
enemy soil and in armor leaped from the ship like someone performing a dance, and then killed sacrificial victims, 11
praying that those lands not unwillingly accept him as
king. In Troy he also conducted funerary rites at tombs of 12
those who had fallen in the Trojan War.

6. Moving on the enemy from there, he kept the soldiers from pillaging Asia, saying they should spare their
own property and not destroy the things for which they
had come. In his army were thirty-two thousand infantry, 2
forty-five hundred cavalry and one hundred and eighty-
two ships.[15] With such a small a force it is debatable which 3
is more amazing, that he conquered the whole world or
that he actually dared make the attack. When raising an 4
army for such a perilous war, he did not choose sturdy
youngsters or men in the first flower of youth, but veterans, mostly even beyond military age, who had fought beside his father and uncles, so you would think it was not so 5
much soldiers being chosen as soldiers' teachers! The 6
ranks, too, were led by no one under sixty,[16] so if you
looked at the camp's headquarters you would say you saw
the senate of some republic of bygone days. So no one in 7

sed victoriam cogitavit; nec in pedibus cuiquam spes, sed
in lacertis fuit.

8   Contra rex Persarum Darius fiducia virium nihil astu
agere, adfirmans suis occulta consilia victoriae furtivae
9 convenire, nec hostem regni finibus arcere, sed in inti-
mum regnum accipere, gloriosius ratus repellere bellum
10 quam non admittere. Prima igitur congressio in campis
11 Adrasteis fuit. In acie Persarum sexcenta milia militum
fuere, quae non minus arte Alexandri quam virtute Macedonum superata terga verterunt. Magna itaque caedes
12 Persarum fuit. De exercitu Alexandri novem pedites, cen-
13 tum XX equites cecidere, quos rex inpense ad ceterorum
solacia humatos statuis equestribus donavit cognatisque
14 eorum inmunitates dedit. Post victoriam maior pars Asiae
15 ad eum defecit. Gessit et plura bella cum praefectis Darii,
quos iam non tam armis quam terrore nominis sui vicit.

7. Dum haec aguntur, interim indicio captivi ad eum
defertur insidias ei ab Alexandro Lyncesta, genero Antipa-
2 tri, qui praepositus Macedoniae erat, parari. Ob quam
causam timens, ne quis interfecto eo in Macedonia motus
3 oreretur, in vinculis eum habuit. Post haec Gordien urbem
petit, quae posita est inter Phrygiam maiorem et mino-
4 rem; cuius urbis potiundae non tam propter praedam
cupido eum cepit, sed quod audierat in ea urbe in templo
Iovis iugum Gordii positum, cuius nexum si quis solvisset,
eum tota Asia regnaturum antiqua oracula cecinisse.

---

17 This is the battle at the Granicus River in 334. Numbers
are, as often, variable, but in Latin six hundred thousand can
mean "countless thousands."   18 Arr. *Anab.* 1.16.4 more re-
liably reports eighty-five cavalry and thirty infantrymen slain.

19 Notably at Miletus and Halicarnassus.

20 See above, 11.2.1.

battle thought of flight, only of victory; nor was it in his feet that a man's hope lay but in his muscles.

The Persian king Darius for his part would from con- 8 fidence in his strength employ no subterfuge, telling his men that deceptive strategy meant a stolen victory; he did not keep his enemy from his borders, but admitted him 9 into the heart of his kingdom, thinking there more glory in repelling war than not facing it. So the first clash was in 10 the plains of Adrasteia.[17] In the Persian line were six hun- 11 dred thousand men, who, defeated no less by the tactics of Alexander than by the valor of the Macedonians, turned and fled. So Persian casualties were heavy. From the army 12 of Alexander nine infantrymen fell and one hundred and twenty cavalrymen;[18] and the king buried these at great 13 expense to console the others, awarded them equestrian statues and granted their relatives tax exemption. After his 14 victory the greater part of Asia defected to him. He also 15 fought more battles with prefects of Darius,[19] whom he defeated less by armed force than the panic that his name inspired.

7. In the course of all this he was meanwhile brought news, based on information from a prisoner, of a plot being hatched against him by Alexander the Lyncestian, a son-in-law of Antipater, who had been put in charge of Macedonia. So fearing that if he executed him there might be a 2 rebellion in Macedonia, he kept him in chains.[20] After this 3 he made for the city of Gordium, which lies between Greater and Lesser Phrygia; an urge to take this city seized 4 him not so much for spoils as because he had heard that in the temple of Jupiter in that city lay the yoke of Gordius, and ancient oracles had foretold that anyone untying its knot would rule all Asia.

5   Huius rei causa et origo illa fuit. Gordius cum in his
regionibus bubus conductis araret, aves eum omnis gene-
6 ris circumvolare coeperunt. Profectus ad consulendos
augures vicinae urbis obviam in porta habuit virginem
eximiae pulchritudinis; percontatus eam, quem potissi-
7 mum augurem consuleret; illa audita causa consulendi,
gnara artis ex disciplina parentum, regnum ei portendi
respondit polliceturque se et matrimonii et spei sociam.
8
9   Tam pulchra condicio prima regni felicitas videbatur. Post
10 nuptias inter Phrygas orta seditio est. Consulentibus de
fine discordiarum oracula responderunt regem discordiis
11 opus esse. Iterato quaerentibus de persona regis, iubentur
eum regem observare, quem reversi primum in templum
12 Iovis euntem plaustro repperissent. Obvius illis Gordius
13 fuit, statimque eum regem consalutant. Ille plaustrum,
quo vehenti regnum delatum fuerat, in templo Iovis posi-
14 tum maiestati regiae consecravit. Post hunc filius Mida
regnavit, qui ab Orpheo sacrorum sollemnibus initiatus
Phrygiam religionibus inplevit, quibus tutior omni vita
15 quam armis fuit. Igitur Alexander capta urbe cum in templum Iovis venisset, iugum plaustri requisivit, quo ex-
16 hibito, cum capita loramentorum intra nodos abscondita
reperire non posset, violentius oraculo usus gladio lora-
menta caedit atque ita resolutis nexibus latentia in nodis
capita invenit.

    8. Haec illi agenti nuntiatur Darium cum ingenti exer-
2 citu adventare. Itaque timens angustias magna celeritate

---

21 On the Latin expression here (*huius rei causa et origo*, literally, "the cause and origin of this state of affairs") possibly coming
directly from Pompeius Trogus, see Mineo ad loc.

Why and how this came about[21] is as follows. When 5
Gordius was plowing in these regions with some hired
oxen, birds of all kinds began fluttering around him. Set- 6
ting out to consult soothsayers in a neighboring city he met
at the city gate a young woman of exceptional beauty, and
he asked her who would be the best soothsayer for him to
consult, and she on hearing the reason for the consultation 7
and being skilled in that art, having been taught by her
parents, replied that he was destined for royal power, and
she promised to marry him and share his prospects. Such 8
a fine match seemed to augur well the start of his rule.
After the wedding sedition arose among the Phrygians. 9
When they consulted about ending the discord the oracles 10
replied that they needed a king. After another question 11
about such a king's identity, they were told to take as king
the first man whom on their return they met going to Jupiter's temple in a wagon. The man they met was Gordius, 12
and they immediately hailed him as king. He placed in 13
Jupiter's temple the wagon he was riding when the kingdom was conferred on him and consecrated it to regal
majesty. After him reigned his son Midas, who after initia- 14
tion by Orpheus in his sacred rites filled Phrygia with religious cults, by which he was throughout his life better
protected than by weapons So after Alexander captured 15
the city and came into the temple of Jupiter, he asked
about the wagon yoke; and when it was shown to him and 16
he could not find the ends of the thongs hidden within the
knots, he interpreted the oracle in a more forceful manner, slashed through the thongs with a sword and thus
undoing the tangles found the ends hidden in the knots.

8. While he was doing this it was reported that Darius 2
was approaching with a huge army. So fearing the re-

Taurum transcendit, in qua festinatione quingenta stadia
3 una die cursu fecit. Cum Tarsum venisset, captus Cydni
fluminis amoenitate per mediam urbem fluentis proiectis
armis plenus pulveris ac sudoris in praefrigidam undam se
4 proiecit, cum repente tantus nervos eius occupavit rigor,
ut interclusa voce non spes modo remedii, sed nec dilatio
5 periculi inveniretur. Vnus erat ex medicis, nomine Philippus, qui solus remedium pollicetur; sed et ipsum Parme-
nionis pridie a Cappadocia missae epistulae suspectum
6 faciebant, qui ignarus infirmitatis Alexandri scripserat, a
Philippo medico caveret, nam corruptum illum a Dario
7 ingenti pecunia esse. Tutius tamen ratus dubiae se fidei
8 medici credere quam indubitato morbo perire. Accepto
igitur poculo epistulas medico tradidit atque ita inter bi-
9 bendum oculos in vultum legentis intendit. Ut securum
conspexit, laetior factus est sanitatemque quarta die recepit.

9. Interea Darius cum CCCC milibus peditum ac cen-
2 tum milibus equitum in aciem procedit. Movebat haec
multitudo hostium respectu paucitatis suae Alexandrum,
sed interdum reputabat, quantas res cum ista paucitate
3 gessisset quantosque populos fudisset. Itaque cum spes
metum vinceret, periculosius differre bellum ratus, ne
desperatio suis cresceret, circumvectus suos singulas
4 gentes diversa oratione adloquitur. Illyrios et Thracas
opum ac divitiarum ostentatione, Graecos veterum bello-

---

22 Roughly 50–60 miles (80–100 km.).

23 The disease may have been malaria, or possibly pneumonia.
Only Justin has Parmenion in Cappadocia at this time.

24 The battle of Issus in November 333. The Persians' numbers and losses are again grossly exaggerated.

stricted terrain, he swiftly crossed the Taurus Mountains, covering in his haste five hundred stades in a one day march.[22] On reaching Tarsus he was taken by the beauty 3 of the River Cydnus that flows through the center of the town, and being covered with dust and sweat he threw down his weapons and hurled himself into its icy waters, when suddenly such stiffness gripped his muscles that his 4 voice was stifled and no hope could be found not just of a cure but even of slowing it.[23] One of his doctors, by the 5 name of Philip, alone promised a cure; but he was also brought under suspicion by a letter sent from Cappadocia the previous day by Parmenion, who unaware of Alexan- 6 der's illness had written telling him to beware of the doctor Philip, for he had been bribed by Darius with a great amount of money. He, however, thought trusting a doctor 7 of dubious loyalty was safer than facing certain death. So 8 taking the cup he handed the letter to the doctor, and while drinking fixed his eyes the man's face as he read it. When he saw him unperturbed, he cheered up and recov- 9 ered three days later.

9. Meanwhile Darius proceeded into the battle line with four hundred thousand infantry and a hundred thou- sand cavalrymen.[24] Such a multitude of enemies com- 2 pared with his own small numbers worried Alexander, but he would occasionally reflect on what great things he had achieved with that small force and what great peoples he had defeated. And so as hope overcame fear, and he 3 thought postponing battle more dangerous if despon- dency grew among the troops, he rode around his men and addressed the various races with different harangues. The 4 Illyrians and Thracians he would animate by pointing to

rum memoria internecivique cum Persis odii accendebat;
5 Macedonas autem nunc Europae victae admonet, nunc
Asiae expetitae, nec inventos illis toto orbe pares viros
6 gloriatur; ceterum et laborum finem hunc et gloriae cu-
7 mulum fore. Atque inter haec identidem consistere aciem
iubet, ut hac mora consuescant oculis turbam hostium
8 sustinere. Nec Darii segnis opera in ordinanda acie fuit;
quippe omissis ducum officiis ipse omnia circumire, singulos hortari, veteris gloriae Persarum imperiique perpe-
tuae a diis inmortalibus datae possessionis admonere.
9   Post haec proelium ingentibus animis committitur. In
eo uterque rex vulneratur. Tam diu certamen anceps fuit,
10 quoad fugeret Darius. Exinde caedes Persarum secuta est.
Caesa sunt peditum sexaginta unum milia, equitum decem milia; capta XL milia. Ex Macedonibus cecidere pe-
11 destres CXXX, equites CL. In castris Persarum multum
12 auri ceterarumque opum inventum. Inter captivos castrorum mater et uxor eademque soror et filiae duae Darii
13 fuere. Ad quas visendas hortandasque cum Alexander
veniret, conspectis armatis invicem se amplexae, velut sta-
14 tim moriturae, conplorationem ediderunt. Provolutae deinde genibus Alexandri non mortem, sed, dum Darii cor-
15 pus sepeliant, dilationem mortis deprecantur. Motus tanta
mulierum pietate Alexander et Darium vivere dixit et ti-

their enemy's wealth and opulence, the Greeks by remind-
ing them of their past wars and their deadly hatred of the
Persians. The Macedonians he reminded now of Europe   5
which they had conquered, now of Asia their present tar-
get, and he boasted that nowhere on earth had there been
soldiers found to match them; but this fight would be both   6
the end of their labors and the height of their glory. And   7
meanwhile he would repeatedly order the line to halt so
that by such pauses they would have their eyes accustomed to the enemy numbers. Nor was Darius slow de-   8
ploying his battle line; for, disregarding his generals' usual
duties he did all the rounds himself, encouraged the men
individually, and reminded them of the earlier glory of the
Persians and their everlasting possession of an empire
granted them by the immortal gods.

After this battle was joined with immense fervor. In it   9
both kings suffered wounds. The outcome long remained
doubtful until Darius began to flee. There then followed   10
a slaughter of Persians. sixty-one thousand of their infantry and ten thousand cavalry were killed; forty thousand
were taken prisoner. Of the Macedonians a hundred and
thirty infantry were lost and a hundred and fifty cavalrymen. In the camp of the Persians large amounts of gold   11
and other treasures were found. Among the prisoners in   12
the camp were Darius' mother, his wife, who was also his
sister, and his two daughters. When Alexander came to   13
visit and encourage them, they embracing one other as if
facing imminent death, let out sorrowful cries. Then,   14
throwing themselves at Alexander's feet they begged not
to be spared death, only postponement of execution until
they buried Darius' body. Moved by such loyalty from the   15
women Alexander told them that Darius was still alive,

mentibus mortis metum dempsit easque et haberi et salu-
16 tari ut reginas praecepit; filias quoque non sordidius dignitate patris sperare matrimonium iussit.

10. Post haec opes Darii divitiarumque adparatum
2 contemplatus admiratione tantarum rerum capitur. Tunc
primum luxuriosa convivia et magnificentiam epularum
sectari, tunc et Barsinen captivam diligere propter formae
3 pulchritudinem coepit, a qua postea susceptum puerum
4 Herculem vocavit. Memor tamen adhuc Darium vivere
Parmeniona ad occupandam Persicam classem aliosque
5 amicos ad recipiendas Asiae civitates misit, quae statim
audita fama victoriae ipsis Darii praefectis cum auri
magno pondere tradentibus se in potestatem victorum
6 venerunt. Tunc in Syriam proficiscitur, ubi obvios cum
7 infulis multos Orientis reges habuit. Ex his pro meritis
singulorum alios in societatem recepit, aliis regnum ade-
8 mit suffectis in loca eorum novis regibus. Insignis praeter
ceteros fuit Abdalonymus, rex ab Alexandro Sidoniae con-
9 stitutus, quem Alexander, cum operam oblocare ad puteos
exhauriendos hortosque inrigandos solitus esset, misere
vitam exhibentem regem fecerat spretis nobilibus, ne generis id, non dantis beneficium putarent.

10 Tyriorum civitas cum coronam auream magni ponderis
per legatos in titulum gratulationis Alexandro misisset,
grate munere accepto Tyrum se ire velle ad vota Herculi

---

25 These treasures were in fact taken later at Damascus, along
with Barsine.   26 In antiquity, the wearing of such headbands/
fillets was a common symbol for people thus craving favor.

27 Around the turn of 333/2. Abdalonymus in reality was a
royal kinsman; he reigned for some forty years.

and he dispelled their fear of execution and ordered them treated and addressed as queens; and he also told the daughters to expect marriage not beneath their father's status. 16

10. Examining Darius' treasures and display of wealth after this he was overcome with wonder at such possessions.[25] That was when he first started to hold lavish banquets and magnificent feasts, then too that he started to 2 fall for the captive Barsine because of her beauty (the son 3 he had by her later on he named Hercules). Aware, how- 4 ever, that Darius was still alive, he sent Parmenion to commandeer the Persian fleet and other friends to take over the cities of Asia, which immediately on news of the vic- 5 tory fell into the conquerors' hands since Darius' governors themselves surrendered to their conquerors with large amounts of gold. He then set out for Syria, where he 6 was met by many eastern kings wearing suppliant headbands.[26] A number he accepted as allies according to their 7 merits; from others he took away their kingdom, replacing them with new rulers. Oustanding above all the others was 8 Abdalonymus, who was appointed king of Sidon by Alexander;[27] and Alexander made him king although he had 9 earlier been eking out a wretched existence as a hired laborer, drawing water and irrigating gardens, noble candidates being passed over so people would not think it an appointment due to birth, not the benefactor's wishes.

When the city of Tyre sent him through delegates a 10 heavy crown of gold as a token of congratulation, he, gratefully accepting the gift, said he wished to go to Tyre to

11   reddenda dixit. Cum legati rectius id eum Tyro Vetere et
antiquiore templo facturum dicerent, deprecantes eius
12   introitum, ita exarsit, ut urbi excidium minaretur; confestimque exercitu insulae adplicato, non minus animosis
13   Tyriis fiducia Karthaginiensium, bello excipitur. Augebat
enim Tyriis animos Didonis exemplum, quae Karthagine
condita tertiam partem orbis quaesisset, turpe ducentes,
si feminis suis plus animi fuisset in imperio quaerendo
14   quam sibi in tuenda libertate. Amota igitur inbelli aetate
Karthaginem et arcessitis mox auxiliis non magno post
tempore per proditionem capiuntur.

    11. Inde Rhodum Alexander, Aegyptum Ciliciamque
2   sine certamine recepit. Ad Iovem deinde Hammonem
pergit consulturus et de eventu futurorum et de origine
3   sua. Namque mater eius Olympias confessa viro suo Philippo fuerat, Alexandrum non ex eo se, sed ex serpente
4   ingentis magnitudinis concepisse. Denique Philippus ul-
timo prope vitae suae tempore filium suum non esse pa-
5   lam praedicaverat. Qua ex causa Olympiada velut stupri
6   conpertam repudio dimiserat. Igitur Alexander cupiens
originem divinitatis adquirere, simul et matrem infamia
liberare, per praemissos subornat antistites, quid sibi re-
7   sponderi vellet. Ingredientem templum statim antistites

---

28 The siege of Tyre lasted seven months, into July or August
332. Old Tyre was on the mainland nearby.

29 See 18.4ff., where the lady is called Elissa.

30 This temple stood in the oasis of Siwa in the Western Desert of Egypt, 330 miles (560 km.) from the Nile.

31 See above, 9.5.9. For the serpent, see Plut. *Vit. Alex.* 2.6,
3.1ff.

discharge his vows to Hercules. When the delegates said 11
that he would be better doing that at Old Tyre and in a
temple of greater antiquity—they were trying to prevent
him from entering—he became so angry that he threatened to destroy the city;[28] and immediately bringing his 12
army to the island, he faced war with the Tyrians who were
no less confident of support from the Carthaginians. For 13
the Tyrians' spirits were raised by the example of Dido,
who after founding Carthage had acquired a third of the
world,[29] and they thought it shameful if their women had
shown more courage in acquiring an empire than did they
themselves in guarding their freedom. So they removed 14
those not of fighting age to Carthage and presently asked
them for help, but not much later they were captured
through treachery.

11. Alexander next took Rhodes, Egypt and Cilicia
without opposition. He then went on to the temple of 2
Jupiter Hammon to consult it about the future and his own
birth.[30] For his mother Olympias had confessed to her 3
husband Philip that it was not by him that she had conceived Alexander, but by a huge serpent. Eventually, al- 4
most at the end of his life, Philip had openly declared that
Alexander was not his son. Because of that he had divorced 5
Olympias as guilty of adultery.[31] So wishing to claim divine 6
birth and at the same time clear his mother of infamy,
Alexander, using men he sent ahead, prepared the priests
to give the response he wanted.[32] The moment he entered 7
the temple the priests hailed him as the son of Hammon.

[32] Justin is the only extant source to contain the imputation of
bribery.

8 ut Hammonis filium salutant. Ille laetus dei adoptione hoc
9 se patre censeri iubet. Rogat deinde, an omnes interfec-
tores parentis sui sit ultus. Respondetur patrem eius nec
interfici posse nec mori; regis Philippi plene peractam
10 ultionem. Tertia interrogatione poscenti victoriam omnium bellorum possessionemque terrarum dari responde-
11 tur. Comitibus quoque suis responsum, ut Alexandrum
12 pro deo, non pro rege colerent. Hinc illi aucta insolentia
mirusque animo increvit tumor exempta comitate, quam
et Graecorum litteris et Macedonum institutis didicerat.
13 Reversus ab Hammone Alexandream condidit et coloniam
Macedonum caput esse Aegypti iubet.

12. Darius cum Babyloniam perfugisset, per epistulas
Alexandrum precatur, redimendarum sibi captivarum potestatem faciat, inque eam rem magnam pecuniam pollice-
2 tur. Sed Alexander pretium captivarum regnum omne,
3 non pecuniam petit. Interiecto tempore aliae epistulae
Darii Alexandro redduntur, quibus filiae matrimonium et
4 regni portio offertur. Sed Alexander sua sibi dari rescripsit
iussitque supplicem venire, regni arbitria victori permit-
5 tere. Tunc spe pacis amissa bellum Darius reparat et cum
quadringentis milibus peditum, centum milibus equitum
6 obviam vadit Alexandro. In itinere nuntiatur uxorem eius
ex conlisione abiecti partus decessisse, eiusque mortem
inlacrimatum Alexandrum exequiasque benigne prosecu-
tum, idque eum non amoris, sed humanitatis causa fecisse;

---

33 The foundation of Alexandria probably equates with April
7, 331 (R. Bagnall, "The Date of the Foundation of Alexandria,"
American Journal of Ancient History 4 [1979]: 46ff.), but it did
not become capital of Egypt until 320 or 312 at the instigation of
Ptolemy.

He, pleased with his adoption by the god, ordered he be 8
considered born of this father. He then asked whether he 9
had punished all his father's killers. The reply was that his
father could neither be assassinated nor die, but vengeance for King Philip was fulfilled. On his asking a third 10
question the reply was that he was granted victory in all
wars and possession of the world. His companions also 11
received a response: they were to venerate Alexander as a
god, not as a king. After this his arrogance grew and his 12
conceit swelled to a startling degree, removing the cour-
tesy he had acquired from Greek scholarship and Macedonian customs. Returning from Hammon he founded 13
Alexandria and gave orders for the Macedonian colony to
be the capital of Egypt.[33]

12. After fleeing to Babylonia, Darius appealed in letters to Alexander to grant him leave to ransom his female
prisoners, and for that he promised a large amount of
money. But as the price of the captives, Alexander asked 2
for his entire kingdom, not money. Some time later other 3
letters from Darius came to Alexander, in which he was
offered marriage to his daughter and part of his kingdom.
But Alexander replied that he was being given his own 4
possessions and told him to come to him as a suppliant and
leave decisions about the kingdom to the victor. Then after 5
hope of peace was lost Darius resumed the war and with
four hundred thousand infantry and a hundred thousand
cavalry marched to meet Alexander. En route he was in- 6
formed that his wife had died following a miscarriage, that
Alexander had wept over her death and given her a gener-
ous funeral and done so not from love for her but humane

7   nam semel tantum eam Alexandro visam esse, cum ma-
8   trem parvulasque filias eius frequenter consolaretur. Tunc
    se ratus vere victum, cum post proelia etiam beneficiis ab
    hoste superaretur, gratumque sibi esse, si vincere ne-
9   queat, quod a tali potissimum vinceretur. Scribit itaque et
    tertias epistulas et gratias agit, quod nihil in suos hostile
10   fecerit. Offert deinde et maiorem partem regni usque
    Euphratem flumen et alteram filiam uxorem, pro reliquis
11   captivis XXX milia talentum. Ad haec Alexander gratiarum
12   actionem ab hoste supervacaneam esse respondit; nec a se
    quicquam factum in hostis adulationem, nec quod in du-
    bios belli exitus aut in leges pacis sibi lenocinia quaereret,
13   sed animi magnitudine, qua didicerit adversus vires ho-
14   stium, non adversus calamitates contendere; polliceturque
    praestaturum se ea Dario, si secundus sibi, non par haberi
15   velit. Ceterum neque mundum posse duobus solibus regi,
    nec orbem summa duo regna salvo statu terrarum habere.
16   Proinde aut deditionem ea die aut posteram aciem paret;
    nec polliceatur sibi aliam, quam sit expertus, victoriam.

     13. Postera die aciem producunt, cum repente ante
    proelium confectum curis Alexandrum somnus adripuit.
2   Cum ad pugnam solus rex deesset, a Parmenione aegre
    excitatus, quaerentibus somni causas omnibus inter peri-
3   cula, cuius etiam in otio semper parcior fuerit, magno se
    aestu liberatum ait, somnumque sibi a repentina securi-

---

34 The battle of Gaugamela in October 331.

kindness; for only once was she seen by Alexander, whereas   7
he was frequently consoling her mother and her little
daughters. He then understood that he was truly beaten,   8
surpassed now by his enemy even in benevolence, and he
was pleased that if he could not win he would be defeated
by such a man. So he even wrote a third letter and thanked   9
him for not taking any untoward action against his family.
He then even offered him most of his empire up to the   10
Euphrates River and one of his daughters in marriage,
plus thirty thousand talents for the rest of the prisoners.
Alexander's reply was that thanks from an enemy were   11
unnecessary: nothing he had done was meant to ingratiate   12
himself with his enemy nor, while the outcome of the war
remained uncertain, to seek lenient peace terms for himself, but from a magnanimity with which he had learned   13
to fight against his enemies' strengths, not his misfortunes;
and he promised he would grant Darius' wishes if he were   14
ready to be considered second to him, not his equal. But   15
the world could not be guided by two suns, he said, nor
could the globe hold two supreme kingdoms if its lands
were to be safe. So he must prepare to surrender on that   16
day or do battle on the next; nor should he promise himself
any other victory than he had already encountered.

13. The next day they brought out the armies into the
battle line[34] when suddenly, just before they engaged,
Alexander, exhausted from worry, was overcome by
sleep. Since only the king was missing for the battle, he   2
was with difficulty roused by Parmenion, and when everyone was asking how he could sleep amid the danger, especially when he took so little sleep even when he was at
leisure, he replied that he had been freed from great
anxiety and been granted sleep by a sudden release from   3

tate datum, quod liceat cum omnibus Darii copiis confli-
gere; veritum se longam belli moram, si Persae exercitum
4 divisissent. Ante proelium utraque acies hostibus specta-
5 culo fuit. Macedones multitudinem hominum, corporum
magnitudinem armorumque pulchritudinem mirabantur,
6 Persae a tam paucis victa suorum tot milia stupebant. Sed
7 nec duces circuire suos cessabant. Darius vix denis Arme-
8 niis singulos hostes, si divisio fieret, evenire dicebat; Alexander Macedonas monebat, ne multitudine hostium, ne
corporis magnitudine vel coloris novitate moverentur;
9 tantum meminisse iubet, cum isdem se tertio pugnare; nec
meliores factos putarent fuga, cum in aciem secum tam
tristem memoriam caedium suarum et tantum sanguinis
10 duobus proeliis fusi ferrent; et quemadmodum Dario mai-
11 orem turbam hominum esse, sic virorum sibi. Hortatur,
spernant illam aciem auro et argento fulgentem, in qua
plus praedae quam periculi sit, cum victoria non ornamen-
torum decore, sed ferri virtute quaeratur.

14. Post haec proelium committitur. Macedones in ferrum cum contemptu totiens a se victi hostis ruebant: con-
2 tra Persae mori quam vinci praeoptabant. Raro in ullo
3 proelio tantum sanguinis fusum est. Darius cum vinci suos
videret, mori et ipse voluit, sed a proximis fugere conpul-
4 sus est. Suadentibus deinde quibusdam, ut pons Cydni
fluminis ad iter hostium inpediendum intercluderetur,
non ita se saluti suae velle consultum ait, ut tot milia socio-

---

35 "Armenians" translates the text, but their presence here is
inexplicable and probably a manuscript error. Professor A. Mac-
Gregor suggests the reading "Achaemenians."

worry since he could now fight all of Darius' troops together—he had feared a long war if the Persians had divided their army. Before the battle each army provided 4
their enemies with an impressive sight. The Macedonians 5
were amazed at the Persian numbers, their sturdiness, and
the beauty of their weapons; the Persians were astonished
that so many thousands of their people had been defeated
by so few. But the leaders did not stop making the rounds 6
their men, either. Darius kept saying that if counted there 7
would hardly be one enemy for every ten Armenians;[35]
and Alexander kept telling the Macedonians not to be 8
cowed by the enemy's numbers, size, or strange color. He 9
ordered them to remember only that this was their third
battle with the same enemy; they should not think flight
had made the Persians better soldiers, for they took into
battle with them the sad memory of past defeats and so
much blood spilled in two battles; and although Darius 10
had larger numbers, he had more real men himself. He 11
urged them to feel contempt for that army gleaming with
gold and silver, in which for them there was more plunder
than danger, since victory was to be sought not with ornate
equipment but prowess with the sword.

14. After that the battle began. The Macedonians
charged into the fray with disdain for an enemy so often
beaten by them; the Persians on their side preferred death
to defeat. Rarely in any battle was so much blood shed. 2
When he saw his men go down, Darius wanted to die 3
himself but was made to flee by his kinsmen. Then when 4
some urged him to have the bridge over the River Cydnus
cut down so the enemy's advance could be blocked, he said
he did not want such concern shown for his safety as would
throw so many thousands of allies to the enemy; others

rum hosti obiciat; debere et aliis fugae viam patere, quae patuerit sibi.

5   Alexander autem periculosissima quaeque adgrediebatur, et ubi confertissimos hostes acerrime pugnare conspexisset, eo se semper inmergebat periculaque sua esse,
6 non militis volebat. Hoc proelio Asiae imperium rapuit,
7 quinto post acceptum regnum anno; cuius tanta felicitas fuit, ut post hoc nemo rebellare ausus sit patienterque Persae post imperium tot annorum iugum servitutis acce-
8 perint. Donatis refectisque militibus XXXIV diebus prae-
9 dam recognovit. In urbe deinde Susa XL milia talentum
10 invenit. Expugnat et Persepolim, caput Persici regni, urbem multis annis inlustrem refertamque orbis terrarum
11 spoliis, quae interitu eius primum apparuere. Inter haec octingenti admodum Graeci occurrunt Alexandro, qui poenam captivitatis truncata corporis parte tulerant, rogantes, ut sicuti Graeciam se quoque ab hostium crudeli-
12 tate vindicaret. Data potestate redeundi agros accipere maluerunt, ne non tam gaudium parentibus quam detestandum sui conspectum reportarent.

15. Interea Darius in gratiam victoris a cognatis suis aureis conpedibus catenisque in vico Parthorum Thara
2 vincitur, credo ita diis inmortalibus iudicantibus, ut in terra eorum, qui successuri imperio erant, Persarum reg-
3 num finiretur. Alexander quoque citato cursu postera die supervenit; ibi cognovit Darium clauso vehiculo per noc-
4 tem exportatum. Iusso igitur exercitu subsequi cum sex milibus equitum fugientem insequitur; in itinere multa et

---

36 The name is another detail found only in Justin.
37 Namely the Parthians; see Book 41.

should also have open the same means of escape as was open to him.

Alexander was now attacking all the most dangerous 5 areas, and where he saw the enemy densest and the fighting keenest that was where he was always diving in, and he wanted the dangers to be his, not his men's. With this 6 battle he seized power over Asia, in the fifth year after acquiring his throne; and so complete was his success that 7 after this none dared to rebel and the Persians after so many years of empire submissively accepted the yoke of servitude. When his men had been rewarded and given 8 thirty-four days' rest he took inventory of the spoils. In the 9 city of Susa he then found forty thousand talents. He also 10 captured Persepolis, capital of the Persian Kingdom, a city renowned through many years and full of spoils from all over the world that came to light only after its fall. Mean- 11 while some eight hundred Greeks came to meet Alexander, men who had been mutilated and kept in captivity, and they asked him to avenge them, just as he had Greece, for the barbarous treatment they had received at the enemy's hands. Although given the opportunity to return 12 home, they preferred to accept land, so as not to be bringing their kinsmen not joy but their repulsive appearance.

15. Meanwhile, to conciliate the conqueror, Darius was bound by his own kinsmen with golden fetters and chains in the Parthian village of Thara,[36] the immortal gods, I believe, judging that it was in the land of those destined 2 to succeed to it that the Persian Kingdom should come to an end.[37] Alexander after a speedy journey also arrived the 3 following day; and there he learned that Darius had been taken off at night in a covered wagon. So ordering the 4 army to follow, he chased the fugitive with six thousand

243

5 periculosa proelia facit. Emensus deinde plura milia passuum cum nullum Darii indicium repperisset, respirandi
   equis data potestate unus e militibus, dum ad fontem
   proximum pergit, in vehiculo Darium multis quidem
6 vulneribus confossum, sed spirantem adhuc invenit; qui
   applicito captivo cum civem ex voce cognovisset, id saltim
   praesentis fortunae habere se solacium dixit, quod apud
   intellecturum locuturus esset nec incassum postremas
7 voces emissurus. Perferri haec Alexandro iubet: se nullis
   in eum meritorum officiis maximorum illi debitorem mori,
   quod in matre liberisque suis regium eius, non hostilem
   animum expertus felicius hostem quam cognatos propin-
8 quosque sortitus sit; quippe matri et liberis suis ab eodem
   hoste vitam datam, sibi a cognatis ereptam, quibus et vi-
9 tam et regna dederit. Quamobrem gratiam illis eam futu-
10 ram, quam ipse victor volet. Alexandro referre se, quam
   solam moriens potest, gratiam, precari superum infe-
   rumque numina et regales deos, ut illi terrarum omnium
11 victori contingat imperium. Pro se iustam magis quam
12 gravem sepulturae veniam orare. Quod ad ultionem per-
   tineat, iam non suam, sed exempli communemque omnium regum esse causam, quam neglegere illi et indecorum et periculosum esse; quippe cum in altero iustitiae
13 eius, in altero etiam utilitatis causa versetur. In quam rem
   unicum pignus fidei regiae, dextram se ferendam Alexan-

cavalry; and on the road he fought many hazardous battles. Then after going many miles and finding no trace of Da- 5 rius, he gave the horses a rest, at which point one of his men on approaching a nearby spring found Darius in his carriage with many stab wounds, but still breathing. When 6 a prisoner was brought to him and from his speech Darius recognized him as a citizen, he said he at least had this solace in his present misfortune, that he would be talking to someone able to understand him and not be uttering his final words in vain. He then ordered this message be 7 taken to Alexander: although he had done the Macedonian no favors, he died indebted to him for the greatest of services, since in the matter of his mother and children he had found Alexander's character to be that of a king not an enemy, and he had been more blessed in the enemy allotted him by fate than in his own relatives and kinsmen; for 8 his wife and children had been granted their lives by that same enemy and he had been deprived of his by his relatives, to whom he had given both their lives and their powers. For this they would receive a recompense the 9 victor himself would choose. To Alexander he gave the 10 only thanks a dying man could, he said, by praying to the gods above and below and to the patron deities of kings that he as victor be granted dominion of the whole world. For himself he begged a favor fair rather than onerous, his 11 burial. As for revenge, justification for it was now not only 12 himself but setting a precedent and supporting the common cause of all kings, ignoring which was both dishonorable and perilous; for it was a matter both of justice on the one hand and expediency on the other. On that, he said, 13 he gave him his right hand, the supreme guarantee of regal trust, to be taken to Alexander. He then stretched

14 dro dare. Post haec porrexit manum expiravit⟨que⟩. Quae
ubi Alexandro nuntiata sunt, viso corpore defuncti tam
15 indignam illo fastigio mortem lacrimis prosecutus est cor-
pusque regio more sepeliri et reliquias eius maiorum tu-
mulis inferri iussit.

out his hand and died.[38] When this was reported to Alex- 14
ander, he on seeing the dead man's body wept that he had
succumbed to a death so unbecoming of his exalted position, and he ordered that the body be given a royal burial 15
and his remains laid in his ancestors' tombs.

[38] In July 330.

LIBER XII

1. Alexander in persequendo Dario amissos milites magnis funerum inpensis extulit, reliquis expeditionis eius sociis
2 tredecim milia talentum divisit. Equorum maior pars
3 aestu amissa, inutiles etiam qui superfuerant facti. Pecunia omnis, CXC milia talentum, Ecbatana congesta eique Parmenio praepositus.

4 Dum haec aguntur, epistulae Antipatri a Macedonia ei redduntur, quibus bellum Agidis, regis Spartanorum, in Graecia, bellum Alexandri, regis Epiri, in Italia, bellum
5 Zopyrionis, praefecti eius in Scythia continebatur. Quibus varie adfectus plus tamen laetitiae cognitis mortibus duorum aemulorum regum quam doloris amissi cum Zopy-
6 rione exercitus cepit. Namque post profectionem Alexandri Graecia ferme omnis in occasionem reciperandae libertatis ad arma concurrerat, auctoritatem Lacedaemo-
7 niorum secuta, qui Philippi Alexandrique et pacem soli spreverant et leges respuerant; dux huius belli Agis, rex
8 Lacedaemoniorum, fuit. Quem motum Antipater con-

---

[1] Parmenion remained at Ecbatana as Alexander journeyed east.

[2] For Alexander of Epirus, uncle of Alexander the Great, see below, 2.1; for Zopyrion, 2.16ff. On Agis' movement there is an additional contemporary source in Aeschin. 3.165. The Spartans

BOOK XII

1. Alexander went to great expense in burying the soldiers lost in the pursuit of Darius, and among his other allies in the campaign he distributed thirteen thousand talents. Most of the horses had been lost in the heat, and even 2 those that had survived were disabled. All his money, one 3 hundred and ninety thousand talents, was deposited at Ecbatana and Parmenion put in charge of it.[1]

While this was taking place he was brought dispatches 4 from Antipater in Macedonia with news of a war with the Spartan king Agis in Greece, of a war fought by Alexander, king of Epirus, in Italy, and of his governor Zopyrion's war in Scythia.[2] While having different reactions to them he 5 had greater joy on learning of the death of his two royal rivals than distress over the loss of the army with Zopyrion. For after Alexander's departure almost all of Greece had 6 rushed to arms to seize an opportunity to recover its freedom, following the lead of the Spartans, who alone had 7 rejected Philip and Alexander's peace and ignored its conditions; the leader of this war was Agis, king of the Spartans. That insurrection Antipater with his assembled 8

had not joined the Greek alliance (cf. 11.2.7n.). Agis was in fact supported by most of the Peloponnesians, but Thebes had been destroyed and the Athenians held back.

9 tractis militibus in ipso ortu oppressit. Magna tamen
10 utrimque caedes fuit. Agis rex cum suos terga dantes videret, dimissis satellitibus, ut Alexandro felicitate, non virtute inferior videretur, tantam stragem hostium edidit, ut
11 agmina interdum fugaret. Ad postremum etsi a multitudine victus, gloria tamen omnes vicit.

2. Porro Alexander, rex Epiri, in Italiam auxilia Tarentinis adversus Bruttios deprecantibus sollicitatus, ita cupide profectus fuerat, velut in divisione orbis terrarum
Alexandro, Olympiadis, sororis suae, filio, Oriens, sibi
2 Occidens sorte contigisset, non minorem rerum materiam
in Italia, Africa Siciliaque, quam ille in Asia et in Persis
3 habiturus. Huc accedebat, quod, sicut Alexandro Magno
Delphica oracula insidias in Macedonia, ita huic responsum Dodonaei Iovis urbem Pandosiam amnemque Ache-
rusium praedixerat. Quae utraque cum in Epiro essent,
4 ignarus eadem et in Italia esse, ad declinanda fatorum
5 pericula peregrinam militiam cupidius elegerat. Igitur
cum in Italiam venisset, primum illi bellum cum Apulis
6 fuit, quorum cognito urbis fato brevi post tempore pacem
7 et amicitiam cum rege eorum fecit. Erat namque tunc
temporis urbs Apulis Brundisium, quam Aetoli secuti
fama rerum in Troia gestarum clarissimum et nobilissi-
8 mum ducem Diomeden condiderant; sed pulsi ab Apulis
consulentes oracula responsum acceperant, locum qui
9 repetissent perpetuo possessuros. Hac igitur ex causa per
legatos cum belli comminatione restitui sibi ab Apulis

---

3 See Livy 8.24, where Alexander is said to have died in the
same year as the foundation of Alexandria, which is 331/0, not
Livy's 326.

4 Neither the oracle nor the plot is known from elsewhere.

forces quelled right at its start. Casualties were heavy on 9
both sides however. When King Agis saw his forces turn 10
to flee he, dismissing his bodyguard in order to appear
Alexander's inferior only in fortune, not in courage,
brought such slaughter on his enemy that he was sometimes routing hordes of them. Although finally overcome 11
by superior numbers, in glory he outdid them all.

2. Now Alexander, the king of Epirus, lured into Italy
when the Tarentines sought his help against the Bruttii,[3]
eagerly undertook the expedition as if in a partition of the
world the East had fallen to Alexander, son of his sister
Olympias, and the West to him; he thought he would have 2
no less an opportunity for action in Italy, Africa and Sicily
than Alexander would in Asia and Persia. In addition to 3
this, just as the Delphic Oracle had forewarned Alexander
the Great of a plot in Macedonia,[4] so an oracular response
from Jupiter at Dodona had warned him against the city
of Pandosia and the Acherusian River. Since both lay in
Epirus and he did not know that identically named places 4
existed in Italy, he in trying to avoid the perils of destiny
had been more inclined to a campaign abroad. Now when 5
he reached Italy, his first war was with the Apulians, but 6
on learning what was fated for their city he soon concluded
a peace treaty with their king. Now at that time Brundi- 7
sium was a city of the Apulians, which Aetolians had
founded after following Diomedes, a man of great renown
and distinction for his exploits in Troy; but after being 8
driven out by the Apulians and consulting oracles they had
received the response that those reclaiming the land
would possess it for ever. So in light of this, they had de- 9
manded through delegates and with a threat of war, that

10   urbem postulaverant; sed ubi Apulis oraculum innotuit, interfectos legatos in urbe sepelierant, perpetuam ibi sedem habituros. Atque ita defuncti responso diu urbem
11   possederunt. Quod factum cum cognovisset Alexander,
12   antiquitatis fata veneratus bello Apulorum abstinuit. Gessit et cum Bruttiis Lucanisque bellum multasque urbes cepit; cum Metapontinis et Poediculis et Romanis foedus
13   amicitiamque fecit. Sed Bruttii Lucanique cum auxilia a
14   finitimis contraxissent, acrius bellum repetivere. Ibi rex iuxta urbem Pandosiam et flumen Acheronta, non prius fatalis loci cognito nomine quam occideret, interficitur moriensque non in patria fuisse sibi periculosam mortem,
15   propter quam patriam fugerat, intellexit. Corpus eius Thurini publice redemptum sepulturae tradiderunt.

16   Dum haec in Italia aguntur, Zopyrion quoque, praefectus Ponti ab Alexandro Magno relictus, otiosum se ratus, si nihil et ipse gessisset, adunato XXX milium exercitu
17   Scythis bellum intulit caesusque cum omnibus copiis poenas temere inlati belli genti innoxiae luit.

    3. Haec cum nuntiata in Parthia Alexandro essent, simulato maerore propter Alexandri cognationem exercitui
2   suo triduo luctum indixit. Omnibus deinde velut perpetrato bello reditum in patriam expectantibus coniugesque ac liberos suos animo iam quodam modo conplectentibus
3   ad contionem exercitum vocat. Ibi nihil actum tot egregiis

---

5 Cf. 2.3.4, 37.3.2. Zopyrion was general in Thrace.

6 That is, Alexander of Epirus.

7 On the basis that the aims of the crusade against Persia seemed to have been achieved.

the city must be restored to them by the Apulians; but   10
when the oracle became known to the Apulians they had
murdered the ambassadors and buried them in the city so
they should always have their home there. And after thus
fulfilling the oracle they had the city for a long time. When   11
he learned of the matter Alexander, venerating the ancient
prophesies, renounced war with Apulians. He also fought   12
wars with the Bruttii and Lucanians and captured many
cities; and he concluded treaties and alliances with the
Metapontines, Poediculi and Romans. But the Bruttii and   13
the Lucanians after acquiring auxiliary forces from their
neighbors resumed the war more fiercely. There the king   14
was killed near the city of Pandosia and the River Acheron,
unaware of the fateful region's name before he fell, and
dying he realized that it was not in his country that the
death over which he had fled his country been a threat to
him. His body the people of Thurii ransomed and com-   15
mitted to burial at public expense.

While this was taking place in Italy, Zopyrion, left gov-   16
ernor of Pontus by Alexander the Great and thinking himself useless if he took no personal action, also assembled
an army of thirty thousand, attacked the Scythians, and   17
being cut down with all his troops paid the penalty for a
reckless attack on an innocent people.[5]

3. When these events were reported to Alexander in
Parthia, he affected sorrow because of his kinship with
Alexander[6] and declared a three-day mourning period for
his army. Then when they all assumed the war to be over[7]   2
and were expecting to be returning home and in their
minds already embracing their wives and children, he
called the army to an assembly. There he said that nothing   3
had been accomplished by so many outstanding battles if

proeliis ait, si incolumis orientalis barbaria relinquatur;
nec se corpus, sed regnum Darii petisse; persequen-
4 dosque eos esse, qui a regno defecerint. Hac oratione
velut ex integro incitatis militum animis Hyrcaniam Mar-
5 dosque subegit. Ibi ei occurrit Thalestris sive Minythia,
Amazonum regina, cum CCC mulieribus XXXV dierum
inter confertissimas gentes itinere confecto ex rege liberos
6 quaesitura; cuius conspectus adventusque admirationi
omnibus fuit et propter insolitum feminis habitum et
7 propter expetitum concubitum. Ob hoc tredecim diebus
otio a rege datis, ut est visa uterum implesse, discessit.
8 Post haec Alexander habitum regum Persarum et diadema insolitum antea regibus Macedonicis, velut in leges
9 eorum, quos vicerat, transiret, adsumit. Quae ne invidio-
sius in se uno conspicerentur, amicos quoque suos longam
10 vestem auratam purpureamque sumere iubet. Ut luxum
quoque sicut cultum Persarum imitaretur, inter paelicum
regiarum greges electae pulchritudinis nobilitatisque noc-
11 tium vices dividit. His rebus ingentes epularum apparatus
adicit, ne ieiuna et destricta luxuria videretur, convivium-
12 que iuxta regiam magnificentiam ludis exornat, inmemor
prorsus tantas opes amitti his moribus, non quaeri solere.

4. Inter haec indignatio omnium totis castris erat, a
Philippo illum patre tantum degenerasse, ut etiam patriae

---

8 See 2.4.33, 42.3.7.

9 This translates the received text "inter confertissimas gentes." Supposing a better sense could be gained, F. R. D. Goodyear
(*Proceedings of the African Classical Associations* 16 [1982]: 10)
strongly advocated the old emendation "infestissimas," thus having the journey proceed "through most hostile peoples."

the eastern barbarians were left secure, that his objective
had not been Darius' life but his kingdom, and they must
hunt down those who had defected from his rule. With the   4
soldiers' hearts freshly stirred by this speech, he subdued
Hyrcania and the Mardians. There he was met by Thales-   5
tris (also called Minythyia), the queen of the Amazons,[8]
together with three hundred women, and she had traveled
thirty-five days through thickly populated[9] lands to have
children by the king; and her appearance and arrival sur-   6
prised everyone both because she was strangely dressed
for a woman and was also coming for sexual intercourse.
For this a thirteen-day pause was taken by the king and   7
she left when she thought she had conceived.

After this Alexander assumed the dress of Persian kings   8
and a diadem, something hitherto unknown for Macedonian kings, as if accepting the conventions of those he had
defeated. Not to face animosity if seen only on him, he also   9
ordered his friends to adopt long, gilded, purple clothing.
To match the Persians in extravagance as well as dress, he   10
divided his nights among groups of strikingly beautiful and
nobly born concubines. To this he added huge, sumptuous   11
banquets for his extravagance not to appear paltry and
meager, and a dinner party he would magnificently embel-
lish with games on a regal scale, completely forgetting that   12
by this conduct such great power is usually lost, not gained.

4. Meanwhile there was general resentment throughout the camp at his having so far deteriorated from his
father Philip as to disown even his own country's glory and

nomen eiuraret moresque Persarum adsumeret, quos
2 propter tales mores vicerat. Sed ne solus vitiis eorum,
quos armis subiecerat, succubuisse videretur, militibus
quoque suis permisit, si quarum captivarum consuetudine
3 tenerentur, ducere uxores, existimans minorem in patriam
reditus cupiditatem futuram habentibus in castris imagi-
4 nem quandam larum ac domesticae sedis; simul ex labore
5 militiae molliorem fore dulcedinem uxorum. In supple-
menta quoque militum minus exhauriri posse Macedoniam, si veteranis patribus tirones filii succederent milita-
6 turi in vallo, in quo essent nati, constantioresque futuri, si
non solum tirocinia, verum et incunabula in ipsis castris
7 posuissent. Quae consuetudo in successoribus quoque
8 Alexandri mansit. Igitur et alimenta pueris statuta et instrumenta armorum equorumque iuvenibus data, et patri-
9 bus pro numero filiorum praemia statuta. Si quorum
patres occidissent, nihilo minus pupilli stipendia patrum
trahebant, quorum pueritia inter varias expeditiones mili-
10 tia erat. Itaque a parvula aetate laboribus periculisque
indurati invictus exercitus fuere, neque aliter castra quam
patriam neque pugnam aliud umquam quam victoriam
11
12 duxere. Haec suboles nomen habuit Epigoni. Parthis deinde domitis praefectus his statuitur ex nobilibus Persa-

---

10 Reinforcements had from time to time come from Macedon; see A. B. Bosworth, "Alexander the Great and the Decline
of Macedon," *Journal of Hellenic Studies* 106 (1986): 1ff.

11 This term, "Epigoni," is properly applied to the thirty thousand young men of native extraction whom Alexander ordered to
be recruited before he left Bactria for India (Curt. 8.5.1), but who
did not join him until he returned to Susa in 324. These "Descen-

adopt Persian customs, people he had defeated because
of such customs. But not to appear alone in having suc- 2
cumbed to the vices of those he had defeated in battle, he
also allowed his soldiers to take as wives any captive
women with whom they were involved, thinking they 3
would be less eager to return to the fatherland if they had
some form of home and domestic setting in the camp; and 4
also that after the rigors of the campaign having wives
would be all the sweeter. To supplement his forces he also 5
felt it less of a drain on Macedon if veteran fathers were
replaced by their sons who, as young recruits, would be
serving on the rampart on which they were born, and they 6
would be all the more steadfast if they had spent not only
their training but even their infancy right there in the
camp.[10] This practice remained even under the successors 7
of Alexander. So they were given a statutory food allow- 8
ance as boys, and as young men they were also equipped
with weapons and horses, while fathers were rewarded
according to the number of their children. When fathers 9
fell in battle, the orphans continued to draw their pay, and
their boyhood years were spent on various military campaigns. So, toughened by hardship and danger from their 10
early years, they formed an invincible army, and they
thought their camp nothing other than home and a battle
never anything but a victory. These children were called 11
"The Descendants."[11] Then when the Parthians were de- 12
feated one of the Persian noblemen Andragoras was ap-

dants" could have been at most only five or six years old at Alexander's death!

rum Andragoras; inde postea originem Parthorum reges
habuere.

5. Interea et Alexander non regio, sed hostili odio sae-
2 vire in suos coepit. Maxime indignabatur carpi se sermo-
nibus suorum Philippi patris patriaeque mores subver-
3 tisse. Propter quae crimina Parmenio quoque senex,
dignitate regi proximus, cum Philota filio, de utroque
4 prius quaestionibus habitis, interficitur. Fremere itaque
omnes universis castris coepere innoxii senis filiique ca-
sum miserantes, interdum se quoque non debere melius
5 sperare dicentes. Quae cum nuntiata Alexandro essent,
verens, ne haec opinio etiam in Macedoniam divulgaretur
et victoriae gloria saevitiae macula infuscaretur, simulat se
ex amicis quosdam in patriam victoriae nuntios missurum.
6 Hortatur milites suis scribere, rariorem habituros occa-
7 sionem propter militiam remotiorem. Datos fasces epistu-
8 larum tacite ad se deferri iubet; ex quibus cognito de se
singulorum iudicio in unam cohortem eos, qui de rege
durius opinati fuerant, contribuit, aut consumpturus eos
aut in ultimis terris in colonias distributurus.

9 Inde Drancas, Euergetas vel †Arimaspos†, Parapame-
sadas ceterosque populos, qui in radice Caucasi moraban-
10 tur, subegit. Interea unus ex amicis Darii Bessus vinctus

---

12 There is evident confusion here. Arr. *Anab*. 3.25.7 suggests
the name was Arsaces. There was a Seleucid satrap named Andragoras, who was defeated by the Arsaces who was founder of
the Parthian Kingdom (see 41.4.6ff.).

13 Philotas had not passed on information brought to him of a
plot in late 330; now in 329 he was condemned and executed, and
his father murdered (though not tortured, as his son had been).

pointed their governor; from him the kings of Parthians were later descended.[12]

5. Meanwhile Alexander also began to treat his own men savagely, not with the hatred of a king but an enemy. He was particularly angered by criticism in their gossip 2 that he had broken with the traditions of his father Philip and his country. Over such charges the elderly Parmenion, 3 next in authority after the king, was also put to death together with his son Philotas, both of them after torture.[13] So throughout the camp everyone began angrily grum- 4 bling over the fate of an innocent old man and his son, sometimes adding that they should expect no better for themselves. When this was reported to Alexander, he 5 feared that such talk might even become common in Macedonia and the glory of his victory be darkened by the stain of cruelty, so he pretended that he was going to send some of his friends home to report their victory. He urged 6 the soldiers to write to their families since they would have less opportunity as the campaign became more remote. Their bundles of letters he covertly had brought to him; 7 and on seeing each man's opinion of him he placed in a 8 single company those who had been quite critical in judging their king, intending either to kill them or distribute them in colonies in distant lands.

He next subdued the Drancae, the Euergetae or †Ari- 9 maspi†,[14] the Parapamesadae, and the other tribes living in the foothills of the Caucasus, Meanwhile Bessus, one of 10

[14] This is an addition to the text in a form commonly found (see Hdt. 4.13.1), though it belongs better to a Scythian tribe, and the correct form is probably "Ariaspi" (so Arr. *Anab.* 3.27.4).

perducitur, qui regem non solum prodiderat, verum et
11 interfecerat. Quem in ultionem perfidiae excruciandum
fratri Darii tradidit, reputans non tam hostem suum fuisse
12 Darium quam amicum eius, a quo esset occisus. Et ut his
terris nomen relinqueret, urbem Alexandream super amnem Tanaim condidit, intra diem septimum decimum
muro sex milium passuum consummato, translatis in eam
13 trium civitatum populis, quas Cyrus condiderat. In Bac-
trianis quoque Sogdianisque XII urbes condidit, distribu-
tis his, quoscumque in exercitu seditiosos habebat.

6. His ita gestis sollemni die amicos in convivium
2 convocat, ubi orta inter ebrios rerum a Philippo gestarum
mentione praeferre se patri ipse rerumque suarum magnitudinem extollere caelo tenus coepit adsentante maiore
3 convivarum parte. Itaque cum unus e senibus, Clitos, fiducia amicitiae regiae, cuius palmam tenebat, memoriam
Philippi tueretur laudaretque eius res gestas, adeo regem
offendit, ut telo a satellite rapto eundem in convivio tru-
4 cidaverit. Qua caede exultans mortuo patrocinium Phi-
5 lippi laudemque paternae militiae obiectabat. Postquam
satiatus caede animus conquievit et in irae locum successit
aestimatio, modo personam occisi, modo causam occi-
6 dendi considerans, pigere eum facti coepit; quippe pater-
nas laudes tam iracunde accepisse se quam nec convicia
debuisset, amicumque senem et innoxium a se occisum
7 inter epulas et pocula dolebat. Eodem igitur furore in

---

15 The Jaxartes.   16 That is, Cyrus the Great in the sixth
century.   17 Versions of this incident differ in detail. Clitus
had been an important commander, but at this time, autumn 328,
was chosen to succeed to the satrapy of Bactria (Curt. 8.1.19).

the friends of Darius, was brought in chains, the man who had not only betrayed but also murdered him. To punish 11 him for his treason he passed him on to Darius' brother for torture, thinking Darius had been less his enemy than his "friend" by whom he was killed. And to leave his name 12 in these lands, he founded the city of Alexandria on the River Tanais,[15] completing in seventeen days a wall that measured six miles and transferring into it populations from three towns that Cyrus had founded.[16] In Bactria and 13 Sogdiana he also founded twelve cities, dispersing among them any in the army he considered mutinous.

6. This done, he invited his friends to a banquet on a feast day,[17] and when mention of Philip's achievements 2 arose among some drunken men, he started setting himself above his father and praising his own great exploits to the skies, with most of the diners in agreement. So when 3 one of the older men, Clitus, confident in the king's friendship. in which he held first place, started defending Philip's memory and praising his achievements, he so offended the king that he took a spear from a guard and murdered him at the banquet. Reveling in the bloodshed he began 4 taunting the dead man for championing Philip and praising his father's soldiering. When, sated with bloodshed, his 5 temper cooled and anger gave way to reflection, he started thinking now about the person he had killed and now about his reason for killing him, and he began to regret what he had done; for he had taken praise of his father 6 with such anger as even insults had not merited, and an elderly, innocent friend had been killed by him in a setting of feasting and drinking. So as shaken with remorse as he 7

8   paenitentiam quo pridem in iram versus mori voluit. Primum in fletus progressus amplecti mortuum, vulnera tractare, quasi audienti confiteri dementiam, adreptumque telum in se vertit peregissetque facinus, nisi amici inter-
9   venissent. Mansit haec voluntas moriendi etiam sequenti-
10 bus diebus. Accesserat enim paenitentiae nutricis suae et sororis Cliti recordatio, cuius absentis eum maxime pude-
11 bat: tam foedam illi alimentorum suorum mercedem redditam, ut, in cuius manibus pueritiam egerat, huic iuvenis
12 et victor pro beneficiis funera remitteret. Reputabat deinde, quantum in exercitu suo, quantum apud devictas gentes fabularum atque invidiae, quantum apud ceteros
13 amicos metum et odium sui fecerit, quam amarum et triste reddiderit convivium suum, non armatus in acie
14 quam in convivio terribilior. Tunc Parmenion et Philotas, tunc Amyntas consobrinus, tunc noverca fratresque interfecti, tunc Attalus, Eurylochus, Pausanias aliique Macedo-
15 niae extincti principes occurrerunt. Ob haec illi quadriduo perseverata inedia est, donec exercitus universi precibus
16 exoratus est, precantis, ne ita morte unius doleat, ut universos perdat, quos in ultimam deductos barbariam inter
17 infestas et irritatas bello gentes destituat. Multum profuere Callisthenis philosophi preces; condiscipulatu apud

---

18 Arrian (*Anab.* 4.9.3) calls her Lanice; Curtius (8.1.21), Hellanice. A great deal is made of such details by E. D. Carney, "The Death of Clitus," *Greek, Roman, and Byzantine Studies* 22 (1981): 149ff.

19 The figures from Parmenion to Attalus have been mentioned earlier. Eurylochus was the one who revealed to Alexander the conspiracy of the pages, which came later, so there is confu-

had earlier been with rage, he wished to die. First bursting   8
into tears he embraced the dead man, touched his wounds
and, as if he could hear, confessed that he had lost his
mind; and seizing a weapon he turned it on himself and
would have completed the act had his friends not inter-
vened. This wish to die remained even through the days   9
that followed. For his regret had been deepened by the   10
memory of his own nurse, Clitus'[18] sister, who although
absent aroused in him the deepest shame; so foul had been   11
her reward for nursing him, he thought, for after spending
his infancy in her arms he now when young and victorious
was repaying her with a death, not kindness! He then   12
started to think about how much idle rumor and animosity
he had aroused in his army, how much among the peoples
he had conquered, and how much fear and hatred among
his other friends, and into what a bitter and sad affair he   13
had turned his own banquet, a man no more frightening
when armed in battle than at a banquet! Then Parmenion   14
and Philotas came to mind, then his cousin Amyntas, then
his murdered stepmother and brothers, then Attalus, Eurylochus, Pausanias and the other Macedonian chieftains
he had eliminated.[19] Because of this he went four days   15
without eating, until he was brought round by the troops,
who together begged him not to allow grief over one man's
death to destroy them all, for after leading them to the   16
furthest frontier of barbarian territory he would be leaving
them among hostile tribes roused to war. Of great help   17
were the pleas of the philosopher Callisthenes; the two of

sion of some sort here. Pausanias seems to be the assassin of
Philip, and the others could be the Lyncestians, including Alexander of Lyncestis (cf. 11.2.1, 7.1).

Aristotelem familiaris illi et tunc ab ipso rege ad prodenda
18 memoriae acta eius accitus. Revocato igitur ad bella animo
Chorasmos et Dahas in deditionem accepit.

7. Dein, quod primo ex Persico superbiae regiae more
distulerat ne omnia pariter invidiosiora essent, non salu-
2 tari, sed adorari se iubet. Acerrimus inter recusantes Callisthenes fuit. Quae res et illi et multis principibus Macedonum exitio fuit, siquidem sub specie insidiarum omnes
3 interfecti. Retentus tamen est a Macedonibus modus salu-
tandi regis explosa adoratione.
4 Post haec Indiam petit, ut Oceano ultimoque Oriente
5 finiret imperium. Cui gloriae ut etiam exercitus ornamenta convenirent, phaleras equorum et arma militum
argento inducit exercitumque suum ab argenteis clipeis
6 Argyraspidas appellavit. Cum ad Nysam urbem venisset,
oppidanis non repugnantibus fiducia religionis Liberi patris, a quo condita urbs erat, parci iussit, laetus non mili-
7 tiam tantum, verum et vestigia se dei secutum. Tunc ad
spectaculum sacri montis duxit exercitum, naturalibus

---

[20] Callisthenes of Olynthus is also said to have been a nephew
of Aristotle.

[21] Normal Persian practice ("proskynesis" in Greek), this did
not to his subjects imply the divinity of the Persian king; but for
Greeks and Macedonians it was an honor reserved for immortals.
The consequences for Callisthenes and others, including the
royal pages who conspired, are told in greater (and not wholly
consistent) detail in other accounts.

[22] These "silver shields" were not the whole army, but a kind
of special unit, their exact nature being a matter of debate. They
seem to have numbered three thousand.

them having been pupils of Aristotle, he was friendly with him and also had been personally invited by the king to compile his chronicles.[20] So brought back to his wars 18 he accepted the surrender of the Chorasmians and the Dahae.

7. Then came some typically Persian regal vanity, adopting which he had deferred for all the more offensive things not to arrive together: he ordered he not be saluted but receive obeisance.[21] The most outspoken of those ob- 2 jecting was Callisthenes. This meant death both for him and many leading Macedonians, since they were all executed, ostensibly for treason. However the usual manner 3 of saluting the king was retained by the Macedonians and obeisance rejected.

After this he headed for India so his empire would end 4 at the Ocean and the Orient's furthest limits. For that 5 glorious aspiration also to be matched by the army's equipment he had the horses' trappings and men's weapons overlaid with silver, and from their silver shields he named his army "the Argyraspids."[22] When he reached the city of 6 Nisa and met no resistance from its townspeople, who were confident in their cult of Father Liber[23] by whom their city was founded, he ordered them spared, pleased that he had not only emulated the god's campaign but even followed his footsteps. He then led the army to view the 7 holy mountain, which was as luxuriantly covered with a

[23] Dionysus, hence the identification of the city as Dionysopolis. The holy mountain was called Meros or Meron. Dionysus is another figure whom Alexander consciously imitated. Nisa stood near modern Ashgabat in southern Turkmenistan.

bonis, vite hederaque, non aliter vestiti, quam si manu
8 cultus colentiumque industria exornatus esset. Sed exercitus eius, ubi ad montem accessit, repentino impetu mentis in sacros dei ululatus instinctus cum stupore regis sine
noxa discurrit, ut intellegeret non tam oppidanis se par-
9 cendo quam exercitui suo consuluisse. Inde montes Dae-
dalos regnaque Cleophidis reginae petit. Quae cum se
dedidisset ei, concubitu redemptum regnum ab Alexandro recepit, inlecebris consecuta, quod armis non poterat;
10 filiumque ab eo genitum Alexandrum nominavit, qui
11 postea regno Indorum potitus est. Cleophis regina propter
prostratam pudicitiam scortum regium ab Indis exinde
12 appellata est. Peragrata India cum ad saxum mirae aspe-
ritatis et altitudinis, in quod multi populi confugerant,
pervenisset, cognoscit Herculem ab expugnatione eius-
13 dem saxi terrae motu prohibitum. Captus itaque cupidine
Herculis acta superare cum summo labore ac periculo
potitus saxo omnes eius loci gentes in deditionem accepit.

8. Vnus ex regibus Indorum fuit, Porus nomine, viribus
2 corporis et animi magnitudine pariter insignis, qui bellum
iam pridem audita Alexandri opinione in adventum eius
3 parabat. Commisso itaque proelio exercitum suum Macedonas invadere iubet, sibi regem eorum privatum hostem
4 deposcit. Nec Alexander pugnae moram fecit; sed prima

---

24 Curt. 8.10.36 attests to the son, but neither he nor any other
author asserts Alexander's paternity. Trogus' readers may have
been reminded of Cleopatra, who bore a son to Caesar and is
called "whore queen" at Prop. 3.11.39 and Plin. *HN* 9.119.

25 The height was called Aornus (Birdless). Probably the peak

natural growth of vine and ivy as if cultivated by hand and
carefully tended by gardeners. But his army, when it 8
reached the mountain, rushed off in a sudden frenzy calling out the god's holy cry without harm, stupefying the
king, so he should understand that in sparing the townspeople he had been serving not so much the citizens as his
own army. From there he made for the Daedalian Moun- 9
tains and the kingdom of Queen Cleophis. After she surrendered to him, she regained her kingdom from Alexander through sleeping with him, gaining by seduction what
she could not by weapons; and the child fathered by him 10
she named Alexander,[24] who later rose to power over the
Indians. Queen Cleophis because she surrendered her 11
virtue was subsequently called the "royal whore" by the
Indians. After traversing India he arrived at an extremely 12
high and precipitous crag on which many tribes had sought
refuge, and there was told that Hercules had been prevented from taking it by an earthquake. So taken with an 13
urge to outdo Hercules' feats, he despite facing extreme
hardship and danger, took the rock and accepted the surrender of all the tribes in that area.[25]

8. One of the Indian kings, Porus by name, was equally
renowned for his physical strength and greatness of spirit,
and having already heard of Alexander's reputation he was 2
preparing for war on his arrival.[26] So when battle was 3
joined, he ordered his army to attack the Macedonians,
but claimed for himself their king as his own personal foe.
And Alexander did not delay the fight; but his horse being 4

of the Pir-Sar heights, above Islamabad, Pakistan. For emulation
of Hercules, see 11.4.5.

[26] This is the battle at the Hydaspes (Jhelum) River in 326.

congressione vulnerato equo cum praeceps ad terram
5 decidisset, concursu satellitum servatur. Porus multis
6 vulneribus obrutus capitur. Qui victum se adeo doluit, ut,
cum veniam ab hoste accepisset, neque cibum sumere
voluerit neque vulnera curari passus sit aegreque sit ab eo
7 obtentum, ut vellet vivere. Quem Alexander ob honorem
8 virtutis incolumem in regnum remisit. Duas ibi urbes
condidit; unam Nicaeam, alteram ex nomine equi Buce-
9 phalen vocavit. Inde Adrestas, †Catheanos†, Praesidas,
10 Gangaridas caesis eorum exercitibus expugnat. Cum ad
Sophitis ⟨regnum⟩ venisset, ubi eum hostium CC milia
⟨peditum et XX milia⟩ equitum opperiebantur, exercitus
omnis non minus victoriarum numero quam laboribus fes-
11 sus lacrimis eum deprecatur, finem tandem bellis faceret;
aliquando patriae reditusque meminisset, respiceret mili-
12 tum annos, quibus vix aetas ad reditum sufficeret.
Ostendere alius canitiem, alius vulnera, alius aetate con-
13 sumpta corpora, alius cicatricibus exhausta; solos se esse,
qui duorum regum, Philippi Alexandrique, continuam
14 militiam pertulerint. Tantum orare, ut reliquias saltim
suas paternis sepulcris reddat, quorum non studiis deficia-
15 tur quam annis, ac, si non militibus, vel ipsi sibi parcat, ne
16 fortunam suam nimis onerando fatiget. Motus his tam
iustis precibus velut in finem victoriae castra solito
magnificentiora fieri iussit, quorum molitionibus et hostis
17 terreretur et posteris admiratio sui relinqueretur. Nullum

---

27 There are problems of identification and chronology. The
readings "Catheani" here and "Sophites" in the next sentence
appear by emendation.

28 This is the mutiny at the Hyphasis (Sutlej) River.

wounded in the first clash, he fell headlong to the ground
and was saved by attendants who rushed to his aid. Porus,   5
overcome by many wounds, was taken prisoner. So dis-   6
tressed was he over his defeat that, although spared by his
enemy, he refused to take food or have his wounds tended
to, and was only with difficulty persuaded to remain alive.
From respect for his courage Alexander sent him back to   7
his kingdom unharmed. He founded two cities there; one   8
he called Nicaea, the other, after his horse, Bucephala. He 9
then defeated the Adrestae, Catheani, Praesidae, and
Gangaridae, wiping out their armies.[27] When he reached   10
the kingdom of Sophites, where he found two hundred
thousand enemy infantry and twenty thousand cavalry
waiting for him, his entire army, wearied no less by its
numerous victories than the hardships it had faced, tearfully begged him finally to bring the wars to an end; at   11
some point he should think about returning home and
consider the ages of soldiers who scarcely had enough   12
years left for their return.[28] One showed his gray hair,
another his wounds, another his body decrepit with age
and another his weakened with scars; they alone had borne   13
uninterrupted service under both kings, Philip and Alexander, they said. Their only prayer was that he at least take 14
their remains back to the graves of their fathers—it was
not spirit but youth that they lacked; and if he would not   15
spare his soldiers he should at least spare himself, not to
wear out his good fortune by overtaxing it! Moved by such   16
just entreaties and to add the final touch to his victory he
ordered camp set up on a grander scale than usual, both
so the enemy should be intimidated and also for admiration for him to live on in posterity. There was no task that 17

opus laetius milites fecere. Itaque caesis hostibus cum gra-
tulatione in eadem reverterunt.

9. Inde Alexander ad amnem Acesinem pergit; per
2 hunc in Oceanum devehitur. Ibi Agensonas Sibosque,
3 quos Hercules condidit, in deditionem accepit. Hinc in
Mandros et Sudracas navigat, quae gentes eum armatis
LXXX milibus peditum et LX milibus equitum excipiunt.
4 Cum proelio victor esset, exercitum ad urbem eorum
5 ducit. Quam desertam a defensoribus cum de muro, quem
primus ceperat, animadvertisset, in urbis planitiem sine
6 ullo satellite desiliit. Itaque cum eum hostes solum
conspexissent, clamore edito undique concurrunt, si possint in uno capite orbis bella finire et ultionem tot gentibus
7 dare. Nec minus Alexander constanter restitit et unus
8 adversus tot milia proeliatur. Incredibile dictu est, ut eum
non multitudo hostium, non vis magna telorum, non tantus lacessentium clamor terruerit, solus tot milia ceciderit
9 ac fugaverit. Vbi vero obrui multitudine se vidit, trunco
10 se, qui tum propter murum stabat, adplicuit, cuius auxilio
tutus cum diu agmen sustinuisset, tandem cognito periculo eius amici ad eum desiliunt, ex quibus multi caesi;
11 proeliumque tam diu anceps fuit, quoad omnis exercitus
12 muris deiectis in auxilium veniret. In eo proelio sagitta sub
mamma traiectus cum sanguinis fluxu deficeret, genu
posito tam diu proeliatus est, donec eum, a quo vulneratus
13 fuerat, occideret. Curatio vulneris gravior ipso vulnere
fuit.

---

[29] In fact, the army came first to the Acesines (Chenab) and
thence to the Hydaspes to meet a fleet, late in 326. The readings
"Agensonae," "Oxydracae," and "Sudracae" are emendations
based on Arrian and other sources. The "Mandri" are the Mal-
lians.

the men accepted more happily. And so after sacrificial
offerings they joyfully turned back.

9. From there Alexander proceeded to the River Acesines and down it sailed to the Ocean. There he received   2
the surrender of the Agensonae[29] and Sibi, whose founder
was Hercules. From here he sailed to the Mandri and   3
Sudracae, tribes who faced him with an armament of
eighty thousand infantry and sixty thousand cavalry.
Defeating them in battle, he led the army to their city.   4
When from the wall, which he scaled first, he observed   5
that it was without defenders, he leaped down onto a level
part of the city without any attendant. So when the enemy   6
saw him alone, they raised a shout and charged at him
from every side, hoping that with the one life they could
end worldwide wars and take revenge for so many nations. Alexander nevertheless stoutly resisted and single-   7
handedly fought against many thousands. Amazing to say,   8
he was not terrified by the enemy numbers, the dense
shower of spears, or the loud clamor of his attackers; on
his own he cut down or drove back many thousands. When   9
he saw that he was being overwhelmed by their numbers,
however, he pressed himself against the trunk of a tree
that then stood close the wall and helped by its cover   10
staved off the hordes until his friends, finally aware of his
danger, leaped down to him, many to their deaths; and the   11
battle long remained undecided until when the wall was
breached the whole army come to his aid. Struck beneath   12
the breast by an arrow in that battle and weakened from
loss of blood, he dropped to one knee and kept fighting
until he killed the man by whom he had been wounded.
Treating the wound was more serious than the wound it-   13
self.

10. Itaque ex magna desperatione tandem saluti redditus Polyperconta cum exercitu Babyloniam mittit, ipse
cum lectissima manu navibus conscensis Oceani litora
2 peragrat. Cum venisset ad urbem Ambi regis, oppidani
invictum ferro audientes sagittas veneno armant atque ita
gemino mortis vulnere hostem a muris submoventes plu-
3 rimos interficiunt. Cum inter multos vulneratus etiam
Ptolomeus esset moriturusque iam iamque videretur, per
quietem regi monstrata in remedia veneni herba est, qua
in potu accepta statim periculo liberatus est maiorque pars
4 exercitus hoc remedio servata. Expugnata deinde urbe
reversus in navem Oceano libamenta dedit, prosperum in
5 patriam reditum precatus; ac veluti curru circa metam
acto, positis imperii terminis, quatenus aut terrarum solitudines prodire passae sunt aut mare navigabile fuit, se-
6 cundo aestu ostio fluminis Indi invehitur. Ibi in monumenta a se rerum gestarum urbem Barcem condidit
arasque statuit relicto ex numero amicorum litoralibus
7 Indis praefecto. Inde iter terrestre facturus, cum arida
loca medii itineris dicerentur, puteos opportunis locis fieri
praecepit, quibus ingenti dulci aqua inventa Babyloniam
8 redit. Ibi multae devictae gentes praefectos suos accusa-

---

[30] Craterus was the major figure sent, though Polyperchon
(the correct Greek spelling) may well have gone with him. Carmania would be the precise destination, but Justin is vague. At
this point Alexander had not reached the coast but was following
the Indus. The king next mentioned is otherwise called Sambus.
The story about Ptolemy is held to be fiction.

[31] Otherwise unknown. The governor was Peithon, son of
Agenor.

10. So when he was after great despair finally restored to health he sent Polypercon to Babylonia with the army, while he himself boarded ships with a carefully selected group of men and followed the ocean coastline.[30] When 2 he reached the city of King Ambus, the townspeople, hearing him to be unbeatable with the sword, dipped their arrows in poison, and driving their enemy from their walls with doubly lethal wounds killed them in large numbers. Among the many casualties was Ptolemy, and he time and 3 again seemed on the point of death; but then a herb that would provide an antidote to the poison was revealed to the king in a dream, and after taking it in a drink he was immediately free from danger, and most of the army was saved by this antidote. Then after storming the city Alex- 4 ander returned to his ship and offered sacrifices to the Ocean, praying for a safe return home; and as though his 5 chariot had passed its turning point and he had set his empire's boundaries as far as deserts permitted advance on land or as far as the sea could be sailed, he came on a favorable tide into the mouth of the River Indus. There in 6 commemoration of his achievements he founded the city of Barce[31] and erected altars, leaving one of his friends as governor of the Indian coast. Then, when he was about to 7 begin the overland journey and was informed of deserts along his route, he ordered wells to be dug at appropriate points, and after much sweet water was found in them he returned to Babylonia.[32] There many subject nations 8

[32] Gross misrepresentation of the hellish trek through the Gedrosian Desert. Again, Carmania is the actual arrival point (see above, n. 30). The marriages took place at Susa, which Alexander reached in spring 324.

verunt, quos sine respectu amicitiae Alexander in con-
9 spectu legatorum necari iussit. Filiam post haec Darii
10 regis Statiram in matrimonium recepit; sed et optimatibus
Macedonum lectas ex omnibus gentibus nobilissimas virgines tradidit, ut communi facto crimen regis levaretur.

11. Hinc ad contionem exercitus vocat et promittit se
aes alienum omnium propria inpensa soluturum, ut prae-
2 dam praemiaque integra domos ferant. Insignis haec mu-
nificentia non summa tantum, verum etiam titulo muneris
fuit nec a debitoribus magis quam creditoribus gratius
excepta, quoniam utrisque exactio pariter ac solutio diffi-
3
4 cilis erat. XX milia talentum in hos sumptus expensa. Di-
5 missis veteranis exercitum iunioribus supplet. Sed retenti
veteranorum discessum aegre ferentes missionem et ipsi
flagitabant nec annos, sed stipendia sua numerari iube-
bant, pariter in militiam lectos pariter sacramento solvi
6 aequum censentes. Nec iam precibus, sed convicio agebant, iubentes eum solum cum patre suo Hammone inire
7 bella, quatenus milites suos fastidiat. Contra ille nunc cas-
tigare milites, nunc lenibus verbis monere, ne gloriosam
8 militiam seditionibus infuscarent. Ad postremum cum
verbis nihil proficeret, ad corripiendos seditionis auctores
e tribunali in contionem armatam inermis ipse desiluit et
nemine prohibente tredecim correptos manu sua ipse—
9 ad supplicium duxit. Tantam vel illis moriendi patientiam

---

33 These events took place at Opis in the summer of 324.

brought charges against their governors, and without consideration of friendship, he ordered them executed in the delegates' sight. After this he married Darius' daughter 9 Statira; but he also presented his Macedonian noblemen 10 with unmarried girls chosen from all the peoples' best families, so that by the communal act there would be less criticism of the king.

11. He then summoned the troops to an assembly and promised to discharge everyone's debts at his own expense for them to take their booty and prizes home intact.[33] Such 2 generosity was remarkable not only for the amount involved but also because it was a gift, and creditors were as grateful as the indebted since collection and payment were equally difficult for one as for the other. Twenty 3 thousand talents were spent on this outlay. Demobilizing 4 the veterans he supplemented his army with younger men. But the men retained, resenting the veterans' discharge, 5 also started to demand demobilization themselves and insisted that not age but years of service be counted, since they thought it fair for those recruited together to be released from their oath together. No longer were they now 6 using entreaties, but insults, telling him go into his wars alone with his father Hammon, since he had no concern for his soldiers. He for his part was now rebuking the men, 7 and then advising them with soothing words not to tarnish their glorious campaign with mutiny. Finally, when he was 8 making no progress with words, he jumped down from his tribunal into the armed assembly, unarmed himself, to seize the mutiny's ringleaders, and meeting no opposition he seized thirteen with his own hands and led them off for execution. So far did fear of their king make them willing 9

metus regis vel huic exigendi supplicii constantiam disciplina militaris dabat.

12. Inde separatim auxilia Persarum in contione adloquitur. Laudat perpetuam illorum cum in se tum in pristinos reges fidem; sua in illos beneficia commemorat, ut numquam quasi victos, sed veluti victoriae socios habuerit, denique se in illorum, non illos in gentis suae morem transisse, adfinitatibus conubiorum victos victoribus miscuisse. Hinc quoque ait custodiam corporis sui non Macedonibus tantum se, verum et illis crediturum. Atque ita mille ex his iuvenes in numerum satellitum legit auxiliorumque portionem formatam in disciplinam Macedonum exercitui suo miscet. Quam rem aegre Macedones tulerunt, iactantes hostes suos in officium suum a rege subiectos. Tunc universi flentes regem adeunt; orant, suppliciis suis potius saturaret se quam contumeliis. Qua modestia obtinuerunt, ut undecim milia militum veteranorum exauctoraret. Sed et ex amicis dimissi senes Polypercon, Clitos, Gorgias, Polydamas, ⟨Ammadas,⟩ Antigenes. Dimissis Crateros praeponitur, iussus praeesse Macedonibus in Antipatri locum, Antipatrumque cum supplemento tironum in locum eius evocat. Stipendia revertentibus veluti militantibus data.

Dum haec aguntur, unus ex amicis eius Hephaestion decedit, dotibus primo formae pueritiaeque, mox obsequiis regi percarus. Quem contra decus regium Alexander

to die, and so far did military discipline give him the resolve to carry out the execution.

12. Then, separately, he addressed the Persian auxiliaries at a meeting. He praised their unfailing loyalty both 2 to him and to their earlier kings; and he reminded them of his services to them, how he had never considered them defeated foes but partners in victory, and finally how he had gone over to their customs and not imposed his own people's on them, and how by marriage bonds he had united the conquered and conqueror. He also said that he 3 would in future entrust his personal protection not only to Macedonians but also to them. And with that he chose 4 from them a thousand young men to join his bodyguard and incorporated in his army some auxiliaries for Macedonian training. This the Macedonians took badly, complain- 5 ing that their duties had been transferred to their enemies by the king. Then they all tearfully approached the king 6 and begged him to vent his displeasure by punishing them rather than humiliating them. By such restraint they ob- 7 tained the discharge of eleven thousand veterans. But 8 some of his older friends were also dismissed: Polyperchon, Clitus, Gorgias, Polydamas, ⟨Ammadas⟩ and Antigenes. Discharged men came under the authority of 9 Craterus, who was ordered to replace Antipater as governor of Macedonia, and he summoned Antipater with a force of new recruits to replace him. Those returning were 10 paid as if still in service.

In the course of this one of his friends died, Hephaes- 11 tion, who was very dear to the king, at first for his good looks and boyish charms, and later for his devotion to him. Breaking with regal decorum Alexander long mourned for 12

diu luxit tumulumque ei duodecim milium talentum fecit eumque post mortem coli ut deum iussit.

13. Ab ultimis litoribus Oceani Babyloniam revertenti nuntiatur legationes Karthaginiensium ceterarumque Africae civitatium, sed et Hispaniarum, Siciliae, Galliae, Sardiniae, nonnullas quoque ex Italia adventum eius Ba-
2 byloniae opperiri. Adeo universum terrarum orbem nominis eius terror invaserat, ut cunctae gentes veluti destinato
3 sibi regi adularentur. Hac igitur ex causa Babyloniam festinanti, velut conventum terrarum orbis acturo, quidam ex magis praedixit, ne urbem introiret, testatus hunc locum
4 ei fatalem fore. Ob haec omissa Babylonia in Borsipam
5 urbem trans Euphraten, desertam olim, concessit. Ibi ab Anaxarcho philosopho conpulsus est rursus magorum praedicta contemnere ut falsa et incerta et, si fatis constent, ignota mortalibus ac, si naturae debeantur, inmutabilia.
6 Reversus igitur Babyloniam multis diebus otio datis inter-
7 missum olim convivium sollemniter instituit; totusque in laetitiam effusus cum diei noctem pervigilem iunxisset, recedentem iam e convivio Medius Thessalus instaurata
8 comisatione et ipsum et sodales eius invitat. Accepto po-
9 culo media potione repente velut telo confixus ingemuit elatusque convivio semianimis tanto dolore cruciatus est, ut ferrum in remedia posceret tactumque hominum velut
10 vulnera indolesceret. Amici causas morbi intemperiem

---

34 Hephaestion, Alexander's closest friend, died at Ecbatana in October 324. Strictly speaking, he was worshipped as a hero, not a god, with his shrine in Egypt.   35 The seers were the Median priestly class; in other accounts they are Chaldaean astrologers. Borsipa was not deserted until much later.

him and he built him a tomb costing twelve thousand talents and ordered him posthumously worshipped as a god.[34]

13. Returning to Babylonia from the farthest shores of the ocean, he was informed that embassies from the Carthaginians and other African states, as well as embassies from Spain, Sicily, Gaul and Sardinia, and several from Italy, were awaiting his arrival in Babylonia. So far had the 2 whole world been touched by the terror of his name that all nations were fawning on him as their preordained king. Now while he was for that reason hurrying to Babylonia to 3 preside over what seemed to be a worldwide assembly, one of the seers warned him against entering the city, saying the place would be fatal for him.[35] He therefore bypassed 4 Babylon and withdrew across the Euphrates to the long-deserted city of Borsipa. There he was pushed by the phi- 5 losopher Anaxarchus into ignoring the seer's predictions as being false and unreliable: what was subject to fate lay beyond the knowledge of mortals, and what was due to nature was immutable. So returning to Babylon and giving 6 the army several days' rest, he resumed his long discontin-ued habit of the ceremonial banquet; and totally abandon- 7 ing himself to revelry he went a day and a night without sleep, and as he was leaving the dinner, the Thessalian Medius revived the festivities and invited him and his companions to join in. Taking a cup he was half way 8 through the drink when he suddenly uttered a groan as if pierced by a spear, and carried half-conscious from the 9 banquet he was racked with such pain that he asked for a sword to end it, and men's touch was as excruciating as wounds. His friends reported that the cause of his illness 10

ebrietatis disseminaverunt, re autem vera insidiae fuerunt, quarum infamiam successorum potentia oppressit.

14. Auctor insidiarum Antipater fuit, qui cum carissimos amicos eius interfectos videret, Alexandrum Lynces-
2 tam, generum suum, occisum, se magnis rebus in Graecia gestis non tam gratum apud regem quam invidiosum esse,
3 a matre quoque eius Olympiade variis se criminationibus
4 vexatum. Huc accedebant ante paucos dies supplicia in
5 praefectos devictarum nationum crudeliter habita. Ex quibus rebus se quoque a Macedonia non ad societatem
6 militiae, sed ad poenam vocatum arbitrabatur. Igitur ad occupandum regem Cassandrum filium dato veneno subornat, qui cum fratribus Philippo et Iolla ministrare
7 regi solebat, cuius veneni tanta vis fuit, ut non aere, non ferro, non testa contineretur, nec aliter ferri nisi in ungula equi potuerit; praemonito filio, ne alii quam Thessalo et
8 fratribus crederet. Hac igitur causa apud Thessalum para-
9 tum repetitumque convivium est. Philippus et Iollas praegustare ac temperare potum regis soliti in aqua frigida venenum habuerunt, quam praegustatae iam potioni supermiserunt.

15. Quarto die Alexander indubitatam mortem sentiens agnoscere se fatum domus maiorum suorum ait, nam
2 plerosque Aeacidarum intra XXX annum defunctos. Tumultuantes deinde milites insidiisque perire regem suspicantes ipse sedavit eosque omnes, cum prolatus in editissimum urbis locum esset, ad conspectum suum admisit

---

[36] A very confident assertion of something which is (and was) at least debatable.　　　[37] See 11.7.1.

[38] Alexander was almost thirty-three in 323.

was excessive drinking, but in fact it was a conspiracy, the scandal of it suppressed by the power of the successors.[36]

14. The man responsible for the conspiracy was Antipater, who could see that his closest friends had been executed, that his son-in-law Alexander the Lyncestian had been killed by him,[37] that by his own achievements in Greece he had made the king not so much grateful as envious, and that he had also been the object of various accusations made by his mother Olympias. Then there were also the cruel executions of governors of conquered nations a few days earlier. Reflecting on this he started to think that he had also been called from Macedonia not to join the campaign but to face punishment. So to anticipate the king he suborned his own son Cassander who, together with his brothers Philip and Iollas, used to wait on the king, and they gave him a poison of such virulence that it could not be contained by bronze, iron or earthenware and could be carried only in a horse's hoof, warning him to trust no one except his brothers and the Thessalian. This was why the drinking party was arranged and restarted in the Thessalian's quarters. Philip and Iollas who used to taste and regulate the king's drinks put the poison in cold water and added it to his cup after the tasting.

15. On the fourth day Alexander, feeling his death inevitable, said he recognized the fate that had overtaken the house of his forefathers,[38] for most of the Aeacids were dead by their thirtieth year. Then when the soldiers became disorderly and suspected the king was dying as a result of treachery, he personally calmed them down and had himself carried to the highest spot in the city, where he permitted them all to come to see him, and as they wept

3 osculandamque dexteram suam flentibus porrexit. Cum
lacrimarent omnes, ipse non sine lacrimis tantum, verum
sine ullo tristioris mentis argumento fuit, ut quosdam in-
patientius dolentes consolatus sit, quibusdam mandata ad
4 parentes eorum dederit: adeo sicuti in hostem, ita et in
mortem invictus animus fuit.

5 Dimissis militibus circumstantes amicos percontatur,
6 videanturne similem sibi reperturi regem. Tacentibus
cunctis tum ipse, ut hoc nesciat, ita illud scire vaticina-
rique se ac paene oculis videre dixit, quantum sit in hoc
certamine sanguinis fusura Macedonia, quantis caedibus,
7 quo cruore mortuo sibi parentatura. Ad postremum cor-
8 pus suum in Hammonis templum condi iubet. Cum defi-
cere eum amici viderent, quaerunt, quem imperii faciat
9 heredem. Respondit "dignissimum." Tanta illi magnitudo
animi fuit, ut, cum Herculem filium, cum fratrem Arridaeum, cum Roxanen uxorem praegnantem relinqueret,
oblitus necessitudinum dignissimum nuncuparit here-
10 dem: prorsus quasi nefas esset viro forti alium quam virum
fortem succedere, aut tanti regni opes aliis quam probatis
11 relinqui. Hac voce veluti bellicum inter amicos cecinisset
aut malum Discordiae misisset, ita omnes in aemulationem consurgunt et ambitione vulgi tacitum favorem
12 militum quaerunt. Sexta die praeclusa voce exemptum
digito anulum Perdiccae tradidit, quae res gliscentem

---

39 These maudlin details are fiction; Alexander lost the ability
to speak during his final few days.
40 Roxane was the daughter of the Sogdian Oxyartes and had
married Alexander in 327. Her child would be Alexander IV.

he held out his hand for them to kiss. When all were weep-   3
ing, he himself was so far from tears that he showed no
sign of low spirits and was actually comforting some who
were grieving uncontrollably and giving others messages
for their parents; so far, just as when facing the enemy, was   4
his spirit undaunted facing death.[39]

When the soldiers were dismissed he asked the friends   5
at his bedside if they thought they would ever find a king
like him. When they all fell silent he then said himself that,   6
although he did not know that, he did know this one thing,
which he could predict and almost see with his own eyes—
how much blood Macedonia would shed in this struggle,
and with what slaughter and gore it would appease his
shade. Finally he ordered his body to be buried in the   7
temple of Hammon. When his friends saw him failing,   8
they asked whom he appointed heir to the empire. He
replied "the worthiest man." Such was the greatness of his   9
soul that although leaving a son, Hercules, a brother, Arridaeus, and a wife, Roxane, who was pregnant, he ignored
family ties and nominated "the worthiest man" as his successor,[40] clearly meaning that it was wrong for a brave man   10
to be succeed by anyone but a brave man, or for the power
of a great kingdom to be left to any but those of proven
worth. As if by these words he had given a war cry among   11
his friends or thrown the apple of Discord,[41] they all rose
to compete with each other and canvassing the mob furtively sought the favor of the troops. On the sixth day his   12
voice failed and he took off his ring and handed it to Per-

[41] The golden apple thrown into the banquet celebrating the
marriage of Peleus and Thetis that ultimately brought about the
Trojan War.

13   amicorum dissensionem sedavit. Nam etsi non voce
nuncupatus heres, iudicio tamen electus videbatur.

    16. Decessit Alexander mense Iunio, annos tres et XXX
natus, vir supra humanam potentiam magnitudine animi
2   praeditus. Qua nocte eum mater Olympias concepit, visa
per quietem est cum ingenti serpente volutari, nec de-
cepta somnio est, nam profecto maius humana mortalitate
3   opus utero tulit; quam cum Aeacidarum gens ab ultima
saeculorum memoria et regna patris, fratris, mariti ac
deinceps maiorum omnium inlustraverint, nullius tamen
4   nomine quam filii clarior fuit. Prodigia magnitudinis eius
5   ipso ortu nonnulla apparuere. Nam ea die, qua natus est,
duae aquilae tota die perpetes supra culmen domus patris
eius sederunt, omen duplicis imperii, Europae Asiaeque,
6   praeferentes. Eadem quoque die nuntium pater eius dua-
rum victoriarum accepit, altera belli Illyrici, altera certaminis Olympici, in quod quadrigarum currus miserat,
quod omen universarum terrarum victoriam infanti por-
7   tendebat. Puer acerrimis litterarum studiis eruditus fuit.
8   Exacta pueritia per quinquennium sub Aristotele doctore,
9   inclito omnium philosophorum, crevit. Accepto deinde
imperio regem se terrarum omnium ac mundi appellari
10   iussit tantamque fiduciam sui militibus fecit, ut illo
11   praesente nullius hostis arma nec inermes timuerint. Itaque cum nullo hostium umquam congressus est, quem
non vicerit, nullam urbem obsedit, quam non expugnaverit,
12   nullam gentem adiit, quam non calcaverit. Victus denique
ad postremum est non virtute hostili, sed insidiis suorum
et fraude civili.

---

42 See 11.11.3.

diccas, which calmed the growing dissension among his
friends. For while not verbally designated the heir, he still 13
seemed the one chosen by him.

16. Alexander died in the month of June at the age of
thirty-three, a man endowed with superhuman greatness
of spirit. On the night that his mother Olympias conceived 2
him, she saw in her sleep that she was entwined with a
huge serpent, and she was not misled by the dream, for
what she carried in her womb was certainly more than
mortal;[42] and although her renown came from her descent 3
from the Aeacids, a family dating back to earliest times,
and from her father, brother, husband and all her ancestors being kings, from nobody's name did she have greater
fame than her son's. Prodigies foretelling his greatness 4
appeared right at his birth. For on the day he was born two 5
eagles settled all day on the roof of his father's house, an
omen of the twin empire of Europe and Asia. That very 6
day his father also received word of two victories, one in
the Illyrian War, the other in a race at Olympia in which
he had entered four-horse chariots, an omen that was pre-
dicting worldwide conquest for the infant. As a boy he was 7
a dedicated student of literature. His boyhood over, he 8
grew up having five years' instruction under Aristotle, a
man renowned among all philosophers. Then on coming 9
to power he ordered he be called the king of all lands and
of the world and such confidence did he inspire in his men 10
that, when he was present, they feared no enemy's army
even if unarmed themselves. So it was that he fought no 11
adversary that he did not defeat, besieged no city that he
did not take, and attacked no people that he did not tram-
ple underfoot. He was finally overcome not by an enemy's 12
valor but his own men's plotting and internal treachery.

LIBER XIII

1. Extincto in ipso aetatis ac victoriarum flore Alexandro Magno triste apud omnes tota Babylonia silentium fuit.
2 Sed nec devictae gentes fidem nuntio habuerunt, quod ut
3 invictum regem ita inmortalem esse crediderant, recordantes quotiens praesenti morte ereptus esset, quam saepe pro amisso repente se non sospitem tantum suis,
4 verum etiam victorem obtulisset. Ut vero mortis eius fides adfuit, omnes barbarae gentes paulo ante ab eo devictae
5 non ut hostem, sed ut parentem luxerunt. Mater quoque Darii regis, quae amisso filio a fastigio tantae maiestatis in captivitatem redacta indulgentia victoris in eam diem vitae non paenituerat, audita morte Alexandri mortem sibi
6 ipsa conscivit, non quod hostem filio praeferret, sed quod pietatem filii in eo, quem ut hostem timuerat, experta es-
7 set. Contra Macedones versa vice non ut civem ac tantae maiestatis regem, verum ut hostem amissum gaudebat, et severitatem nimiam et adsidua belli pericula execrantes.

---

1 The major narrative source for the successors of Alexander is Diodorus Siculus, from Book 18 onward, generally thought to depend (as probably did Trogus) on Hieronymus of Cardia along with Duris of Samos. Arrian also covered the successors, and in addition there are Plutarch's biographies of Eumenes and Deme-

BOOK XIII

1. When Alexander the Great died in the prime of life and the flush of victory there was a mournful silence among everyone throughout Babylonia.[1] But the conquered nations had no confidence in the report because while they had thought their king invincible they had also thought him immortal, remembering how often he had been snatched from imminent death, and how often when believed lost he had suddenly appeared to his men not only unscathed but even victorious. When confirmation of his death arrived, all the barbarian tribes recently defeated by him mourned for him not as an enemy, but as a father. The mother of King Darius had after losing her son been reduced to captivity from such an exalted position, but not until that day had she grown weary of life, and now on hearing of Alexander's death she committed suicide, not because she preferred an enemy to her son but because she had felt the affection of a son in someone she had feared as an enemy. The Macedonians on the other hand were rejoicing, thinking not that they had lost a fellow citizen or a king of great majesty, but an enemy, and they cursed his extreme severity and the endless dangers they

trius (which parallel Justin to the end of Book 14). See in general Hammond, *A History of Macedonia*, 3:95ff.

8 Huc accedebat, quod principes regnum et imperia, vulgus militum thesauros et grande pondus auri velut inopinatam praedam spectabant, illi successionem regni, hi opum ac

9 divitiarum hereditatem cogitantes. Erant enim in thesauris L milia talentum et in annuo vectigali tributo tricena

10 milia. Sed nec amici Alexandri frustra regnum spectabant. Nam eius virtutis ac venerationis erant, ut singulos reges

11 putares; quippe ea formae pulchritudo et proceritas corporis et virium ac sapientiae magnitudo in omnibus fuit, ut qui eos ignoraret, non ex una gente, sed ex toto terra-

12 rum orbe electos iudicaret. Neque enim umquam ante Macedonia vel ulla gens alia tam clarorum virorum pro-

13 ventu floruit, quos primo Philippus, mox Alexander tanta cura legerat, ut non tam ad societatem belli quam in suc-

14 cessionem regni electi viderentur. Quis igitur miretur talibus ministris orbem terrarum victum, cum exercitus

15 Macedonum tot non ducibus, sed regibus regeretur? Qui numquam sibi repperissent pares, si non inter se concurrissent, multosque Macedonia provincia Alexandros habuisset, nisi Fortuna eos aemulatione virtutis in perniciem mutuam armasset.

2. Ceterum occiso Alexandro non ut laeti ita et securi

2 fuere omnibus unum locum conpetentibus, nec minus milites quam invicem se timebant, quorum et libertas

3 solutior et favor incertus erat. Inter ipsos vero aequalitas

had faced in battle. In addition the leaders were contem- 8
plating the kingdom and positions of power, the common
soldiers treasures and great hoards of gold, like an unexpected prize, the ones' eyes focused on succession to the
throne, the others' on inheriting wealth and riches. For in 9
the treasury there were fifty thousand talents, and in annual tribute there were three hundred thousand a year.
But neither were Alexander's friends unreasonable in hav- 10
ing eyes on the kingdom. For such were their qualities and
such the respect they enjoyed that you might think any of
them a king; for there were such handsome features, fine 11
physiques, and great physical and mental attributes in all
of them that anyone not knowing them might have supposed them drawn not from one people but from all over
the world. For never before that time was Macedonia or 12
any other nation blessed with a crop of such outstanding
men, men whom Philip first and Alexander after him had 13
selected with such care that they appeared chosen less as
comrades in arms than as successors to the throne. Who 14
then should be surprised at the world being conquered by
such officers, when the army of the Macedonians was under so many men who were not generals but kings? They 15
could never have been equaled had they not clashed
among themselves, and the province of Macedonia would
have had many Alexanders had not Fortune by making
them rivals in courage armed them for mutual destruction.

2. But while pleased with Alexander's murder they
were not also secure since they were all competing for one
position, and they had no less fear of their soldiers than 2
they did of each other, their license being greater and their
sympathies unpredictable. The equality among them- 3

discordiam augebat nemine tantum ceteros excedente, ut ei aliquis se submitteret.

4   Armati itaque in regiam coeunt ad firmandum rerum
5 praesentium statum. Perdicca censet Roxanes expectari partum, quae exacto mense octavo matura iam ex Alexandro erat, et si puerum peperisset, hunc dari successorem
6 patri. Meleager negat differenda in partus dubios consilia, neque expectandum, dum reges sibi nascerentur, cum iam
7 genitis uti liceret; seu puer illis placeat, esse Pergami filium Alexandri natum ex Barsine, nomine Herculem, seu
8 mallent iuvenem, esse in castris fratrem Alexandri Arridaeum, comem et cunctis non suo tantum, verum et patris
9 Philippi nomine acceptissimum. Ceterum Roxanen esse originis Persicae, nec esse fas, ut Macedonibus ex sanguine eorum, quorum regna deleverint, reges constituan-
10 tur, quod nec ipsum Alexandrum voluisse dicit; denique
11 morientem nullam de eo mentionem habuisse. Ptolomeus recusabat regem Arridaeum non propter maternas modo sordes, quod ex Larissaeo scorto nasceretur, sed etiam propter valetudinem maiorem, quam patiebatur, ne ille
12 nomen regis, alius imperium teneret; melius esse ex his legi, qui prae virtute regi suo proximi fuerint, qui provincias regant, quibus bella mandentur, quam sub persona
13 regis indignorum imperio subiciantur. Vicit Perdiccae
14 sententia consensu universorum. Placuit itaque Roxanes expectari partum, et, si puer natus fuisset, tutores Leona-

---

2 On Roxane and her child (Alexander IV) and Hercules, see 12.15.9. Arridaeus (below), considered to be feebleminded, was about thirty-four years old; his mother was no whore (see below), but Philina of the Aleuadae of Larissa in Thessaly.

selves actually increased their discord since no one so far surpassed the others as to have anyone defer to him.

So they assembled under arms at the palace to resolve the present situation. Perdiccas recommended that they wait for the birth of the child of Roxane, who was then eight months pregnant by Alexander, and if she had a boy he should be his father's successor.[2] Meleager said plans should not be delayed by doubt over what might be born, and they should not wait for kings when they had recourse to some already born; if they wanted a boy, there was at Pergamum Alexander's son by Barsine, Hercules by name, or if they preferred a young man, there was in the camp Alexander's brother Arridaeus, an affable fellow and most acceptable to everyone not only in himself but also through of his father Philip. Roxane, however, was of Persian descent, and it was not right for kings to be appointed for Macedonians from the bloodline of those whose kingdoms they had destroyed, something not even Alexander himself had wanted—in fact when dying he had made no mention of the child. Ptolemy opposed Arridaeus as king not only because of his mother's low birth, since she was born of a Larissan prostitute, but also because of the serious disability he suffered, which might leave him as titular king while another held the power; better for one to be chosen from those closest the king in personal qualities, men who governed provinces and were entrusted with military campaigns, than to be subjected to the rule of unworthy men under a puppet king. Perdiccas' opinion prevailed with unanimous agreement. It was therefore decided that they await the birth of Roxane's child, and, should a boy be born, they appointed Leonatus, Perdiccas,

tum et Perdiccam et Crateron et Antipatrum constituunt
confestimque in tutorum obsequia iurant.

3. Cum equites quoque idem fecissent, pedites in-
dignati nullas sibi consiliorum partes relictas Arridaeum,
Alexandri fratrem, regem appellant satellitesque illi ex
tribu sua legunt et nomine Philippi patris vocari iubent.
2 Quae cum nuntiata equitibus essent, legatos ad mitigan-
dos eorum animos duos ex proceribus, Attalum et Melea-
grum mittunt, qui potentiam ex vulgi adulatione quae-
3 rentes omissa legatione militibus consentiunt. Statim et
4 seditio crevit, ubi caput et consilium habere coepit. Tum
ad delendum equitatum cuncti in regiam armati inrum-
5 punt, quo cognito equites trepidi ab urbe discedunt ca-
strisque positis et ipsi pedites terrere coeperunt.
6
7 Sed nec procerum inter se odia cessabant. Attalus ad
interficiendum Perdiccam, ducem partis alterius, mittit,
8 ad quem armatum et ultro provocantem cum accedere
percussores ausi non fuissent, tanta constantia Perdiccae
fuit, ut ultro ad pedites veniret et in contionem vocatos
9 edoceret, quod facinus molirentur. Respicerent contra
quos arma sumpsissent: non illos Persas, sed Macedonas,
non hostes, sed cives esse, plerosque etiam cognatos eorum, certe conmilitones, eorundem castrorum ac pericu-
10 lorum socios; edituros deinde egregium hostibus suis
spectaculum, ut quorum armis victos se doleant, eorum
mutuis caedibus gaudeant, parentaturosque sanguine suo
manibus hostium a se interfectorum.

Craterus and Antipater as the child's guardians and they immediately swore allegiance to the guardians.

3. When the cavalry also did the same, the infantry, furious at being left no say in the matter, declared Alexander's brother Arridaeus king, appointed guards for him from among their number, and ordered that he be addressed by his father's name, Philip. When this was reported to the cavalry, they sent as delegates two of their officers, Attalus and Meleager, to calm them down, but these while seeking power by currying favor with the crowd abandoned their mission and joined the soldiers. The mutiny immediately grew when it began to have leadership and a plan of action. Then in order to eliminate the cavalry they all burst in arms into the royal tent, and at the news the cavalrymen fled in panic from the city, pitched camp, and themselves began to intimidate the infantry.

But there was no end to the animosity between the leaders. Attalus sent men to kill Perdiccas, the leader of the other party, but as he was armed and even challenging them and the assassins had not dared confront him, so fearless was Perdiccas that he even came to the infantry and calling them to a meeting told then clearly the crime they were be committing They should consider against whom they had taken up arms, he said; these were not Persians but Macedonians, not enemies but fellow citizens, most of them even their blood relatives and certainly their comrades in arms, men who had shared with them the same camp and same dangers: a fine sight would they then be providing for their foes, their internecine slaughter bringing joy to men still smarting from defeat at their hands, and with their own blood appeasing the spirits of enemies killed by them.

4. Haec cum pro singulari facundia sua Perdicca pero-
rasset, adeo movit pedites, ut probato consilio eius dux ab
2 omnibus legeretur. Tum equites in concordiam revocati in
3 Arridaeum regem consentiunt. Servata est portio regni
4 Alexandri filio, si natus esset. Haec agebant posito in medio Alexandri corpore, ut maiestas eius testis decretorum
esset.

5 His ita compositis Macedoniae et Graeciae Antipater
praeponitur, regiae pecuniae custodia Cratero traditur,
castrorum et exercitus et rerum cura Meleagro et Perdic-
6 cae adsignatur; iubeturque Arridaeus rex corpus Alexandri
7 in Hammonis templum deducere. Tunc Perdicca, infensus
seditionis auctoribus, repente ignaro collega lustrationem
castrorum propter mortem regis in posterum edicit.
8 Postquam armatum exercitum in campo constituit, consentientibus universis evocatos, dum transit, de singulis
9 manipulis seditiosos supplicio tradi occulte iubet. Reversus inde inter principes provincias dividit, simul ut et aemulos removeret et munus imperii beneficii sui faceret.
10 Prima Ptolomeo Aegyptus et Africae Arabiaeque pars
sorte venit, quem ex gregario milite Alexander virtutis

---

3 This was hardly an effective arrangement. Craterus was in
fact made guardian of Arridaeus' kingdom, and Perdiccas remained chiliarch, a vague "first man after the king," Meleager
being his right-hand man. The King Arridaeus next mentioned is
a different man, later satrap of Hellespontine Phrygia. The words
"its affairs" here translate the Latin *rerum* of the manuscripts.
Seel, however, prints Madvig's *regum*, "kings"; the post of super-
visor is attested elsewhere, but at this point there was only one
king to be concerned with.

4. When Perdiccas presented these arguments with his superb eloquence, he so impressed the infantry that his advice was taken and he was chosen as leader by everyone. The cavalry were then reconciled and they agreed on Arridaeus as their king. Part of the kingdom was reserved for Alexander's son, if one were born. These arrangements they made with Alexander's body set among them so that his majestic presence should witness their decisions. 2 3 4

These matters thus settled, Antipater was appointed governor of Macedonia and Greece, Craterus was given charge of the royal treasury, and Meleager and Perdiccas were assigned the camp, the army and its affairs;[3] and King Arridaeus was instructed to escort the body of Alexander to the temple of Hammon.[4] Then Perdiccas, furious with the instigators of the mutiny, suddenly and without consulting his colleague announced a ceremonial purification of the camp for the king's death on the following day. After he drew up the armed troops on an open plain, he with everyone's approval called out the mutinous elements from each maniple[5] as he passed along the lines and secretly ordered their execution. Returning from there he divided the provinces among the officers, both to remove any rivals and also make the award of a command a favor from him. First Egypt and part of Africa and Arabia came by lot to Ptolemy, whom Alexander had promoted from 5 6 7 8 9 10

[4] Perdiccas intended Alexander's body to go for traditional burial at Aegae in Macedon, but it ended up in Alexandria after the machinations of Ptolemy.

[5] A maniple was a Roman infantry company; Justin applies it here to the subordinate units of the Macedonian army. Meleager was also murdered at this time.

11 causa provexerat; cui ad tractandam provinciam Cleo-
12 menes, qui Alexandriam aedificaverat, additur. Confinem
huic provinciae Syriam Laomedon Mytilenaeus, Ciliciam
13 Philotas accipiunt. Pitho Illyrius Mediae maiori, Atropatos
14 minori, socer Perdiccae, praeponitur. Susiana gens Coeno,
15 Phrygia maior Antigono, Philippi filio, adsignatur. Lyciam
et Pamphyliam Nearchus, Cariam Cassander, Lydiam
16 Menander sortiuntur. Leonato minor Phrygia evenit;
Thracia et regiones Pontici maris Lysimacho, Cappadocia
17 cum Paphlagonia Eumeni data. Summus castrorum tribu-
18 natus Seleuco, Antiochi filio, cessit. Stipatoribus regiis
19 satellitibusque Cassander, filius Antipatri, praeficitur. In
Bactriana ulteriore et Indiae regionibus priores praefecti
20 retenti. Seras inter amnes Hydaspem et Indum Taxiles
21 habebat. In colonias in Indis conditas Pithon, Agenoris
filius, mittitur. Parapamenos, finem Caucasi montis,
22 Oxyartes accepit. Arachossi Cedrossique Sibyrtio tradun-
23 tur; Drancae et Arei Stasanori. Bactrianos Amyntas sor-
titur, Sogdianos †Soleus† Staganor, Parthos Philippus,
Hyrcanos Phrataphernes, Carmanos Tleptolemus, Persas
Peucestes, Babylonios Archon Pellaeus, Arcesilaus Meso-
24 potamiam. Haec divisio velut fatale munus singulis conti-

---

6 This Philotas was not Parmenion's executed son but one of
Alexander's friends.

7 Atropatos, or Atropates, was a Persian nobleman; his daughter's name is unknown.

8 This term usually indicates the Chinese, but that is clearly
not so here. It must refer to Taxila, the kingdom of Taxiles, an
Indian ruler and ally since 326 of Alexander.

9 *Soleus Staganor* and other MSS readings are scribal errors
due to the mention of Stasanor above and the Sogdians below.

the ranks for his courage; to administer the province he 11
was also assigned Cleomenes, who had built Alexandria.
The province adjacent to it, Syria, was given to Laomedon 12
the Mitylenian, and Cilicia to Philotas.[6] Pithon the Illyrian 13
was made governor of Greater Media, and Atropatos, Perdiccas' father-in-law, was made governor of Lesser Media.[7] The people of Susiana were assigned to Coenus, and 14
Greater Phrygia to Antigonus, son of Philip. Lycia and 15
Pamphylia were allotted to Nearchus, Caria to Cassander,
and Lydia to Menander. To Leonatus fell Lesser Phrygia; 16
to Lysimachus Thrace and the coastline of Pontus, and to
Eumenes Cappadocia together with Paphlagonia. Overall 17
command of the camp fell to Seleucus, son of Antiochus.
The royal entourage and guards were put under Cas- 18
sander son of Antipater. In further Bactria and regions of 19
India their former governors were retained. The Seres[8] 20
between the rivers Hydaspes and Indus came under Taxiles' jurisdiction. Pithon, son of Agenor, was sent out to the 21
colonies established in India. The Parapameni, in the farthest Caucasus range, were taken by Oxyartes. The Ara- 22
chosians and Cedrosians were assigned to Sibyrtius, the
Drancae and Arei to Stasanor. Amyntas was allotted the 23
Bactrians, †Soleus Staganor† the Sogdians,[9] Philip the
Parthians, Phrataphernes the Hyrcanians, Tleptolemus
the Carmanians, Peucestes the Persians, Archon of Pella
the Babylonians, and Arcesilaus Mesopotamia. While this 24
division became a fatal gift for some, it presented an op-

Other evidence shows that the Philip mentioned next was made
satrap of both Bactria and the Sogdians (roughly Afghanistan),
and Phrataphernes satrap of Parthia and Hyrcania (in the north
and northeast, respectively, of modern Iran).

gisset, ita magna incrementorum materia plurimis fuit;
25 siquidem non magno post tempore, quasi regna, non prae-
fecturas divisissent, sic reges ex praefectis facti magnas
opes non sibi tantum paraverunt, verum etiam posteris
reliquerunt.

5. Dum haec in Oriente aguntur, in Graecia Athenienses et Aetoli bellum, quod iam vivo Alexandro move-
2 rant, summis viribus instruebant. Causae belli erant, quod
reversus ab India Alexander epistulas in Graeciam scripserat, quibus omnium civitatium exules, praeter caedis
3 damnati, restituebantur. Quae recitatae praesenti universa
Graecia in mercatu Olympiaco magnos motus fecerunt,
4 quia plurimi non legibus pulsi patria, sed per factionem
principum fuerunt, verentibus isdem principibus, ne re-
5 vocati potentiores in re publica fierent. Palam igitur iam
tunc multae civitates libertatem bello vindicandam freme-
6 bant. Principes tamen omnium Athenienses et Aetoli
7 fuere. Quod cum nuntiatum Alexandro esset, mille naves
longas sociis imperari praeceperat, quibus in Occidente
bellum gereret, excursurusque cum valida manu fuerat ad
8 Athenas delendas. Igitur Athenienses contracto XXX milium exercitu et ducentis navibus bellum cum Antipatro,
cui Graecia sorte evenerat, gerunt eumque detractantem
proelium et Heracleae urbis moenibus tuentem se obsi-
9 dione cingunt. Eodem tempore Demosthenes, Athenien-

---

10 Of course, a great deal of shifting and rearrangement occurred first, and the power that became kingship devolved on only
a few.

11 The Lamian War, put down in 322. Alexander's letter had
been read at the Olympic games of 324. Additional sources are

portunity to acquire power for most; for not much later, as   25
though they had divided kingdoms, not provinces, they
became kings instead of governors and not only acquired
great power for themselves but also left it to their descendants.[10]

5. While this was occurring in the East, in Greece the
Athenians and Aetolians were prosecuting with all their
might a war that they had earlier started while Alexander
was still alive.[11] What caused the war was that after return-   2
ing from India Alexander had written a letter to Greece
by which exiles from all the city-states, were being rein-
stated apart from condemned murderers. When this was   3
read out in the presence of all of Greece at the Olympic
festival it caused great alarm, because large numbers had   4
been driven from home not by due legal process but by a
faction of leading citizens, and these same leading citizens
now feared that if recalled those people would become
more powerful in their state. Thus many cities were then   5
already openly chafing to assert their freedom by war.
Foremost among them, however, were the Athenians and   6
Aetolians. When this was reported to Alexander, he had   7
ordered a thousand warships to be levied from the allies
for fighting a war in the West and was going to set out with
a powerful force to destroy Athens. So the Athenians   8
raised a force of thirty thousand men and two hundred
ships and made war on Antipater, to whom Greece had
been allotted, and when he refused to meet them in battle
and sought refuge within the city walls of Heraclea, they
laid siege to him. At that same time the Athenian orator   9

Plut. *Vit. Phoc.* 23ff.; Plut. *Vit. Dem.* 27ff.; *AO* 406ff. (the years
323/2 and 321/0).

sis orator, pulsus patria ob crimen accepti ab Harpago
auri, qui crudelitatem Alexandri fugerat, quod civitatem
in eiusdem Alexandri bellum inpelleret, forte Megaris
10   exulabat. Qui ut missum ab Atheniensibus Hyperidem
legatum cognovit, qui Peloponneson in societatem armorum sollicitaret, secutus eum Sicyona, Argos et Corinthum
ceterasque civitates eloquentia sua Atheniensibus iunxit.
11   Ob quod factum missa ab Atheniensibus obviam navi ab
exilio revocatur.
12   Interim in obsidione Antipatri Leosthenes, dux Atheniensium, telo a muris in transeuntem iacto occiditur.
13   Quae res tantum animorum Antipatro dedit, ut etiam val-
14   lum rescindere auderet. Auxilium deinde a Leonato per
legatos petit, qui cum venire cum exercitu nuntiatus esset,
obvii ei Athenienses cum instructis copiis fuere, ibique
15   equestri proelio gravi vulnere ictus extinguitur. Antipater
tametsi auxilia sua videret victa, morte tamen Leonati lae-
tatus est; quippe et aemulum sublatum et vires eius acces-
16   sisse sibi gratulabatur. Statim igitur exercitu eius recepto,
cum par hostibus etiam proelio videretur, solutus obsi-
17   dione in Macedoniam concessit. Graecorum quoque copiae finibus Graeciae hoste pulso in urbes dilapsae.
    6. Interea Perdicca bello Ariarathi, regi Cappadocum,

---

12 That is, Harpalus.

13 Justin conflates campaigns in Cappadocia (322) and Pisidia
(321); see Diod. Sic. 18.16.1ff. and 18.22.

Demosthenes, who had been banished from his homeland
on a charge of accepting gold from Harpagus,[12] who had
fled from Alexander's brutal reprisals, happened to be in
exile in Megara because he was pressing his city into war
with the same Alexander. When he learned that Hyperides   10
had been sent as a delegate by the Athenians to induce the
Peloponnese to join their uprising, he accompanied him
and with his oratory brought Sicyon, Argos, Corinth and
other cities over to the Athenian cause. For this service a   11
ship was sent by the Athenians to meet him and he was
recalled from exile.

   Meanwhile, when Antipater was under siege, the Athe-   12
nian leader Leosthenes was killed by a weapon hurled at
him from the city walls as he was passing by. This incident   13
so raised Antipater's spirits that he even ventured to break
down the Athenian siege rampart. He then sought assis-   14
tance from Leonatus by means of delegates, but when the
Athenians were then informed that he was approaching
with an army they moved to confront him in battle forma-
tion and there he died from a serious wound received in
a cavalry engagement. Although Antipater saw that his   15
reinforcements had been defeated, he was still pleased
with the death of Leonatus; for he could congratulate himself both on both removing his rival and also acquiring
his forces. So he immediately commandeered Leonatus'   16
army, and since he now thought himself a match for the
enemy even in battle, he broke out of the siege and withdrew to Macedonia. The Greek forces, with the enemy   17
now driven from Greek soil, also slipped away to their
various cities.

   6. Meanwhile Perdiccas had made war on Ariarathes,
the king of Cappadocia,[13] but after defeating him in battle

inlato proelio victor nihil praemii praeter vulnera et peri-
2 cula rettulit. Quippe hostes ab acie in urbem recepti occisis coniugibus et liberis domos quisque suas cum omnibus
3 copiis incenderunt; eodem congestis etiam servitiis semet
ipsi praecipitant, ut nihil hostis victor suarum rerum prae-
4 ter incendii spectaculo frueretur. Inde, ut viribus auctoritatem regiam adquireret, ad nuptias Cleopatrae, sororis
Alexandri Magni et alterius Alexandri quondam uxoris,
5 non aspernante Olympiade, matre eius, intendit, sed prius
Antipatrum sub adfinitatis obtentu capere cupiebat.
6 Itaque fingit se in matrimonium filiam eius petere, quo
facilius ab eo supplementum tironum ex Macedonia ob-
7 tineret. Quem dolum praesentiente Antipatro, dum duas
8 eodem tempore uxores quaerit, neutram obtinuit. Post
9 haec bellum inter Antigonum et Perdiccam oritur. Antigono Crateros et Antipater auxilium ferebant, qui facta
cum Atheniensibus pace Polyperconta Graeciae et Mace-
10 doniae praeponunt. Perdicca alienatis regibus, Arridaeo et
Alexandro, Magni filio, in Cappadocia, quorum cura illi
mandata fuerat, de summa belli ⟨amicos⟩ in consilium
11 adhibet. Quibusdam placebat bellum in Macedoniam
transferri, ad ipsum fontem et caput regni, ubi et Olym-
12 pias esset, mater Alexandri, non mediocre momentum
partium et civium favor propter Alexandri Philippique
13 nomina; sed in rem visum est ab Aegypto incipere, ne in

---

[14] Alexander of Epirus, who had died in 331 (12.2.1ff.).
Cleopatra's daughter was named Nicaea.

[15] Arrangements with Athens had been made in 322, the previous year. At this time, they were concerned with the Aetolians
(Diod. Sic. 18.25).

he left with no prize other than wounds and the dangers
he had faced. For the enemy on returning to their city   2
from the battle killed their wives and children, set fire to
their homes together with all their possessions; and even   3
throwing in their slaves hurled themselves into the flames
so their victorious enemy should enjoy nothing of their
possessions but the sight of them burning. Then, to ac-   4
quire regal sanction for his power, he turned his thoughts
to marriage with Cleopatra, sister of Alexander the Great
and former wife of the other Alexander,[14] a match to which
her mother Olympias had no objection, but first he wanted   5
to ensnare Antipater with the pretext of a family alliance.
So he pretended that he wished to marry his daughter, his   6
true aim being to gain from him more easily fresh levies
of recruits from Macedonia. When Antipater saw through   7
the ruse, however, his simultaneous courting of two
women left him with neither. After this, war arose be-   8
tween Antigonus and Perdiccas. Antigonus was brought   9
support by Craterus and Antipater, who made peace with
the Athenians, and appointed Polypercon governor of
Greece and Macedonia.[15] Perdiccas sent off to Cappado-   10
cia Arridaeus and the son of Alexander the Great, the
kings who had been placed in his charge, and consulted
his friends on the conduct of the war. Some favored having   11
the war transferred to Macedonia, the very source and
heart of the empire, where there was also Olympias, the
mother of Alexander, no little support for their cause, and   12
also approved by the citizens because of the names Alexander and Philip; but it seemed expedient to start with   13

14 Macedoniam profectis Asia a Ptolomeo occuparetur. Eumeni praeter provincias, quas acceperat, Paphlagonia et
15 Caria et Lycia et Phrygia adiciuntur. Ibi Crateron et Antipatrum opperiri iubetur; adiutores ei dantur cum exerci-
16 tibus suis frater Perdiccae Alcetas et Neoptolemus; Clito
cura classis traditur; Cilicia Philotae adempta Philoxeno
datur; ipse Perdicca Aegyptum cum ingenti exercitu petit.
17 Sic Macedonia in duas partes discurrentibus ducibus in
sua viscera armatur, ferrumque ab hostili bello in civilem
sanguinem vertit, exemplo furentium manus ac membra
sua ipsa caesura.
18 Sed Ptolomeus in Aegypto sollerti industria magnas
19 opes parabat. Quippe et Aegyptios insigni moderatione in
favorem sui sollicitaverat et reges finitimos beneficiis ob-
20 sequiisque devinxerat; terminos quoque imperii adquisita
Cyrene urbe ampliaverat factusque iam tantus erat, ut non
tam timeret hostem quam timendus ipse hostibus esset.

7. Cyrene autem condita fuit ab Aristaeo, cui nomen
2 Battos propter linguae obligationem fuit. Huius pater Grinus, rex Therae insulae, cum ad oraculum Delphos propter dedecus adulescentis filii nondum loquentis deum
deprecaturus venisset, responsum accepit, quo iubebatur
filius eius Battos Africam petere et urbem Cyrenen
3 condere; usum ibi linguae accepturum. Cum responsum

---

16 As Eumenes had been given Paphlagonia in 323, perhaps
Pamphylia is meant here.

17 For the details of which see Diod. Sic. 18.19ff.

18 For versions of the founding of Cyrene, which took place
around 630, see Hdt. 4.150ff., where Battos' father is Polymnes-
tos, and Grinus is the son of Aesanius; compare Pind. *Pyth.* 4. The

Egypt, so that after they left for Macedonia Asia would not
be seized by Ptolemy. Eumenes, apart from the provinces   14
that he had already received, was also given Paphlagonia,[16]
Caria, Lycia and Phrygia. There he was ordered to wait for   15
Craterus and Antipater; and as assistants he was given,
together with their armies, Perdiccas' brother Alcetas, and
Neoptolemus; Clitus was put in charge of the fleet; Cilicia   16
was taken from Philotas and given to Philoxenus; Perdiccas himself made for Egypt with a huge army. Thus Mace-   17
donia, its leaders splitting into two factions, armed itself
to stab its own vitals, and turned its sword from fighting a
foe to shedding its people's blood, ready like lunatics to
lacerate its own hands and limbs.

But in Egypt Ptolemy was with his shrewd energy ac-   18
cumulating considerable resources. He had both won the   19
Egyptians over to him with his exceptional restraint and
also put neighboring kings under obligation to him through
his benefactions and services; the bounds of his empire he   20
had also extended by acquiring the city of Cyrene,[17] and
so great had he now become that he did not fear any enemy as much as he was himself feared by his enemies.

7. Cyrene had been founded by Aristaeus, who had the
name Battos from being tongue-tied.[18] His father Grinus,   2
king of the island of Thera, had come to the oracle at
Delphi to beg for the god's help, being ashamed that his
adolescent son could not yet speak, and he received the
response that his son Battos was ordered to head for Africa
and found the city of Cyrene; there he would gain use of

Battiad kings ruled until about 440. Thera is the island called
Santorini today.

ludibrio simile videretur propter solitudinem Therae insulae, ex qua coloni ad urbem condendam in Africam tam vastae regionis proficisci iubebantur, res omissa est.
4 Interiecto deinde tempore velut contumaces pestilentia deo parere conpelluntur, quorum tam insignis paucitas fuit, ut vix unam navem conplerent.

5 Cum venissent in Africam, pulsis accolis montem Cyran et propter amoenitatem loci et propter fontis uber-
6 tatem occupavere. Ibi Battos, dux eorum, linguae nodis solutis loqui primum coepit, quae res animos eorum ex promissis dei iam parte percepta in reliquam spem con-
7 dendae urbis accendit. Positis igitur castris opinionem veteris fabulae accipiunt, Cyrenen, eximiae pulchritudinis virginem, a Thessaliae monte Pelio ab Apolline raptam perlatamque in eiusdem montis iuga; cuius collem occupaverant, a deo repletam quattuor pueros peperisse, No-
8 mium, Aristaeum, Autuchum, Agraeum, missos a patre Hypseo, rege Thessaliae, qui perquirerent virginem, loci amoenitate captos in isdem terris cum virgine resedisse;
9 ex his pueris tres adultos in Thessaliam reversos avita re-
10 gna recepisse; Aristaeum in Arcadia late regnasse, eumque primum et apium et mellis usum et lactis ad coagula hominibus tradidisse solstitialisque ortus sideris primum
11 invenisse. Quibus auditis Battos virginis nomine ex responsis agnito urbem Cyrenen condidit.

---

19 The constellation will be that of Sirius, the Dog Star.

his tongue. As the oracle seemed absurd since the island 3
of Thera was sparsely populated and yet colonists were
being instructed to go from there to found a city in Africa,
which covered such a vast territory, the matter was ignored. Then some time later their defiance of the god was 4
punished with a plague, but so incredibly small were their
numbers that they barely filled a single ship.

When they arrived in Africa, they drove off the indig- 5
enous population and took over Mount Cyra, both because
of the attractiveness of the region and also because of its
plentiful supply of water. There Battos, their leader, find- 6
ing his tongue loosened, for the first time started to speak,
something that since they now saw the god's prophecy
partially fulfilled encouraged them to achieve their hope
of founding a city. So on encamping there they heard 7
about an old tale, that Cyrene, a virgin of striking beauty,
had been abducted from Mount Pelion in Thessaly by
Apollo and brought to the very mountain range that included the hill that they had occupied; that impregnated
by the god, she had given birth to four boys, Nomius,
Aristaeus, Autuchus and Agraeus; that men had then been 8
sent by Cyrene's father, Hypseus, king of Thessaly, to
search for the girl, but struck by the beauty of the area had
settled in the same place together with the girl; three of 9
Cyrene's sons had returned to Thessaly on reaching manhood and there inherited their grandfather's kingdom; and 10
Aristaeus had ruled over extensive lands in Arcadia, and
he had been the first to have taught men how to keep bees,
produce honey, and make cheese, and the first to have
discovered the rising of the constellation at the solstice.[19]
On hearing this Battos, recognizing the girl's name from 11
the oracle, founded the city of Cyrene.

8. Igitur Ptolomeus huius urbis auctus viribus bellum
2 in adventum Perdiccae parabat. Sed Perdiccae plus odium
adrogantiae quam vires hostium nocebat, quam exosi
3 etiam socii ad Antipatrum gregatim profugiebant. Neoptolemus quoque in auxilium Eumeni relictus non solum
transfugere, verum etiam prodere partium exercitum vo-
4 luit. Quam rem cum praesensisset Eumenes, cum prodi-
5 tore decernere proelio necesse habuit. Victus Neoptolemus ad Antipatrum et Polyperconta profugit eisque
persuadet, ut continuatis mansionibus laeto ex victoria et
6 securo fuga sua Eumeni superveniant. Sed res Eumenen
non latuit. Itaque insidiae in insidiatores versae, et qui
securum adgressuros se putabant, securis in itinere et per-
7 vigilio noctis fatigatis occursum est. In eo proelio Poly-
8 percon occiditur. Neoptolemus quoque cum Eumene
congressus diu mutuis vulneribus acceptis conluctatus est;
9 in summa victus occumbit. Victor igitur duobus proeliis
continuis Eumenes adflictas partes transitione sociorum
10 paululum sustentavit. Ad postremum tamen Perdicca occiso ab exercitu hostis cum Pithone [et] Illyrio et Alceta,
fratre Perdiccae, appellatur bellumque adversus eos Antigono decernitur.

---

20 The narrative goes back to the year 321. From section 3 the
scene switches to the Hellespont.

21 Here and at 8.7 the name should be Craterus, as in the
Prologue to the book.

22 Perdiccas was killed in Egypt, and Antigonus' appointment
as "General of Asia" came only when the army had reached Tripa-
radeisus in northern Syria, where a new distribution of satrapies
took place.

8. So Ptolemy with his strength increased by acquisition of this city was preparing for when Perdiccas should arrive.[20] But Perdiccas was harmed more by hatred felt for his arrogance than he was by his enemy's strength, for, detesting that, even his allies were deserting to Antipater in large numbers. Neoptolemus, too, who had been left behind to assist Eumenes, wanted not only to desert but even to betray his side's army. Since Eumenes had sensed this he thought it necessary to decide the issue with the traitor in battle. Defeated, Neoptolemus fled to Antipater and Polypercon[21] and persuaded them to overtake Eumenes by forced marches while he was still jubilant from his victory and unconcerned because of Neoptolemus' flight. But Eumenes was not duped. So the ambush was turned back on the ambushers, and men who thought they would be taking someone by surprise were themselves taken by surprise, on the road and exhausted, in the middle of the night. In that battle Polypercon was killed. Neoptolemus also clashed with Eumenes in a long struggle in which they both wounded each other; he was finally overcome and killed. So as the victor in two consecutive battles Eumenes somewhat revived the fortunes of a side badly damaged by the desertion of allies. Finally however Perdiccas was killed, Eumenes was declared a public enemy along with Pitho the Illyrian and Alcetas, brother of Perdiccas, and the war against them was assigned to Antigonus.[22]

LIBER XIV

1. Eumenes ut Perdiccam occisum, se hostem a Macedonibus iudicatum bellumque Antigono decretum cognovit,
2 ultro ea militibus suis indicavit, ne fama aut rem in maius
3 extolleret aut militum animos rerum novitate terreret; simul an, ut circa se animati essent cognosceret, sumpturus
4 consilium ex motu universorum. Constanter tamen praefatus est, si cui haec terrori essent, habere eum discedendi
5 potestatem. Qua voce adeo cunctos in studium partium suarum induxit, ut ultra bellum omnes hortarentur rescis-
6 surosque se ferro decreta Macedonum adfirmarent. Tunc exercitu in Aeoliam promoto pecunias civitatibus imperat,
7 recusantes dare hostiliter diripit. Inde Sardas profectus ad Cleopatram, sororem Alexandri Magni, ut eius voce centuriones principalesque confirmarentur, existimaturos ibi maiestatem regiam verti, unde soror Alexandri staret.
8 Tanta veneratio magnitudinis Alexandri erat, ut etiam per vestigia mulierum favor sacrati eius nominis quaereretur.
9   Cum reversus in castra esset, epistulae totis castris abiectae inveniuntur, quibus his, qui Eumenis caput ad Antigonum detulissent, magna praemia definiebantur.

---

[1] In northwestern Asia Minor; the year is 320. Cleopatra had moved to Sardis in 321.   [2] Again, Roman military terms are used for Macedonian forces.

BOOK XIV

1. When Eumenes discovered that Perdiccas had been killed, that he had himself been judged an enemy by the Macedonians and that the war had been entrusted to Antigonus, he volunteered the information to his soldiers so 2 rumor should not exaggerate matters or frighten the men with unexpected news; and it was also to ascertain how 3 they felt about him so that he could base his strategy on their overall morale. He insisted, however, that anyone 4 frightened by the situation was free to leave. In saying that 5 he so completely won everyone over to his side that they all actually urged him to war and swore they would rescind the decrees of the Macedonians with the sword. Then 6 moving the army forward into Aeolia[1] he levied money from the cities and savagely plundered any refusing to pay. From there he went on to Sardis, to Cleopatra, sister of 7 Alexander the Great, in order to have his centurions[2] and senior officers confirmed by her words so they should think that regal authority rested where the sister of Alexander was standing. Such respect was there for Alexan- 8 der's greatness that even through women was the favor of his hallowed name to be sought.

When he returned to camp, letters were found scat- 9 tered through the camp in which large rewards were offered for any who brought Eumenes' head to Antigonus.

311

10 His cognitis Eumenes vocatis ad contionem militibus
primo gratias agit, quod nemo inventus esset, qui spem
11 cruenti praemii fidei sacramenti anteponeret, tum deinde
callide subnectit confictas has a se epistulas ad experiun-
12 dos suorum animos esse. Ceterum salutem suam in omnium potestate esse, nec Antigonum nec quemquam ducum sic velle vincere, ut ipse in se exemplum pessimum
13 statuat. Hoc facto et in praesenti labantium animos deter-
ruit et in futurum providit, ut, si quid simile accidisset,
non se ab hoste corrumpi, sed ab duce temptari arbitra-
14 rentur. Omnes igitur operam suam certatim ad custodiam
salutis eius offerunt.

2. Cum interim Antigonus cum exercitu supervenit ca-
2 strisque positis postera die in aciem procedit. Nec Eumenes moram proelio fecit; qui victus in munitum quod-
3 dam castellum confugit. Vbi cum videret se fortunam
obsidionis subiturum, maiorem exercitus partem dimisit,
ne aut consensu multitudinis hosti traderetur aut obsidio
4 ipsa multitudine gravaretur. Legatos deinde ad Antipatrum, qui solus par Antigoni viribus videbatur, supplices
mittit, a quo cum auxilia Eumeni missa Antigonus didicis-
5 set, ab obsidione recessit. Erat quidem solutus ad tempus
metu mortis Eumenes, sed nec salutis dimisso exercitu
magna spes erat.
6 Omnia igitur circumspicienti optimum visum est ad
Alexandri Magni Argyraspidas, invictum exercitum et tot
7 victoriarum praefulgentem gloria, decurrere. Sed Argy-

---

3 This is the battle of Orcynii in early 319, after which
Eumenes was besieged at Nora (the fortress).

4 Antipater died in autumn 319. Antigonus came to terms with
Eumenes after the siege had lasted a year.

On learning of this Eumenes called the men to an assem-   10
bly and first thanked them that nobody had been found
who would put the prospect of blood money above loyalty
to his oath of allegiance, and then craftily added that the   11
letters had been written by him to sound out his men's
feelings. But his safety lay in everyone's hands, he said,   12
and neither Antigonus nor any of the generals wanted a
victory that would set a terrible precedent for him. By this   13
he both for the present deterred any waverers and for the
future ensured they would think not that they were being
bribed by the enemy but being tested by their commander.
So they all competed with one another in offering to serve   14
as his bodyguard.

2. Meanwhile Antigonus arrived with his army, pitched
camp and the following day proceeded to the battle line.[3]
Eumenes did not delay the battle either; defeated, he   2
sought refuge in some fortified stronghold. When he saw   3
himself facing the risk of a siege, he dismissed most of his
army in order not to be surrendered to his enemy by a
majority vote or have the siege worsened by sheer numbers. He then sent delegates to Antipater, who alone   4
seemed Antigonus' equal in strength, begging for aid, and
when Antigonus learned that reinforcements had been
sent to Eumenes by Antipater he raised the siege.[4] So for   5
the moment Eumenes was freed from fear of death, but
with his army demobilized his hope of survival was not
great.

So taking everything, into account he thought it best to   6
turn to Alexander the Great's Argyraspids, an invincible
army and one covered with glory from so many victories.[5]

---

[5] See 12.7.5 and note 22 there.

raspides post Alexandrum omnes duces fastidiebant, sordidam militiam sub aliis post tanti regis memoriam existi-
8 mantes. Itaque Eumenes blandimentis agere, suppliciter
singulos adloqui, nunc conmilitones suos, nunc patronos
appellans, periculorum orientalium socios, nunc refugia
salutis suae et unica praesidia, commemorans solos esse,
9 quorum virtute Oriens sit domitus, solos, qui militiam
10 Liberi patris, qui Herculis monumenta superarint; per hos
Alexandrum magnum factum, per hos divinos honores et
11 inmortalem gloriam consecutum. Orat, ut non tam ducem
se quam conmilitonem recipiant unumque ex corpore suo
12 esse velint. Receptus hac lege paulatim imperium, primum monendo singulos, mox quae perperam facta erant
blande corrigendo usurpat; nihil in castris sine illo agi,
nihil administrari sine sollertia illius poterat.

3. Ad postremum cum Antigonum venire cum exercitu
2 nuntiatum esset, conpellit in aciem descendere. Ibi cum
ducis imperia contemnunt, hostium virtute superantur.
3 In eo proelio non gloriam tantum tot bellorum cum coniugibus et liberis, sed et praemia longa militia parta per-
4 diderunt. Sed Eumenes, qui auctor cladis erat nec aliam
5 spem salutis reliquam habebat, victos hortabatur. Nam et
virtute eos superiores fuisse adfirmabat, quippe ab his V
milia hostium caesa, et si in bello perstent, ultro hostes
6 pacem petituros. Damna, quibus se victos putent, duo
milia mulierum et paucos infantes et servitia esse, quae
melius vincendo possint reparare quam deserendo victo-

---

6 The narrative now jumps from 318 to winter 317/16. Justin
(following Trogus?) is far more interested in the drama and rhetoric of Eumenes' fall than in the military details.

But after Alexander the Argyraspids looked down on all   7
leaders, thinking service under others beneath them after
their memory of so a great king. So Eumenes resorted   8
to flattery and humbly entreated them one by one, calling them now his "comrades," now his "protectors," now
his allies in facing the perils of the East, now the guardians
of his safety and his only protection; by their valor was the   9
east conquered, he said, they alone had eclipsed Father
Liber's campaigns and Hercules' monumental achievements; through them had Alexander become great, through   10
them had he achieved divine honors and immortal glory.
He begged them to accept him not so much as their leader   11
as a comrade and to want him to be one of their own body.
Accepted on these terms he, by first advising individuals   12
and then only leniently correcting misconduct, gradually
took command; nothing in camp could be done without
him, no action taken without his expertise.

3. When it was finally reported that Antigonus was approaching with an army, he forced them to go into battle.[6]
There, since they ignored the leader's orders, they were   2
defeated by a courageous enemy. In that battle they lost   3
not only the glory won from so many campaigns together
with their wives and children, but also the rewards gar-
nered during their long service. But Eumenes, who was   4
responsible for the defeat and had no other hope of saving
himself, kept encouraging his defeated men. For, he   5
would assure them, they were superior in valor since five
thousand of their enemies had been killed by them, and if
they persisted with the war, it would be the enemy who
would sue for peace. The losses by which they thought   6
they had been defeated amounted to two thousand women
and a few children and slaves, which they could better

7 riam. Porro Argyraspides neque fugam se temptaturos
dicunt post damna patrimoniorum et post coniuges amis-
8 sas, neque bellum gesturos contra liberos suos; ultroque
eum conviciis agitant, quod se post tot annos emeritorum
stipendiorum redeuntes domum cum praemiis tot bellorum ab ipsa missione rursus in novam militiam inmen-
9 saque bella revocaverit, et a laribus iam quodam modo suis
et ab ipso limine patriae abductos inanibus promissis de-
10 ceperit, nunc quoque amissis omnibus felicis militiae
quaestibus ne victos quidem in misera et inopi senecta
11 quiescere sinat. Ignaris deinde ducibus confestim ad Antigonum legatos mittunt petentes, ut sua reddi iubeat. Is
12 redditurum se pollicetur, si Eumenen sibi tradant. Quibus
cognitis Eumenes cum paucis fugere temptavit; sed
retractus desperatis rebus, cum concursus multitudinis
factus esset, petit ut postremum sibi adloqui exercitum
liceret.

4. Iussus ab universis dicere facto silentio laxatisque
vinculis prolatam, sicut erat catenatus, manum ostendit.
2 "Cernitis, milites" inquit, "habitum atque ornamenta ducis vestri, quae mihi non hostium quisquam inposuit; nam
3 hoc etiam solacio foret. Vos me ex victore victum, vos me
ex imperatore captivum fecistis, qui ter intra hunc annum
4 in mea verba iure iurando obstricti estis. Sed ista omitto,
5 neque enim miseros convicia decent; unum oro, si propo-
sitorum Antigoni in meo capite summa consistit, inter vos
6 me velitis mori. Nam neque illius interest, quemadmo-

---

7 It is indicative of the rhetorical freedom of ancient historiography that the speech at Plut. *Vit. Eum.* 17.6ff. is different in
content.

recoup by conquest than conceding victory. The Argyras-   7
pids said they would not attempt flight after the destruction of their property and the loss of their wives, but neither would they fight a war against their own children; and   8
they even berated him for bringing them back to a new
campaign and interminable wars when after so many years
of service they were now going home laden with spoils
from numerous wars, and by somehow abducting them   9
from their homes and the very threshold of their fatherland he had deceived them with empty promises, and not   10
even now, having lost all the gains from a successful campaign and even after being defeated would he allow them
to remain at peace in a wretched, impoverished old age.
Then behind their officers' backs they hurriedly sent del-   11
egates to Antigonus to ask for their property to be restored
to them. He promised to return it if they surrendered
Eumenes to him. On hearing of this Eumenes tried to   12
escape with a few men; but brought back and in despair
when a crowd of soldiers converged on him, he asked that
he be allowed a final address to the army.

4. When he was ordered to speak by everybody, silence
fell, his bonds were loosened, and he stretched out his
hand, which was manacled.[7] "Men," he said, "you see the   2
clothing and decorations of your leader, which no enemy
has put on me—even that might have been some consolation. It was you who turned me from victor to defeated   3
man, from commander to captive—you who three times
this year swore the oath of loyalty to me. But that I pass   4
over, for recriminations ill suit men in wretched circumstances; one thing I do ask, that if Antigonus' greatest wish   5
is for my death, let me die among you. For to him it means   6

dum aut ubi cadam, et ego fuero ignominia mortis libera-
7 tus. Hoc si inpetro, solvo vos iure iurando, quotiens vos
8 sacramento mihi devovistis. Aut si ipsos pudet roganti vim
adhibere, ferrum huc date et permittite, quod vos facturos
pro imperatore iurastis, imperatorem pro vobis sine reli-
9 gione iuris iurandi facere." Cum non obtineret, preces in
10 iram vertit. "At vos," ait, "devota capita, respiciant dii pe-
riuriorum vindices talesque vobis exitus dent, quales vos
11 ducibus vestris dedistis. Nempe vos idem paulo ante et
Perdiccae sanguine estis aspersi et in Antipatrum eadem
12 moliti. Ipsum denique Alexandrum, si fas fuisset eum
mortali manu cadere, interempturi, quod maximum erat,
13 seditionibus agitastis. Vltima nunc ego perfidorum victima
14 has vobis diras atque inferias dico: ut inopes extorresque
omne aevum in hoc castrensi exilio agatis devorentque vos
arma vestra, quibus plures vestros quam hostium duces
absumpsistis."

15 Plenus deinde ira custodes suos praecedere ad Anti-
16 goni castra coepit. Sequitur exercitus prodito imperatore
suo et ipse captivus, triumphumque de se ipse ad victoris
17 castra ducit, omnia auspicia regis Alexandri et tot bellorum palmas laureasque una secum victori tradentes;
18 et ne quid deesset pompae, elephanti quoque et auxilia
19 orientalia subsecuntur. Tanto pulchrior haec Antigono
quam Alexandro tot victoriae fuerunt, ut, cum ille Orientem vicerit, hic etiam eos, a quibus Oriens victus fuerat,

nothing how or where I die, and I shall be spared a shameful death If I am granted this, I release you from the oath 7
by which you have so often bound yourselves to me. Or if 8
you are yourselves ashamed to do violence to the man who
asks for it, pass me a sword and on your behalf, without
the obligation of an oath, allow your general do for you
what you have sworn to do for your general." When unable 9
to have it, he turned from pleas to anger. "You accursed 10
scoundrels," he said "may the gods that punish perjury
take note and bring you such fortunes as you have brought
your leaders. Of course it was you who a short time ago 11
were bespattered with Perdiccas' blood and had the same
fate in store for Antipater, too. You would actually have 12
killed Alexander himself, had heaven willed that he die by
a mortal hand, and doing your worst, you plagued him with
mutinies. Now as the last victim of your treachery I call 13
down upon you this infernal curse: may you spend all eter- 14
nity poverty-stricken and homeless exiled to this camp and
be destroyed by your own weapons, with which you have
destroyed more of your own generals than you have your
enemy's."

Then full of rage he proceeded to go ahead of his body- 15
guards to Antigonus' camp. He was followed by an army 16
also itself captive after betrayal by its leader, and he led a
triumphal procession over himself to the victor's camp,
surrendering all of King Alexander's authority and the 17
palms and laurels of so many campaigns to the victor, together with himself And for the procession to lack nothing, 18
elephants and eastern auxiliary troops also brought up the
rear. Far finer for Antigonus was this than were all of Al- 19
exander's victories, for while that man had conquered the
East, this one had triumphed even over those by whom

20 superaverit. Igitur Antigonus domitores illos orbis exer-
21 citui suo dividit, redditis eorum quae in victoria ceperat.
Eumenen verecundia prioris amicitiae in conspectum
suum venire prohibitum adsignari custodibus praecepit.

5. Interea Eurydice, uxor Arridaei regis, ut Polyperconta a Graecia redire in Macedoniam cognovit et ab eo
2 arcessitam Olympiada, muliebri aemulatione perculsa,
3 abutens valetudine viri, cuius officia sibi vindicabat, scribit regis nomine Polyperconti, Cassandro exercitum tra-
dat, in quem regni administrationem rex transtulerit. Ea-
4 dem et in Asiam Antigono per epistulas nuntiat. Quo
beneficio devinctus Cassander nihil non ex arbitrio mulie-
5 bris audaciae gerit. Dein profectus in Graeciam multis
6 civitatibus bellum infert. Quarum excidio velut vicino incendio territi Spartani urbem, quam semper armis, non
muris defenderant, tunc contra responsa fatorum et veterem maiorum gloriam armis diffisi murorum praesidio
7 includunt. Tantum eos degeneravisse a maioribus, ut, cum
multis saeculis murus urbi virtus civium fuerit, tunc cives
salvos se non existimaverint fore, nisi intra muros laterent.
8 Dum haec aguntur, Cassandrum a Graecia turbatus
9 Macedoniae status domum revocavit. Namque Olympias,
mater Alexandri regis, cum ab Epiro in Macedoniam prosequente Aeacida, rege Molossorum, veniret prohibe-
10 rique finibus ab Eurydice et Arridaeo rege coepisset, seu

the East was won. So Antigonus divided those world con-   20
querors among his own troops, restoring to them what he
had taken from them in victory. Eumenes from consider-   21
ation of their earlier friendship he refused to allow into his
sight and had him assigned to guards.

5. Meanwhile Eurydice, the wife of King Arridaeus,
learned that Polypercon was returning from Greece to
Macedonia and that Olympias had been summoned by
him; and struck with female jealousy, and profiting from   2
the illness of her husband, whose duties she was starting
to usurp she wrote to Polypercon in the king's name for   3
him to delegate the army to Cassander, to whom the king
had transferred administration of the kingdom. She sent
the same message by letter to Antigonus in Asia. Indebted   4
for the favor, Cassander did nothing that did not accord
with the whims of the headstrong woman. Then setting off   5
for Greece he made war on many cities. By their destruc-   6
tion the Spartans were terrified as if by a neighbor's fire,
and ignoring prophesies and their forefathers' glorious
reputation, they lost confidence in their weapons and surrounded with protective walls the city they had always
defended with weapons, not walls. So far had they degen-   7
erated from their ancestors that although for many centuries the valor of its citizens had been their wall, they now
did not think themselves secure unless they hid within
walls.

While this was taking place, unsettled conditions in   8
Macedonia brought Cassander home from Greece. For   9
when Olympias, the mother of King Alexander, was coming from Epirus to Macedonia accompanied by Aeacides,
king of the Molossians, Eurydice and King Arridaeus had
tried to prevent her from entering the country; and either   10

memoria mariti seu magnitudine filii et indignitate rei
moti Macedones ad Olympiada transiere, cuius iussu et
Eurydice et rex occiditur, sex annis post Alexandrum potitus regno.

6. Sed nec Olympias diu regnavit. Nam cum principum
passim caedes muliebri magis quam regio more fecisset,
2 favorem sui in odium vertit. Itaque audito Cassandri adventu diffisa Macedonibus cum nuru Roxane et nepote
3 Hercule in Pydnam urbem concedit. Proficiscenti Deidamia, Aeacidae regis filia, et Thessalonice privigna, et ipsa
clara Philippi patris nomine, multaeque aliae principum
matronae, speciosus magis quam utilis grex, comites fuere.
4 Haec cum nuntiata Cassandro essent, statim citato cursu
5 Pydnam venit et urbem obsidione cingit. Cum fame fer-
roque urgeretur, Olympias longae obsidionis taedio pacta
6 salute victori se tradidit. Sed Cassander ad contionem
vocato populo, sciscitaturus quid de Olympiade fieri velint, subornat parentes interfectorum, qui sumpta lugubri
7 veste crudelitatem mulieris accusarent. A quibus accensi
Macedones sine respectu pristinae maiestatis occidendam
8 decernunt, inmemores prorsus, quod per filium eius vi-
rumque non solum vitam ipsi inter finitimos tutam habuissent, verum etiam tantas opes imperiumque orbis
9 quaesissent. Sed Olympias ubi obstinatos venire ad se
armatos videt, veste regali, duabus ancillis innixa ultro

from the memory of her husband or the greatness of her son and the indignity of such an act, the Macedonians shifted allegiance to Olympias, on whose orders both Eurydice and the king were killed. He had held the throne for three years after Alexander's death.

6. But Olympias' rule was not long either. For since she wrought wholesale slaughter on leading men by acting more like a woman than a ruler, she turned her popularity into hatred. So on hearing of Cassander's arrival and distrusting the Macedonians, she withdrew to the city of Pydna with her daughter-in-law Roxane and her grandson Hercules. Setting out with her as companions were Deidamia, daughter of King Aeacides, her stepdaughter Thessalonice, who herself also enjoyed some distinction through the name of her father Philip, and many other mothers of leading men, a group more impressive than capable. When this was reported to Cassander, he immediately came to Pydna by forced marches and laid siege to the city. When beset by hunger and military force Olympias, wearied by the long siege, bargained for her life and surrendered to the victor. But Cassander, summoning the people to an assembly to ascertain what they wanted done with Olympias, then bribed the parents of those who had been killed to put on mourning dress and denounce the woman's atrocities. Incited by these people the Macedonians, with no respect for her former grandeur, decreed that she must be executed, forgetting indeed that it had been through her son and husband that they had not only enjoyed safe lives among their neighbors but also gained such great wealth and worldwide power. But when she saw determined armed men coming to her, Olympias, in her regal clothing and leaning on two maidservants, readily

10 obviam procedit. Qua visa percussores adtoniti fortuna maiestatis prioris et tot in ea memoriae occurrentibus regum suorum nominibus substiterunt, donec a Cassandro

11 missi sunt, qui eam confoderent, non refugientem gladium sed nec vulnera aut muliebriter vociferantem, sed virorum fortium more pro gloria veteris prosapiae morti succumbentem, ut Alexandrum posses etiam in moriente

12 matre cognoscere. Compsisse insuper expirans capillos et veste crura contexisse fertur, ne quid posset in corpore

13 eius indecorum videri. Post haec Cassander Thessalonicen, regis Arridaei filiam, uxorem duxit; filium Alexandri cum matre in arcem Amphipolitanam custodiendos mittit.

went forward to meet them. At this sight the assassins 10
halted in astonishment, reflecting on her former majesty
and the names of all the kings that she brought to mind,
until soldiers were sent by Cassander to run her through. 11
She did not recoil from the sword or their blows or scream
like a woman, but yielded to death as brave men would,
upholding the glorious reputation of her ancient family, so
you could recognize Alexander even in his dying mother.
She is also said to have arranged her hair as she lay dying 12
and covered her legs with her dress so that nothing undig-
nified could be seen in her body. Later on Cassander mar- 13
ried Thessalonice, daughter of King Arridaeus;[8] and the
son of Alexander he sent to the citadel of Amphipolis together with his mother to be kept under guard.

[8] Actually, daughter of Philip II, not Arridaeus (Philip III).

LIBER XV

1. Perdicca et fratre eius, Eumene ac Polyperconte cete-
risque ducibus diversae partis occisis finitum certamen
inter successores Alexandri Magni videbatur, cum repente
2 inter ipsos victores nata discordia est. Quippe postulantibus Ptolomeo et Cassandro et Lysimacho, ut pecunia in
praeda capta provinciaeque dividerentur, Antigonus nega-
vit se in eius belli praemia socios admissurum, in cuius
3 periculum solus descenderit; et ut honestum adversus
socios bellum suscipere videretur, divulgat se Olympiadis
mortem a Cassandro interfectae ulcisci velle et Alexandri,
regis sui, filium cum matre obsidione Amphipolitana libe-
4 rare. His cognitis Ptolomeus et Cassander inita cum Lysimacho et Seleuco societate bellum terra marique enixe
instruunt.
5   Tenebat Ptolomeus Aegyptum cum Africae parte maiore et Cypro et Phoenice. Cassandro parebat Macedonia
6 cum Graecia. Asiam et partes Orientis occupaverat Antigonus, cuius filius Demetrius prima belli congressione a
7 Ptolomeo apud Galamam vincitur. In quo proelio maior

---

[1] As at 13.8.5, 7, Justin should mean Craterus. Polyperchon
lived at least until the end of the century. We have reached the
winter of 316/5 and Diod. Sic. 19.57.   [2] So Justin, but the
battle is that of Gaza in 312, as in *Prologue* 15.

BOOK XV

1. With Perdiccas and his brother, and Eumenes, Polyper-con[1] and the other generals on the other side, all now killed, the war among the successors of Alexander the Great seemed to have come to an end, when suddenly there was discord among the victors themselves. For when 2 Ptolemy, Cassander and Lysimachus insisted that all money taken as plunder as well as the provinces should be divided between them, Antigonus said he would not con-sider giving the allies rewards for a war in which he alone had faced the danger; and so that the war he was undertak- 3 ing against his allies might seem honorable, he claimed that he wished to avenge the death of Olympias, who had been killed by Cassander, and free the son of Alexander, his king, together with his mother from their imprison-ment in Amphipolis. On hearing this, Ptolemy and Cas- 4 sander made an alliance with Lysimachus and Seleucus and strenuously prepared for war on land and sea.

Ptolemy held Egypt together with most of Africa as 5 well as Cyprus and Phoenicia. Under Cassander was Macedonia together with Greece. Asia and parts of the 6 East had been taken over by Antigonus, whose son Deme-trius was defeated by Ptolemy in the first operation of the war at Galama.[2] In that battle Ptolemy's clemency earned 7

Ptolomei moderationis gloria quam ipsius victoriae fuit;
8 siquidem et amicos Demetrii non solum cum suis rebus,
verum etiam additis insuper muneribus dimisit et ipsius
Demetrii privatum omne instrumentum ac familiam red-
9 didit adiecto honore verborum, non se propter praedam,
sed propter dignitatem inisse bellum, indignatum, quod
Antigonus devictis diversae factionis ducibus solus communis victoriae praemia corripuisset.

2. Dum haec aguntur, Cassander ab Apollonia rediens
incidit in Audariatas, qui propter ranarum muriumque
2 multitudinem relicto patrio solo sedes quaerebant; veritus, ne Macedoniam occuparent, facta pactione in societatem eos recepit agrosque iis ultimos Macedoniae ad-
3 signat. Deinde, ne Hercules, Alexandri filius, qui annos
XIV excesserat, favore paterni nominis in regum Macedoniae vocaretur, occidi eum tacite cum matre Barsine iubet
corporaque eorum terra obrui, ne caedes sepultura pro-
4 deretur, et quasi parum facinoris in ipso primum rege,
5 mox in matre eius Olympiade ac filio admisisset, alterum
quoque filium cum matre Roxane pari fraude interfecit,
scilicet quasi regnum Macedoniae, quod adfectabat, aliter
consequi quam scelere non posset.
6 Interea Ptolomeus cum Demetrio navali proelio iterato congreditur et amissa classe hostique concessa victo-

---

³ Cassander acquired this city in southern Illyria in 314; cf.
17.3.16ff.

⁴ Though the fourteenth birthday is symbolic of reaching
manhood, Hercules was, at the time of his death in 309, seventeen
or eighteen years old. Justin alone notes his mother's death, but
it is likely enough, given the fate of Roxane and Alexander IV.

him more glory than the victory itself; for not only did he   8
release the friends of Demetrius together with their property, but he even added further gifts and also restored
all Demetrius' personal belongings and slaves, adding
the magnanimous comment that he had not gone to war   9
for plunder but honor, angry that after the leaders of
their opposition had been defeated Antigonus alone had
snatched the rewards of a communal victory.

2. In the meantime Cassander while returning from
Apollonia[3] came upon the Audariatae, who had left their
native soil because of an infestation of frogs and mice and
were then seeking a new home; and fearing that they   2
might seize Macedonia, he made an agreement with them,
accepted them as his allies and assigned to them the most
remote lands in Macedonia. Then, so Hercules, Alexan-   3
der's son, who was now past his fourteenth birthday,
should not be called to the kingdom of Macedonia from
respect for his father's name, he ordered that he and his
mother Barsine should be secretly murdered and their
bodies buried without ceremony so murder should not to
be revealed by a burial;[4] and as if he had committed too   4
small a crime against the king himself and then against the
king's mother Olympias and her son, he also murdered the   5
other son together with his mother Roxane in the same
treacherous manner, thinking of course that he could not
gain the Macedonian throne he hankered after other than
by crime.

Meanwhile Ptolemy clashed with Demetrius in a sec-   6
ond naval battle and after losing his fleet[5] and conceding

[5] The battle of Salamis in the spring of 306; Diod. Sic.
20.47.7ff.

7 ria in Aegyptum refugit. Demetrius filium Ptolomei Leon-
tiscum et fratrem Menelaum amicosque eius cum privati
instrumenti ministerio, pari provocatus antea munere,
8 Aegyptum remittit; et ut appareret eos non odii, sed dignitatis gloria accensos, donis muneribusque inter ipsa
9 bella contendebant. Tanto honestius tunc bella gereban-
10 tur quam nunc amicitiae coluntur. Hac victoria elatus
Antigonus regem se cum Demetrio filio appellari a populo
11 iubet. Ptolomeus quoque, ne minoris apud suos auctorita-
12 tis haberetur, rex ab exercitu cognominatur. Quibus auditis Cassander et Lysimachus et ipsi regiam sibi maiestatem
13 vindicaverunt. Huius honoris ornamentis tam diu omnes
abstinuerunt, quam diu filii regis sui superesse potuerunt.
14 Tanta in illis verecundia erat, ut cum opes regias haberent,
regum tamen nominibus aequo animo caruerint, quoad
15 Alexandro iustus heres fuit. Sed Ptolomeus et Cassander
ceterique factionis alterius duces cum carpi se singulos ab
Antigono viderent, dum privatum singulorum, non commune universorum bellum ducunt nec auxilium ferre alter
16 alteri volunt, quasi victoria unius, non omnium foret, per
epistulas se invicem confirmantes tempus, locum coeundi
17 condicunt bellumque communibus viribus instruunt. Cui
cum Cassander interesse propter finitimum bellum non
posset, Lysimachum cum ingentibus copiis in auxilium
sociis mittit.

3. Erat hic Lysimachus inlustri quidem Macedoniae
loco natus, sed virtutis experimentis omni nobilitate cla-

---

6 Not an immediate reaction: Ptolemy did not employ the tide
until early 304.

victory to his enemy fled to Egypt. Demetrius sent Ptol-   7
emy's son Leontiscus, his brother Menelaus and his friends
back to Egypt together with their personal entourage and
belongings; and so it might seem that their motivation had   8
been not hatred but glory and honor, they started to compete with each other in gifts and kindnesses right in the
midst of their wars. So much more honorably were wars   9
fought then than friendships are cultivated now! Elated by   10
this victory Antigonus ordered that both he and his son
Demetrius should be addressed as "kings" by the people.
Ptolemy, too, so he should have no less authority among   11
his people, was given the title "king" by the army.[6] On   12
hearing this Cassander and Lysimachus also claimed royal
status for themselves. All of them refrained from adopting   13
this position's insignia for as long the sons of their king
were able to survive. Such was the respect they felt that,   14
although they had regal power, they willingly eschewed
the title of "king" for as long as there was a legitimate heir
for Alexander. But although Ptolemy, Cassander and the   15
other generals of the opposing faction could see themselves being picked off one by one by Antigonus, they
thought of the war as belonging to each of them individually, not as one fought together, and they were unwilling
to give each other assistance, thinking that victory would
belong to one and not all of them. So reassuring each other   16
with letters, they agreed on a time and place to assemble
and prepared for war with their forces united. Since Cas-   17
sander could not be there because of a war with his neighbors, he sent Lysimachus with massive forces to assist his
allies.

3. This Lysimachus was actually born to a distinguished
Macedonian family, but all his pedigree paled before the

2 rior, quae tanta in illo fuit, ut animi magnitudine philoso-
phiam ipsam viriumque gloria omnes, per quos Oriens
3 domitus est, vicerit. Quippe cum Alexander Magnus Callisthenen philosophum propter salutationis Persicae inter-
pellatum morem insidiarum, quae sibi paratae fuerant,
4 conscium fuisse iratus finxisset eumque truncatis crudeliter omnibus membris abscisisque auribus ac naso labiisque
5 deforme ac miserandum spectaculum reddidisset, insuper
in cavea cum cane clausum ad metum ceterorum circum-
6 ferret: tunc Lysimachus, audire Callisthenen et praecepta
ab eo virtutis accipere solitus, miseratus tanti viri non cul-
pae, sed libertatis poenas pendentis, venenum ei in reme-
7 dia calamitatium dedit. Quod adeo Alexander aegre tulit,
8 ut eum obici ferocissimo leoni iuberet. Sed cum ad conspectum eius concitatus leo impetum fecisset, manum
amiculo involutam Lysimachus in os leonis inmersit
9 abreptaque lingua feram exanimavit. Quod cum nuntiatum regi esset, admiratio in satisfactionem cessit, cari-
oremque eum propter constantiam tantae virtutis habuit.
10 Lysimachus quoque magno animo regis veluti parentis
11 contumeliam tulit. Denique omni ex animo huius facti
memoria exturbata post in India insectanti regi quosdam
palantes hostes, cum a satellitum turba equi celeritate

---

[7] There is some confusion as to Lysimachus' origins. For Callisthenes, who was more historian than philosopher, see 12.6.17;
the manner of his death is variously reported. For a parallel treatment of Lysimachus, see Paus. 1.9.5ff. The story of the lion was
legendary, but for an alternative see Curt. 8.1.14ff.

[8] The claim about Callisthenes' vicious mutilation is not found
in any other source; ironically the same mistreatment was alleg-

clear instances of his moral worth, which was so great in
him that in magnanimity he surpassed the teachings of   2
philosophy, and in reputation for physical strength surpassed all those by whom the East was conquered.[7] Now   3
Alexander the Great was furious with the philosopher Callisthenes' opposition to his use of the Persian method of
salutation, and he falsely charged him with involvement in
a conspiracy that was afoot against him; and, after brutally   4
mutilating all his limbs and cutting off his ears, nose and
lips he had reduced him to a hideous and pitiful spectacle,
and even had him carried around shut up in a cage with a   5
dog to intimidate the others.[8] Then Lysimachus, who had   6
been a student of Callisthenes and often took his advice
on moral issues, feeling pity for this great man being punished not for a crime but for speaking his mind, gave him
poison to relieve his sufferings. So incensed by this was   7
Alexander that he ordered him thrown to a ferocious lion.
But when the lion leaped at him, excited at the sight of his   8
victim, Lysimachus wrapped his hand in his cloak, plunged
it into the lion's mouth, ripped out its tongue, and killed
the beast. When this was reported to the king, his admira-   9
tion led to forgiveness, and his affection for the man increased because of his unshakable courage. Lysimachus   10
also magnanimously accepted the king's humiliation of
him as if it was coming from a father. Eventually, memory   11
of this incident completely left his mind, and later on, in
India, when the king was in pursuit of some enemy strag-
glers and became separated from his troop of attendants

edly inflicted by Lysimachus himself later on a Rhodian who
joked about his wife (Sen. *De ira* 3.17.3–4; Athenaeus 14.616c).

desertus esset, solus ei per inmensas harenarum moles
12 cursus comes fuit. Quod idem antea Philippus, frater eius,
13 cum facere voluisset, inter manus regis expiraverat. Sed
Lysimachum desiliens equo Alexander hastae cuspide ita
in fronte vulneravit, ut sanguis aliter cludi non posset
quam diadema sibi demptum rex adligandi vulneris causa
14 capiti eius inponeret. Quod auspicium primum regalis
15 maiestatis Lysimacho fuit. Sed et post Alexandri mortem,
cum inter successores eius provinciae dividerentur, fero-
cissimae gentes quasi omnium fortissimo adsignatae sunt.
16 Adeo etiam consensu universorum palmam virtutis inter
ceteros tulit.

4. Priusquam bellum inter Ptolomeum sociosque eius
adversum Antigonum committeretur, repente ex Asia maiore digressus Seleucus novus Antigono hostis accesserat.
$\frac{2}{3}$ Huius quoque virtus clara et origo admirabilis fuit; siquidem mater eius Laodice, cum nupta esset Antiocho, claro
inter Philippi duces viro, visa sibi est per quietem ex
4 concubitu Apollinis concepisse, gravidamque factam munus concubitus a deo anulum accepisse, in cuius gemma
anchora sculpta esset; iussaque donum filio, quem pepe-
5 risset, dare. Admirabilem fecit hunc visum et anulus, qui
postera die eiusdem sculpturae in lecto inventus est, et
figura anchorae, quae in femore Seleuci nata cum ipso
6 parvulo fuit. Quamobrem Laodice anulum Seleuco eunti
cum Alexandro Magno ad Persicam militiam, edocto de
7 origine sua, dedit. Vbi post mortem Alexandri occupato

---

9 In 328/7; see Curt. 8.2.33ff.

10 Nothing more is known of his parents. The ring story is
found in App. *Syr.* 56.

because his horse was so swift, it was Lysimachus alone who accompanied him across the huge sand dunes. (Although his brother Philip ad earlier wanted to perform 12 the same service, he had died in the king's arms.⁹) But 13 while dismounting from his horse Alexander accidentally wounded Lysimachus on the forehead with the tip of his spear, so seriously that the only way of staunching the flow of blood was to take the diadem from his own head and place it on Lysimachus' to close up the wound. This was 14 the first omen of royal authority coming to Lysimachus. But also after Alexander's death, when provinces were di- 15 vided among the successors, it was to him, as being the bravest of them all, that the fiercest tribes were assigned. So far in everyone's opinion did he exceed the others in 16 courage.

4. Before the start of the war that pitted Ptolemy and his allies against Antigonus, Seleucus, suddenly returning from Greater Asia, had appeared as a new enemy for Antigonus. This man's courage was also renowned and his 2 birth amazing;¹⁰ for his mother Laodice, when she had 3 married Antiochus, who stood out among Philip's officers, dreamed that she had conceived after sleeping with Apollo, that when pregnant she had received from the god 4 as a present for sleeping with him a ring that had a stone with an anchor carved on it; and that she was ordered to give it to the son she bore. What made this dream aston- 5 ishing was both that a ring was found in the bed the next day bearing that very motif, and also that the shape of an anchor appeared on the infant Seleucus' thigh at his birth. Laodice therefore gave the ring to Seleucus when he went 6 off with Alexander the Great on the Persian campaign, informing him of how he had been born. When he became 7

regno Orientis urbem condidit, ibi quoque geminae origi-
8 nis memoriam consecravit. Nam et urbem ex Antiochi
patris nomine Antiochiam vocavit et campos vicinos urbi
9 Apollini dicavit. Originis eius argumentum etiam in posteris mansit, siquidem filii nepotesque eius anchoram in
femore veluti notam generis naturalem habuere.

10 Multa in Oriente post divisionem inter socios regni
11 Macedonici bella gessit. Principio Babyloniam cepit; inde
12 auctis ex victoria viribus Bactrianos expugnavit. Transitum
deinde in Indiam fecit, quae post mortem Alexandri, veluti cervicibus iugo servitutis excusso, praefectos eius occi-
13 derat. Auctor libertatis Sandrocottus fuerat, sed titulum
14 libertatis post victoriam in servitutem verterat; siquidem
occupato regno populum, quem ab externa dominatione
15 vindicaverat, ipse servitio premebat. Fuit hic humili quidem genere natus, sed ad regni potestatem maiestate
16 numinis inpulsus. Quippe cum procacitate sua Nandrum
regem offendisset, interfici a rege iussus salutem pedum
17 celeritate quaesierat. Ex qua fatigatione cum somno captus iaceret, leo ingentis formae ad dormientem accessit
sudoremque profluentem lingua ei detersit expergefac-
18 tumque blande reliquit. Hoc prodigio primum ad spem
regni inpulsus contractis latronibus Indos ad novitatem
19 regni sollicitavit. Molienti deinde bellum adversus praefectos Alexandri elephantus ferus infinitae magnitudinis
ultro se obtulit et veluti domita mansuetudine eum tergo
excepit duxque belli et proeliator insignis fuit.

---

11 Seleucus, Lysimachus, Cassander, and Ptolemy. Seleucus
took Babylon in 312. See App. *Syr.* 54ff.   12 Chandragupta
Maurya, ruler of the kingdom of Magadha ca. 322 to 291.

master of the east after Alexander's death and founded a
city, he there also hallowed the memory of his double
conception. For he both named the city Antioch after his   8
father and also dedicated its adjacent fields to Apollo. His   9
birthmark continued in the succeeding generations, since
his sons and grandsons had an anchor on the thigh as a
congenital indicator of their ancestry.

He fought many wars in the East after the partition of   10
the Macedonian Empire among the allies,[11] First he took   11
Babylon; then with his strength increased by the victory
he conquered the Bactrians. He next crossed into India,   12
which after Alexander's death had shaken the yoke of servitude from its shoulders and killed its governors. The   13
author of its liberation had been Sandrocottus,[12] but after
his victory he had turned the so-called liberty back into
servitude; for after seizing power he himself began   14
oppressing with slavery the people he had championed
against foreign domination. He was a man of low birth but   15
called to royal power by divine authority. With his outspo-   16
kenness he had irked King Nandrus, and when sentenced
to death by the king had relied on his fleetness of foot to
escape. While overtaken by sleep from exhaustion, a huge   17
lion approached him as he lay sleeping and with its tongue
licked away the sweat that was pouring from him, and
when he awoke it calmly left him. By this strange incident   18
he was first led to hopes of royal power and gathering together a band outlaws, he incited the Indians to revolu-
tion. Then as he was preparing for war against the gover-   19
nors Alexander, a wild elephant of immense size actually
approached him and as if tamed took him on its back and
was his guide in the war and a remarkable fighter in battle.

20   Sic adquisito regno Sandrocottus ea tempestate, qua
Seleucus futurae magnitudinis fundamenta iaciebat, In-
21 diam possidebat, cum quo facta pactione Seleucus conpo-
sitisque in Oriente rebus in bellum Antigoni descendit.
22 Adunatis igitur omnium sociorum copiis proelium committitur; in eo Antigonus occiditur, Demetrius, filius eius,
23 in fugam vertitur. Sed socii profligato hostili bello denuo
in semet ipsos arma vertunt et, cum de praeda non con-
24 venirent, iterum in duas factiones diducuntur. Seleucus
Demetrio, Ptolomeus Lysimacho iunguntur. Cassandro
25 defuncto Philippus filius succedit. Sic quasi ex integro
nova Macedoniae bella nascuntur.

Having gained the kingdom in this way, Sandrocottus 20 was then ruler of India at just the time that Seleucus was laying the ground for his future greatness, and after 21 making a truce with him and settling matters in the East Seleucus returned to the war with Antigonus.[13] The allies 22 therefore combined their forces and battle was joined; in it Antigonus was killed and his son Demetrius put to flight. But with the war against their enemy terminated, the allies 23 again turned their weapons on each other, and when they could not agree over the spoils,[14] they again split into two factions. Seleucus became allied with Demetrius, Ptolemy 24 with Lysimachus. When Cassander died his son Philip succeeded him. So as if from the start there were new wars 25 arising for Macedonia.

[13] The Peace with Chandragupta was perhaps made in 303. Justin has moved to the battle of Ipsus in Phrygia in 301, at which Cassander and Ptolemy were not in fact present; Diod. Sic. 21.1.4; Plut. *Vit. Demetr.* 29ff.

[14] That is, Coele-Syria, claimed by Seleucus, but annexed by Ptolemy. Cassander died in 297; his sons, Philip, Antipater, and Alexander, ruled less than four years altogether.

LIBER XVI

1. Post Cassandri regis filiique eius Philippi continuas mortes Thessalonice regina, uxor Cassandri, non magno post tempore ab Antipatro filio, cum vitam etiam per
2 ubera materna deprecaretur, occiditur. Causa parricidii fuit, quod post mortem mariti in divisione inter fratres
3 regni propensior fuisse pro Alexandro videbatur. Quod facinus eo gravius omnibus visum est, quod nullum mater-
4 nae fraudis vestigium fuit, quamquam in parricidio nulla
5 satis iusta causa ad sceleris patrocinia praetexi potest. Post haec igitur Alexander in ultionem maternae necis cum
6 fratre gesturus bellum auxilium a Demetrio petit. Nec Demetrius spe invadendi Macedonici regni moram fecit.
7 Cuius adventum verens Lysimachus persuadet genero suo Antipatro, ut malit cum fratre in gratiam reverti quam
8 paternum hostem in Macedoniam admitti. Incohatam igitur inter fratres reconciliationem cum praesensisset De-
9 metrius, per insidias Alexandrum interfecit occupatoque Macedoniae regno caedem apud exercitum excusaturus in contionem vocat.

---

1 See 15.4.24. Continuing sources are Diod. Sic. 21.7ff.; Plut. *Vit. Demetr.* 36ff.; Plut. *Vit. Pyrrh.* 6ff. In this chapter we reach the year 294. For events from Ipsus to the Roman conquest, see *A History of Macedonia*, 3:199ff. (F. W. Walbank); A. M. Eckstein,

BOOK XVI

1. After the successive deaths of King Cassander and his son Philip[1] Queen Thessalonice, the wife of Cassander, was not long afterward murdered by her son Antipater, although she pleaded for her life by the breasts that suckled him. The motive for the killing was that after the death 2 of her husband she seemed to have favored Alexander in the partition of the kingdom between the brothers. The 3 crime seemed all the more heinous to everyone because there was no hint of foul play on the mother's part, though 4 for killing a parent no satisfactory plea can be offered in its defense. So after this Alexander in order to avenge his 5 mother's murder sought help from Demetrius to make war on his brother. And Demetrius, hoping to invade the king- 6 dom of Macedon, did not hesitate to comply. Fearing his 7 coming Lysimachus persuaded his son-in-law Antipater to choose reconciliation with his brother rather than have his father's enemy allowed into Macedonia. So when Deme- 8 trius sensed some reconciliation between the brothers ahead, he trapped and killed Alexander, seized the king- 9 dom of Macedonia, and called the army to an assembly to justify the murder.

Mediterranean Anarchy, Interstate War, and the Rise of Rome (Berkeley, 2006).

10   Ibi priorem se petitum ab Alexandro adlegat, nec fe-
11 cisse se, sed occupasse insidias. Regem autem se Macedoniae vel aetatis experimentis vel causis iustiorem esse.
12 Patrem enim suum et Philippo regi et Alexandro Magno
13 socium in omni militia fuisse; liberorum deinde Alexandri
ministrum et ad persequendos defectores ducem extitisse.
14 Contra Antipatrum, avum horum adulescentium, ama-
riorem semper ministrum regni quam ipsos reges fuisse.
15 Cassandrum vero patrem, extinctorem regiae domus, non
feminis, non pueris pepercisse nec cessasse, quoad om-
16 nem stirpem regiae subolis deleret. Horum scelerum
ultionem, quia nequisset ab ipso Cassandro exigere, ad
17 liberos eius translatam. Quamobrem etiam Philippum
Alexandrumque, si quis manium sensus est, non interfec-
tores suos ac stirpis suae, sed ultores eorum Macedoniae
18 regnum tenere malle. Per haec mitigato populo rex Mace-
19 doniae appellatur. Lysimachus quoque cum bello Dromi-
chaetis, regis Thracum, premeretur, ne eodem tempore
adversus eum dimicare necesse haberet, tradita ei altera
parte Macedoniae, quae Antipatro, genero eius, obvene-
rat, pacem cum eo fecit.

    2. Igitur Demetrius totis Macedoniae regni viribus in-
structus cum Asiam occupare statuisset, iterato Ptolomeus, Seleucus et Lysimachus, experti priore certamine,
quantae vires essent concordia, pacta societate aduna-
tisque exercitibus bellum adversus Demetrium transfe-
2 runt in Europam. His comitem se et belli socium iungit

---

2 Not really true: Antigonus had remained in Asia Minor in
333 and became Alexander's satrap of Greater Phrygia. For the
rest of his exploits, see Books 14 and 15.

There he claimed that he had been attacked by Alex- 10
ander first, that he had not set a trap but averted one. It 11
was he who was the more legitimate king of Macedon, he
said, whether from the experience of age or for other co-
gent reasons. For his father had been an ally to King Philip 12
and Alexander the Great on all their campaigns;[2] and then 13
had been guardian of the children of Alexander and the
leader in hunting down the rebels. Antipater, however, 14
the grandfather of these young men, had always been a
harsher governor of the kingdom than the kings themselves. Their father Cassander, exterminator of the royal 15
house, had certainly not spared either women or children,
and had not stopped before eliminating every descendant
of the royal line. Since he could not exact vengeance for 16
these crimes from Cassander himself, he had brought it
on the man's children. So Philip and Alexander, if the 17
shades of the dead have any feeling, would also prefer to
see not those who murdered them and their family but
rather the avengers of those men as holders of the kingdom of Macedonia. The people being appeased by this, 18
Demetrius was declared the king of Macedonia. Lysima- 19
chus, under pressure in a war with the Thracian king
Dromichaetes and fearing he might have to fight Demetrius at the same time, also ceded to him the other part of
Macedonia, which had fallen to his son-in-law Antipater,
and made peace with him.

2. So when Demetrius, equipped with all the forces of
the Macedonian Kingdom, decided to seize Asia, Ptolemy,
Seleucus, and Lysimachus, who from experience in the
earlier conflict had learned what strength lay in coopera-
tion, again formed an alliance, joined forces, and shifted
the war against Demetrius to Europe. Joining them as 2

343

Pyrrus, rex Epiri, sperans non difficilius Demetrium amit-
3 tere Macedoniam posse quam adquisierat. Nec spes frustra fuit; quippe exercitu eius corrupto ipsoque in fugam
acto regnum Macedoniae occupavit.
4   Dum haec aguntur Lysimachus generum suum Antipatrum regnum Macedoniae ademptum sibi fraude soceri
querentem interficit filiamque suam Eurydicen, querela-
5 rum sociam, in custodiam tradit, atque ita universa Cassandri domus Alexandro Magno seu necis ipsius seu stirpis
extinctae poenas partim caede, partim supplicio, partim
6 parricidio luit. Demetrius quoque a tot exercitibus circumventus, cum posset honeste mori, turpiter se dedere
Seleuco maluit.
7   Finito bello Ptolomeus cum magna rerum gestarum
gloria moritur. Is contra ius gentium minimo natu ex filiis
ante infirmitatem regnum tradiderat eiusque rei populo
8 rationem reddiderat; cuius non minor favor in accipiendo
9 quam patris in tradendo regno fuerat. Inter cetera patris
et filii mutuae pietatis exempla etiam ea res amorem populi iuveni conciliaverat, quod pater regno publice ei tradito privatus officium regi inter satellites fecerat omnique
regno pulchrius regis esse patrem duxerat.
    3. Sed inter Lysimachum et Pyrrum regem, socios
paulo ante, adsiduum inter pares discordiae malum bel-
2 lum moverat. Victor Lysimachus pulso Pyrro Macedoniam

---

3 In the year 287.

4 Cf. 12.14. He was captured in Cilicia and drank himself to
death in 283 after three years in captivity.

5 Probably not the youngest, Ptolemy II Philadelphus reigned
from 282 to 246.

companion and ally in the war was Pyrrhus, king of Epirus, who was hoping that Demetrius would have no more difficulty in losing Macedonia than he had acquiring it. Nor 3 was it a futile hope; for bribing his army and putting the man himself to flight, he seized the throne of Macedonia.[3]

While this was taking place Lysimachus executed his 4 son-in-law Antipater who was complaining that the kingdom of Macedon had been treacherously taken from him by his father-in-law and he imprisoned his own daughter Eurydice who shared his complaints, and so Cassander's 5 entire household paid Alexander the Great the penalty either for his own killing or the extinction of his line, some of them murdered, some tortured, some through assassination. Demetrius was also surrounded by many armies, 6 and although he could die with honor he preferred a disgraceful surrender to Seleucus.[4]

At the end of the war Ptolemy died with a glorious record of achievements to his name. Contrary to the usual practice of nations he had passed the throne to the youngest of his sons before he became infirm[5] and had explained that to the people, who were no less pleased to accept his 8 rule than the father had been to pass it to him. Among the 9 various instances of mutual affection of father and son the following had also won the people's love for the young man: after officially passing him the kingdom his father served the king as an ordinary subject among his bodyguards and had considered being the king's father finer than any kingdom.

3. But between Lysimachus and King Pyrrhus, allies a little earlier, the apple of discord, ever a problem among equals, had started a war. The victor Lysimachus, after 2 driving out Pyrrhus, had seized Macedonia. He had then 3

3 occupaverat. Inde Thraciae ac deinceps Heracleae bellum intulerat, cuius urbis et initia et exitus admirabiles fuere.

4 Quippe Boeotiis pestilentia laborantibus oraculum Delphis responderat, coloniam in Ponti regione sacram Herculi conderent. Cum propter metum longae ac periculo-

5 sae navigationis mortem in patria omnibus praeoptantibus res omissa esset, bellum his Phocenses intulerunt, quorum

6 cum adversa proelia paterentur, iterato ad oraculum decurrunt; responsum idem belli quod pestilentiae reme-

7 dium fore. Igitur conscripta colonorum manu in Pontum delati urbem Heracleam condiderunt, et quoniam fatorum auspiciis in eas sedes delati erant, brevi tempore mag-

8 nas opes paravere. Multa deinde huius urbis adversus finitimos bella, multa etiam domesticae dissensionis mala fuere. Inter cetera magnifica vel praecipue illud memora-

9 bile fuit. Cum rerum potirentur Athenienses victisque Persis Graeciae et Asiae tributum in tutelam classis descripsissent, omnibus cupide ad praesidium salutis suae conferentibus soli Heracleenses ob amicitiam regum Per-

10 sicorum conlationem abnuerant. Missus itaque ab Atheniensibus Lamachus cum exercitu ad extorquendum quod negabatur, dum relictis in litore navibus agros Heracleensium populatur, classem cum maiore parte exercitus nau-

11 fragio repentinae tempestatis amisit. Itaque cum neque

---

6 For what follows see S. M. Burstein, *Outpost of Hellenism: The Emergence of Heraclea on the Black Sea* (Berkeley and Los Angeles, 1976). The founding of the city, most of whose colonists were Megarian, probably took place shortly after 570. It had a native historian named Nymphis, who was perhaps Trogus' source.

made war on Thrace and after that on Heraclea, a city
whose early history and final days were both remarkable.[6]
For when the Boeotians were afflicted with a plague the   4
Delphic oracle's response had been that they should in the
Pontus region found a colony sacred to Hercules. When   5
from fear of a long and dangerous voyage they all preferred a death in their own country and the matter was
dropped, the Phocians made war on them, and after they   6
suffered some defeats they again approached the oracle,
receiving the same response, that the remedy for the war
would be the same as for the plague. So after conscripting   7
a band of colonists and sailing to Pontus they founded the
city of Heraclea, and since it was with the blessing of the
Fates that they had been brought to that spot they quickly
amassed great wealth. There were then many wars with   8
neighboring peoples faced by this city, and also many dire
instances of internal dissension. In its generally rich history, the following was particularly memorable. When the   9
Athenians were ascendant and the Persians defeated, they
had assessed the tribute payable by Greece and Asia for
maintenance of a fleet; and while everyone else readily
contributed to maintaining their security only the Heracleans had, from their friendship with the Persian kings,
refused a contribution. So Lamachus was sent with an   10
army by the Athenians to wrest from them what was being
refused, but while raiding the Heracleans' lands with his
ships left on the shore he lost his fleet together with most
of his army when it was wrecked in a sudden storm.[7] So   11

---

[7] Lamachus' expedition was in 424; see *AO* 132. Thuc. 4.75
makes no mention of the kindness of the Heracleans.

mari posset amissis navibus, neque terra auderet cum parva manu inter tot ferocissimas gentes reverti, Heracleenses honestiorem beneficii quam ultionis occasionem
12 rati instructos commeatibus auxiliisque dimittunt, bene agrorum suorum populationem inpensam existimantes, si quos hostes habuerant amicos reddidissent.

2 4. Passi sunt inter plurima mala etiam tyrannidem; siquidem cum plebs et tabulas novas et divisionem agrorum divitum inpotenter flagitarent, diu re in senatu tractata
3 cum exitus rei non inveniretur, postremum adversus plebem nimio otio lascivientem auxilia a Timotheo, Atheniensium duce, mox ab Epaminonda Thebanorum petivere.
4 Utrisque negantibus ad Clearchum, quem ipsi in exilium
5 egerant, decurrunt. Tanta calamitatium necessitas fuit, ut cui patriam interdixerant, eum ad tutelam patriae voca-
6 rent. Sed Clearchus, exilio facinorosior redditus et dissensionem populi occasionem invadendae tyrannidis existi-
7 mans, primo tacitus cum Mithridate, civium suorum hoste, conloquitur et inita societate paciscitur, ut revocatus in patriam prodita ei urbe praefectus eius constitue-
8 tur. Postea autem insidias, quas civibus paraverat, in ipsum
9 Mithridatem verterat. Namque cum velut arbiter civilis discordiae exilio reversus esset, statuto tempore, quo urbem Mithridati traderet, ipsum cum amicis suis cepit,
10 captum accepta ingenti pecunia dimisit. Atque ut in illo

---

8 See Diod. Sic. 15.81.5f., under 364/3, and for Clearchus' death, 16.36.3, under 353/2, which account does not square with Justin's on the setting and names Clearchus' successor as his son Timotheus; Memnon, *FGrH* 434 F 2.1, agrees with Justin. For Timotheus see *AO* 262.

since he could neither return by sea after losing the ships, and would not dare to return overland with a small band of men amid so many savage tribes, the Heracleans, seeing a more honorable opportunity for kindness than for revenge, sent them off equipped with supplies and an escort, thinking themselves well recompensed for the destruction 12 of their land if they had turned former enemies into friends.

4. They also endured, among their many other hardships, a tyranny;[8] for when their plebs outrageously de- 2 manded both debt cancellation and distribution of rich people's lands and the matter was long discussed in the senate but no solution was found, they finally sought help 3 against their plebs, who were becoming undisciplined from having too much free time, first from the Athenian general Timotheus and then from Epaminondas of Thebes. When 4 both refused they turned to Clearchus, whom they had themselves driven into exile. So dire was their situation 5 that a man they had debarred from their country they were now calling on for the protection of the country! But 6 Clearchus, coming out of exile an even worse scoundrel and seeing in dissension among the people an opportunity for seizing a tyranny, first quietly conferred with Mithri- 7 dates, the enemy of his own citizens, and negotiating a pact with him agreed that if recalled he would betray the city to him and be made its governor. Later, however, he 8 had turned the plot he had prepared for the citizens against Mithridates himself. For when he, supposedly as 9 an arbiter of civil discord, had returned from exile and a time was arranged for delivering the city to Mithridates, he arrested the man himself together with his friends, and after arresting him released for a huge sum of money. And, 10

subitum se ex socio fecit hostem, sic ex defensore senato-
11 riae causae repente patronus plebis evasit et adversus auctores potentiae suae, a quibus revocatus in patriam, per
quos in arce conlocatus fuerat, non solum plebem accendit, verum etiam nefandissima quaeque tyrannicae crude-
12 litatis exercuit. Igitur populo ad contionem vocato neque
adfuturum se amplius grassanti in populum senatui ait;
13 intercessurum etiam, si in pristina saevitia perseveret;
quodsi pares se crudelitati senatorum arbitrentur, abitu-
rum cum militibus suis neque civilibus discordiis inter-
14 futurum; sin vero diffidant viribus propriis, vindictae se
15 civium non defuturum. Proinde consulant sibi ipsi: iu-
beant abire se, an sibi malint, vel causae populari socium
16 remanere. His verbis sollicitata plebs summum ad eum
imperium defert et, dum senatus potentiae irascitur, in
servitutem se tyrannicae dominationis cum coniugibus et
17 liberis tradit. Igitur Clearchus LX senatores conprehensos
(nam ceteri in fugam dilapsi erant) in vincula conpingit.
18 Laetari plebs, quod a duce potissimum senatorum senatus
deleretur, versaque vice auxilium eorum in exitium con-
19 versum esse. Quibus dum mortem passim omnibus mina-
20 tur, cariora eorum pretia fecit, siquidem Clearchus magna
pecunia, quasi minis populi occulte eos subtracturus, accepta spoliatos fortunis vita quoque spoliavit.

    5. Cognito deinde quod bellum sibi ab iis, qui profuge-
rant, misericordia in auxilium sollicitatis civitatibus para-

just as he had in his case suddenly turned himself from ally
to enemy, so, after acting as defender of the senate's cause,
he suddenly appeared as patron of the plebs, and against 11
the authors of his power, men by whom he had been recalled to his country and through whom he had been installed in the citadel, he not only inflamed the plebeians
but also inflicted all the atrocities of a ruthless tyranny. So 12
summoning the people to an assembly he said that he
would no longer support senatorial repression of the people; he would even intervene if it continued its earlier
brutality; but if they thought they could tolerate the ruth- 13
lessness of the senators, he would leave with his soldiers
and take no part in their civil disputes; if, however, they 14
lacked confidence in their own strength he would not fail
to vindicate his fellow citizens. So they must decide for 15
themselves: they could order him to leave if they liked, or
to remain as an ally of the people's cause. Disturbed by 16
such talk the people conferred supreme power on him,
and through anger over their senate's power surrendered
themselves to a despotic tyranny together with their wives
and children. So Clearchus arrested sixty senators (for the 17
others had slipped away in flight) and clapped them in
irons. The plebs were happy that the senate was being 18
destroyed by its very own leader, and that with the tables
turned the anticipated help had turned into their downfall. While he randomly threatened everyone with death, 19
he increased their ransom prices; for Clearchus, taking 20
large sums of money, ostensibly to rescue them secretly
from threats from the people, robbed them of their fortunes and also of their lives.

5. Hearing then of war being fomented against him by
those who had fled, with some states coming their aid out

2 retur, servos eorum manumittit et, ne quid mali adflictis
honestissimis domibus deesset, uxores eorum filiasque
nubere servis suis proposita recusantibus morte conpellit,
3 ut eos sibi fidiores et dominis infestiores redderet. Sed
matronis tam lugubres nuptiae graviores repentinis fune-
4 ribus fuere. Itaque multae se ante nuptias, multae in ipsis
nuptiis occisis prius novis maritis interficiunt et se tam
funestis calamitatibus virtute ingenui pudoris eripiunt.
5 Proelium deinde committitur, quo victor tyrannus captivos senatores in triumphi modum per ora civium trahit.
6 Reversus in urbem alios vincit torquetque alios, alios occi-
7 dit; nullus locus urbis a crudelitate tyranni vacat. Accedit
8 saevitiae insolentia, crudelitati adrogantia. Interdum ex
successu continuae felicitatis obliviscitur se hominem,
9 interdum Iovis filium dicit. Eunti per publicum aurea
10 aquila velut argumentum generis praeferebatur, veste
purpurea et cothurnis regum tragicorum et aurea corona
11 utebatur, filium quoque suum Ceraunon vocat, ut deos
non mendacio tantum, verum etiam nominibus inludat.

12 Haec illum facere duo nobilissimi iuvenes, Chion et
Leonides, indignantes patriam liberaturi in necem tyranni
13 conspirant. Erant hi discipuli Platonis philosophi, qui virtutem, ad quam cotidie perfectius praeceptis magistri eru-
diebantur, patriae exhibere cupientes L cognatos veluti
14 clientes in insidiis locant. Ipsi more iurgantium ad tyran-

---

9 Which means "thunderbolt," signifying the power of Zeus.

10 The Latin here is *cognatos veluti clientes*. A *cliens* was "a
free man who entrusted himself to another and received protection in return" (*OCD* s.v. cliens), but Justin's point is unclear.

of sympathy, he freed the slaves of those people and so the   2
most reputable families should not be spared any misfortune he made their wives and daughters marry their slaves,
threatening any refusal with death in order to make them
more loyal to him and more hostile to their masters. But   3
for married women such wretched marriages were worse
than swift deaths. Many of them therefore killed them-   4
selves before a marriage and many during the marriage
itself after first killing their new husbands, and thus saved
themselves from such dismal fates by their moral probity.
A battle then followed, in which the victorious tyrant   5
dragged his captive senators before the eyes of the citizens
as if in a triumph. After returning to the city he imprisoned   6
some, tortured others, and others again he executed; no   7
place in the city avoided the tyrant's brutality. His inso-
lence approached callousness and his arrogance cruelty.
Sometimes after an unbroken run of success he would   8
forget he was a man, and sometimes he said he was the
son of Jupiter. When he went in public a golden eagle was   9
carried before him as the symbol of his lineage, and he   10
wore purple clothes, the buskins worn by kings in tragedy,
and a golden crown; and he also called his son Ceraunus,[9]   11
making a mockery of the gods not only by his own preten-
sions but even his choice of names.

Outraged by such conduct two very wellborn young   12
men, Chion and Leonides, in order to free their country,
conspired to kill the tyrant. These were students of the   13
philosopher Plato, who being eager to show their country
the qualities in which they were daily improving themselves in following their master's precepts, enlisted fifty of
their relatives to assist them,[10] and set them in ambush.
They themselves, as though in dispute, went in person to   14

15 num veluti ad regem in arcem contendunt; qui iure familiaritatis admissi, dum alterum priorem dicentem intentus
16 audit tyrannus, ab altero occupatur. Sed et ipsi sociis tar-
17 dius auxilium ferentibus a satellitibus obruuntur. Qua re
factum est, ut tyrannus quidem occideretur, sed patria non
18 liberaretur. Nam frater Clearchi Satyrus eadem via tyrannidem invadit, multisque annis per gradus successionis
Heracleenses regnum tyrannorum fuere.

the tyrant in the citadel as if to a king; and, allowed entry   15
through their family connections, while the tyrant was
preoccupied listening to the one speaking first he was
struck down by the other. But since their associates were   16
too late bringing help they were overwhelmed by the
bodyguard. Thus it turned out that although the tyrant was   17
assassinated the country was not liberated. For Clearchus'   18
brother Satyrus seized the tyranny by the same means, and
for many years, as power passed down by succession, the
Heracleans remained under the rule of tyrants.

LIBER XVII

1. Per idem ferme tempus Hellesponti et Chersonesi re-
2 gionibus terrae motus fuit, maxime tamen Lysimachia
urbs, ante duos et XX annos a Lysimacho rege condita,
3 eversa est. Quod portentum dira Lysimacho stirpique eius
ac regni ruinam cum clade vexatarum regionum porten-
4 debat. Nec ostentis fides defuit, nam brevi post tempore
Agathoclem, filium suum, quem in successionem regni
ordinaverat, per quem multa bella prospere gesserat, non
solum ultra patrium, verum etiam ultra humanum morem
5 perosus ministra Arsinoe noverca veneno interfecit. Haec
illi prima mali labes, hoc initium inpendentis ruinae fuit.
6 Nam parricidium principum secutae caedes sunt luentium
7 supplicia, quod occisum iuvenem dolebant. Itaque et ii,
qui caedibus superfuerant, et ii, qui exercitibus praeerant,
8 certatim ad Seleucum deficiunt eumque pronum iam ex
aemulatione gloriae bellum Lysimacho inferre conpellunt.
9 Vltimum hoc certamen conmilitonum Alexandri fuit et
10 velut ad exemplum fortunae par reservatum. Lysimachus

---

1 We return to the late 280s, where Justin left off at 16.3.3.

2 The daughter of Ptolemy I, on whom see further below.

3 The end was the battle of Corupedium in 281. See App. *Syr.*
62ff.

BOOK XVII

1. At about the same time[1] areas of the Hellespont and
Chersonese were struck by an earthquake, but most im- 2
portantly the city of Lysimachia, founded twenty-two years
earlier by King Lysimachus, was destroyed. This was an 3
omen portending a grim future for Lysimachus and his
descendants and ruin for his kingdom with the destruction of the afflicted areas. Nor did the portents lack cred- 4
ibility, for shortly afterward he conceived for his own son
Agathocles, whom he had appointed as successor to the
throne and through whom he had successfully conducted
many wars, a hatred abnormal not only in a father but in
any human being, and he had him poisoned by his stepmother Arsinoë.[2] This was his first disastrous step, this the 5
start of his impending downfall. For the murder was fol- 6
lowed by a massacre of leading citizens for grieving over
the young man's killing. So both those who had survived 7
the killings and those in command of armies rushed to 8
defect to Seleucus and pushed him into attacking Lysimachus, to which he was already inclined from envy of the
king's reputation. This was the last fight between the com- 9
rades of Alexander[3] and the two had been virtually kept in
reserve as a demonstration of the vagaries of fortune. Ly- 10

357

quattuor et LXX annos natus erat, Seleucus septem et
11 LXX. Sed in hac aetate utrique animi iuveniles erant impe-
12 riique cupiditatem insatiabilem gerebant; quippe cum
orbem terrarum duo soli tenerent, angustis sibi metis in-
clusi videbantur vitaeque finem non annorum spatio, sed
imperii terminis metiebantur.

2. In eo bello Lysimachus amissis ante variis casibus
quindecim liberis non instrenue moriens postremus do-
2 mus suae ruinae cumulus accessit. Laetus tanta victoria
Seleucus et, quod maius victoria putat, solum se de cohorte Alexandri remansisse victoremque victorum extitisse, non humanum esse opus, sed divinum munus gloria-
3 tur, ignarus prorsus non multo post fragilitatis humanae se
4 ipsum exemplum futurum. Quippe post menses admodum septem a Ptolomeo, cuius sororem Lysimachus in
5 matrimonio habuerat, per insidias circumventus occiditur
regnumque Macedoniae, quod Lysimacho eripuerat, cum
6 vita pariter amittit. Igitur Ptolomeus cum et in gratiam
memoriae Magni Ptolomei patris et in favorem ultionis
Lysimachi ambitiosus ad populares esset, primo Lysi-
7 machi filios conciliare sibi statuit nuptiasque Arsinoae,
sororis suae, matris eorum, petit puerorum adoptione pro-
8 missa, ut cum in locum patris eorum successisset, nihil illi
moliri vel verecundia matris vel appellatione patris au-
derent.

9   Fratris quoque, regis Aegypti, concordiam per epistulas deprecatur, professus deponere se offensam erepti

---

4 Ptolemy Ceraunus (Thunderbolt) was the half brother of
Arsinoë; his full brother, Philadelphus, had the succession in
Egypt.

simachus was seventy-four years old, Seleucus seventy-seven. But at that age both were young in spirit and had 11 an insatiable lust for power; for while the two alone held 12 the world in their hands, they still felt themselves confined within narrow limits and measured their life's term not by the passing of years but by their empires' boundaries.

2. In that war Lysimachus, who had earlier lost fifteen children from various misfortunes, died fighting bravely and added the last touch to his family's demise. Seleucus 2 was pleased with so great a victory and also, something he thought greater than the victory, by the thought that only he remained from Alexander's circle and was the conqueror of conquerors—no human achievement, he boasted, but a gift from heaven, little realizing that not 3 much later he too would be an example of the frailty of the human condition. For some seven months later he was 4 caught in a trap and killed by Ptolemy,[4] to whose sister Lysimachus had been married, and he lost the kingdom of 5 Macedon, which he had wrested from Lysimachus, and with it he also lost his life. So Ptolemy, being eager to ex- 6 ploit his father Ptolemy the Great's memory among the people and also win favor for avenging Lysimachus, de- cided first to win over Lysimachus' sons and sought a mar- 7 riage with Arsinoë, his own sister and the boys' mother, with a promise to adopt the boys, so that once he had re- 8 placed their father the boys, either from respect for their mother or because he was nominally their father, would not dare oppose him.

He also sought an accord with his brother, the king of 9 Egypt, by letter, claiming he would put aside any resent-

paterni regni neque amplius a fratre quaesiturum, quod
10 honestius a paterno hoste perceperit, omnique arte adu-
latur eum, ne Antigono Demetrii filio, Antiocho filio Seleuci, cum quibus bellum habiturus erat, tertius sibi hostis
11 accederet. Sed nec Pyrrus, rex Epiri, omissus, ingens
12 momentum futurus, utri parti socius accessisset, qui et
ipse spoliare singulos cupiens omnibus se partibus vendi-
13 tabat. Itaque Tarentinis adversus Romanos laturus auxilium ab Antigono naves ad exercitum in Italiam deportan-
dum mutuo petit, ab Antiocho pecuniam, qui opibus quam
militibus instructior erat, ab Ptolomeo Macedonum mili-
14 tum auxilia. Sed Ptolomeus, cui nulla dilationis ex infirmitate virium venia esset, quinque milia peditum, equitum
IV milia, elephantos L non amplius quam in biennii usum,
15 dedit. Ob haec Pyrrus filia Ptolomei in matrimonium accepta vindicem eum regni reliquit, pacificatus cum omnibus finitimis, ne abducta in Italiam iuventute praedam
hostibus regnum relinqueret.

3. Sed quoniam ad Epiri mentionem ventum est, de
2 origine regni eius pauca narranda sunt. Molossorum pri-
3 mum in ea regione regnum fuit. Post Pyrrus, Achillis filius,
amisso per absentiam Troianis temporibus paterno regno
in his locis consedit: qui Pyrridae primo, postea Epirotae

---

5 The rule of Antigonus II Gonatas in Macedonia began in 276
and ran to (probably) 239. Antiochus I Soter ruled from 281 to
261. For Pyrrhus, who crossed to Italy in 281/0, see Plut. *Vit.
Pyrrh.* 13ff. Though the Latin uses the spelling "Pyrrus," we re-
tain the familiar form of the well-known name in the translation.

6 Plut. *Vit. Pyrrh.* 15.1 does not mention such a loan. For the
marriage cf. 24.1.8, though there is no evidence it ever took place,

ment over the seizure of their father's kingdom and no
longer ask of his brother what he had more honorably
gained from their father's enemy, and he plied him with   10
all manner of flattery not have him become his third enemy by joining Antigonus son of Demetrius and Antiochus
son of Seleucus, with whom he was about to go to war.[5]
But Pyrrhus, king of Epirus, was not overlooked either, a   11
man who could be a great asset to whichever side he joined
and who himself, being eager to prey on them individually,   12
was ingratiating himself with all sides. So, in order to bring   13
the Tarentines help against the Romans, he asked Antigonus to lend him ships for ferrying an army to Italy; Antiochus, who had more wealth than troops, he asked for
money; and Ptolemy he asked for Macedonian auxiliary
forces. Ptolemy, who had no excuse for holding back on   14
grounds of lack of troops, gave him five thousand infantry,
four thousand cavalry and fifty elephants for a period no
more than two years.[6] In return Pyrrhus received Ptole-   15
my's daughter in marriage and left him to safeguard his
kingdom, having first made peace with all his neighbors so
when he took his young troops off to Italy he would not
have the kingdom fall prey to his enemies.

3. But since we have reached mention of Epirus, a
little must be said about the origin of that kingdom. The   2
Molossians' kingdom was first in that region. Later Pyr-   3
rhus, Achilles' son, settled in this area after losing the
kingdom of his father during his absence in the time of the
Trojan War; the people were first called Pyrrhidae and

perhaps because Ceraunus died in 279. Pyrrhus' wives are recorded at Plut. *Vit. Pyrr.* 9.

4 dicti sunt. Sed Pyrrus cum in templum Dodonaei Iovis ad
consulendum venisset, ibi Lanassam, neptem Herculis,
5 rapuit, ex cuius matrimonio octo liberos sustulit. Ex his
nonnullas virgines nuptum finitimis regibus tradidit opes-
6 que adfinitatium auxilio magnas paravit. Atque ita Heleno,
filio Priami regis, ob industriam singularem regnum Chao-
num et Andromachan Hectoris e matrimonio suo, quos in
divisione Troianae praedae acceperat, uxorem tradidit,
7 brevique post tempore Delphis insidiis Orestae, filii Aga-
8 memnonis, inter altaria dei interiit. Successor huic Piales
filius fuit.

9 Per ordinem deinde regnum ad Tharybam descendit,
10 cui, quoniam pupillus et unicus ex gente nobili superesset,
intentiore omnium cura servandi eius educandique pu-
11 blice tutores constituuntur. Athenas quoque erudiendi
gratia missus. Quanto doctior maioribus suis, tanto et
12 populo gratior fuit. Primus itaque leges et senatum an-
13 nuosque magistratus et rei publicae formam conposuit, et
ut a Pyrro sedes, sic vita cultior populo a Tharyba statuta.
14 Huius filius Neoptolemus fuit, ex quo nata est Olympias,
15 mater magni Alexandri, et Alexander, qui post eum regnum Epiri tenuit et in Italia bello gesto in Bruttiis interiit.
16 Post eius mortem frater Aeacidas regno successit, qui
adsiduis adversus Macedonas bellorum certaminibus pop-
17 ulum fatigando offensam civium contraxit ac propterea in
exilium actus Pyrrum filium, bimum admodum parvulum,

---

7 Usually spelled "Tharyps" or "Tharypas"; he ruled in the late
fifth century.

later Epirotae. But when Pyrrhus came to the temple of 4
Jupiter at Dodona to consult the oracle, he there abducted
Lanassa the granddaughter of Hercules, and from their
marriage had eight children. Of these he gave several girls 5
in marriage to neighboring kings and with the help of such
family ties acquired great wealth. So to King Priam's son 6
Helenus, in recognition of his outstanding service, he
passed on the kingdom of Chaonia and also Andromache,
Hector's widow, whom he had himself married after receiving her in the partition of the Trojan spoils; and a little 7
later he was waylaid at Delphi by Orestes, son of Agamem-
non, and died amid the altars of the god. His successor was 8
his son Piales.

In order of succession, the throne then came down to 9
Tharybas;[7] and since he was a minor and sole survivor of 10
the noble line and everyone was all the more concerned
for his protection and education, guardians were officially
appointed for him. He was also sent to Athens for school- 11
ing. The more he surpassed his ancestors in learning, the
more pleased with him were the people. So he was the first 12
to found laws, a senate, annual magistracies, and a regular
constitution, and although the country was founded by 13
Pyrrhus, a more civilized life for its people was founded
by Tharybas. This man's son was Neoptolemus, from 14
whom Olympias, Alexander the Great's mother, was born,
as was the Alexander who succeeded him on the throne of 15
Epirus and died in Italy in a war fought in Bruttium. After 16
his death he was succeeded in the kingdom by his brother
Aeacides, who after exhausting his people with interminable wars against the Macedonians, earned the citizens'
disapproval, and when he was therefore driven into exile 17
he left his son Pyrrhus, a mere infant just two years old, as

18 in regno reliquit. Qui et ipse, cum a populo propter odium
patris ad necem quaereretur, furtim subtractus in Illyrios
19 defertur traditusque est Beroae, Glauciae regis uxori,
20 nutriendus, quae et ipsa genus Aeacidarum erat. Ibi eum
seu misericordia fortunae eius seu infantilibus blandimentis inductus rex adversum Cassandrum, Macedoniae regem, qui eum sub belli comminatione deposcebat, diu
21 protexit, addito in auxilium etiam adoptionis officio. Quibus rebus moti Epirotae odio in misericordiam verso annorum XI eum in regnum revocaverunt, datis tutoribus,
22 qui regnum usque adultam eius aetatem tuerentur. Adulescens deinde multa bella gessit tantusque rerum successu haberi coeptus est, ut Tarentinos solus adversus
Romanos tueri posse videretur.

ruler. When because of the hatred felt for his father he 18
was himself also sought for execution by the people, he
was furtively taken away to the Illyrians, and entrusted 19
for nurturing to Beroa, wife of King Glaucias, herself of
Aeacid descent.[8] There, either from pity for his sad cir- 20
cumstances or induced by his infant charms, the king long
defended him against Cassander, the king of Macedonia,
who was demanding his rendition with a threat of war,
even going so far as formal adoption to protect him. By 21
this the Epirotes' hatred was turned to pity and they recalled him to the throne at the age of eleven, giving him
guardians to maintain the kingdom until he came of age.
As a young man he then fought many wars and from his 22
successes he began to gain such a reputation that only he
seemed capable of defending the people of Tarentum
against the Romans.[9]

[8] On the claimed lineage of the Molossian royal house, see
11.4.5, 12.16.3.
[9] Suffice it to say that Pyrrhus' career was not as smooth as
Justin's last sentence suggests.

LIBER XVIII

1. Igitur Pyrrus, rex Epiri, cum iterata Tarentinorum legatione additis Samnitium et Lucanorum precibus, et ipsis
auxilio adversus Romanos indigentibus fatigaretur, non
tam supplicium precibus quam spe invadendi Italiae im-
2 perii inductus venturum se cum exercitu pollicetur. In
quam rem inclinatum semel animum praecipitem agere
coeperant exempla maiorum, ne aut inferior patruo suo
Alexandro videretur, quo defensore idem Tarentini adversus Bruttios usi fuerant, aut minores animos Magno
Alexandro habuisse, qui tam longa a domo militia Orien-
3 tem subegit. Igitur relicto custode regni Ptolomeo filio
annos XV nato exercitum in portu Tarentino exponit, duobus parvulis filiis, Alexandro et Heleno, in solacia longinquae secum expeditionis adductis.
4   Cuius audito adventu consul Romanus Valerius Laevinus festinans, ut prius cum eo congrederetur, quam auxilia
5 sociorum convenirent, exercitum in aciem educit. Nec
rex, tametsi numero militum inferior esset, certamini

---

1 Continued from 17.2. The story goes on in Plut. *Vit. Pyrrh.*
16ff.; other sources at *MRR* 1.191ff.; P. Valerius Laevinus was
consul in 280; C. Fabricius Luscinus' embassy occurred in 279.
Pyrrhus' final defeat in Italy came in 275. For his uncle Alexander,
see 12.2.1ff.

BOOK XVIII

1. Now[1] Pyrrhus, king of Epirus, was tiring of repeated embassies from the Tarentines along with appeals from the Samnites and Lucanians, who were themselves also in need of help against the Romans, and being drawn less by his petitioners' entreaties than hope of seizing power in Italy, he promised he would come with an army. Already 2 inclined to such a move, he was finally prompted to act by the examples of his ancestors, so he should neither appear inferior to his uncle Alexander, whom those same Tarentines had found as their defender against the Bruttii, nor to have had less courage than Alexander the Great, who conquered the East in a campaign so far from home. So, 3 leaving his fifteen-year-old son Ptolemy to guard the kingdom he disembarked his army in the port of Tarentum, taking with him his two young sons Alexander and Helenus as solace on a distant campaign.

On hearing of his arrival the Roman consul, Valerius 4 Laevinus, hastening to encounter him before the auxiliary forces of the king's allies could assemble, led his army into the line of battle. And the king, although nu- 5 merically inferior in soldiers, did not delay the encounter.

6 moram fecit. Sed Romanos vincentes iam invisitata ante elephantorum forma stupere primo, mox cedere proelio coegit, victoresque iam nova Macedonum repente mon-
7 stra vicerunt. Nec hostibus incruenta victoria fuit. Nam et Pyrrus ipse graviter vulneratus est et magna pars militum eius caesa, maioremque gloriam eius victoriae quam lae-
8 titiam habuit. Huius pugnae eventum multae civitates
9 secutae Pyrro se tradunt. Inter ceteras etiam Locri prodito
10 praesidio Romano ad Pyrrum deficiunt. Ex ea praeda Pyrrus CC captivos milites gratis Romam remisit, ut cognita virtute eius Romani cognoscerent etiam liberalitatem.
11 Interiectis deinde diebus, cum sociorum exercitus supervenisset, iterato proelium cum Romanis facit, in quo par fortuna priori bello fuit.

2. Interea Mago, dux Karthaginiensium, in auxilium Romanorum cum centum XX navibus missus senatum adiit, aegre tulisse Karthaginienses adfirmans, quod bel-
2 lum in Italia a peregrino rege paterentur. Ob quam causam missum se, ut, quoniam externo hoste oppugnarentur,
3 externis auxiliis iuvarentur. Gratiae a senatu Karthagini-
4 ensibus actae auxiliaque remissa. Sed Mago Punico ingenio post paucos dies tacitus, quasi pacificator Karthaginiensium, Pyrrum adiit speculaturus consilia eius de Sicilia,
5 quo eum arcessi fama erat. Nam Romanis eadem causa mittendi auxilia Karthaginiensibus fuerat, ut Romano

---

2 Actually, in the following year, 279.

3 Polyb. 3.25 marks a treaty between Rome and Carthage at this time.

4 The notion that Carthaginians could not be trusted resounds through Roman writings; see also below, 18.6.2.

But the Romans, though dominant, were first left stunned 6
by the shape of elephants, hitherto unseen by them, and
then forced to retreat; and though victors, were suddenly
defeated by the Macedonians' strange creatures. But for 7
the enemy it was no bloodless victory, either. For Pyrrhus
himself was also seriously wounded and a large number of
his men killed, and from that victory he had more glory
than joy. Many cities awaiting the result of this battle sur- 8
rendered to Pyrrhus. Among the others were also the 9
Locrians, who after betraying the Roman garrison defected to Pyrrhus. From those spoils Pyrrhus sent two 10
hundred captured soldiers back to Rome ransom free, so
the Romans, now aware of his valor, should also be aware
of his generosity. Then a few days later when his allies' 11
army arrived,[2] he fought a second battle with the Romans,
in which the outcome was as in the earlier battle.

2. Meanwhile Mago, general of the Carthaginians, sent
with a hundred and twenty ships to support the Romans,[3]
approached the senate stating that the Carthaginians were
vexed that they were facing war in Italy from a foreign
king. That was why he had been sent, he said. so that since 2
they were being attacked by an enemy from without, they
should also be assisted with aid from without. The Cartha- 3
ginians were thanked by the senate but their reinforcements were returned. Mago, however, with Punic trick- 4
ery,[4] stayed silent for a few days and then approached
Pyrrhus as if a peacemaker from the Carthaginians in order to find out his plans for Sicily, to which rumor had it
he was being summoned. For the Carthaginians had had 5
this same motive for sending help to the Romans: detained

bello, ne in Siciliam transire posset, Pyrrus in Italia detineretur.

6   Dum haec aguntur, legatus a senatu Romano Fabricius
7 Luscinus missus pacem cum Pyrro conponit. Ad quam
confirmandam Cineas Romam cum ingentibus a Pyrro
donis missus neminem, cuius domus muneribus pateret,
8 invenit. Huic continentiae Romanorum simile exemplum
9 isdem ferme temporibus fuit. Nam missi a senatu Aegyptum legati cum ingentia sibi a Ptolomeo rege missa munera sprevissent, interiectis diebus ad cenam invitatis
aureae coronae missae sunt, quas illi ominis causa receptas
10 postera die statuis regis inposuerunt. Igitur Cineas, cum
turbatam cum Romanis pacem ab Appio Claudio renuntiasset, interrogatus a Pyrro, qualis Roma esset, respondit
11 regum urbem sibi visam. Post haec legati Siculorum superveniunt tradentes Pyrro totius insulae imperium, quae
12 adsiduis Karthaginiensium bellis vexabatur. Itaque relicto
Locris Alexandro filio firmatisque sociorum civitatibus
valido praesidio in Siciliam exercitum traiecit.

   3. Et quoniam ad Karthaginiensium mentionem ventum est, de origine eorum pauca dicenda sunt, repetitis
Tyriorum paulo altius rebus, quorum casus etiam do-
2 lendi fuerunt. Tyriorum gens condita a Phoenicibus fuit,

---

5 Justin's wording is clumsy and not easy to follow, but he must
mean that the Carthaginians had the same motive in both offering
help to Rome and offering mediation to Pyrrhus—i.e., to keep
him out of Sicily.

6 Ptolemy II Philadelphus; *MRR* 1.197 places this in 273.

7 The account is resumed at 23.3.

8 Justin is an important source for Carthaginian history. Tro-

in Italy in a Roman war, Pyrrhus would not be able to cross to Sicily.[5]

While this was happening, Fabricius Luscinus, who 6 had been sent as a delegate by the Roman senate, concluded a peace treaty with Pyrrhus. For its ratification 7 Cineas, who was sent to Rome with sumptuous gifts from Pyrrhus, found no one whose home was open to his largesse. Such integrity on the Romans' part was like another 8 of about the same time. For delegates who had been sent 9 to Egypt by the senate had rejected rich gifts offered them by King Ptolemy,[6] and when they were invited to dinner some days later and were sent golden wreaths, they did accept them as a good omen for their mission, but the next day set them on the king's statues. Thus when Cineas re- 10 ported that the treaty with the Romans had been rejected by Appius Claudius and was asked by Pyrrhus what Rome was like, he replied that to him it seemed a city of kings. After this, delegates arrived from Sicily granting Pyrrhus 11 authority over the whole island, which was harassed with ongoing Carthaginian wars. So leaving his son Alexander 12 at Locri and securing his allies' cities with powerful garrisons, he took his army over to Sicily.[7]

3. And since we have now come to mention of the Carthaginians, a little must be said about their origins, with a look back to the history of the Tyrians, whose fortunes were also pitiful.[8] The Tyrian race was founded by the Phoeni- 2

gus derived much from Timaeus for this episode. See in general B. H. Warmington, *Carthage* (London, 1960); S. Lancel, *Carthage: A History* (London, 1995); R. Miles, *Carthage Must Be Destroyed* (London, 2010); D. Hoyos, *The Carthaginians* (London and New York, 2010).

3   qui terrae motu vexati relicto patrio solo ad Syrium sta-
gnum primo, mox mari proximum litus incoluerunt, con-
4   dita ibi urbe, quam a piscium ubertate Sidona appellave-
5   runt; nam piscem Phoenices sidon vocant. Post multos
deinde annos a rege Ascaloniorum expugnati, navibus
appulsi Tyron urbem ante annum Troianae cladis condi-
6   derunt. Ibi Persarum bellis diu varieque fatigati victores
quidem fuere, sed adtritis viribus a servis suis multitu-
7   dine abundantibus indigna supplicia perpessi sunt, qui
conspiratione facta omnem liberum populum cum dominis interficiunt atque ita potiti urbe lares dominorum oc-
cupant, rem publicam invadunt, coniuges ducunt et, quod
ipsi non erant, liberos procreant.
8   Vnus ex tot milibus servorum fuit, qui miti ingenio
senis domini parvulique filii eius fortuna moveretur do-
minosque non truci feritate, sed pia misericordiae huma-
9   nitate respiceret. Itaque cum velut occisos alienasset ser-
visque de statu rei publicae deliberantibus placuisset
regem ex corpore suo creari eumque potissimum quasi
acceptissimum diis, qui solem orientem primus vidisset,
rem ad Stratonem (hoc enim ei nomen erat) dominum
10 occulte latentem detulit. Ab eo formatus, cum medio noctis omnes in unum campum processissent, ceteris in orientem spectantibus solus occidentis regionem intuebatur.
11 Id primum aliis videri furor, in occidente solis ortum quae-

---

9 Tyre in fact existed from the early third millennium; its
Phoenician name was Sor.   10 Latin *liberi*: a play on words,
since *liberi* can mean both "children" and "free men." The story
of the slave rising and the loyal slave of Strato is invented. Justin
puts it in the mid-fourth century (sections 18–19 below).

cians, who after an earthquake left their native land and 3
settled first at the Syrian lake and then on the coastline;
and there they founded a city that they called Sidon from 4
its abundance of fish (for *sidon* is Phoenician for fish).
Then after many years when defeated by the king of the 5
Ascalonians, they took to their ships and founded the city
of Tyre the year before the fall of Troy.[9] There, exhausted 6
from long and intermittently successful wars with the Persians, they were eventually victorious, but their strength
being depleted they suffered shameful treatment from
their teeming number of slaves, who hatched a conspiracy, 7
murdered all free people together with their masters, and
thus taking over the city occupied their masters' homes,
seized the government, took wives and fathered what they
were not themselves, free men.[10]

Among the many thousands of the slaves was one who, 8
having a compassionate nature, was moved to pity by the
plight of his aging master and his young son, and regarded
his masters not with pitiless hostility but with pious and
compassionate devotion. So after he took them away, 9
claiming that they had been killed, and the slaves started
to discuss the constitution of their state, they decided a
king should be appointed from among their number and
that it should be the man who first caught sight of the rising sun, since he in particular would seem very acceptable
to the gods; and the slave then reported the matter to his
master Strato (for such was his name) who was in hiding.
Having this information from him, when at midnight they 10
all went to the same open space and the others looked east,
only he had his gaze fixed westward. This to other people 11
at first seemed crazy, to be looking for the sunrise in the

12 rere. Vbi vero dies adventare coepit editissimisque culmi-
nibus urbis oriens splendere, spectantibus aliis, ut ipsum
solem aspicerent, hic primus omnibus fulgorem solis in
13 summo fastigio civitatis ostendit. Non servilis ingenii ratio
14 visa; requirentibus auctorem de domino confitetur. Tunc
intellectum est, quantum ingenua servilibus ingenia prae-
15 starent, malitiaque servos, non sapientia vincere. Igitur
venia seni filioque data est, et velut numine quodam reser-
16 vatos arbitrantes regem Stratonem creaverunt. Post cuius
mortem regnum ad filium ac deinde ad nepotes transiit.

17 Celebre hoc servorum facinus metuendumque exem-
18 plum toto orbe terrarum fuit. Itaque Alexander Magnus,
cum interiecto tempore in Oriente bellum gereret, velut
ultor publicae securitatis, expugnata eorum urbe omnes,
qui proelio superfuerant, ob memoriam veteris caedis cru-
19 cibus adfixit; genus tantum Stratonis inviolatum servavit
regnumque stirpi eius restituit, ingenuis et innoxiis incolis
insulae adtributis, ut exstirpato servili germine genus urbis
ex integro conderetur.

4. Hoc igitur modo Tyrii Alexandri auspiciis conditi
2 parsimonia et labore quaerendi cito convaluere. Ante cladem dominorum cum et opibus et multitudine abun-
darent, missa in Africam iuventute Uticam condidere.
3 Cum interim rex Mutto Tyro decedit filio Pygmalione et
Elissa filia, insignis formae virgine, heredibus institutis.
4 Sed populus Pygmalioni, admodum puero, regnum tradi-
5 dit. Elissa quoque Acherbae, avunculo suo, sacerdoti Her-
6 culis, qui honos secundus a rege erat, nubit. Huic magnae,

---

[11] Utica was supposedly founded in 1101 BC. Pygmalion and
Elissa date to the late ninth century.

west. But when dawn started breaking and the rising sun   12
began shining on the city's highest points, he, while others
kept watching for a glimpse of the sun itself, was the first
to point out to everyone the sun shining on the city's tallest
roof. It seemed not the reasoning of a slave; and when they   13
asked who was responsible, he confessed about his master.
Then it was understood how far the free intellect sur-   14
passed the servile, and that it was in deception that slaves
were superior, not intelligence. So the old man and his son   15
were pardoned and, feeling that they had been protected
by some deity, they made Strato king. After his death the   16
kingdom passed to his son and then to his grandsons.

This action of the slaves became a famous and fearful   17
example throughout the world. So when Alexander the   18
Great was later campaigning in the East he stormed their
city as the champion law and order, and to mark the earlier
massacre he crucified all who had survived the battle; only   19
Strato's family did he leave untouched and he restored the
kingdom to his descendants, giving the island freeborn
and guiltless settlers, so that with the eradication of servile
stock the city's race could be founded anew.

4. So founded in way this under Alexander's auspices,
Tyre through its thrift and enterprise quickly recovered.
Before the massacre of its masters, when they flourished   2
in both wealth and population, they had sent young men
to Africa and founded Utica.[11] Meanwhile King Mutto   3
died in Tyre leaving his son Pygmalion and his daughter
Elissa, a girl of exceptional beauty, as his heirs. But the   4
people passed the kingdom on to Pygmalion, who was still
a boy, Elissa for her part married her uncle Acherbas, a   5
priest of Hercules, a post next to that of king. He had great   6

sed dissimulatae opes erant, aurumque metu regis non
7 tectis, sed terrae crediderat; quam rem etsi homines igno-
8 rabant, fama tamen loquebatur. Qua incensus Pygmalion
oblitus iuris humani avunculum suum eundemque generum sine respectu pietatis occidit.

9   Elissa diu fratrem propter scelus aversata ad postremum dissimulato odio mitigatoque interim vultu fugam
tacito molitur adsumptis quibusdam principibus in societatem, quibus par odium in regem esse eandemque fu-
10 giendi cupiditatem arbitrabatur. Tunc fratrem dolo adgreditur, fingit se ad eum migrare velle, ne amplius ei mariti
domus cupidae oblivionis gravem luctus imaginem reno-
11 vet neve ultra amara admonitio oculis eius occurrat. Non
invitus Pygmalion verba sororis audivit, existimans cum ea
12 et aurum Acherbae ad se venturum. Sed Elissa ministros
migrationis a rege missos navibus cum omnibus opibus
suis prima vespera inponit provectaque in altum conpellit
eos onera harenae pro pecunia involucris involuta in mare
13 deicere. Tunc deflens ipsa lugubrique voce Acherbam
ciet; orat ut libens opes suas recipiat, quas reliquerit,
14 habeatque inferias, quas habuerat causam mortis. Tunc
ipsos ministros adgreditur; sibi quidem ait optatam olim
mortem, sed illis acerbos cruciatus et dira supplicia in-
minere, qui Acherbae opes, quarum spe parricidium rex
15 fecerit, avaritiae tyranni subtraxerint. Hoc metu omnibus
iniecto comites fugae accepit. Iunguntur et senatorum in

wealth but kept it concealed, and from fear of the king had
entrusted his gold not to his house but to the earth; and   7
although people were unaware of it, rumor still spread.
Aroused by this Pygmalion with no regard for human jus-   8
tice executed the man who was both his uncle and his
brother-in-law, having no respect for family ties.

Elissa long shunned her brother because of the crime,   9
but finally concealing her hatred and meanwhile assuming
a conciliatory demeanor, she secretly prepared her escape,
taking into her confidence some prominent citizens who
she believed had just as much hatred for the king and were
as eager to escape. She then outwitted her brother and   10
pretended she wished to move to his house so that her
husband's home would no longer revive within her, when
she wished to forget, the painful memory of her grief and
so that bitter reminders of him should no longer meet her
eyes. Pygmalion was not displeased to hear his sister's   11
words, thinking that along with her Acherbas' gold would
also come to him. But when the movers had been sent by   12
the king, Elissa put them aboard after nightfall along with
all her possessions, and setting out to sea made them
throw overboard loads of sand packed in bags as though it
were money. Then in tears and in a mournful voice she   13
called upon Acherbas and begged him to willingly accept
the wealth that he had left her, and to take as funerary
offerings what had been the cause of his death. Then she   14
turned to her attendants; for herself, she said, she had long
wished for death, but for them cruel torture and terrible
punishments lay ahead for cheating the greedy tyrant of
Acherbas' riches, for which the king had committed murder. All being filled with fear of that, she accepted them   15
as her companions in flight. She was further joined by

eam noctem praeparata agmina, atque ita sacris Herculis, cuius sacerdos Acherbas fuerat, repetitis exilio sedes quaerunt.

5. Primus illis adpulsus terrae Cyprus insula fuit,
2 ubi sacerdos Iovis cum coniuge et liberis deorum monitu comitem se Elissae sociumque praebuit pactus sibi post-
3 erisque perpetuum honorem sacerdotii. Condicio pro
4 manifesto omine accepta. Mos erat Cypriis virgines ante nuptias statutis diebus dotalem pecuniam quaesituras in quaestum ad litus maris mittere, pro reliqua pudicitia liba-
5 menta Veneri soluturas. Harum igitur ex numero LXXX admodum virgines raptas navibus inponi Elissa iubet, ut et iuventus matrimonia et urbs subolem habere posset.
6 Dum haec aguntur, Pygmalion cognita sororis fuga, cum impio bello fugientem persequi parasset, aegre precibus
7 matris deorumque minis victus quievit; cui cum inspirati vates canerent non inpune laturum, si incrementa urbis toto orbe auspicatissimae interpellasset, hoc modo spatium respirandi fugientibus datum.
8 Itaque Elissa delata in Africae sinum incolas loci eius adventu peregrinorum mutuarumque rerum commercio
9 gaudentes in amicitiam sollicitat, dein empto loco, qui corio bovis tegi posset, in quo fessos longa navigatione socios, quoad proficisceretur, reficere posset, corium in tenuissimas partes secari iubet atque ita maius loci spa-

---

12 "Jupiter" is most likely the Roman interpretation of the Phoenician and Carthaginian chief god Ba'al Hamon, so worshiped at Carthage.   13 "Venus" corresponds to Astarte, who was indeed worshiped in Phoenician Cyprus and other regions, often with ritual prostitution.

crowds of senators already prepared for that night, and so after recovering the sacred objects of Hercules, whose priest Acherbas had been, they sought a home in exile.

5. Their first landfall was the island of Cyprus, where on the gods' advice the priest of Jupiter offered himself to Elissa as a companion, together with his wife and children, on condition that the position of priest forever remain with him and his descendants.[12] The agreement was accepted as a clear omen of good fortune. It was customary for the Cyprians to send young girls down to the coast on appointed days before their marriage to earn dowry money by prostitution, and then offer Venus libations for the preservation of their virtue thereafter.[13] Elissa therefore ordered some eighty of these girls to be seized and put aboard the ships, so her young men could have wives and her city also have descendants. While this was happening, Pygmalion had on learning of his sister's flight been preparing to hound her with an impious war as she fled, and only with difficulty was he persuaded to desist by his mother's entreaties and warnings from gods; for when inspired soothsayers predicted that he would not go unpunished if he impeded the growth of a city that enjoyed the most auspicious foundation in the world, the fugitives were thus given some respite.

So Elissa, on arriving in a gulf of Africa, cultivated an acquaintanceship with the inhabitants of the region, who were pleased to see foreigners arriving with whom they could conduct barter trade. She then bought enough land as could be covered by a cow's hide, on which to refresh her allies, who were wearied after their long voyage, and she had the hide cut into the finest strips and thereby took

tium, quam petierat, occupat, unde postea ei loco Byrsae
10 nomen fuit. Confluentibus deinde vicinis locorum, qui spe
11 lucri multa hospitibus venalia inferebant, sedesque ibi sta-
tuentibus ex frequentia hominum velut instar civitatis ef-
12 fectum est. Uticensium quoque legati dona ut consanguineis adtulerunt hortatique sunt, urbem ibi conderent, ubi
13 sedes sortiti essent. Sed et Afros detinendi advenas amor
14 cepit. Itaque consentientibus omnibus Karthago conditur
15 statuto annuo vectigali pro solo urbis. In primis funda-
mentis caput bubulum inventum est, quod auspicium
fructuosae quidem, sed laboriosae perpetuoque servae
16 urbis fuit; propter quod in alium locum urbs translata, ibi
quoque equi caput repertum, bellicosum potentemque
populum futurum significans, urbi auspicatam sedem de-
17 dit. Tunc ad opinionem novae urbis concurrentibus gentibus brevi et populus et civitas magna facta.

6. Cum successu rerum florentes Karthaginis opes essent, rex Maxitanorum Hiarbas decem Poenorum principibus ad se arcessitis Elissae nuptias sub belli denuntia-
2 tione petit. Quod legati reginae referre metuentes Punico
cum ea ingenio egerunt, nuntiantes regem aliquem pos-
3 cere, qui cultiores victus eum Afrosque perdoceat; sed
quem inveniri posse, qui ad barbaros et ferarum more
4 viventes transire a consanguineis velit? Tunc a regina cas-

---

14 Greek for "ox hide." Byrsa was (and is) the hill on which
Carthage's citadel stood.

15 A legendary African king; cf. Verg. *Aen*. 4.196 (with Pease's
note). The Maxitani, or Muxsitani, dwelt near Carthage. They and
the other peoples of North Africa were in ancient times called
Libyans, and were the ancestors of today's Berbers. Virgil in *Ae-*

over a greater area than she had asked for; and from this
the place was later called the Byrsa.[14] Then as neighboring   10
peoples poured in with many goods to sell to the foreigners in the hope of making money, and also establishing   11
homes there, something like a city emerged from the
crowds of people. Delegates from Utica also brought them   12
gifts, as they were their relatives, and urged them to found
a city on the spot where they had chanced to settle. But   13
the Africans were also eager to keep the foreigners. So by   14
unanimous agreement Carthage was founded, with an annual tax fixed for the city's land. When its foundations were   15
first laid an ox's head was found, an omen that while it
would prosper the city would see hardship and always be
enslaved; and for that reason the city was moved to another location, and there too a horse's head was found,   16
indicating that its people would be warlike and mighty,
and so it provided an auspicious site for the city. Then as   17
various tribes came swarming there drawn by the new
city's reputation both the people and the city soon became
great.

6. When through its successes Carthage's wealth was
flourishing, Hiarbas[15] king of the Maxitani summoned ten
of the leading Carthaginians to him and demanded Elissa's
hand in marriage with a threat of war. Since the delegates   2
feared to report this to the queen, they used typical Punic
ingenuity with her, reporting that the king was demanding
someone to instruct him and his Africans a more refined
lifestyle—but who could be found willing to leave their   3
own relatives for barbarians living like animals? Then   4

neid 4 famously tells of Elissa-Dido's suicide, with the anachro-
nistic involvement of the royal Trojan exile Aeneas.

tigati, si pro salute patriae asperiorem vitam recusarent,
cui etiam ipsa vita, si res exigat, debeatur, regis mandata
aperuere, dicentes quae praecipiat aliis, ipsi facienda esse,
5 si velit urbi consultum esse. Hoc dolo capta diu Acherbae
viri nomine cum multis lacrimis et lamentatione flebili
invocato ad postremum ituram se, quo sua et urbis fata
6 vocarent, respondit. In hoc trium mensium sumpto spatio,
pyra in ultima parte urbis instructa, velut placatura viri
manes inferiasque ante nuptias missura multas hostias
7 caedit et sumpto gladio pyram conscendit atque ita ad
populum respiciens ituram se ad virum, sicut praecepe-
8 rint, dixit vitamque gladio finivit. Quam diu Karthago in-
victa fuit, pro dea culta est.

9 Condita est haec urbs LXXII annis ante quam Roma;
10 cuius virtus sicut bello clara fuit, ita domi status variis
11 discordiarum casibus agitatus est. Cum inter cetera mala
etiam peste laborarent, cruenta sacrorum religione et sce-
12 lere pro remedio usi sunt; quippe homines ut victimas
immolabant et inpuberes, quae aetas etiam hostium misericordiam provocat, aris admovebant, pacem deorum sanguine eorum exposcentes, pro quorum vita dii rogari maxime solent.

7. Itaque adversis tanto scelere numinibus, cum in Sicilia diu feliciter dimicassent, translato in Sardiniam bello
amissa maiore exercitus parte gravi proelio victi sunt;
2 propter quod ducem suum Malchum, cuius auspiciis et

---

16 Timaeus dated it to 814/13; modern archaeological finds
seem to show that this was not inaccurate. Whether the Carthaginians practiced child sacrifice, regularly or intermittently, remains debated by scholars.

when they were reprimanded by the queen for refusing to accept a harsher life for the good of the fatherland, to which, if necessary, even one's life was owed, they revealed their king's instructions, saying that what she recommended for others she must do for herself if she wished to serve her city. Caught by this ruse she long called out 5 her husband Acherbas' name with streaming tears and sorrowful lamentation, and finally replied that she would go where her and her city's destiny called her. For this she 6 took a three month period, built a pyre on the furthest outskirts of the city, sacrificed numerous animals as if to placate her husband's shade and send him offerings before her marriage, and taking a sword, she mounted the pyre; then looking back at her people she declared she was go- 7 ing to join her husband, just as they ordered, and ended her life with the sword. For as long as Carthage remained 8 unconquered, she was worshipped as a goddess.

This city was founded seventy-two years before 9 Rome;[16] and though its valor in war was highly praised, its 10 domestic stability was riven by various bouts of dissension. When among other misfortunes its people were also en- 11 during a plague, they resorted to a bloodthirsty and unconscionable form of religious ceremony as a remedy; for 12 they would offer humans as sacrificial victims and bring to their altars children whose age aroused pity even in their enemies, seeking the gods' indulgence with the blood of those for whose lives gods are most often invoked.

7. So, the gods being against them for such criminal behavior, they, although they had long fought successfully in Sicily, now lost most of their army when the war was transferred to Sardinia and they were defeated in a critical battle. Because of that they ordered into exile their gen- 2

Siciliae partem domuerant et adversus Afros magnas res
gesserant, cum parte exercitus, quae superfuerat, exulare
3 iusserunt. Quam rem aegre ferentes milites legatos Karthaginem mittunt, qui reditum primo veniamque infelicis
militiae petant, tum denuntient, quod precibus nequeant,
4 armis se consecuturos. Cum et preces et minae legatorum
spretae essent, interiectis diebus conscensis navibus ar-
5 mati ad urbem veniunt, ubi deos hominesque testati, non
se expugnatum, sed reciperatum patriam venire, ostensu-
6 rosque civibus suis non virtutem sibi priore bello, sed fortunam defuisse, prohibitis commeatibus obsessaque urbe
in summam desperationem Karthaginienses adduxerunt.
7 Interea Karthalo, Malchi exulum ducis filius, cum praeter
castra patris a Tyro, quo decimam Herculis ferre ex praeda
Siliensi, quam pater eius ceperat, a Karthaginiensibus
missus fuerat, reverteretur arcessitusque a patre esset,
prius se publicae religionis officia executurum quam pri-
8 vatae pietatis respondit. Quam rem etsi indigne ferret
pater, non tamen vim adferre religioni ausus est.
9   Interiectis deinde diebus Karthalo petito commeatu a
populo cum reversus ad patrem esset ornatusque purpura
et infulis sacerdotii omnium se oculis ingereret, tum in
10 secretum abducto pater ait: "aususne es, nefandissimum
caput, ista purpura et auro ornatus in conspectum tot
miserorum civium venire et maesta ac lugentia castra cir-

---

[17] Possibly not a true personal name, as the Phoenician *melek*
means "king." "Malchus" is a seventeenth-century guess; MSS
variously have "Mazeus," "Maleus," or "Maceus." The date seems
to be in the mid-sixth century.

eral Malchus,[17] under whose leadership they had both conquered part of Sicily and had great success against the Africans, sending with him part of the army that had survived the campaign. Incensed over this the soldiers sent 3 delegates to Carthage, first to beg for their return from exile and pardon for the unsuccessful campaign, and then to give notice that what they could not gain by entreaty they would gain by armed force. When both appeals and 4 threats from the legates were ignored, they boarded ships a few days later and came to the city under arms. There 5 calling on gods and men to witness that they came not to attack but to recover their country, and to show their compatriots that it was not courage that they had lacked in the earlier war but good fortune, they cut off supplies, 6 laid siege to the city, and brought the Carthaginians to utter despair. Meanwhile Carthalo, son the exiles' leader 7 Malchus, was passing by his father's camp when returning from Tyre, where he had been sent by the Carthaginians to bear Hercules' tithes from the Sicilian plunder that his father had taken, and when summoned by his father he replied that he would discharge the state's religious duties before turning to any personal matter. Although his father 8 was angry over this, he did not dare violate religious observance.

Then some days later when Carthalo after requesting 9 leave of absence from his people went back to his father and was parading himself before the eyes of all his people in the purple robes and fillets of his priesthood, the father then took him aside and said: "Have you, you miserable 10 wretch, dared to come, all dressed up in that purple and gold of yours, into the sight of so many pitiful citizens, and decked out with the insignia of peace and happiness to

cumfluentibus quietae felicitatis insignibus velut exulta-
bundus intrare? Nusquamne te aliis iactare potuisti?
11 Nullus locus aptior quam sordes patris et exilii infelicis
12 aerumnae fuerunt? Quid, quod paulo ante vocatus, non
dico patrem, ducem certe civium tuorum superbe spre-
13 visti? Quid porro tu in purpura ista coronisque aliud quam
14 victoriarum mearum titulos geris? Quoniam igitur tu in
patre nihil nisi exulis nomen agnoscis, ego quoque imperatorem me magis quam patrem iudicabo statuamque in
te exemplum, ne quis posthac infelicibus miseriis patris
15 inludat" Atque ita eum cum ornatu suo in altissimam cru-
16 cem in conspectu urbis suffigi iussit. Post paucos deinde
dies Karthaginem capit evocatoque populo ad contionem
exilii iniuriam queritur, belli necessitatem excusat, conten-
tumque victoria sua punitis auctoribus miserorum civium
17 iniuriosi exilii omnibus se veniam dare dicit. Atque ita
decem senatoribus interfectis urbem legibus suis reddidit.
18 Nec multo post ipse adfectati regni accusatus duplicis, et
19 in filio et in patria, parricidii poenas dedit. Huic Mago
imperator successit, cuius industria et opes Karthaginiensium et imperii fines et bellicae gloriae laudes creve-
runt.

enter a camp full of sadness and dejection, almost beside yourself with joy? Was there nowhere you could show off to other people? Was there nowhere more suitable than where your father was in disgrace and suffering the miseries of a wretched exile? And what about when you were recently summoned and you arrogantly disregarded your— I won't say your father, but at least the leader of your fellow citizens? What on earth are you displaying in that purple and those crowns but the renown of my victories? So since you recognize in your father nothing but an exile's name, I shall also judge myself your commander rather than your father and with you set an example for no one after this to make light of a father's wretched state." And with that he ordered him crucified in his fine regalia on a towering cross in the sight of the whole town. Then some days later he took Carthage and calling the people to an assembly complained of the injustice of his exile, justified the war as unavoidable, and declared that, satisfied with his victory, he granted a general amnesty, punishing only those responsible for their unfortunate compatriots' wrongful exile. And then, after executing ten senators, he returned the city to constitutional rule. Not much later he was himself accused of regal aspirations and punished for a double murder, both his son's and his country's. He was succeeded as general by Mago, through whose energy the Carthaginians' wealth, imperial territory and military renown were all increased.

LIBER XIX

1. Mago, Karthaginiensium imperator, cum primus omnium ordinata disciplina militari imperium Poenorum condidisset viresque civitatis non minus bellandi arte quam virtute firmasset, diem fungitur relictis duobus filiis,
2 Asdrubale et Hamilcare, qui per vestigia paternae virtutis decurrentes sicuti generi, ita et magnitudini patris suc-
3 cesserunt. His ducibus Sardiniae bellum inlatum; adversus Afros quoque vectigal pro solo urbis multorum an-
4 norum repetentes dimicatum. Sed Afrorum sicuti causa
5 iustior, ita et fortuna superior fuit, bellumque cum his
6 solutione pecuniae, non armis finitum. In Sardinia quoque Asdrubal graviter vulneratus imperio Hamilcari fratri tra-
7 dito interiit, cuius mortem cum luctus civitatis, tum et dictaturae undecim et triumphi quattuor insignem fecere.
8 Hostibus quoque crevere animi, veluti cum duce vires
9 Poenorum cecidissent. Itaque Siciliae populis propter adsiduas Karthaginiensium iniurias ad Leonidam fratrem regis Spartanorum, concurrentibus grave bellum natum, in quo et diu et varia victoria fuit proeliatum.

---

[1] We are at the end of the sixth century.

[2] After the victories of "Malchus," the Carthaginians apparently had ceased to pay the tax (see 18.5.14) for the city site.

[3] This seems to refer to the Spartan Dorieus, as at Hdt. 5.43, 46ff.; Diod. Sic. 4.23.3. Dorieus founded a city in western Sicily, around 510, but was soon driven out and later perished in Libya.

BOOK XIX

1. Mago, the Carthaginian general, the very first man to have organized military discipline and founded a Punic Empire, had built up the strength of his state as much by his military prowess as by his courage,[1] and he died leaving two sons, Hasdrubal and Hamilcar; as these trod in the 2 footsteps of their courageous father, so they also succeeded him in greatness. Under their leadership there was 3 an attack made on Sardinia; and there was also war against the Africans who were demanding back many years' revenue from their city's land.[2] But just as the Africans' cause 4 was more righteous, so also was their success greater, and 5 the war with them ended in a financial settlement not a battle. In Sardinia, too, Hasdrubal died from a serious 6 wound after transferring command to his brother Hamilcar, whose death was notable both for his city's grief and 7 his eleven dictatorships and four triumphs. Their enemies' 8 fortitude also grew, as if the Carthaginians' strength had fallen with their leader. The peoples of Sicily therefore 9 united to seek assistance from Leonidas, brother of the Spartan king, over wrongs regularly inflicted them by the Carthaginians, and a serious war arose in which the fighting was long and victory also fluctuating.[3]

Leonidas became king after the death of Dorieus and Cleomenes (Hdt. 7.205).

10 Dum haec aguntur, legati a Dario, Persarum rege, Karthaginem venerunt adferentes edictum, quo Poeni hu-
manas hostias immolare et canina vesci prohibebantur;
11 mortuorum quoque corpora cremare potius quam terra
12 obruere a rege iubebantur; petentes simul auxilia adversus
13 Graeciam, cui inlaturus bellum Darius erat. Sed Karthaginienses auxilia negantes propter adsidua finitimorum
bella ceteris, ne per omnia contumaces viderentur, cupide
paruere.

2. Interea Hamilcar bello Siciliensi interficitur relictis
2 tribus filiis, Himilcone, Hannone, Gisgone. Asdrubali
quoque par numerus filiorum fuit, Hannibal, Asdrubal et
3 Sapho. Per hos res Karthaginiensium ea tempestate rege-
4 bantur. Itaque et Mauris bellum inlatum et adversus Nu-
midas pugnatum et Afri conpulsi stipendium urbis condi-
5 tae Karthaginiensibus remittere. Dein, cum familia tanta
imperatorum gravis liberae civitati esset omniaque ipsi
agerent simul et iudicarent, centum ex numero senatorum
6 iudices deliguntur, qui reversis a bello ducibus rationem
rerum gestarum exigerent, ut hoc metu ita in bello imperia cogitarent, ut domi iudicia legesque respicerent.
7 In Sicilia in locum Hamilcaris imperator Himilco succedit, qui cum navali terrestrique bello secunda proelia

---

4 Darius' supposed messages to the Carthaginians are a fiction.

5 The battle of Himera was thought to have occurred on the
same day as Salamis in 480: Hdt. 7.165ff.; Diod. Sic. 11.20ff.

6 Mid-fifth century; cf. Plin. *HN* 2.169.   7 This body of
100—or 104—judges is described by Aristotle at *Pol.* 2.1272b–
1273a, where it is called the supreme authority of Carthage.

While this was happening, envoys came to Carthage 10
from Darius, king of the Persians, bringing an edict by
which the Carthaginians were barred from conducting human sacrifice and eating dogs' flesh; burning rather than 11
burying the bodies of their dead was also forbidden by the
king; and at the same time the envoys were also requesting 12
assistance against Greece, on which Darius intended to
make war. But while the Carthaginians refused help be- 13
cause of ongoing wars with their neighbors, they, not to
appear totally defiant, readily obeyed the other orders.⁴

2. Meanwhile Hamilcar was killed in a war in Sicily,
leaving three sons, Himilco, Hanno and Gisgo.⁵ Hasdrubal 2
also had the same number of sons: Hannibal, Hasdrubal
and Sapho. It was by these that Carthage was then being 3
ruled. Thus there was war with the Mauretanians,⁶ fight- 4
ing against the Numidians, and the Africans were also
forced to refund to the Carthaginians the tribute paid for
their city's foundation. Then, since such a great family of 5
generals posed a threat to a free state and they were personally taking all actions and decisions, a hundred judges
were chosen from the senatorial body who were to de- 6
mand accountability for their actions from commanders
returning from war, so that by such fear they would frame
their orders in war while respecting their judicial process
and laws at home.⁷

In Sicily Hamilcar was replaced as commander by Hi- 7
milco,⁸ who after fighting successful battles on land and

⁸ See Diod. Sic. 13.80ff. (the year 406/5) and for what follows,
in the summer of 396, 14.70ff. Justin (if not Trogus) has confused
the Hamilcar of 480 with Hannibal, a descendant commanding in
Sicily seventy years later. The epidemic may have been smallpox.

fecisset multasque civitates cepisset, repente pestilentis
8 sideris vi exercitum amisit. Quae res cum nuntiata Karthagine esset, maesta civitas fuit; omnia ululatibus non secus
9 ac si urbs ipsa capta esset personabant, clausae privatae
domus, clausa deorum templa, intermissa omnia sacra,
10 omnia privata officia damnata. Cuncti deinde ad portum
congregantur egredientesque paucos e navibus, qui cladi
11 superfuerant, de suis percontantur. Ut vero dubia antea
spe et suspenso metu, incerta orbitatis expectatione casus
suorum miseris eluxit, tunc toto litore plangentium gemi-
tus, tunc infelicium matrum ululatus et flebiles querelae
audiebantur.

3. Inter haec procedit inops navi sua imperator sordida
servilique tunica discinctus, ad cuius conspectum plangen-
2 tium agmina iunguntur. Ipse quoque manus ad caelum
tendens nunc sortem suam, nunc publicam fortunam de-
3 flet; nunc deos accusat, qui tanta belli decora et tot ornamenta victoriarum, quae ipsi dederant, abstulerint; qui
captis tot urbibus totiensque hostibus terrestri navalique
proelio victis exercitum victorem non bello, sed peste
4 deleverint. Deferre se tamen civibus suis non modica solacia, quod malis eorum hostes gaudere, non gloriari pos-
5 sint; quippe cum neque eos, qui mortui sunt, a se occisos,
neque eos, qui reversi sunt, a se fugatos possint dicere,
6 praedam, quam relictis a se castris abstulerint, non esse
talem, quam velut spolium victi hostis ostentent, sed quam

sea and capturing many towns suddenly lost his army in a
seasonal epidemic. When this was reported in Carthage, 8
the state went into mourning; everything rang with lamentation just as if the city itself had been captured, private 9
homes were closed, temples of the gods closed, all religious activity suspended, all private business canceled.
Everyone then assembled at the harbor, and as the few 10
survivors of the disaster disembarked, they asked for news
of their relatives. Although there had earlier been diffi- 11
dent hope, anxious fear, and uncertain anticipation of loss,
the fate of their kin now became clear to the poor wretches,
and then all along the shore moaning and breast-beating
could be heard, then the unfortunate mothers' wailing and
tearful laments.

3. Meanwhile the hapless general came forward from
his ship dressed in a dirty slave-like tunic, and crowds of
sorrowful people came flocking to catch sight of him. He 2
too, with his hands raised to heaven, lamented now his
own plight, now the fortunes of the state; now he re- 3
proached the gods, who had taken away such great military honors and so many victory trophies that they themselves had granted him; who after the capture of so many
cities and after their enemies had so often been defeated
in battle on land and sea, had now wiped out a victorious
army not with a battle, but with a plague. Nevertheless, he 4
said, he brought his fellow citizens no meager solace, that
though their enemy might gloat over their misfortunes, he
could not take pride in them; for they could neither say 5
that the dead had been killed by them nor that those who
returned had been routed by them, and the booty they 6
took when the camp was abandoned was not something
they could parade as spoils from a defeated foe, but what

possessione vacua fortuitis dominorum mortibus sicuti
7 caduca occuparint. Quod ad hostes pertinet, victores se
8 recessisse; quod ad pestem, victos. Nihil tamen se gravius
ferre, quam quod inter fortissimos viros mori non potuerit
servatusque sit non ad vitae iucunditatem, sed ad ludi-
9 brium calamitatis. Quamquam ubi miseras copiarum reliquias Karthaginem reduxerit, se quoque secuturum com-
10 militones suos ostensurumque patriae non ideo se in eam
diem vixisse, quoniam vellet vivere, sed ne hos, quibus
nefanda lues pepercerat, inter hostium exercitus relictos
11 morte sua proderet. Tali vociferatione per urbem ingressus, ut ad limina domus suae venit, prosecutam multitudi-
12 nem velut postremo adloquio dimisit obseratisque foribus
ac nemine ad se, ne filiis quidem, admissis mortem sibi
conscivit.

they seized after title to it was relinquished by the owners'
accidental deaths and left without inheritors. As regards   7
the enemy, the Carthaginians had emerged as the victors,
as regards the plague as the defeated. But nothing did he   8
find more distressing than being unable to die among the
bravest of men, and instead being saved not for pleasure
in life but to be plaything of Fortune. However, after   9
bringing the pitiful remnants of his troops back to Carthage, he too would follow his comrades and show his
country that his reason for living to that day was not a wish   10
to survive but so he should not by his own death leave men
that the loathsome plague had spared abandoned amid the
armies the enemy. Crying this out as he went through the   11
city, when he reached the threshold of his house, he dismissed the crowd attending him with his final address,   12
and, locking his door and letting no one into him, not even
his sons, he took his own life.

LIBER XX

1. Dionysius e Sicilia Karthaginiensibus pulsis occupatoque totius insulae imperio grave otium regno suo peri-
culosamque desidiam tanti exercitus ratus, copias in Ita-
2 liam traiecit, simul ut et militum vires continuo labore
3 acuerentur et regni fines proferrentur. Prima illi militia
adversus Graecos, qui proxima Italici maris litora tene-
4 bant, fuit; quibus devictis finitimos quosque adgreditur
omnesque Graeci nominis Italiam possidentes hostes sibi
5 destinat; quae gentes non partem, sed universam ferme
6 Italiam ea tempestate occupaverant. Denique multae urbes adhuc post tantam vetustatem vestigia Graeci moris
7 ostentant. Namque Tuscorum populi, qui oram Inferi
8 maris possident, a Lydia venerunt, et Venetos, quos incolas Superi maris videmus, capta et expugnata Troia Ante-
9 nore duce misit, Adria quoque Illyrico mari proxima, quae

---

1 While Trogus' *Prologue* tells us that Dionysius I was mentioned in Book 19, he has not yet appeared in Justin. While Timaeus again looms as the source in the present book, Diodorus
(15.89.3) notes the history of Dionysius by the contemporary
Philistus. Modern treatments include L. J. Sanders, *Dionysius I
of Syracuse and Greek Tyranny* (London, 1987); B. Caven, *Dionysius I: War-lord of Sicily* (New Haven and London, 1990); D.
Hoyos, *Carthage's Other Wars* (Barnsley, UK, 2019). The events

BOOK XX

1. With the Carthaginians driven from Sicily and the whole island now in his power, Dionysius,[1] thinking inactivity hazardous to his rule and keeping such a large army idle and dangerous, ferried his forces over to Italy, and this was also to have his soldiers' strength honed by constant work and the boundaries of his kingdom extended. His first campaign was against the Greeks occupying coastal areas closest to the Italian Sea; and with these defeated he attacked their neighbors and all those of Greek nationality that inhabited Italy he targeted as his enemies; and these peoples had occupied not just a part of Italy but almost all of it by that time. Indeed, many cities after all this time still show traces of Greek culture. For the Etrurian peoples who inhabit the coast of the Lower Sea came from Lydia, and the Veneti, whom we see as inhabitants of the Upper Sea, were sent there under Antenor's leadership after the capture and defeat of Troy,[2] and Adria, which is

here are interspersed in Diodorus Siculus from 13.90 onward, beginning in the year 405 and ending in 367.

[2] For the alleged Lydian origin of the Etruscans, see Hdt. 1.94. The Lower Sea is the Tyrrhenian, the Upper Sea the Adriatic. On the Veneti see Livy 1.1.2 with R. M. Ogilvie, *A Commentary on Livy Books 1–5* (Oxford, 1965), 35ff.

10 et Adriatico mari nomen dedit, Graeca urbs est; Arpos
Diomedes exciso Ilio naufragio in ea loca delatus condidit.

11 Sed et Pisae in Liguribus Graecos auctores habent; et in
Tuscis Tarquinii a Thessalis, et Spina in Vmbris; Perusini

12 quoque originem ab Achaeis ducunt. Quid Caeren urbem
dicam? Quid Latinos populos, qui ab Aenea conditi viden-

13 tur? Iam Falisci, Nolani, Abellani nonne Chalcidensium

14 coloni sunt? Quid tractus omnis Campaniae? Quid Bruttii

15 Sabinique? Quid Samnites? Quid Tarentini, quos Lace-

16 daemone profectos spuriosque vocatos accipimus? Thuri-
norum urbem condidisse Philocteten ferunt; ibique adhuc
monumentum eius visitur, et Herculis sagittae in Apollinis
templo, quae fatum Troiae fuere.

2. Metapontini quoque in templo Minervae ferra-
menta, quibus Epeos, a quo conditi sunt, equum Troia-

2 num fabricavit, ostentant. Propter quod omnis illa pars
Italiae Maior Graecia appellata est.

3 Sed principio originum Metapontini cum Sybaritanis
et Crotoniensibus pellere ceteros Graecos Italia statue-

4 runt. Cum primum urbem Sirim cepissent, in expugnatione eius L iuvenes amplexos Minervae simulacrum sacer-
dotemque deae velatum ornamentis inter ipsa altaria

5 trucidaverunt. Ob haec cum peste et seditionibus vexaren-
tur, priores Crotonienses Delphicum oraculum adierunt.

6 Responsum his est, finem mali fore, si violatum Minervae

7 numen et interfectorum manes placassent. Itaque cum

---

3 See 3.4.

4 "Maior Graecia" rather than the more usual "Magna Graecia," i.e., "Great Greece." Except for the Greek colonies in southern Italy, these supposed origins are fanciful.

close to the Illyrian Sea and gave its name to the Adriatic
Sea, is also a Greek city; Arpi Diomedes founded when he   10
was shipwrecked in those areas after the fall of Troy. But   11
Pisae in Liguria also has Greek founders; and Tarquinii in
Etruria and Spina in Umbria derive their origins from the
Thessalians; and the people of Perusia are also descended
from the Achaeans. Why mention the city of Caere? Why   12
the Latin peoples who are thought to have been founded
by Aeneas? Then there are the Falisci, the Nolans and the   13
Abellani—are they not colonists from Chalcis? What of   14
the whole area of Campania? What of the Bruttii and Sa-
bines? What about the Samnites? What about the Taren-   15
tines, who we are told came from Sparta and were called
"the Illegitimates"?[3] The city of Thurii was founded by   16
Philoctetes, they say; and there visits are still made to his
tomb, and in the temple of Apollo are the arrows of Hercules, which sealed the fate of Troy.

2. The people of Metapontum also have on display in
their temple of Minerva the iron tools with which Epeos,
by whom they were founded, built the Trojan horse. As a   2
result all that area of Italy is called "Greater Greece."[4]

But in their earliest days the Metapontines together   3
with the Sybarites and Crotonites decided to drive all the
other Greeks from Italy. In capturing the city of Siris they   4
during the assault butchered fifty young men among Minerva's very altars as they clung to her statue as well as the
priest of the goddess, dressed his vestments. When they   5
were tormented with plague and dissension because of
this, the Crotonites approached the Delphic Oracle before the others. The response they received was that their   6
troubles would end if they placated Minerva's divine spirit
and the shades of the people they had murdered. So after   7

statuas iuvenibus iustae magnitudinis et in primis Minervae fabricare coepissent, et Metapontini oraculo cognito deorum occupandam manium et deae pacem rati, iuvenibus modica et lapidea simulacra ponunt et deam panificiis

8 placant. Atque ita pestis utrubique sedata est, cum alteri magnificentia, alteri velocitate certassent.

9   Recuperata sanitate non diu Crotonienses quievere.
10 Itaque indignantes in oppugnatione Siris auxilium contra
11 se a Locrensibus latum, bellum his intulerunt. Quo metu
territi Locrenses ad Spartanos decurrunt; auxilium sup-
12 plices deprecantur. Illi longinqua militia gravati auxilium
13 a Castore et Polluce petere eos iubent. Neque legati responsum sociae urbis spreverunt profectique in proximum
14 templum facto sacrificio auxilium deorum inplorant. Litatis hostiis obtentoque, ut rebantur, quod petebant, haud secus laeti quam si deos ipsos secum avecturi essent, pulvinaria iis in navi conponunt faustisque profecti ominibus solacia suis pro auxiliis deportant.

    3. His cognitis Crotonienses et ipsi legatos ad oraculum Delphos mittunt, victoriae facultatem bellique prosperos
2 eventus deprecantes. Responsum prius votis hostes quam
3 armis vincendos. Cum vovissent Apollini decimas praedae, Locrenses et voto hostium et responso dei cognito

they had started to construct life-sized statues of the young men and especially of Minerva, the Metapontines also learned of the oracle of the gods and decided to forestall the Crotonites in securing the favor of the dead souls and the goddess; so they erected smaller statues of stone for the young men and appeased the goddess with sacrificial cakes. And so it was that the plague was halted for 8 both, their rivalry marked by nobility on one side and speed on the other.

With their health restored, the Crotonians did not long 9 remain inactive. So being angry that in their assault on 10 Siris the town had been assisted by the Locrians, they made war on them. Terrified by this, the Locrians turned 11 to the Spartans and begged them for help as suppliants. Being reluctant to face a distant campaign these told them 12 to ask Castor and Pollux for help. Nor did their delegates 13 disregard the answer from an allied city, and setting off for the closest temple, they begged for help from the gods with a sacrificial offering. Since the sacrificial omens were 14 favorable and what they sought was, so they thought, granted, they were as pleased as if they were going to be taking those very gods away with them, and they put cushions down for them in their ship and setting off with their favorable omens brought their people consolation instead of help.

3. On learning of this, the people of Croton also sent delegates to the oracle at Delphi begging for a way to victory and a successful outcome for the war. The answer 2 they received was that the enemy must be defeated by prayers, not weapons. When they had vowed to Apollo a 3 tenth of their spoils, the Locrians then learned of their enemies' vow and the god's oracle and promised a ninth of

nonas voverunt tacitamque eam rem habuere, ne votis
4 vincerentur. Itaque cum in aciem processissent et Croto-
niensium centum viginti milia armatorum constitissent,
Locrenses paucitatem suam circumspicientes (nam sola
XV milia militum habebant) omissa spe victoriae in desti-
5 natam mortem conspirant, tantusque ardor ex desperatione singulos cepit, ut victores se putarent, si non inulti
6 morerentur. Sed dum mori honeste quaerunt, feliciter
vicerunt, nec alia causa victoriae fuit, quam quod despe-
7 raverunt. Pugnantibus Locris aquila ab acie numquam
recessit eosque tam diu circumvolavit, quoad vincerent.
8 In cornibus quoque duo iuvenes diverso a ceteris armorum habitu, eximia magnitudine et albis equis et coccineis
paludamentis pugnare visi sunt nec ultra apparuerunt,
9 quam pugnatum est. Hanc admirationem auxit incredibilis
famae velocitas. Nam eadem die, qua in Italia pugnatum
est, et Corintho et Athenis et Lacedaemone nuntiata est
victoria.

4. Post haec Crotoniensibus nulla virtutis exercitatio,
2 nulla armorum cura fuit. Oderant enim quae infeliciter
sumpserant, mutassentque vitam luxuria, ni Pythagoras
3 philosophus fuisset. Hic Sami de Marato, locuplete nego-
tiatore, natus magnisque sapientiae incrementis formatus
Aegyptum primo, mox Babyloniam ad perdiscendos side-
rum motus originemque mundi spectandam profectus
4 summam scientiam consecutus erat. Inde regressus Cre-

---

5 Evidently, Castor and Pollux; see 20.2.12 above.

6 Athletes of Croton enjoyed remarkable success at the Olympic games from 588 to 484, after which not a single victor is known
from that city. Whether this had anything to do with Pythagoras
is another matter; it seems chronologically impossible. See

their spoils, keeping the matter secret so as not to be out-
bid in vows. So when they marched into battle and one   4
hundred and twenty thousand armed men of Croton made
their stand, the Locrians, looking around at their own
small numbers (for they had only fifteen thousand men),
abandoned hope of victory and agreed to face certain
death; and such fervor gripped each man in their plight   5
that they thought themselves victors if they did not die
unavenged. But while they sought honorable deaths, they   6
luckily prevailed, and for the victory there was no other
cause than their desperation. While the Locrians were in   7
battle an eagle never left the field and flew around them
until they prevailed. On the army's wings two young men   8
were spotted with weapons different from the rest, men
of extraordinary size, with white horses and scarlet cloaks,[5]
and they were no longer seen after the battle. The aston-   9
ishment this raised was increased by the amazing speed of
the report of the battle. For on the very day that it was
fought in Italy, the victory was also announced in Corinth,
Athens and Sparta.

4. After this the people of Croton had no physical
prowess and no interest in weapons.[6] For they hated what   2
they had unsuccessfully undertaken, and they might have
turned to lives of luxury had it not been for the philosopher Pythagoras. This man was born on Samos, the son of   3
Maratus, a wealthy merchant, and after making great
strides in philosophy he had gone first to Egypt and then
Babylonia in order to acquire full knowledge of the move-
ments of the stars and examine the origin of the world, and
he had reached the peak of learning. After returning from   4

W. K. C. Guthrie, *A History of Greek Philosophy*, vol. 1 (Cambridge, 1971), 173ff.

tam et Lacedaemona ad cognoscendas Minois et Lycurgi
5 inclitas ea tempestate leges contenderat. Quibus omnibus
instructus Crotonam venit populumque in luxuriam lap-
6 sum auctoritate sua ad usum frugalitatis revocavit. Lauda-
bat cotidie virtutem et vitia luxuriae casumque civitatium
7 ea peste perditarum enumerabat tantumque studium ad
frugalitatem multitudinis provocavit, ut aliquos ex his
8 luxuriatos incredibile videretur. Matronarum quoque separatam a viris doctrinam et puerorum a parentibus fre-
9 quenter habuit. Docebat nunc has pudicitiam et obsequia
10 in viros, nunc illos modestiam et litterarum studium. Inter
haec velut genetricem virtutum frugalitatem omnibus in-
11 gerebat consecutusque disputationum adsiduitate erat, ut
matronae auratas vestes ceteraque dignitatis suae ornamenta velut instrumenta luxuriae deponerent eaque om-
12 nia delata in Iunonis aedem ipsi deae consecrarent, prae
se ferentes vera ornamenta matronarum pudicitiam, non
13 vestes esse. In iuventute quoque quantum profligatum sit,
14 victi feminarum contumaces animi manifestant. Sed CCC
ex iuvenibus cum sodalicii iure sacramento quodam nexi
separatam a ceteris civibus vitam exercerent, quasi coe-
tum clandestinae coniurationis haberent, civitatem in se
15 converterunt, quae eos, cum in unam domum convenis-
16 sent, cremare voluit. In quo tumultu sexaginta ferme peri-
17 ere; ceteri in exilium profecti. Pythagoras autem cum annos XX Crotone egisset, Metapontum emigravit ibique
18 decessit; cuius tanta admiratio fuit, ut ex domo eius templum facerent eumque pro deo colerent.

there he had gone to Crete and Sparta to acquaint himself
with the legal systems of Minos and Lycurgus, famous at
that time. Having familiarized himself with all this he   5
came to Croton and by his personal authority brought a
people that had lapsed into luxury back to practicing frugality. He would praise virtue every day and list the ills of 6
luxury and the plight of states ruined by that malaise, and 7
such eagerness for temperance did he arouse in the masses
that it seemed incredible that any of them had been prof-
ligate. Teaching wives apart from husbands and children   8
apart from their parents was also his regular practice. He   9
would now be teaching these chastity and obedience to
their husbands, now those decorum and study of literature. Meanwhile he would be impressing on all of them   10
frugality as the mother of virtues, and by ongoing discus-   11
sion he was able to have wives lay aside gold-embroidered
robes and other finery of their rank as being promoters of
extravagance, to take all of these to Juno, and to consecrate
them to the goddess herself, thus openly declaring that the 12
true beauty of wives was their chastity, not their clothing.
With young people his success is also clear from his over-   13
coming the women's obstinacy. But when three hundred   14
of their young men swore an oath of fraternity and started
living apart from the other citizens, they from suspicion of
forming some secret conspiracy turned the community
against them, and when they came together in one house,   15
these citizens wanted to burn them alive. In the fracas   16
about sixty lost their lives; the rest went into exile. Py-   17
thagoras then when he had spent twenty years in Croton
moved to Metapontum and there died; and admiration for   18
him was so great that they made a temple of his house and
worshipped him as a god.

405

5. Igitur Dionysius tyrannus, quem supra a Sicilia exercitum in Italiam traiecisse bellumque Graecis intulisse memoravimus, expugnatis Locris Crotonienses vix vires

2 longo otio ex prioris belli clade resumentes adgreditur, qui fortius cum paucis tanto exercitui eius quam antea cum tot

3 milibus Locrensium paucitati restiterunt. Tantum virtutis paupertas adversus insolentes divitias habet, tantoque insperata interdum sperata victoria certior est.

4 Sed Dionysium gerentem bellum legati Gallorum, qui ante menses Romam incenderant societatem amicitiam-

5 que petentes adeunt, gentem suam inter hostes eius positam esse magnoque usui ei futuram vel in acie bellanti vel

6 de tergo intentis in proelium hostibus adfirmant. Grata legatio Dionysio fuit. Ita pacta societate et auxiliis Gallo-

7 rum auctus bellum velut ex integro restaurat. His autem Gallis causa in Italiam veniendi sedesque novas quaerendi intestina discordia et adsiduae domi dissensiones fuere,

8 quarum taedio cum in Italiam venissent, sedibus Tuscos expulerunt et Mediolanum, Comum, Brixiam, Veronam,

9 Bergomum, Tridentum, Vincentiam condiderunt. Tusci quoque duce Raeto avitis sedibus amissis Alpes occupavere et ex nomine ducis gentem Raetorum condiderunt.

10 Sed Dionysium in Siciliam adventus Karthaginiensium revocavit, qui reparato exercitu bellum, quod deseruerant,

---

7 At 20.1.1. Events here are recounted in Diod. Sic. 14–15; the attack on Croton is at 14.100ff. under the years 390/89 and 389/8; for the Gauls see 14.113ff. (387).

8 Justin means Etruscans dwelling in northern Italy beyond the Apennines.

5. Now the tyrant Dionysius (whom we mentioned above[7] as having taken an army across from Sicily to Italy and made war on its Greeks) defeated the Locrians and proceeded to attack the people of Croton, who were barely recovering their strength during the long peace following their defeat in their earlier war; but even with 2 their small numbers they more bravely resisted his great army than they had earlier a small force of Locrians. Such 3 valor can poverty have when facing arrogant riches, and an unexpected victory is sometimes more certain than one expected.

Now while Dionysius was conducting his campaign, he 4 was approached by delegates from the Gauls who had burned down Rome some months earlier, and they came seeking an alliance and friendly relations; their people 5 were situated amid his foes, they said, and would prove very useful to him either in battle or behind the lines while the enemy was preoccupied with the fight. The embassy 6 pleased Dionysius. So negotiating an alliance and with his strength now augmented by Gallic auxiliaries, he virtually started the war afresh. Now the reason for these Gauls 7 entering Italy and seeking a new home was the internal discord and incessant strife that they suffered at home; and when they tired of it and came into Italy, they drove 8 the Etruscans from their homes[8] and founded Mediolanum, Comum, Brixia, Verona, Bergomum, Tridentum and Vicentia. The Etruscans, too, after losing their ancestral 9 homes occupied the Alps under the leadership of Raetus and founded the Raetian people, named after their leader.

Dionysius, however, was brought back to Sicily by the 10 approach of the Carthaginians, who after rebuilding their army were now renewing with increased vigor the war that

407

11   auctis viribus repetebant. Dux belli Hanno Karthagini-
12   ensis erat, cuius inimicus Suniatus, potentissimus ea tem-
       pestate Poenorum, cum odio eius Graecis litteris Dionysio
       adventum exercitus et segnitiam ducis familiariter prae-
       nuntiasset, conprehensis epistulis proditionis eius damna-
13   tur, facto senatus consulto, ne quis postea Karthaginiensis
       aut litteris Graecis aut sermoni studeret, ne aut loqui cum
14   hoste aut scribere sine interprete posset. Nec multo post
       Dionysius, quem paulo ante non Sicilia, non Italia capie-
       bat, adsiduis belli certaminibus victus fractusque insidiis
       ad postremum suorum interficitur.

they had abandoned.[9] Their leader in the war was the Car- 11
thaginian Hanno, whose personal enemy Suniatus was 12
then the most powerful man in Carthage; through hatred
of Hanno he had forewarned Dionysius in a friendly manner in a letter written in Greek of the army's approach and
its leader's weakness; but the letter was intercepted and
Suniatus was condemned for treason, with a senatorial
decree passed forbidding any Carthaginian thereafter to 13
study Greek writing or language, so nobody might com-
municate with the enemy orally or in writing without an
interpreter. Not much later Dionysius, whom a little ear- 14
lier neither Sicily nor Italy could contain, was defeated
and broken by ongoing warfare and finally killed by a conspiracy of his own people.[10]

[9] In some manuscripts the word *lue* occurs, which could be
correct. If it is, then the translation would be "abandoned because
of the plague."

[10] Diod. Sic. 15.73f. (the year 368/7) says he died of illness,
and this is more likely.